W0007102

Sobhuza II, King of Swaziland, in full Ncwala clothing

SOBHUZA II

NGWENYAMA AND KING OF SWAZILAND

The story of an hereditary ruler and his country

HILDA KUPER

AFRICANA PUBLISHING COMPANY

A division of Holmes & Meier Publishers, Inc.
New York

0746712

First published in the United States of America by
AFRICANA PUBLISHING COMPANY
a division of Holmes & Meier Publishers, Inc.
30 Irving Place, New York, N.Y. 10003

Library of Congress Cataloging in Publication Data

Kuper, Hilda.
    Sobhuza II, Ngwenyama and King of Swaziland.

    Bibliography: p.
    Includes index.
    1. Sobhuza II, King of Swaziland, 1899-
2. Swaziland – Kings and rulers – Biography.
I. Title.
DT971.81.S55K86   1978   968'.3'00994   78–2356
ISBN 0–8419–0383–2

Printed in Great Britain

Contents

Acknowledgments

The writing of a biography is the responsibility of the author, the material is provided by others. It is impossible to acknowledge by name all those who contributed to this particular biography and I can only express my deep appreciation and recognition that it is in many ways a joint effort.

There are, however, a few individuals whose support and assistance were invaluable. My initial acknowledgment is due to His Majesty, Sobhuza II, King of Swaziland, who consented that his biography be written by me, with advice from an editorial committee. While His Majesty also made it clear that this was not a personal biography, but the story of his role in the history of his country, and that it was we who were the interpreters of events, he illuminated many issues raised with him at our various meetings.

The members of the Committee selected by Cabinet were: The Honourable Polycarp L. Dlamini, Minister of Justice; Mr J.S. Mkhulunyelwa Matsebula, then Private Secretary to His Majesty and Swazi historian and author; and Dr S.T. Msindazwe Sukati, Swaziland's first Ambassador to the United States. The committee members were encouraging, helpful, critical and cautious. Our lengthy sessions were to me a challenging learning experience in intellectual co-operation. Thoko Teresa Ginindza served as an indispensable secretary and research worker in the field and in the Swaziland archives made available by Mr V.W. Hiller, Government Archivist.

I have made considerable use of archival material both in Swaziland and in the Public Record Office. However, most of the data have been derived from personal observation and interviews. Not to fatigue the reader, I have limited documentation to essentials and given only main references in the bibliography.

Though it would be invidious to specify the parliamentarians, civil servants, Swazi National Councillors and others who gave generously of their time and knowledge, I would like to give special mention to Prince Makhosini, then Prime Minister.

I cannot adequately express my thanks to all my friends in Swaziland for their warmth and hospitality over many years. I was particularly fortunate to have been the guest in the home of Princess Gcinaphi and her husband Nkominophondo Khumalo for seven months, and it is wonderful to know that I have an open invitation to return there.

In the United States, Sondra Hale and particularly Beth Rosen Prinz were most helpful research assistants. Lillian R. Chodar of the Central Stenographical Pool of UCLA deciphered my writing with patience and efficiency. I received funding from the Ford Foundation, supplemented by the Academic Senate and African Studies Centre of UCLA, for travel and research. The manuscript was completed during my year as a Fellow of the Center for Advanced Study in the Behavioral Sciences, Palo Alto, California.

Professor Isaac Schapera, a friend in deed, checked both galleys and page proofs, while Susan Johnson compiled the Index.

It is with a deep sense of loss that I record the death of Dr Msindazwe Sukati on 23 March 1977. His intimate knowledge of Swazi history, his varied political experience, and his long and close association with the King contributed immeasurably to the substance of this book.

My greatest and enduring gratitude is to my husband, Leo, who not only gave me the moral support and devotion needed to complete a major task, but worked with me through each chapter of the manuscript to put it into final form.

September 1977
University of California,
Los Angeles   H.K.

Illustrations

Frontispiece: Sobhuza II in traditional dress of Kingship

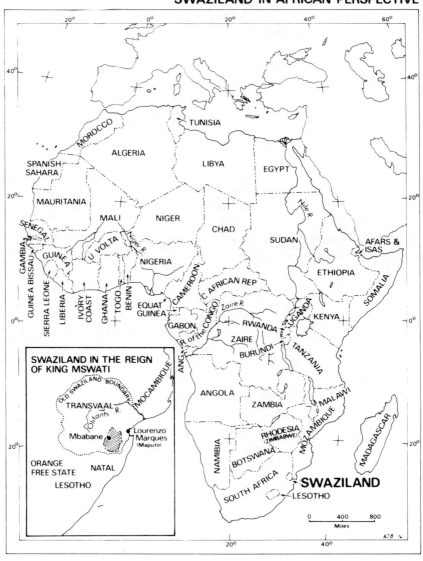

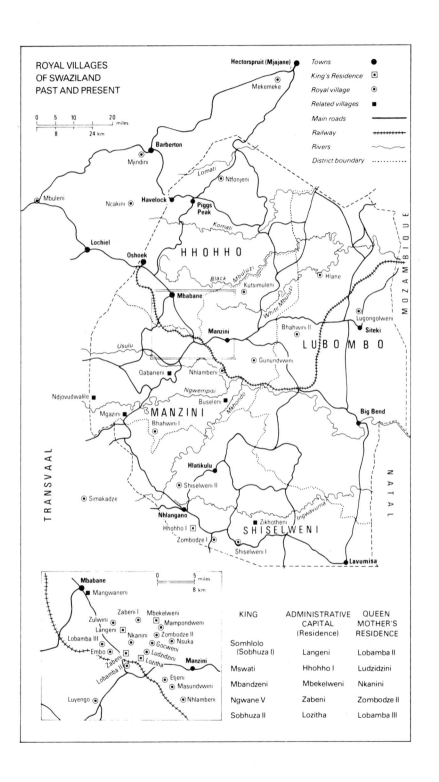

ROYAL VILLAGES
OF SWAZILAND
PAST AND PRESENT

	Towns	●
	King's Residence	▣
	Royal village	◉
	Related villages	■
	Main roads	——
	Railway	+++++++
	Rivers	∿∿
	District boundary	·········

0 5 10   20 miles
8   24 km

Hectorspruit (Mjajane)
Mekemeke

Barberton
Mjindini

Lomati
Ntfonjeni

Mbuleni
Ncakini
Havelock
Piggs Peak

Komati

Lochiel
Oshoek   HHOHHO

Black Mbuluzi
Kutsimuleni
Hlane

Mbabane

White Mbuluzi
Lugongolweni
Bhahwini II   Siteki

Manzini   LUBOMBO

Usulu
Qabaneni   Nhlambeni   Gunundvwini

Ngwempisi
Buseleni
Ndjovudwalile   MANZINI   Mhondo
Mgazini
Bhahwini I   Big Bend

Hlatikulu
Shiselweni II

Simakadze
Nhlangano   Zikhotheni
Hhohho I   SHISELWENI
Zombodze I
Shiselweni I

Lavumisa

TRANSVAAL

MOZAMBIQUE

NATAL

0   5 miles
8 km

Mbabane
Mangwaneni

Zabeni I   Mbekelweni
Zulwini   Mampondweni
Langeni   Nkanini   Zombodze II
Lobamba III   Nsuka
Gocweni
Embo   Ludzidzini
Zabeni   Lozitha   Manzini
Lobamba II
Etjeni
Masundvwini
Luyengo   Nhlambeni

KING	ADMINISTRATIVE CAPITAL (Residence)	QUEEN MOTHER'S RESIDENCE
Somhlolo (Sobhuza I)	Langeni	Lobamba II
Mswati	Hhohho I	Ludzidzini
Mbandzeni	Mbekelweni	Nkanini
Ngwane V	Zabeni	Zombodze II
Sobhuza II	Lozitha	Lobamba III

Glossary

This glossary contains the Swazi words used most frequently in the book. Other Swazi words are defined where they occur.

Bafana – boys; attendants
Bukhosi – sovereignty
Emabutfo (sing. *libutfo*) – age-regiments, warriors
Emadloti (sing. *lidloti*) – ancestors
Emakholwa – Christians
Emakhosikati – queens
Emalangeni – Dlamini princes and princesses
Emaphovela – King's betrothed
Embo – State House
Imbokodvo – grinding stone
Imigubho – solemn chants
Inkosatana – princess
Kukhonta – allegiance
Kungena (literally, to enter), the custom of the levirate
Libandla – Council
Liqoqo – Inner Council
Lusasa – embryonic ritual capital
Ngemandla – with power; applied to the commands of the Ngwenyama
Madlangengwenya – Order-in-Council
Ncwala – annual ritual of kingship
Ndlovukazi – Queen Mother
Ndlunkulu – Great Hut
Ndvuna – Governor
Ndvunankulu – traditional Prime Minister
Ngwenyama – (literally, lion), King of the Swazi
Nkosi – chief, ruler
Sibaya – cattle byre; arena
Sibhimbi – celebration
Sibhimbi sekutfomba – puberty ceremony
Sigodlo – seraglio
Simema – annual ritual during minority of a King
Tingani – lovers
Tinyanga – specialists; priests
Tinkundla – regional committees
Tinsila (sing. *insila*) – ritual blood-brothers
Umcwasho – girls' ceremony
Umntfwana – the child (heir to the throne); also a decorative ornament
Umhlanga Day – Reed Day
Umpakhatsi (literally, the inside), the ritual capital

CHAPTER 1
An Essential Introduction

This is the story of Africa's longest reigning living king, Sobhuza II, a modern statesman steeped in the subtleties of African traditional civilization. Perhaps because his country is small and his principles of government are peaceful, he is less well known than some who strut and fume on the international stage.

My friendship with His Majesty, King Sobhuza II, dates from 1934 when the present independent Kingdom of Swaziland was a neglected British High Commission Territory in which the traditional ruler, labelled Paramount Chief, was subordinate to a local Resident Commissioner. But to his people he was essentially *Ngwenyama* (the Lion), representative of a nation conscious of its rich cultural heritage, rightful heir to powers achieved by ancestors of the Nkosi Dlamini clan in a period of pre-colonial independence. Boundaries imposed by colonial rulers still shape many modern states and Swaziland appears on the map of Africa as a tiny landlocked country (6704.5 square miles) wedged between the Republic of South Africa and the former Portuguese province of Mozambique; but there are many people who identify themselves as Swazi dispersed across the borders as far north as the Zambesi, indicative of the wider area controlled by a Swazi ruler as late as the early nineteenth century. Within the present internationally recognized Kingdom the total population is under half a million, of whom over 90 percent are Swazi by birth.

I first met Ngwenyama, Sobhuza II, at a conference on education held in the Republic (then the Union) of South Africa at the Witwatersrand University, Johannesburg (16-27 July 1934). He was sitting towards the back of the crowded hall when someone pointed to him and said, 'That is Sobhuza.' I observed a man in the mid-thirties, of medium height and build, with a strong face, deep brown in complexion, a wide forehead, broad flared nose, high cheek bones, bright, deep-set penetrating eyes, a short, natural, untrimmed beard, and smiling mouth. But it was not the build or features that set him apart as much as a general impression of animated intensity and personal dignity. He was leaning slightly forward as if to catch each word, and I like to think that I would have singled him out even had I not been told who he was; that I would have sensed that elusive quality which the Swazi describe as 'the shadow of Kingship' and Shakespeare as 'the divinity that doth hedge a King'. On his right was an older man, big-boned with broad squashed-up features, like a good-natured boxer, and on his left a thin, frail-looking individual, with an exceedingly high forehead, and slightly protruding eyes. Later we were introduced. The big man was Benjamin Nxumalo, one of Sobhuza's maternal uncles, the other was Ngolotjeni Motsa, whose unique close relationship with the King emerged only after I came to Swaziland.

I was with three of my teachers, Mrs Winifred Hoernlé of the Witwatersrand University, Professor I. Schapera of Cape Town, and Professor Bronislaw Malinowski of the London School of Economics. Mrs Hoernlé, a woman who combined scholarship with warm sympathy for humanity, had recently been to Swaziland with Schapera to examine the feasibility of a suggestion made by Sobhuza to integrate the traditional age regimental system into western-style schools. Malinowski, tense, brilliant and provocative, had come to present a paper at the conference. I was on my way to Swaziland with a Fellowship from the International Institute of African Languages and Cultures.

Sobhuza was interested in hearing the ideas of experts and put some fundamental questions to us on controversial matters of practical educational and political policy. As the young novitiate, I listened and learned, conscious of the practical limitations of academia. Sobhuza drew his companions into the discussion, inviting their opinions. They were not afraid to express disagreement, but their manner was impressively courteous and formal, and they punctuated their remarks with titles of royal praise such as *Silo* (Powerful Creature), *Mbangazitha* (Cause of Enemies), *Ndlaluselwa* (Eater of the Gourd), *Mbube* (Lion), *Ndlovu'ndvuna* (Male Elephant). Benjamin Nxumalo was a master of English, the others spoke with different degrees of fluency, and broke off now and then to discuss a point among themselves in siSwati. Sobhuza spoke with quick eagerness interrupted by a slight hesitation as though his thoughts raced ahead of his words.

He was acutely aware of problems confronting his people caught between conflicting ways of life, and thought that perhaps anthropology might help provide some solutions. He said, 'Anthropology makes possible comparison and selection of lines of further development. European culture is not all good; ours is often better. We must be able to choose how to live and for that we must see how others live. I do not want my people to be imitation Europeans, but to be respected for their own laws and customs.' On many subsequent occasions he opposed the theory, current among many African as well as white intellectuals of the time, that 'assimilation' with the dominant Europeans would help African people, and he argued instead that the Swazi must choose the best of their own culture and the best of that available from outside in order to maintain their national identity and self-respect. He was not so naive as to believe that the choice would be easy; he recognized that there was no straightforward road, no permanent unequivocal signpost to 'Progress'. With the passing of years he has become increasingly aware of the complexity of alternatives and the difficulties of implementing the simplest decision, but he still has faith that guidelines for a stable future should be selected by the people from their own traditions and that cultural nationalism is a preliminary to political unity.

At the same time, he never fell into the pit of identifying custom with race, and his non-racism, his acceptance of an individual on his or her merits, emerged clearly in our initial meetings. He described racial discrimination as 'very cruel' and 'unjust'. He spoke from personal experience, having suffered the humiliation of routine discrimination in lifts, post office, shops, trains. No African was immune from the pervasive oppression of the system. His attitude to Goli (Johannesburg) was ambivalent – he enjoyed the excitement of variety, but there was always the fear of violence and the danger of infringing on any one of the numerous restrictive laws such that no African could move freely without fear of arbitrary arrest. In Johannesburg he stayed in his house in Sophiatown, a rough district, badly lit and poorly serviced, but the only part of the city where Africans were permitted to own freehold property. His house was a refuge for many friends and also a meeting place for Swazi working in the surrounding gold mines.

Racism defined relations in Swaziland but was less forcibly expressed than in the Union. The South African government, a coalition between General Smuts and General J.B.M. Hertzog, who had founded the first National Party of South Africa in 1914, was pressing for the transfer of the then three High Commission territories (Basutoland, Bechuanaland and Swaziland) to the Union of South Africa. There were rumours that Swaziland would be the first offering. Sobhuza expressed anxiety at the possibility that negotiations were going on with the British, represented in Pretoria by Sir Herbert Stanley as High Commissioner, and that decisions would be made without his knowledge or consent.

Sobhuza invited Malinowski to visit Swaziland, and agreed that I stay at the village of his mother, the *Ndlovukazi*, Lomawa of the Nxumalo Ndwandwe clan. As Ndlovukazi (She Elephant) she held a position in the traditional system of government equal to that of the Ngwenyama, and her residence, Lobamba, was the ritual centre and capital of the Swazi nation. The Swazi had developed a unique dual monarchy over many generations, and the Ndwandwe were renowned as one of the groups that had provided mothers of past Nkosi Dlamini kings.

Sobhuza and his retinue returned by car to Swaziland. Malinowski and I followed later by the mine workers' route – a train from Johannesburg to Breyten, a dust-infested junction in the Eastern

Transvaal, and then by South African railway bus to Mbabane, seat of the British Administration in Swaziland. Both train and bus were strictly segregated. In the bus three white passengers (the third was a young woman coming as governess to a settler's family) sat in a roomy front compartment, while packed close together in the back were the Africans with all the luggage.

Most of the journey was through the flat sourveld of the Eastern Transvaal, marked here and there by a brick farmhouse, a few trees, scattered herds of cattle, and occasional clusters of ramshackle huts of grass or mud. It was the end of winter, the grass was brown and the fields were bare. Roughly every twenty miles we passed a small town marked by a shop, a few simple brick houses and a petrol pump. Then suddenly past Lake Chrissie the entire landscape changed. Fantastically shaped boulders loomed on either side, and in the distance towered serried mountains, ranging in colour through the softest pastels to the deepest purple. The small country had a rich variety of scenery, of climate, and of vegetation falling into four rough zones – the mountainous highveld bordering the Transvaal, undulating midlands merging with the bushveld, and finally a narrow escarpment – the Lubombo, from the top of which on clear days the Indian Ocean glitters in the distance.

When the bus stopped at Oshoek all the passengers at the back jumped out and went shouting joyfully towards some women sitting on the ground under a tree on the other side of a signboard marked 'SWAZILAND'. There was no other sign of a border – no gate, no passport control, no police. The women were selling *tjwala*, a cool home-brewed beer of maize and millet, from big dark clay pots. We all moved on, refreshed. Most of the rest of the journey was dangerous with ruts and rocks but the highland scenery was superb. Cutting into the mountainside were deep gorges marked by clumps of trees and huge ferns. Here and there, merging with granite outcrops, appeared scattered villages, many with traditional beehive-shaped huts of grass arranged in neat clearings surrounded by reed fences.

Mbabane itself was a small country town (the total population under 300), with an unpaved main road stretching from an old-fashioned tavern at one end to an old-fashioned jail at the other. We were met by A.G. Marwick, then Acting Resident Commissioner, who had invited us to stay with him and his wife until we went down to Lobamba. 'A.G.', a friend of long standing to Sobhuza, had come to Swaziland at the end of the Anglo-Boer War (1902) with the first British administrative staff after serving as one of 'Baden Powell's police'. Swazi spoke of him as Ndlavela, of the regiment of Mbandzeni, Sobhuza's grandfather. A.G., who had many of the more admirable qualities of a soldier – self-discipline and integrity, loyalty and courage – was also independent in his thinking, outspoken, as well as obstinate, in his views, and a mine of information. His family, sturdy north countrymen, had settled among the Zulu of Natal, and he was fluent in Zulu and well versed in Zulu culture. To Sobhuza he was a friend and staunch ally in times of crisis.

Sobhuza agreed that we accompany Marwick's nephew, Brian (later Sir Brian), then a young Assistant Commissioner interested in anthropology, and his Swazi informant, Mashiphisa Fakudze, to part of a religious ceremony commemorating the *emadloti* (ancestors). This particular rite was held at the village of Chief Dinabantu, of the Gama clan, who was in charge of some of the royal graves in the Mdzimba mountains. More than a hundred *emabutfo* (warriors) had gathered there; they were dressed in kilts of leopard skin, with flowing capes from the tails of cattle falling over their shoulders, caps of black ostrich feathers on their heads, and they carried shields and sticks. Mashiphisa Fakudze explained that this was 'almost the costume' of the main ritual of Kingship – the *Ncwala* – and also of war. But in the rituals, no weapon could be carried; fighting and bloodshed would anger the ancestors. The dances were superb and solemn, the men in long lines moved slowly in perfect rhythm, and their voices blended in deep harmony. The chief danced blissfully with his age mates, and every now and then a few women in traditional leather skirts and aprons or a group of girls in gay printed cloths (*mahiya*) danced together with the men 'to please them and stir them'. A prince of royal blood, Mshengu, and a senior councillor and some warriors had come from the main royal villages to observe and report back to the rulers. I learnt later that Sobhuza had criticized the fact that the men had performed one dance-song that was reserved for the *Ncwala* proper, and had rebuked Dinabantu for straying from tradition. Ritual, to be effective, had to be correct, innovations could not be random.

On the way back, Malinowski had an unfortunate experience which I relate because it had an interesting sequel. With his Polish aristocratic background, he prided himself on his good horsemanship; I, on the other hand, remained stuck on the back of my horse by sheer willpower. When near home Malinowski leapt down to pluck me a spray of the dazzling red *umsinsi* blossom, and as he presented it his less gallant steed stepped back and trod on his big toe! Funny in restrospect, quite awful at the time. If the pain matched his profanities it must have been unendurable. The government doctor, a grand old Scotsman, Dr Jamieson, summoned to come as quickly as possible, fortunately found no bones broken and provided pain-killers and sleeping pills, and advised frequent hot poultices. Marwick wanted Malinowski to remain in Mbabane but Malinowski decided to keep to the original schedule. Sobhuza was expecting to meet us at 2:30 the following afternoon and preparations had been made for our arrival.

Sobhuza avoided Mbabane – seat of an alien administration – as much as possible, and we had not seen him during the four days we were with the Marwicks. Despite the friendship between the two men, social visits across the colour line were not part of the pattern of the time and it was usually the Resident Commissioner who took the initiative. There was no telephone to Lobamba and though one had recently been installed at the King's office at Lozitha the line was poor, the telephonist untrained, and it was still found more efficient to send messengers by foot.

We had brought no camping equipment and only later did I appreciate how extraordinarily difficult it must have been for Sobhuza to prepare the people for our arrival, more especially since the tent put up for Malinowski was provided by the administration and was similar to that used by District Officers on tax-collecting tours.

Lobamba was only 12 miles from Mbabane, but the roads were rutted and corrugated and twisting up and down steep hills; the journey was slow and, especially in wet weather, hazardous. As Marwick drove us down he expounded local history. Outside Mbabane was Mangwaneni, where Sobhuza's grandmother (the previous Ndlovukazi) Labotsibeni, who earned for herself the name *Gwamile* (The Indomitable), stayed with her attendants when she came with her retinue to do verbal battle with foreign officials for the rights of the people. She had died in 1925, three years after Sobhuza had been fully installed as Ngwenyama, leaving him to continue the struggle.

Below Mangwaneni the road wound sharply down the Malagwane with its superb view of the twin-peaked Lugogo mountains (Rider Haggard's Sheba's Breasts) and the stark granite face of Nyonyane, to the broad fertile valley known as Ezulwini (the place of rain-making). The village of Ezulwini had been established by Sobhuza I in the early 19th century and not far off was the site of Elangeni (in the Sun), his administrative headquarters. Between Mbabane and Lobamba there was a halt on the road at a small single-story hotel with a trading shop and butchery combined, and a few western-styled bungalows.

We later crossed a perilously narrow bridge, spanning the Lusushwana River, but instead of being clean and sparkling the water was the colour of dried blood. Marwick explained that this was the result of the crude method of mining tin, carried out by a few small companies, and he pointed to huge gaps in the mountainside, ravines of erosion. The Swazi had their own less destructive techniques for smelting and smithing, and Sobhuza, in an effort to stop the old craft from being forgotten, had brought an old specialist, Mahudvula Mavuso, to Nsuka, a royal village started by the late King Ngwane V, popularly known as Bhunu, and father of Sobhuza.

The manager of the tin mine had his own electricity plant, and the light on his veranda, the only electric light for miles around, was a beacon for the entire area. Between the mine and Lobamba was St. Mary's, a small Catholic mission.

A few hundred yards further, off the main dirt road, past a small plantation of young wattle trees, branched a short almost nonexistent motor track to an unexpectedly large village. Unlike modern cities, which strike the eye with sharp contours and glitter of glass, Lobamba, the ritual capital, the heart of the nation, revealed itself very gradually and quietly, and the beehive-shaped thatched huts took distinctive shape only as you looked at them.

The village followed the basic blueprint of traditional homesteads, but was on a larger and more impressive scale. In the centre was a huge *sibaya* – a heavily palisaded, unroofed, circular enclosure where the cattle were kept at night. This was also the theatre for national gatherings, and it had a small sanctuary at the upper end for the calves, where the King received ritual treatment of Kingship. Facing it was the *Ndlunkulu* (Great Hut), in the charge of the Ndlovukazi, and conspicuous from the outside was the shrine hut decorated with horned skulls of cattle. To the left of the *Ndlunkulu* curved the *sigodlo* (seraglio) – the separate living quarters of the Queens – outside which stood the King's black Buick. Surrounding these key structures was an irregular semi-circle of citizens' huts, several rows deep, and at either end, guarding access to the heart of the nation and protecting its inhabitants, were the *emalawu* (barracks).

We parked at the entrance to the large courtyard of smooth earth between the cattle byre and the Great Hut and waited to be taken to the Ndlovukazi. An old man moved backwards and forwards dramatically reciting royal praises. A young man came to the car, greeted us, said he would report our arrival to the *Ndvuna* (Governor) and a few minutes later brought along an elderly slow-moving gentleman, Mshudvulwane of the Zwane clan, who welcomed us and conducted us into the *Ndlunkulu* through a narrow gateway, past the shrine hut.

Sitting on the ground, holding court, were Sobhuza and several councillors – some old, others young – and a group of women, one of whom was unmistakably his mother. She was gracious and regal in a black ox-hide skirt and decorative goatskin toga, which she wore like a mantle of purple and ermine on her shapely body; and on her head, beneath a high conical coiffure, lay a coronet of deep brown wooden beads, topped by a vivid red flamingo feather set between two lucky beans; she had the tiniest, most perfectly shaped ears.

Sobhuza rose to greet us. In Johannesburg he had worn a well-tailored western suit, a Stetson hat and fashionable patent leather shoes, and he had sported a walking stick. At Lobamba he was in Swazi dress – a stiff dark grey cloth, with a tiny pattern, knotted around his waist reaching to his knees, and over it a triangular sporran of fine buckskin. Tied toga-wise at the right shoulder flowed a deep blue cloth with a bright floral design. He moved elegantly, his feet bare, his only ornament a necklace of beads.

Sobhuza presented us to his mother, and as we shook hands, bending down to her, I felt her examine us shrewdly but not unkindly. Her face lit marvellously when she smiled, exposing unusually broad teeth. Her wrists and ankles, smooth and slender, were adorned with simple amulets of animal skin, but round her right foot was tied a rather thick and clumsy bandage.

Sobhuza had noticed that Malinowski was limping and after the initial pleasantries and introductions were over, asked what had happened. He translated the conversation to his mother, who expressed her personal sympathy and indicated that she too had a sore foot. A few days before, when walking along the path, something sharp and dangerous had pierced the sole and the wound was not healing. After mutual commiseration she asked Malinowski, who had been introduced as 'Doctor', what remedy he suggested. He promptly replied that they should take the same cure: frequent footbaths in water as hot as each could bear, into which he would put his special medicine, the treatment to begin as soon as possible. In the meantime, however, a young girl had brought in a pot of beer for the visitors, and kneeling gracefully she skimmed off the surface with a delicate grass ladle and took the first sip before passing the pot to us.

The conversation was varied and lively despite the difficulties of interpretation. Sobhuza was a superb raconteur. A story engaged his whole being, and his voice, which was musical and gay, slipped easily into quick spontaneous laughter as he told of his own experiences with a rough horse he rode as a boy. Now he no longer rode; he preferred the speed of a car. Moreover, horses first acquired in the reign of his great grandfather, King Mswati, had been periodically decimated by disease, had never been much used by the people, and their worth could not compare to that of cattle, or even sheep. While we were talking we heard the lowing of herds and the shouts of herdboys bringing the cows into the *sibaya* for the evening milking.

It was late in the afternoon when Marwick, having assured himself that we had all we required, took his leave. Sobhuza escorted him to his car and Malinowski began organizing the foot treatment. This proved extremely effective and companionable, and, as I learned later, did a great deal to reduce the suspicion which had been generated by the preparations for our arrival.

I had been given the most westernized house in the village – a square brick building with a wooden door, glass windows and a partition dividing the room into two. In the front room were a table and six wooden chairs with leather seats – the only chairs in the capital and used mainly for western guests. This house had previously been occupied by relatives on state visits to the capital. A separate ordinary hut served as kitchen. No Swazi village had electricity or running water.

Sobhuza put us in the charge of Ngolotjeni Motsa, whom we had already met in Johannesburg, and Princess Sengcabaphi. We then learnt that Ngolotjeni Motsa was Sobhuza's *insila*, an artificially created blood-brother, in some respects closer to the King than a prince by birth. We were soon aware of his strength of character and his complexity. He was individualistic, industrious, intelligent, a convert and a monogamist, with a varied occupational background – shopkeeper, farmer, cattle dealer, and cook in a hotel. In his new role he commandeered several youngsters to fetch firewood, draw water, run errands and 'watch the pots', and it was he who said specifically, 'No service for Kingship (*umsebenti webukhosi*) is ever degrading.' Rank was no excuse for laziness, and he was a strict, almost harsh disciplinarian.

Sengcabaphi was Sobhuza's sister, by the same father, the late King Bhunu, but not by the same mother. Sengcabaphi's mother had been of the Mndzebele clan, and famous for her beauty, and the name bestowed on her child means – 'Where are those who surpass her'. Her life had not been easy; when Sengcabaphi was only three, her mother had died tragically, killed by jealous co-wives. And now Sengcabaphi's marriage to a chief of the Ndwandwe (the same clan as the Ndlovukazi though a different branch) was complicated by the fact that although many cattle had been given as bridewealth, she had borne no son. She came for long periods to Lobamba where she was *Inkosatana* (princess) of the home, and treated with great deference and respect. Her children, two daughters, were growing up under the care of their grandmother Lomawa, and Sobhuza as their maternal uncle was also their protector.

At Sobhuza's request, Sengcabaphi took me to the *sigodlo* to meet the Queens (*Emakhosikati*) – 'the mothers of the country'. She conducted me first to Lozindaba Matsebula, a woman with the sweetest expression and most gentle manner imaginable, who I learnt was the King's first public Queen. As such she took precedence over all his other wives, also ranked by seniority, and was second only to the Ndlovukazi in national importance. She gathered together the other Queens, beginning with Fongofani Motsa, a big buxom woman with a beaming smile. Clinging to her shyly was a beautiful little boy, Mazini, officially recognized as having a special status among the sons.

LaMatsebula called a young girl to spread a mat for me beside her, and the Queens gathered round in a circle. They were of most pleasing appearance, and despite the fact that they were dressed in identical clothing, with hair done in exactly the same style, I felt the impact of their diverse and vivid personalities as they listened while Sengcabaphi explained my presence. I felt rather lonely and embarrassed, conscious of my awkwardness and ignorance, but they were so courteous and responsive, so helpful and encouraging of my halting efforts at conversation that soon I felt more at ease. A big pot of beer was brought and ceremonially presented to me, and there was much laughter and general enjoyment. After the drinking there was singing and dancing, and those with the most beautiful voices took the lead. Some danced solos and were encouraged and applauded as their feet beat out complicated rhythms to the rattles of cocoons filled with stones tied around their ankles.

Sobhuza stayed most of the time at Lozithehlezi, his administrative residence high on the Lancabane ridge. It was very similar to Lobamba, but the *sibaya* was smaller, the quarters for the Queens were in the centre of the circle of huts, there were more men in the barracks, and the Colonial Government had recently completed a modest building and furnished it with basic office equipment.

The royal villages were lively with children. Apart from the Queens' own children, there were young attendants and also the children of princes and chiefs who had sent their young to be brought up at court. Wherever Sobhuza went he took a couple of small boys or girls with him and it was charming to watch him with them – he spoke to them so fondly, and seriously – and it was clear that they reciprocated his affection, and sought his approval and warm smile.

One day he drove us to the bushveld; the aloes were in bloom, there was a marvellous variety of indigenous trees, and the glimpse of an occasional buck – this was once an area rich in game. But on the journey I also noticed stretches where the grass was high and thick, gleaming like gold, and in between, separated only by strands of barbed-wire fencing, patches where the grass was burnt and stubble, and the earth looked barren. Yet it was in these patches that there were villages and signs of civilization. Sobhuza explained that this was the result of the Land Partition Proclamation passed by Britain in 1907; and in 1936 two-thirds of Swaziland was still owned by whites, who numbered 2,740, less than two per cent of the total population; scattered in between vast farms were some 25 'Native Areas' available for over 150,000 Swazi.

Malinowski stayed for over a week, and by the time he left both he and the Ndlovukazi were walking without pain. Sobhuza came to wish him a·bright road and hoped he would some day return to Swaziland. I went to Johannesburg to buy equipment, and we agreed that on my return I should make a tour in order to get a general impression of the whole country. I was lucky enough to pick up a 1926 Ford Coupe in excellent running condition, and Leo Kuper, then a young lawyer who had just started his practice in Johannesburg, returned with me. My heavy equipment was despatched by rail and bus and would, I hoped, be there when I arrived.

Sobhuza helped map the route and said, only half jokingly, that we should perhaps look for Embo, the mythical home of his predecessors, 'somewhere in the north', but then, more practically, he pointed to a place on the coast of Mozambique where he said his forefathers had stayed for some time before leaving their kin (the Tembe) and moving on until they settled in the area of Shiselweni in the south of modern Swaziland, which he described as 'the navel' of the nation and as a new 'breaking off' or starting point. From here his namesake Sobhuza I, better known as *Somhlolo* (Creator of Wonders), later explored other areas inland and established new royal villages to some of which he gave old names.

A new capital under the Queen Mother is founded in each reign, followed soon after by separate residences of the King, and old royal villages are 'revived' by royal representatives. Sobhuza I was the first Dlamini king to build his capital in the midlands, overlooked by the Mdzimba mountains. He named it Lobamba, after an earlier Lobamba, and the present capital, built for Sobhuza II, was also named Lobamba in accordance with ancient precedent.

As he mentioned the names, places, and areas of chiefs, and their links with the royal line, the whole country seemed drawn together by ties of blood or marriage, stretching into a remote, but surprisingly real, past; and though the names were confusing and my head reeled, the more I listened the more clearly I realized that this was not simply history told for its own interest, but something that was alive, directing present actions and providing a charter for the future. Reconstruction did not mean the retention of old buildings but the perpetuation of historic links in a great national network. It came as no surprise that when Swaziland regained its independence Sobhuza II gave the name Embo to the new State House where he received ambassadors from foreign countries.

To guide Leo and me on our journey, Sobhuza selected Mnyakaza Gwebu, a youngish man who had grown up under his patronage and who described himself as 'an orphan cared for by the Ngwenyama'. Mnyakaza knew Swaziland intimately and had worked at different times in South Africa and in Mozambique; he enlightened us at each stage of our journey, which steadily took on the character of an adventurous pilgrimage.

Sobhuza's ancestors were among the pioneers, known in the literature as Bembo Nguni, who explored and finally settled in southern Africa. With them, from their homeland (Embo), they had brought cattle and sheep, a variety of seeds for cultivation, and hand-made utensils of grass, skin, wood, clay, copper and iron. They did not use their herds for transport, and being their own beasts of burden, they travelled light. But they also carried with them the heritage of all immigrants: the knowledge, memories, and experiences of the past from societies they left behind. With these they were able to shape their lives anew – borrowing, adapting and creating.

Their migrations did not follow any single trail. Groups hived off in different directions, sometimes in search of pasture for their herds and land to cultivate, sometimes to assert autonomy or escape hostilities. At the core of each group were male kin under an accepted head, and ties with the original patriclan were retained in clan praise-names. Marriage within the clan was generally prohibited, and marriage extended ties across clan boundaries. A man with many wives had a large following and a range of potential allies.

Dlamini, a founding leader of one branch of Nkosi, led his followers across the Lubombo Range, an achievement recorded to this day in the praises of the ruling clan of the nation: 'Nkosi Dlamini. You scourged the Lubombo in your flight, carrying a small bundle of medicines' (which became part of the heritage of his descendants). The name Dlamini, as well as Ngwane, Mswati, and Sobhuza, recurs in the royal genealogy, which goes back some twenty-five generations.

It was Ngwane III, eight generations back, who brought his following across the Pongola River, towards the northwest, in what is now southeastern Swaziland, and the people frequently speak of themselves as 'The People of Ngwane'. Across the arbitrary boundary between modern Swaziland and the Republic of South Africa stands the Stone of Ngwane, a huge boulder, where Ngwane III is said to have rested before deciding on his next move. He entered an area occupied by a clan of the Nsibandze, whose leader was forced to recognize his greater power and accept his overlordship. But Ngwane did not destroy the occupants. He respected their hereditary line, and built his capital, which he named Zombodze ('the place of the long-winding trail'), in their territory.

The Nsibandzes have ever since been appointed governors and caretakers of royal villages. Indeed, they have played so memorable a role in Swazi kingship that Phuhlaphi Nsibandze, great-great-great-grandson of the early leader, had the honour of witnessing the signatures to the document drawn up by the British officially restoring the title 'King' to Sobhuza II, Ngwenyama of the Swazi, in 1967. It was Phuhlaphi who described the role of the Nsibandzes as 'throning' Swazi kings in the past, the first occasion being when Lohhiya, his great-great-grandfather, had fetched Sobhuza I (Somhlolo) from his mother's people, the Simelane, where he had been 'hidden for safety', and had presented the youth to the Council of Princes, which chose him above all other children of the late King Ndvungunye, son of Ngwane III. After Sobhuza I died, Mkhuzanto Nsibandze, Phuhlaphi's great-grandfather, had gone 'willingly and joyfully singing' into the royal grave 'to accompany his King to the ancestors'. And even more relevant to the present was the fact that, immediately after the Boer War, when Sobhuza was still a baby, and Bhunu his father was dead, Phuhlaphi's own father, Silele, had been one of four messengers sent by Labotsibeni, then Queen Regent, to Pretoria, to announce that 'We still have our king. He is very young and is there back home. He is Sobhuza and we are his guardians.' Phuhlaphi concluded proudly: 'This king was throned by my father and Somhlolo by Lohhiya.'

The Nsibandzes were but one of several new clans incorporated into the nation in the region that became known as Shiselweni, according to some informants a name signifying that there were still fires in the hearths of occupants found in the area. The clans which acknowledged the kingship of Sobhuza I when he expanded his control from Shiselweni described themselves as Bemdzabuko ('those who broke off', i.e., the originals), to distinguish themselves from clans of Emakhandzambili ('those found ahead', the prior occupants of the country). Some clans were subdued by force, others entered into friendly alliances, and defeat of the fighting forces of an enemy did not necessarily involve the extinction of a group or a lasting hostility to the victors. The permanence of hereditary chieftainship was acknowledged, and in several cases sons whose fathers were killed were brought up at court, and later reinstated, or given special positions in the nation. Subsequently, a number of immigrants (exiles and refugees from adjacent areas) sought protection and gave formal allegiance (*kukhonta*) to Somhlolo's successors and became a third element, described as Labefikamuva (those who came after). As *tikhonti*, they were also Swazi citizens, automatically recruited into the age-regiments, accepted as members of the Council, granted recognition in ritual, and entitled to the use of land ultimately controlled by the King.

On our return from a journey that also took us to the little towns of Mankayane, Mahamba, Hlatikulu, Goedgegun (now Nhlangano), Siteki and Piggs Peak (in Hhohho), Sobhuza questioned us closely on what we had seen – and understood. His detailed knowledge of the whole country was overwhelming; and when he did not know something himself, he would refer to someone who might remember. He wanted 'the truth'.

Leo returned reluctantly to his legal practice in Johannesburg and I settled in at Lobamba. Mnyakaza Gwebu continued as my guide, interpreter, cook and travelling companion. He was a born teacher who had taught himself to read and write, and in addition to a wide knowledge of different African languages he spoke a graphic English as well as some Afrikaans and Portuguese.

After I had been in Lobamba a few weeks, there was a meeting in the *sibaya* which the Ndlovukazi invited me to attend with her. Before discussing national affairs the governor, Mshudvulwane Zwane, announced (according to Mnyakaza), 'You see this strange white person, you will see her everywhere. The Ngwenyama says: Do not trouble her. Teach her. She is here to write books about our civilisation. She will see we are not wild animals. She will see our *buntfu* (humanity). If she is troubled, help her. If her motorcar sticks in the mud, take it out. So says *Silo*.'

I lived at Lobamba for more than two years, moving for a short period to outlying villages. After I left Swaziland I took every opportunity to return to see old friends: Swaziland had become my spiritual home.

In 1967 when Sobhuza II was recognized as head of the budding independent Kingdom of Swaziland, I asked if I could become a citizen by *khonta* (the offer of traditional allegiance). In June of 1970, when I was again on a visit, Sobhuza signed the necessary letter of acceptance, and Mfundza Sukati, the first Deputy Prime Minister, the official certificate. I felt proud and happy, and hoped to settle in Swaziland as soon as possible. Though for reasons beyond my control

I still reside and work in America, I remain a Swazi citizen, travelling on only a Swaziland passport.

In April, 1972, I was privileged to be appointed to write this official biography advised by a Committee also selected by Cabinet and approved by the King. In the period between starting and completing this task, many major changes have taken place, reflected in miniature in new positions held by members of the Committee: Mkhulunyelwa Matsebula, having served seven years as King Sobhuza II's Private Secretary, was appointed in 1974 Chief Executive Officer of the National Trust Commission; Dr Samuel Msindazwe Sukati, who returned home after six years as Ambassador in New York and Washington, D.C. was sent (in November, 1975) as Swaziland's first Ambassador to Maputo (formerly Lourenço Marques) in the newly independent country of Mozambique; Mr Hiller has retired and left Swaziland to live in South Africa; Thoko Ginindza qualified for the post of Ethnographer and Curator in charge of the National Museum. Only the position of Polycarp Dlamini as Minister of Justice remains nominally unchanged, but after April, 1973 the context of his appointment was no longer the constitution drawn on a British model. 1973, which marked a climax in Sobhuza's struggle for full Swazi sovereignty, therefore served as a cut-off point in the description of the more detailed events of this national biography. The epilogue indicates more general trends and the work that lies ahead of a great leader.

The writing of this biography has been an exciting but immensely difficult task, in the course of which there have been several interruptions and mishaps – including 'the loss' of a trunk with tapes and documents – resulting in unforeseen and regrettable delays so that I often recall the ominous words of Dr Sukati when he phoned from Washington to tell me of the decision: *'umuntfu lobekiwe usukebulewe'* – literally, 'a person appointed (to a high position) is in process of being killed'. He explained it: 'Unhappy lies the head that wears a crown.'

An official biography is by definition selective; but it does not follow that it is less true. This biography is the history not only of an outstanding man but of the culture with which he has deliberately identified himself; and it is the story not only of a great King but of the institution of a traditional Kingship in a complex world of power politics. Over the years Sobhuza has shown intelligence without arrogance, strength without brutality, nationalism without racialism. He has used traditional culture as a guideline in planning the future, not as a fetter to chain his people to the past. So we thank him, with a traditional song composed and chanted by Mabuntane Mdluli, in 1967, translated by Thoko Ginindza:

It is he, Bhuza among the high who overshadows all.
Thunderous dancer,

Dancer on black shields of *jojo*[1]
You played on shields of *shikane*.

Black bewildering widow bird
You grew plumes in winter
When other widow birds are bare.

Where you build
Stubborn black one of Hhili,[2]
Only he who perseveres survives
He who does not persevere must flee.

Claw of the lion that is heavy
You trod the ocean,
The ocean surged
The ocean built its waves,
The ocean swirled in currents.

They said Sobhuza would not clasp the hand
of George King of England
But he clasped the hand with lightning of heaven
Twice the heavens flashed
Within the palace of the English
They praised you with wonder
'This manhood, so great, whence did it come?'
Rock-thrush of Ngwane, of Mahlokohla,
You said, you inherited it from the navel,
Here, from Ndvungunye,
Here from Somhlolo.

Strength of the leopard
Strength of the lion
Eater of the fruit of the gourd of our country of Ngwane,
Here at our home, Lobamba,
It encircled the palace,
You proved yourself calf of the eater of the fruit of the gourd,
Player upon black shields.

They are calling you, they are giving you a message,
King of the inner circle!
They were not calling you for nothing,
They were calling you to a war of nations, stabbing and killing.

Again you entered battle,
You gave the fighting to the Sikhonyane,
The Balondolozi remained to protect the orphan,
You, yourself orphan born,
Feared one, brother of Ntfoli, brother of Mnengwase,
Who does not lie with one who moves in sleep,
Who until dawn disturbs the peace of rest.
Bushy tail of the bull, it is dark it is fearsome,

[1] Jojo is the male widow bird and shikane the female. The ordinary male grows beautiful long plumes in summer but the King, likened to a miraculous bird, has the power of the plumage even in winter.
[2] One of the names of Sobhuza's father,

Bushy tail of the bull, it is dark by Banganoma's place
Royal plume,
Circling the ridge of Lancabane,
Devouring herds of men.

Bhuza play with water,
That the waters of Ngwane
Reflect their admiration.

You of the inner circle!
Male elephant of the Swazi!
Old one whom age does not diminish!
Old one of the country of Ngwane!
Bayethe your Majesty!

Traditional African history is recorded in such *tibongo* (praises) recited on public occasions. Different bards, or oral historians, present their own selection of events and the same events may receive different emphasis and conflicting interpretations.

A biography, like *tibongo*, though based on written as well as oral sources, reflects a particular version of the events and the meaning of the life of an individual. This is the first national biography focussed on Sobhuza II as King of Swaziland. We hope that it will not be the last.

CHAPTER II
Child of the Nation

In 1967, with the approach of self-government and the reacquisition of independence, Swazi officials decided that the calendar of the colonial regime needed to be remodeled to commemorate events of their own national history, and that Sobhuza's birthday, not that of a British sovereign, should be a public celebration. The year, the season, and even the moon were known. The year, 1899, was marked by two major events – the formal outbreak of war (10 October) between Boers and British, and the sudden death, in December, of his father, Bhunu. The season was winter, a time of hunting and building, and the month, July, with its Swazi equivalent *Kolwane* named after the hawk that breeds in that moon. Only the exact day was not known; this Sobhuza wanted to discover.

A birth was a joyous event; the news was shouted from the main yard for all to hear, work in the fields was prohibited and the cattle were let loose to pasture near the home. It was essentially a group affair, the family rather than the individual was considered blessed. Subsequent birthdays were not personalized, nor did the date affect acceptance into the main educational institution, the *emabutfo* (the age regiments). When Sobhuza went to a western school and the matter of his birthday was first raised, he had asked various relatives and elders, but had received no definite answer, and had on occasion been 'given' the fourth of July for the record. Now, as head of a developing country, with its emphasis on technology and statistics, he was not prepared to accept a day bestowed on him by a teacher or government official, however well intentioned.

Every birth, though not recorded in writing, was vividly remembered by the mother, and Sobhuza's mother Lomawa, who had died in 1938, had told him of certain special auspicious signs that marked his arrival. The moon was full, and the day following would have been prescribed by custom for threshing an ancient variety of sorghum, on the national field known as *Imfabantfu* (where people died). He gave all this information to Mfundza Sukati, the first Deputy Prime Minister in the new government, whose office was responsible for the regulation of public holidays, and said: 'Find out the day that I was born.' Sukati, energetic and enterprising, consulted a number of people in and outside government and sent the clues – year, month and moon – to the meteorological station at Pretoria; the

answer came back: the 22nd of July, 1899. After careful consideration
Sobhuza accepted this as correct, and, since 1968 the 22nd of July has
been a great official celebration.

The birth took place at Zombodze, then capital of the nation and
residence of his paternal grandmother, Ndlovukazi Labotsibeni
Mdluli. In the reign of her husband King Mbandzeni, she was a
power behind the scenes. After his death in 1889, she held the centre
of the stage, first as Queen Mother for her son Bhunu, and then, on
his death in 1899, as Queen Regent until 1921, when her grandson,
Sobhuza II, was fully installed as Ngwenyama. She then handed over
the rain medicines and all other powers of Ndlovukazi to his own
mother, Lomawa Ndwandwe, but continued to be revered and
consulted until she died in 1925. She must then have been almost one
hundred years old.

Her birth name was Labotsibeni, recording that she was born at a
time when her natural father Matsanjana was with a regiment of
Mswati, attacking a Pedi chief Tsibeni, but the present generation
knows her better as Gwamile, or simply Mgwami, from the verb
gwamile – stand firm and unshakable, to be indomitable, adamant – a
woman deservedly commemorated by the nation in 1975,
International Women's Year. Events of her early life are among the
essentials of Sobhuza's story and are recounted by him on many
occasions. I will describe them briefly and selectively: they can be
found in less personalized versions in Blue Books and other studies.[1]

Her paternal ancestors, the Mdluli, were among the 'original
Swazi' incorporated in the earliest days of nation-building, and were
renowned for knowing secrets of military skill that qualified selected
members for onerous national honours. One branch remained in the
Shiselweni area in the south and has in every reign provided the Nkosi
Dlamini king with a unique official, titled *insila* (fictive blood brother)
'of the right hand', the battle hand, a counterpart to the *insila* 'of the
left hand', the protective hand, who, as I mentioned in my
introduction, was selected from the Motsa clan. Another branch was
established as administrators and military governors in the Hhohho
area in the north. Labotsibeni was of this group and when her natural
father died, his brother, Mvelase, chief of the Mdluli, took over his
role. Labotsibeni's mother, a Mabuza, moved with her children to the
national capital of Ludzidzini, where Mvelase had his regimental
residence. Labotsibeni, described in her praises as 'red-winged
starling of Mvelase', grew up in royal villages, acquiring from
childhood knowledge of court etiquette, insight into the politics of the
period, and self-assurance. She served her early apprenticeship under
the Ndlovukazi laZidze (daughter of Zidze), whose appropriate
personal name was Tsandzile, meaning 'the Loved'. She could not

[1] See particularly Matsebula, 1972; Commands 5,089, 1887; 6,200, 1890; 6,201, 1890; 6,217,
1890; 7,212, 1893; 7,611, 1895; and 9,200, 1899, Kuper, 1947.

have had a better and more experienced mentor.

Somhlolo, strategist and statesman more interested in incorporating foreign elements than destroying them, had sought a marriage alliance with Zidze, the Ndwandwe ruler then at the height of his military power, and had sent emissaries to make a formal request. Zidze agreed somewhat reluctantly and from all his unmarried daughters, the envoys selected a lovely, virginal, and altogether charming little girl, Tsandzile. Asked if she were willing to go to the King of the Swazi, and if so to place her hand on the special stick brought to symbolize the royal mission, she did so with deep solemnity; the contract was sealed, her position assured. The Swazi envoys escorted her proudly to her new home, accompanied, in accordance with custom, by sisters to ease her loneliness and become her *tinhlanti*, subsidiary co-wives.

At Lobamba, then the capital, Tsandzile was put under the strict and watchful eye of the ruling Ndlovukazi, Lojiba Simelane, until ripe for marriage to Somhlolo. The ceremony was performed with a unique ritual, indicating her position as main wife and future Ndlovukazi. When she moved from the Great Hut of her mother-in-law into the harem with Somhlolo's other wives, there were some who resented her, knowing the honoured position she would hold, but she is said to have won most of them over by her patience and sweet disposition. She had more than high birth and extraordinary beauty. She was lively, talented, an artist in beadwork, a composer of dance and song (to her are attributed two of the chants still sung in the soft dialect of her people during the *Ncwala*, sacred ritual of Kingship), and she was also wise, compassionate and peace-loving.

When in 1836 Somhlolo died, having foretold the time and circumstances of his own peaceful death at a very ripe old age, laZidze (Tsandzile) was publicly installed as Ndlovukazi, and the Council enthroned her surviving son Mswati, a young man not yet married, as Ngwenyama. Mswati was the greatest of the Swazi fighting kings. He reorganized the warriors into age regiments that cut across local and kinship ties. Pursuing the policy of conquest and diplomatic alliances set by his father, Somhlolo, he expanded, consolidated and enriched the nation by the incorporation of foreigners; and he gave protection to refugees from rival and more despotic rulers. Wars were sporadic, waged when least work was required from the men, and seldom lasted more than a few months.

There was least security along the borders, and the Swazi were greatly threatened by the Zulu under the rule of their king Mpande. Following a major battle fought in 1854 on Swazi soil, subsequent Zulu raids were curtailed as a result of an appeal by Mswati to Theophilus (later Sir Theophilus) Shepstone, Diplomatic Agent of Natives in Natal, to whom with traditional diplomacy and courtesy he also sent a princess as a potential bride.

The conflicts in this period of African nation-building were sharpened by the simultaneous process of European empire building. Though no whites had settled in the country during the reign of Somhlolo, their existence was well known, and their presence considered a potential threat. They were labelled *Balumbi* (workers of esoteric deeds) and Somhlolo, guided by the voice of ancestral wisdom heard in a dream, warned his people never to shed their blood. They would bring with them two gifts, *umculu*, later identified as the Bible, and *indilinga*, money – the first they should accept, of the second they should be wary. It was in Mswati's reign that whites, mainly hunters and traders, came to the Court and were well received. Mswati also sent messengers to a Mission Conference to invite bearers of *umculu* to the country. The first mission,established in 1843 by a Wesleyan minister, Rev. James Allison, was temporarily abandoned when the missionary and his converts fled during the course of an internal conflict, unaware that Mswati had ordered his warriors to do them no harm. Boer and British and, to a lesser extent, Portuguese were competing for control over rich resources in land and minerals, and in Mswati's reign the first concessions were made, precursors to an economic conquest of the country, backed ultimately by the threat of force.

But despite warfare and raiding and the presence of foreigners, life in royal villages, more especially in the capital, was generally orderly and cultivated. Plants, grasses, birds, game, seeds, fruits, stones and soils were seen as manifestations of the power of an original and awesome creator, and were approached with respect and transformed with skill to human use. The technology was simple but the designs and effects were subtly expressed in a material culture of iron, leather, beads, feathers, pottery, basketry, and wood. Interpersonal relations were governed by elaborate patterns of deference related to perceptions of kinship, age, locality and nationality.

When Mswati died, in 1868, after having ruled with laZidze for some twenty-eight years, the Swazi state appeared strong and intact. The regiments were well organized, the generals successful and loyal, and subjects could anticipate protection from external foes and security of person and property within a centralized system of law. LaZidze was in her prime. From Mswati's queens and many children the Royal Council selected as main wife Sisile Khumalo, who had an only child, an adolescent boy, Ludvonga. LaZidze was recognized as Regent together with Prince Ndwandwa, another of Somhlolo's sons, whose mother, Fife, had come as laZidze's junior sister and co-wife to Mswati. A new capital, Nkanini, was founded for Sisile Khumalo, the potential Ndlovukazi, but in the interim laZidze remained in control from Ludzidzini. Labotsibeni was one of her attendants.

Then tragedy struck. Ludvonga died suddenly without having fathered a child. The Council agreed that one of Mswati's other sons be chosen to rule with Sisile. But which one of the many aspirants? The princes finally turned to laZidze for advice. That wise woman said to the young bereaved mother: 'You are the one who has lost a child. It is for you to say who will now be your son.'[2] Sisile chose Mbandzeni, a handsome, gentle, generous youth who had lost his own mother, Nandzi, as an infant. He had been cared for by other 'mothers' – his mother's co-wives – three of whom were of her clan, the Nkambule, living in the royal village of Gunundwini. One of them, Tibati, had been specially chosen by her husband Mswati to care for the motherless child.

The Council accepted Sisile's choice of Mbandzeni although some of the princes wished otherwise. Mbandzeni himself felt little pleasure in his selection. He had been made a king, but knew that he, a child of an Nkambule woman, had not been born for kingship. A first principle of Swazi constitutional law states that 'a King is King by the blood [of his father]' but also specifies that 'a King is King through his mother'. There was, however, no way to avoid or refuse the appointment. Kingship was to be his burden. He would carry it to the best of his ability. He named his private residence Nhlambeni (from *inhlamba*, an insult) and his administrative headquarters Mbekelweni (from *umbekelo*, a patch or substitute).

It was his duty to continue the line of Kingship. There was constant visiting between peoples of different villages, and Mbandzeni had on many occasions seen the strong vital girl Labotsibeni at the capital of Ludzidzini and had been attracted to her. She was no easy conquest and an episode still recounted with much laughter is how on one occasion when he sought her love she responded with spirit, 'I cannot be courted by a person from a common village.' After his coronation the situation had obviously changed and Labotsibeni came willingly into the *sigodlo* not as his first queen but as one whom he had selected for himself.

A commando of Boers, under G.M. Rudolph, representing the government of the South African Republic, had arrived at Nkanini for Mbandzeni's installation in June 1875.[3] They recorded this as a demonstration of their authority; the Swazi considered it nothing more than an act of courtesy and with this attitude willingly entered, on 1 July 1875, into a reciprocal agreement. The Swazi promised to protect Boers who were in the country, and Boer and Swazi leaders agreed to give each other mutual military aid. It was around this time that Labotsibeni bore her first child, a boy, who received the name Bhunu (Boer), and moved from Ludzidzini to Nkhanini. Though Labotsibeni's position at Nkhanini was not specially privileged, she was obviously a personality to be considered, having already learned and experienced much under la Zidze's tutelage.

Trouble, however, developed between King Mbandzeni and the Ndlovukazi Sisile. Though her son Ludvonga had died without issue,

[2] Matsebula, 1972, p. 38.
[3] C.M. Rudolph, Command 6,200, 1890, p. 134.

he had been betrothed to a daughter of a Hlubi chief married to a senior Swazi princess. Mbandzeni had been warned by the Ndlovukazi not to take the girl for himself lest he be regarded as siring a child for the deceased, by which in accordance with the custom of the levirate, the child would then be the heir. However, Mbandzeni did not heed the warning. As King he had the right to many queens and the girl was willing. When she bore him a son, intrigue and rumour spread. The boy died mysteriously. Murder on Mbandzeni's orders was suspected. Sisile fled taking with her the sacred insignia of her high office, and accompanied by two of the regiments of Nkanini. The governor of Nkanini, Mbovane Fakudze, tried to dissuade them from deserting the King, but they would not listen. When this was reported to Mbandzeni he is said to have wept; he had no alternative but to send the regiments from Mbekelweni in pursuit. They were told to remove the *ematinta*, the potent and symbolic crown placed on her brow on installation, and then to kill her, not by the violence of spear or club – her blood must not be spilled – but by throttling with a narrow noose. So it was done. The *ematinta* was brought back and the body carefully buried. After a short decisive battle the regiments of the King had triumphed.   Now it was the position of the Ndlovukazi that had to be filled as quickly as possible in order that life could return to normal under the traditional system of dual sovereignity. The Council decided in favour of Tibati Nkambule, the kind, homely woman, affectionately known by her nickname Madvolomafisha (Short Thighs), who had looked after Mbandzeni from infancy. She now had a son of her own, Logcogco, slightly younger than Mbandzeni, who had always been – and would remain – loyal to Mbandzeni and to his descendants Bhunu and Sobhuza.

In the early years of Mbandzeni's reign, the presence of Europeans appeared to have little direct effect on the lives of most Swazi. They continued to grow enough food for their own needs; many men stayed voluntarily for months at a time in barracks at royal villages, responded to the call for labour, played their part in the great national ceremonies, went on sporadic cattle raids, and when summoned by the King engaged in more serious battle. But beneath the surface, and apparent continuity of custom, there were shifts in resources and realignments of alliances. Boer and British asked and on separate occasions received military support against a common enemy. The hardest battle and the one most vividly remembered and frequently referred to took place in 1879. At the request of Sir Evelyn Wood, the Swazi fought as allies of the British against Sikhukhuni, Chief of the Pedi, entrenched in the eastern Transvaal then under British control. In return for Swazi help, the British envoy is said to have promised to guarantee their independence for all time.

Mbandzeni had an additional reason for agreeing to support the British. The Pedi had on a previous occasion defeated the Swazi, and had also given protection to a Swazi Prince considered guilty of an act of treason. The Ndlovukazi laZidze had been opposed to this earlier battle – it was during the period of mourning, following Mswati's death – and she had argued that only a full-fledged King had the right to call out the army for war: the duty of the Regency was to keep the peace and use the regiments solely for defence. However, the senior Prince Ndwandwe and the chief commander of the regiments disagreed, although from the standpoint of Swazi tradition, defeat was inevitable. Many princes had died in that battle.

Now the circumstances were different, and success was predictable. Mbandzeni called up his own age regiment, the Ndlavela, with its local contingents, 6,000 strong, and sent them out with full rites of battle, under the command of Mbovane Fakudze. The British mustered 2,000 men, and British and Swazi fought together, co-ordinating their tactics. The Swazi crouched behind their shields, jumping forward 'like frogs', and finally scaled the steep mountain slopes, penetrating the Pedi fortress. Chief Sikhukhuni was captured and imprisoned by the British.

This was the last great battle fought by Swazi against another African people, and though it only lasted some two months in all, it was, in the perspective of those times, a costly victory: five hundred Swazi were estimated killed or wounded, double that number of Pedi, and 52 British.[4] Mbandzeni welcomed the survivors, praised them for their valour and had them purified and strengthened against the contamination of death and blood lust. The British had rewarded them with many cattle, which they presented to Mbandzeni, who had some killed for feasting and placed the others at a national cattle post, as was the custom.

In September 1881, Sir Evelyn Wood, then Deputy High Commissioner, came in person to Swaziland and told the King-in-Council that the British would never forget the help they had received, and that Boers and British had both agreed, in a treaty signed at Pretoria, that the Swazi nation be recognized as independent.[5] However, after the battle, the Swazi had raised the question of the actual area over which the Swazi King could exercise his jurisdiction, and the British had appointed a Royal Commission on which Swazi, as well as Boer and British, were represented. But the opinions and protests of the Swazi were ignored and the boundaries as finally drawn reduced Swazi territory by more than one-third.

Rumours that the country was rich in minerals, together with a discovery of gold, in 1880, lured an increasing number of European prospectors and fortune hunters to Swaziland. Adventurers with their worldly wealth slung in knapsacks over their shoulders trudged along the footpaths; the more fortunate travelled in wagons that laboriously

---

[4] G.M. Theal, *History of South Africa*, 2nd Edition, vol. V, 1919.

[5] See Convention for the Settlement of the Transvaal Territory, 1881, and the London Convention, 1884.

carved tracks over hills and valleys till they reached Mbekelweni. Companies were floated, largely with capital from overseas, and the possibilities of a harbour and a railway were investigated. Concessiónaires brought liquor, guns, cash, horses, dogs, blankets, and other products of the 'civilized world'; all they requested in return was that the King and councillors make crosses on documents before them. Some concessionaires drifted away after a while; others settled in as traders and farmers.

To them principles for incorporating alien Africans were applied. They received from the King the right to live in the country, permission to use the land, and a limited protection of person and property. In return, Mbandzeni required them to recognize him as sovereign in Swaziland, to acknowledge his authority, and to obey his judgments in all matters affecting the Swazi people. At the same time the whites held a unique position; they were not assimilated into Swazi life; they did not serve the Swazi King, and they employed his subjects as their servants. They came as individuals without the quality of high birth, and yet commanded the privileges of chiefs; they took no part in national ceremonies and followed their own religious practices; they were in language and cultural traits distinct, and frequently showed in their treatment of the Swazi that they felt they were superior. Finally, they maintained loyalties beyond the borders with their own national groups.

Among the whites were a few lawless men who, respecting neither the life nor the property of others, flouted all authority. Mbandzeni's subjects complained that Boers along the western border demanded tax, stole cattle, seized children, moved beacons, and treated Swazi of all ranks with injustice and brutality. Raids for stock and labourers were a constant menace.

European governments outside Swaziland abstained from taking action against miscreant whites in Mbandzeni's country. Learning of a threatened Boer invasion, Mbandzeni appealed to Sir Hercules Robinson, Governor and High Commissioner in South Africa; Sir Hercules advised him 'that if his country were entered and occupied without his permission by a gang of marauders, he should not remain inactive, but should collect a force and expel them'.[6] But Mbandzeni was cautious as well as peace-loving; he knew from the fate of other African leaders that it was disastrous to fight against the whites. Unable to control them either as groups or as individuals, and appreciating the danger of conflict between Boer and Briton and between them and his own people, Mbandzeni introduced new administrative machinery. The treatment of all inhabitants on the same terms was impossible. Persuaded by some of the more responsible concessionaires, he appealed to the British High Commissioner for protection – not control – by a British Agent. This

[6] Command 5,089, 1887, p. 40.

was refused. He thereupon made use of a basic strategy of government developed among his own people – control through appointment of an official from a trusted family. He turned to Sir Theophilus Shepstone, who had effectively responded to Mswati's appeal to restrain the attacks of the Zulu, and asked him to send 'one of his house' to help the Swazi in their dealings with whites.

Thus it came about that on 18 February 1887 Theophilus Shepstone, Junior, was formally installed by the Swazi King as Resident Advisor and Agent of the Swazi nation. The terms of employment were made clear. He was to act as advisor to the Swazi King only on matters concerning whites.[7] He was specifically excluded from interfering in Swazi affairs. He was not a chief, he had no subjects and no right to allocate land. He received a high salary for his services and could be dismissed if the Swazi government lost confidence in him.

Mbandzeni also attempted to control the Europeans through their own institutions. With his sanction, Shepstone called a meeting of concessionaires, and a White Committee representing land, mining, and other interests was elected, with five additional members as King's nominees. To this committee Mbandzeni gave somewhat reluctantly[8] a charter of self-government, expressly reserving to himself the right to veto any decisions. He told the whites that he was still the King, that nobody should force his people to work on concessions or beat them if they refused. He stated publicly that he had not sold the ground, but simply leased it to white men; that he would be displeased if they interfered with the girls, or burned grass, or made roads where his cattle grazed, or demanded payment from his subjects for thefts without first proving guilt; and that he considered he had the right to maintain his position over his own people by force, administered in accordance with Swazi law.[9]

For a brief period, 13 January to 2 October 1889, during which a prodigious number of industrial monopoly concessions were granted, Shepstone's position was held by Allister Miller (*Mabhala*, a scribe), a journalist as well as a concession seeker. He later obtained for himself a concession which Sobhuza, on assuming Kingship of the nation, would challenge in a test case before the highest available courts.

Mbandzeni died on 7 October 1889. In the fourteen years of his reign he had seen his domain restricted by European Boundary Commissions, his power questioned by European governments, his people treated with brutality by individuals over whom he had no authority. His people mourned his death. They recognized him as a good and generous King duped by unscrupulous white men posing as his friends. It would be one of Sobhuza's duties to clear his name of

[7] Memo by Sir T. Shepstone, 20 April 1889. Command 6,200, 1890, p. 148.
[8] He was finally swayed by the advice of Prince Jokova, a leading councillor who wanted whites to live their lives without impinging on his people.
[9] Command 5,089, 1887, pp. 69-74.

the slanders of those who had described him as 'a King who sold his country'.

The choice of Mbandzeni's successor, made without bloodshed, was the fourteen-year-old Bhunu, not due to his own qualities but to those of his mother, Labotsibeni. No girl of high pedigree had been fetched as Mbandzeni's main wife, and some of the Inner Selection Council argued strongly for the daughter of Ntjingila, Chief of the Simelane, the clan of the mother of Somhlolo, and mother of a young son, Masumphe. But the section backed by the Ndlovukazi Tibati and Prince Logcogco favoured Labotsibeni. Her son Bhunu was about the right age, so that there would not be a long regency. Mbandzeni himself had expressed a wish that she be appointed; her son would sire the true successor to Kingship. Though she had two other sons (Malunge and Lomvazi) and a cautionary idiom in the oral Constitution states that 'a King should not be followed by blood brothers', the consideration that finally turned the choice in Labotsibeni's favour was her outstanding intelligence, ability, character and experience. Without formal education, her wisdom, her perception, her wit and determination were already recognized and respected. The Simelane queen, despite her pedigree, was judged not to have as suitable a character for a Queen Mother; her son Masumphe would be designated *liphosa-kubekwa* (the nearly appointed).

On 3 September 1890, before the year of mourning ended, Labotsibeni was publicly acknowledged as Ndlovukazi, and Bhunu was shown to his people as their King. Until Bhunu reached full manhood, Tibati acted officially as Regent, assisted by Logcogco and many able advisors. Labotsibeni attended the discussions, taking an active part in making decisions, and the centre of Swazi action shifted from Nkanini to the new capital, a 'new Zombodze'. Her branch of the Mdluli clan was given the distinctive title of Mdluli Bhekiswako.

The Swazi population numbered some 63,000 and whites some 750, of whom about 450 claimed British nationality.[10] The whites lacked an accepted leader and their affairs were chaotic. The White Committee had failed to exercise control; from the beginning Boer extremists refused to support any Englishman; decisions were frustrated by personal intrigues; members were untrained and inefficient; their executive powers were challenged. A Joint Commission, appointed by the two European governments in spite of written protests by Mbandzeni, arrived after his death to investigate the racial and economic situation. Its report, drafted by Sir Francis de Winton, began by reaffirming the integrity of the Swazi nation and declared that no inroad on its independence should be allowed. It then recommended the appointment of a Provisional Government representing the three groups; Shepstone was the Swazi nominee.

[10] Sir F. de Winton, Report. Command 6,201, 1890, p. 8.

One of the first acts of 'the Triumvirate' was to establish a Concession Court, with Shepstone again speaking for the Swazi. This Court confirmed 352 out of 364 sought concessions. For three years the 'Provisional Government' muddled along torn by personal and national rivalry and with ever-increasing liabilities.

The Boers persistently advanced reasons why Swaziland should be annexed by the Republic. It had acquired for itself the vital concessions of railways, posts, telegraphs, navigation and surveying, and other rights which were essentially powers of government. In return for Swaziland and other territories required by his people, President Kruger offered that the Republic would (according to British phraseology) 'withdraw her pretensions to extend her influence north of the Limpopo' (i.e., subsequently Rhodesia). In 1893, after lengthy correspondence, the Republic received permission from the British government to negotiate with the Swazi for control over the administration of the country, short of actual incorporation, but the British High Commission stipulated that the free assent of the Swazi was an essential preliminary.[11] The document, spoken of as an Organic Proclamation, was placed before the Queen Regent and her Council. They read it with amazement and refused to sign.[12] How could England betray her promises and hand them over to her own enemies? They decided to make representations directly to the Queen of England.

In October 1894 an official delegation of five Swazi elders headed by Prince Longcanga, accompanied by two interpreters (one European, the other African) and a European legal advisor, sailed for England with a memorandum entreating British protection.

We consider that we are the Queen of England's children. You have protected us ever since the Zulu war and it is now with sorrow that we learn our Mother the Queen wants to send us from under her wing and hand us over to the hawks that will devour us. Whenever you, our Mother, have asked us to assist your troops, we have obeyed, even to the shedding of our blood in your cause. But this was nothing but what we, as your children, were in duty bound to do, and we did it willingly, knowing that our Mother would always, as long as we did no wrong, take care of us.

We have always been afraid of the Boers. We have lived beside them ever since they came into the Transvaal. The country they occupy adjacent to our territory was once ours, but our people have been driven from the land by reason of the unjust and cruel acts of their Boer masters, and now there are scarcely any living on the farms.[13]

The Colonial Secretary, Lord Ripon, handed them a written reply stating that while the British Queen 'is sensible of the confidence in the justice of her rule which is implied in the offer of allegiance ... she

---

[11] The following section is based upon Command 7,212, 1893, pp. 12-15, 101, 142, and 123ff. Also *Hansard*, vol. 347, 3rd Series, pp. 1,138 and 1,715, for correspondence and discussion between the British Colonial Office and the South African Republic.

[12] Command, 7,611, 1895, p.17.

[13] Command, 7,611, 1895, p. 28.

is precluded by her treaty engagements from accepting the allegiance which you have tendered'.[14]

The two European governments were not diverted from their plans by the opposition of the Swazi. On 16 December 1894, Sir Henry Loch, British High Commissioner, met with Paul Kruger, President of the South African Republic, in a railway carriage on a bridge joining Natal and the Transvaal, and after a few days of discussion signed a new convention similar in essentials to the previous document but with one crucial difference ... this time the consent of the Swazi was not required. When this was presented to the Queen Regent and Council and they again refused to sign, it did not matter. The country was proclaimed a 'protected dependency' of the South African Republic. Unwilling to suffer the doom of openly rebellious African nations, the Swazi temporarily submitted.

For the next four years, until the outbreak of the Anglo-Boer War, Swaziland was administered by the South African Republic through a Special Commissioner – Johannes Krogh (Nkoseluhlaza – Raw Chief) – and the British appointed a Consul, Johannes Smuts. Political and economic authority – the basis of power – was vested in a white minority with headquarters at Bremersdorp, and separate from Zombodze in place and outlook.

The Swazi rulers received an annual stipend of £12,000 from the Boer administration under what was known as the King's Private Revenue Concession, recognized by the Concession Court. But they and their subjects were finding white control oppressive; many were required as labourers, and treated cruelly as *Emakhafula* (Kafirs). Moreover, the 1894 Convention provided for the introduction of a 'native hut tax' after the expiration of three years. Tax was not tribute, and the idea of working for money demanded by an alien government – 'to keep the white man in the country' – was widely resented. There were rumours that the Swazi would resist the collectors and that specialists in war ritual had been summoned to prepare Swazi regiments for attack.

The Regency was over; Bhunu now wore the waxen headring symbolizing the privileges and the responsibilities of a married man. He was in his early twenties – passionate and headstrong – more occupied with hunting, riding and shooting than with the affairs of state. He spent much of his time with his regiment, Ingulube ('The Pig'). But warfare, which in former reigns gave young men the opportunity to prove their courage and bring back booty, was now prohibited. Enforced inactivity was frustrating. There was growing tension between Labotsibeni and the young King. She was suspicious of his activities at Mampondweni, his residential retreat in the mountains, and he feared her obvious preference for her younger son, Malunge. The tension between them was expressed in an internal

---

[14] 16 November 1894 in Command 7,611, 1895.

political episode which gave the Boer government the opportunity to intervene directly in Swazi affairs.[15]

On the night of 9 April 1898, Labotsibeni's loyal governor at Zombodze, Mbhabha Nsibandze, was killed. Bhunu was implicated, and the Special Commissioner summoned Bhunu for trial before the Landdrost's Court at Bremersdorp, claiming this power by reason of a clause in the 1894 Convention granting him 'the usual powers of Paramount Chief [only] insofar as the same are not inconsistent with civilized laws and customs'. At first Bhunu refused to appear, arguing that the Swazi had not agreed to and had never accepted that Convention. He came a week later, causing more tension, because he brought with him his regiments, fully armed. The Republican government rushed in commandos from the Transvaal with artillery. Rumours circulated that Bhunu would be sentenced to death; his regiments called for war. Bloodshed appeared inevitable. It was averted at the last hour. In a tense private session, Councillors persuaded Bhunu to seek asylum with British authorities in Natal. They sent with him some twenty brave men who knew the way; and a party of Boers who rode in hot pursuit to Zombodze were diverted in the opposite direction.

When Bhunu came before the British Resident Magistrate at Ngwavuma he said, 'I have fled my country because Boers are invading it, and bringing in arms to kill me. I have seen their troops with my own eyes. I have stolen no sheep and shed no white man's blood.' The British intervened on behalf of the Swazi, holding that there was no court then in existence competent to try the King. The State President of the Republic, in one of the innumerable letters between the two governments, admitted that he was anxious to be 'rid of a Paramount Chief after Bhunu', and considered that by his flight he had already abandoned his throne. The Swazi insisted that 'If the King is dead, the Queen is King'. The British contended that it was premature to treat the King as nonexistent, but eventually agreed to send him back to Swaziland provided his safety be guaranteed. At the end of a trial lasting two weeks, it could not be proved that he had committed 'murder', but he was found guilty of permitting public violence in the royal homestead. For this he was heavily fined, the amount to be deducted from the 'King's Private Revenue Concession', which he would continue to receive.

He was ostensibly reinstated, but a Protocol, signed on 5 October 1898 by the British Agent and the State Secretary of the Republic, removed all criminal jurisdiction from Swazi authorities, and in effect changed the status of the King to that of a Paramount Chief, subject, like his people, to foreign courts of law.

However, tension between Boer and British was also heightening. Swazi cooperation could be helpful to either side, Swazi antagonism

[15] Command 9,206, 1899, pp. 1-157.

was a hindrance. The Boer government made a public gesture of reconciliation to Bhunu, who might be a useful ally in an area where most of his people appeared to be more sympathetic to the British. In April of 1899, he came to Pretoria, accompanied by 1,000 warriors, at the invitation of the State President Paul Kruger and was treated with courtesy. But the Protocol which had removed criminal jurisdiction from the Swazi was not changed.

On 10 October 1899, Britain officially declared war against the Republic. The Boers withdrew their administrative officials from Bremersdorp and advised European civilians to leave the country; the Boer Commandant-General wrote to Bhunu advising him 'purely as a friend to rule Swaziland well and in peace'.

The general attitude of the Swazi was one of neutrality. The issue precipitating the Anglo-Boer War, an issue of franchise, was not their concern. They had their own more familiar troubles close at hand. The *Ncwala*, the great annual ritual of Kingship, was approaching, and no matter what was happening in the rest of the country, it had to be correctly performed. National priests, known as Bemanti (People of the Water), were sent from the capital to collect essential ingredients from the ocean, from rivers and from forests. They travelled secretly, avoiding soldiers of both sides and returned safely with their precious burdens. But it would be a difficult *Ncwala*. Bhunu had alienated many of his people and it was common knowledge that Labotsibeni preferred her younger son, Malunge, and that she had gone so far as to try to make him bathe with potions specific to Kingship. But when Malunge, who was said to be as good and as intelligent as he was beautiful, realized what his mother was trying to do, he had cried out in protest and refused to accept his elder brother's birthright.

When the ritual was reaching its climax, and the King, centre of activities, was in his sanctuary receiving the ministrations of the priests, he suddenly collapsed. Soon after he was dead. The people outside could not be informed. The dancing and singing had to continue. If the ritual were to be interrupted, there would be confusion and disaster. Labotsibeni and special elders acted quickly and secretly. The body was carried to a special hut, trusted men held watch, and priests of the Ngwenya clan, keepers of much of the sacred lore of Dlamini Kingship, were summoned to perform the task of traditional embalming.

In the meantime Labotsibeni conferred with other members of the royal family council attending the ritual and privileged to choose the heir. Bhunu had started his own generation of royal children in accord with custom from the time of his assumption of full Kingship three years earlier. On his death he left behind six widows with one child each, a seventh widow who was pregnant, and several girls betrothed but still childless. The widows with children were:

laDludlu (mother of Ladluli, a girl)
laNkambule (mother of Ncindi, a boy)
laMndzebele (mother of Sengcabaphi, a girl)
laNdwandwe (mother of Nkhotfotjeni, a boy)
laSimelane (mother of Mlumbi, a boy)
laMkhonta (mother of Siboshiwe, a girl)
laMavimbela (who was pregnant with Makhosikhosi,
   a boy, born after Bhunu's death)

Though the numbers were relatively few, the choice was difficult. The princes deliberated and argued, referring to precedent and manipulating complicated principles of succession, starting from the rules that a king is king by the blood of kings, and a king is king by his mother. LaDludlu and laMkhonta were fairly easily eliminated though their respective daughters were, and always would be, highly ranked; Ladluli was not only the senior princess, but also Bhunu's first child. LaNkambule had a better chance, but Mbandzeni himself had suffered from the fact that the Nkambule could not claim to be among the more prestigious clans described as 'bearers of Kings'. Moreover, Ncindi was Bhunu's first-born son, and several senior princes argued that it was contrary to Swazi law to confuse this position, specifically termed 'the first circumcised', with that of the heir, 'the eater of the inheritance'. Prince Logcogco stood to gain most if Ncindi were king, but he was not prepared to push for him in face of stronger claims.

There remained the three queens, laMndzebele, laSimelane and laNdwandwe. However, the Mndzebele queen had no son, only a daughter, Sengcabaphi, and though it would have been possible to give her a son by another of Bhunu's queens, there was a danger that this would result in a repetition of the tragic conflict which had taken place between the Ndlovukazi Sisile and her adopted son Mbandzeni. Supporters of the Simelane queen and her son Mlumbi inevitably included Masumphe, the prince who had been 'nearly appointed' in place of Bhunu. But Masumphe's mother was still alive and had never reconciled herself to being passed over in favour of Labotsibeni. The Ndwandwe queen, mother of Nkhotfotjeni, had the most favourable image. The Ndwandwe were renowned for courage and wisdom, and the memory of laZidze was revered.

Unable to reach a unanimous decision, the princes sent Princess Tongotongo, Labotsibeni's only daughter, to report their deliberations and their dilemma to her mother, the Ndlovukazi. She listened and then summoned the Ndwandwe queen, Lomawa, took her baby from her and gave him to Tongotongo. Tongotongo put the baby on her back, carried him to the princes, and announced, 'Here is the Ndlovukazi's reply.' The Council applauded 'Nkosi'. Henceforth he would be 'Child of the Nation'. His kingly name would be Sobhuza. His legacy would be tradition, re-interpreted in the process of re-creating a Kingdom.

CHAPTER III
The Power of the Crocodile

Labotsibeni, as mother of Bhunu, was responsible for the physical and spiritual well-being of his wives and children. It was her duty to call in doctors to treat the royal babies with potions and drugs of the *Emalangeni* (Children of the Sun), and to see that the regiments decorated the birth hut, which was outside the queens' normal quarters, with branches of the *lugagane*, an evergreen shrub, and that the nursing mother was provided with a distinctive necklace of dark wooden beads. Lomawa was the third of Bhunu's queens to give him a manchild, and runners carried the good news to her parents, the Ndwandwe of Zikhoteni. They acknowledged it with appropriate gifts, but as yet no one knew that this baby would be the future king.

For the first three months he remained indoors, close to his mother, and they were attended by an old woman and a young handmaiden, supervised by Labotsibeni, and allowed only privileged and selected people as visitors. In accordance with Swazi custom, Bhunu, as father, was not allowed into the birth hut and he spent most of his time at his own residence, Mampondvweni. Mother and baby were still in seclusion when the Anglo-Boer war broke out.

On the fourth full moon after the birth Lomawa returned to court and the baby was shown to his father. When Bhunu took him in his arms for the first time, the infant cried, whereupon Bhunu said with astonishment and pride, 'Look! Look! He weeps copious tears. He will cause the heavens to pour waterfalls.' From his father the baby received his first name, Nkhotfotjeni – a small beautifully marked lizard that slides out of the rocks.

Bhunu's death, some two months later, evoked deep currents of fear and dangerous rumours of foul play. Who but evildoers and traitors would have caused the death of so young a king? The corpse, shrouded in black ox-hide, was placed beside the remains of his father in a cave in the Mdzimba mountains. The nation went into formal mourning; the widows would have to mourn the longest. Lomawa, as chief mourner, was placed in charge of the grave hut where her late husband had lain in state, and which had been carried at night a short distance from the capital. Around it a few other huts for her attendants would be erected and a cattle byre constructed of stone for a special herd of cattle. This village, described as *umtsangala* (stone-wall), was to be her residence for three years but the child could not be with her.

Childhood is always a dangerous period and in this case the infant was particularly vulnerable. Labotsibeni gave him a new additional name *Mona* (meaning jealousy) which later became more generally known than Nkhotfotjeni, recording that jealousy, source of hate and fear, had killed his father. A Swazi king may not be in bodily contact with death, so Nkhotfotjeni was abruptly weaned and sent with all speed and secrecy to his mother's home. The task of carrying him the long distance was entrusted to two men, Lozishina and Ntjwebe, both of the Hlophe clan, associated with special knowledge supporting Dlamini kingship. Unlike other children who are tied in a sling of goatskin, his was the pelt of a silver monkey, an animal endowed with the quality of long life.

At Zikhotheni, Lomawa's mother, Msindvose Ndlela, welcomed him with joy and love, and when she put him to her breast he sucked and milk came and he drank and flourished. She and her husband, Ngolotjeni, guarded him closely but did not isolate him from the people of the community. They fetched a young girl, Lambuli (also known as laMatukisa), from the nearby royal village of Sigombeni to act as nurse and carry him around to play and be with other children. Lambuli's father Matukisa, a war captive who never rejoined his own people, had married a Swazi girl whose mother was an Ndlela, the clan of Lomawa's mother. Also at Zikhoteni were several women whom Lomawa called 'sisters' and treated as such and who, in the Swazi system, were 'mothers' to the child. One of them was a bright and intelligent girl, Nukwase, Lomawa's full sister, recognized as potential junior co-wife to Bhunu. There were also several maternal uncles (*bomalume* – male mothers) who showed him much affection and influenced him in later life. Among the senior uncles was Makhanandela, a kindly man, who many years later would receive the marriage cattle provided by the nation for his sister Lomawa.

In a nearby homestead was Ngolotjeni's brother, Elijah, one of the first Swazi preachers of Christianity. Differences in religious practice did not affect Swazi family relations and Elijah was welcomed when he came to Ngolotjeni's village to pray; he knew that he and his family were never excluded from appeals made to the ancestors for the well being of all. His children, Benjamin, Philemon, Naphthali and Norman, received a good education in mission schools in Natal. Benjamin would become one of Sobhuza's main advisors. His close playmates were his younger maternal uncles Mzululeki and Bholojane, who would later be sent to high school with him.

Lambuli, who died in 1976, described Nkhotfotjeni as a 'happy and beautiful child with his own strength'. There was little to indicate to the public that he was unique, but at the approach of the southern summer solstice, the time when the year is renewed and the green gourds ripen, special priests brought potions to strengthen and sanctify him. The power of the ritual would be related to the growth of the child, until on reaching manhood the full ritual of Kingship, the

Ncwala, could be performed. At Zikhotheni he was still young and weak, 'with the strength of a small calf.' After he had been there for more than a year and was able to walk sturdily, Labotsibeni and her advisors decided that he should be brought nearer to the capital. The Ndwandwe accepted the inevitable call and made the necessary arrangements. LaNdlela, Nukwase and Lambuli would return with the child under the protection of a few strong men including the two Hlophes, Ntjwebe and Lozishina.

The journey back was slow and perilous. There were Boer and British soldiers roaming about, and it had been decided that much of the travelling be done at night, resting the day at the homes of trusted people. They walked in single file, the men armed and on the alert leading the way and hiding the child; behind them came the women and in the rear, a few young warriors and a small herd of milking cows. The rains had come and the rivers were full. When they reached the Mkhondvo it was in flood and flowing swiftly. They called for help from the chief in the area, Mutsimunye Nkambule, who sent his strongest swimmer. The body of a king must not be washed by ordinary water and the swimmer had to hold the child above his head. To the horror of the onlookers, they saw the swimmer pulled by the current towards a crocodile-infested pool. The men on the bank jumped into the water, encircling the swimmer, forming a human bulwark against the crocodiles and current. The swimmer reached the shallows. The child was safe and dry. The rest of the party crossed without mishap; only the herder had fled in terror and the cattle were left on the other side.

The travellers remained for some days at Buseleni, the home of Chief Mutsimunye, and then moved to the homestead of Velakubi, a son of Somhlolo. They chose their route carefully, and wherever they rested they were welcomed. On the way they saw the signs of the war – untended fields and occasional deserted homes whose owners in their haste had left their goods behind. They reached the turbulent Ngwempisi. As is recorded in one of Sobhuza's praises: 'He swam against strong currents. He left the crocodiles of the Mkhondvo and Ngwempisi.' Eventually they approached Zombodze. Lozishina reported to Labotsibeni, who told him that the party should not come into the capital, but stay nearby at Etjedze (the high rock which carries another). In the field of Imfabantfu where the traditional red sorghum was cultivated, there was a large beautifully built hut occupied by Sikhupe Dlamini, one of Labotsibeni's trusted attendants. They remained there for a short while, the women and the child sleeping inside, the men on guard outside.

Then they moved to Gocweni, an old royal village, where two of Bhunu's queens (laMavimbela and laMkhonta) had once stayed. Mkhulunyelwa Vilakati, a good and trusted man, was in charge, and he took care of the young child and his company; and laNdlela, knowing her grandchild was in good hands, returned to Zikhotheni.

The bond between the people of Gocweni and the young child was deep and enduring. Gocweni was in easy walking distance of the stone-walled village of mourning and Lomawa sent a messenger to ask Lambuli to visit her. On seeing her she inquired anxiously, 'How is your child?' She did not say 'How is my child?' She was so happy to hear how well he had grown, but still was not allowed to be with him. However, special quarters were built for him a short distance from her enclosure, and then she was able to peep at him through the little spaces between the reeds in the fences that separated them. And he was well cared for.

Fighting between the whites drew close to the capital and Labotsibeni's spies reported to her on the movement of the troops. On 23 July 1901 a Boer commando drove the British out of Bremersdorp, took thirty soldiers prisoner, seized their cattle, horses and wagons, and on leaving set the town on fire. But they also freed a Swazi Prince, Mancibane, whom the British had captured near his home on the northwestern border believing him to be a spy for the enemy. That night the Boers camped on the Lancabane ridge, near Zombodze, and the following morning went to greet Labotsibeni and her Council. She had seen the flames, and though she accepted some of the loot and thanked the Boers for their treatment of Prince Mancibane – they had also given him one of the plundered wagons – she emphasized that the Swazi were not taking part in the fighting, and expressed her grief at the burning of the town.

In the winter of 1902, in the third year of mourning, at the full moon, Bhunu's widows were brought together at Zombodze; their widows' weeds were removed, their coiffures raised, and they emerged in their full beauty ready to resume normal life.

Prince Malunge, according to the ancient custom of the levirate (*kungena*), was publicly given the main duty of looking after them, and they would bear children in the name of their deceased husband. Included among these women was Lomawa's sister, Nukwase. Only Lomawa, as future Ndlovukazi and mother of the King, had to remain alone and aloof and have no intimate relationship with any man. By law, on pain of death, she could bear no more children.

She had left the death hut and all things associated with the stone-walled mourning village, which became a type of sanctuary known as *Ligangadvo*, under a trusted caretaker who had never to leave it unattended.[1] A new village, the future capital, had been built for her. Here she would be together with 'the Child of the Nation'. This village too had its distinctive architecture and was described as *Lusasa* because of its style of fence.

Nkhotfotjeni was given his own quarters and though he was now

---

[1] Ligangadvo is an enclosure surrounded by indigenous trees, where a ruler is buried and cattle have been specially brought in to trample down (*gangadzela*) the earth making the earth hard and the grave inviolate. The cattle are stabled there for all time.

allowed to visit his mother, she could not go into that part of his area which in later years would be developed into the quarters for his queens. While sovereignty (*bukhosi*) was one and indivisible, the two future rulers were recognized and respected as 'twins', linked but not identical, both equally essential. Each received appropriate treatment and instructions.

He had his own close attendants. The two Hlophes, Lozishina and Ntjwebe, were joined by Mncele, a young kinsman, and, in addition to the affectionate Lambuli Matukisa who had been Mona's nurse since Zikhotheni, Labotsibeni chose another young girl, Ncandzekile Mabuza, to tend him. Ncandzekile was of the same clan, the Mabuza, as Labotsibeni's own mother, and under Swazi customary law a suitable wife for Labotsibeni's beloved son Malunge; and she did indeed later marry him and, after his death, was selected as mother of his heir.

Since Zombodze was not far off and princes and governors of royal villages and chiefs of clans were often required at court, Mona learned who they were in terms of their descent and local bases of authority. To all he had to show respect, but some he trusted less than others. Among the many senior Princes were Logcogco of Gunundwini, Makhahleleka of Dlovunga, Maveletiveni, and Labotsibeni's own sons, Malunge and Lomvazi; among the governors were Makhambane Fakudze, son of the General Mbovane of Nkhanini, and Lomadokola Sukati of Zabeni; among the chiefs were Dinabantu Gama of Dlangeni and Bokweni Mamba of Ngudzeni.

Sobhuza considers these early years as not very different from those of other Swazi children. His life was simple, active, and disciplined. He was taught to behave with courtesy, to listen without interrupting, and to obey those older than himself. When the regiments danced in the cattle byre, he would take part with deep enjoyment of music and movement. By accompanying the herders he learned to distinguish edible and poisonous plants and to know the habits of birds and animals. He was quick to learn and his wit was sharpened by riddles and his memory tested by tongue-twisting verses. Best of all he loved to listen to the folktales of his people told in the hut in the evening.

When I asked Sobhuza if he had had a happy childhood he was surprised at the question and said, 'Of course it was happy, like that of all children', adding: 'naturally I was sad when I was punished'. Though punishment was generally 'by the mouth', he recalled that he was also 'beaten when necessary', since 'it is the duty of the elders to be strict and we had to bear our punishment with strength and beg forgiveness'.

It was only in subtle ways that he was distinguished from other Swazi children. He was dressed in the style of other boys, but his first loinskin was of the *inyankhabetane*, a feline animal with special powerful attributes, and later a leopardskin with the claws kept in, and while amulets were general, his were unique. His food was the simple diet of corn, millet, pumpkin, and various beans and greens, but he could not drink plain water or eat from the general dish of princes. An epidemic of Rinderpest had devastated the heads of cattle, and meat was a luxury. Since it was a sign of meanness to eat quite alone, in the very early years Prince Mshede, a son of Mbandzeni by the levirate, was selected to share his meals; later boys of special non-Dlamini clans would be allowed to eat from his bowl.

By the time he had lost his milk teeth he was expected to have a sense of responsibility, and, at this stage, his Swazi identity should have been inscribed by a small slit cut into the lobe of each ear, symbolizing the hearing of new things and the end of the more carefree years of childhood. It may be surprising that in his case this was not done; the explanation was pragmatic. When the operation had been performed on his father, the cuts had not healed for a long time and there had been complications, and though Mona would have liked to be like the others, instead he set a different example, and fewer people felt it an essential mark of Swazi identity.

The Anglo-Boer War ended officially with the Treaty of Vereeniging on 31 May 1902. When the news of the British victory reached the Queen Regent, Labotsibeni, she is reported to have responded, 'It is good', but to have added cautiously, 'We will see what happens next.' In August 1902, a small British administrative staff and a mounted force of 150 men came to Swaziland. Preferring the temperate highlands to the malarial midlands they camped on a hill in the area of Chief Mbabane Kunene, near to the Mbabane River (named from *lubabe*, a specially valued grazing grass) and called their administrative headquarters 'Mbabane'. In charge as Special Commissioner was Enraght Moony (soon known as Muni) with instructions 'To put a stop to the barbarous practices of "killing off" and "eating up" which had been actively resorted to during the war; to act as guardian to the infant son of the late Paramount Chief; and to select if practicable a Council of leading natives to act with him as assessors in native matters.'[2]

When Enraght Moony, accompanied by some of his men, paid an official visit to Zombodze, Labotsibeni and her Council welcomed him; they also 'mourned' the death of Queen Victoria, and expressed the hope that the promises made to the Swazi would be honoured. Moony in turn expressed his sympathy at the death of Bhunu, and the readiness of the British government to protect his heir whom he asked to see. Labotsibeni explained that it was not the custom to point to a child still too young to be able to speak for himself.

The caution expressed by Labotsibeni on hearing of a British victory appeared justified. The Swazi had hoped for protection, not domination; for a restoration of their independent jurisdiction, not

[2] Swaziland Archives. C.O. African (South) 729 Further Correspondence; Kuper 1947, 24-76.

increased restrictions. But by Order-in-Council of 1903, graphically translated as *Madlangengwenya* (The Power of the Crocodile), Swaziland was placed directly under the government of the Transvaal, and in the following year, the laws of the Transvaal were extended to Swaziland. The nation sent a petition to Sir Alfred Milner, as Governor of the Transvaal, protesting that the aim of the Order-in-Council was 'to destroy our national life and put an end to our separate existence, merging us indiscriminately among the scattered tribes of the Transvaal' (Petition dated 30/12/1904).

Milner was succeeded in April 1905 by Lord Selborne, who appointed a Concession Commission in an attempt to settle the land issue once and for all. The spokesman for the Commission, Johannes Smuts, previously British Consul when Swaziland was under Boer administration, explained at a meeting at Zombodze (17/7/1905), 'We are going to see for ourselves where the natives live and how much land they are using and we are going to put up beacons and make a plan on paper which we are going to show to the Governor when we return to Pretoria.'[3] Initially, the Regent and her Council provided six senior councillors to help the commissioners in their investigations, but as the work proceeded the Swazi felt increasingly threatened, and, realizing that participation might subsequently be interpreted as compliance, the councillors were withdrawn. When the commissioners complained that they 'could not understand' this action, the Regent and 70 chiefs set forth their position with strength and clarity. Enraght Moony, however, considered this document was 'sent in an improper manner', and added, 'You always seem to choose the darkest and worst way of sending your request.' He also expressed the opinion that he was 'uncertain whether it has really come from the Swazis'.[4] The Queen Regent, in a dignified reply, explained 'The Proclamation turned me out of the country ... [it] would place us in the position of "Kaffirs" to the Whites. ... We paid homage to the late Queen. I am not satisfied with the Proclamation ... and I ask to be allowed to represent the case in England.'[5] A deputation was permitted to go to Pretoria to see Lord Selborne,[6] and the following year (1906) Lord Selborne paid an official visit to the country to hear the views of both Swazi and concessionaires, but since the legality of

[3] Members of the Swaziland Concessions Commission were: Johannes Smuts (President), J.C. Krogh, W.H. Gilfillan, Enraght Moony. Swaziland Archives, J. 138/1905.
[4] Interview between Resident Magistrate for Swaziland, Queen Regent and Council. 132/1905. Swaziland Archives, J. 138/1905.
[5] *Ibid.*
[6] The leading members were Princes Logcogco, Malunge, Masuku, Mboziswa, Tikhuba, Magongo, and Chiefs Silele Nsibandze, Bokweni Mamba, Alpheus Nkosi, Lomadokola Sukati, Ndlela Mdluli, Mgudlula Mtsetfwa, Sishobane, Manikiniki Nkambule. An official of the Native Affairs Department was attached to them with instructions to be present at every interview with J.M. Parsonson, an attorney from Maritzburg, Natal, chosen by the Regents as their spokesman and representative, to discuss major issues. Swaziland Archives, 4/7/1905.

the concessions had been recognized by a British court, the odds were against the Swazi from the start.

By an Order-in-Council (dàted 1 December 1906) Swaziland, together with Basutoland and Bechuanaland, was placed under the High Commissioner for South Africa, Lord Selborne. A British colonial regime was next proclaimed with a Resident Commissioner in place of the Special Commissioner, and Enraght Moony was given the new position. Swazi chiefs, including the rulers, were recognized as essential but separate subordinates in the system. In October of 1907 Moony was retired and Robert Coryndon appointed; he brought with him previous experience from Basutoland, an awareness of the diversity of African cultures, and a respect for the knowledge of men on the spot, more particularly, de Symon Honey (his Government Secretary), and A.G. Marwick and B. Nicholson (Assistant Commissioners). The Swazi named him *Msindazwe* (literally translated as 'Heavy-on-the-country', euphemistically interpreted as 'prestigious').

The relationship between the Swazi and the British government was complicated by the ambivalent attitude of leading local officials to the Regent Labotsibeni. While they admired her shrewdness and determination, they were interested in having a more docile leader with less radical advisers. They informed Coryndon that Labotsibeni wanted her own son Malunge to be King, and advised him of the necessity of watching over the health as well as the interests of the true heir. At a meeting called by Coryndon on 2 May 1907, and attended by Labotsibeni, Lomawa and several councillors, including the princes Jokovu ('son' of Sobhuza I) and Malunge, and the councillors Lomadokola Sukati and Manikiniki Nkambule, Coryndon spoke of the 'young chief Bhuza', saying: 'You must remember that he is the most important boy in Swaziland, and he is the heart of the nation. Whenever you, Malunge and the Ndlovukazi come into Mbabane I want you to bring Bhuza with you so that I can see him and see how he is getting on ... '[7] When he had finished speaking he called aside Labotsibeni and Lomawa, with whom he shook hands, and he then stated that he would not shake hands with Malunge for reasons they would understand. The message was indeed clear; the British handshake was reserved for the rulers.

In June Coryndon wrote to Selborne describing Labotsibeni as 'an autocrat who has not only shown herself to be intemperately selfish and ambitious, but who has frequently established a dangerous credulity for the advice of irresponsible, and I am afraid at times unscrupulous adventurers – both white and black'.[8] In August he repeated his accusations, stating:

[7] African (South) Public Records Office. London.
[8] H.C. Correspondence. 6/6/1907 Public Records Office.

The bulk of the people have grown somewhat weary of the virtual tyranny which the Ndlovukazi has wielded for many years ... [she] deliberately violated many of the old tribal customs connected with a young chief ... [and the chiefs are] naturally incensed that they are not consulted on the disposal of the comparatively large subsidy [£150 per month] which she receives from government ... At the same time they have a constant fear and respect which she has earned from almost the whole tribe that has prevented them hitherto from taking any steps to establish Sobhuza's rights. There's a widespread belief ... that the Regent is very anxious to obtain the Paramount Chieftainship for her son Malunge ... I have personally and definitely informed the Regent that Her Majesty's Government would not under any circumstances consider any suggestions in this direction.[9]

A week later he wrote again:

I would venture here to emphasise the point that the formal nomination of Sobhuza as a Paramount Chief is a wise and necessary act in itself, apart entirely from the fact that such nomination would happen to follow closely upon another event of such national importance as the (land) settlement.[10]

To this Lord Selborne replied cautiously that no moves should be made at this stage, and that suggestions should originate from the Swazi.[11]

While there is substantial evidence that Labotsibeni would have wished Malunge to be recognized as King, Malunge himself was absolutely loyal to his brother's child and once Labotsibeni accepted this, she did what she could to educate 'the Child of the Nation'. Her main ambition was to regain the rights of her people; Malunge was her staunch and eloquent ally, and while local officials denounced her 'virtual tyranny' the bulk of her people praised her; 'Your body does not crack from men's insults.' The young King, living under the protective eye of the Hlophes and of his mother in the village of Lobamba, was only later aware of the intrigues of the court of Zombodze, and his feelings towards Labotsibeni were of admiration and respect rather than hate and fear.

Coryndon was given the task of explaining to the Swazi the harsh decision of the Concessions Commission embodied in the Land Partition Proclamation (1907). According to the Commission, the Swazi had granted their entire country to concessionaires; however, to meet Swazi needs, one-third of each concession was to be given to the Swazi nation; the rest – two-thirds – was treated as belonging to Europeans and to the Crown. Swazi outside of 'native area' would not be affected for a period of five years; thereafter they could only remain with the permission of the European owner and on his terms.

The concessionaires were more than satisfied – many had been prepared to settle for less – the Swazi were aghast. The whole country was treated as a British possession which had been given away for all

---

[9] Swaziland Archives, 22/8/1907, File 45/07/1418: 7.
[10] Swaziland Archives, 28/8/1907, File 45/07/1418:10.
[11] Swaziland Archives, 9/9/1907, File 45/07/1418.

time, though the Commission agreed that many of the Concessions were aptly named 'the wicked' concessions, (Sir F. de Winton 25/2/1890), and that most were made when the King Mbandzeni was physically broken and fatally ill.[12] Even where Mbandzeni had made the concession leasehold for 50 or 90 years with a right of renewal for 50 years, the title could at the choice of the holder be converted on expiry of the period into freehold or else revert to the British Crown.

The partition of the land, already reduced by the arbitrary demarcation of the boundaries, threatened the existence of every Swazi. For them the future looked gloomy. They were essentially a peasantry dependent on the soil for their subsistence. The land was a focus of national sentiment. Their King was custodian of the land; to lose their land was to lose their identity and their livelihood. Chiefs from all over the country converged at the capital to protest against the Proclamation, but it was left to the Regent and the Inner Council to decide on the strategy.

The Swazi requested permission to send a deputation to put the case before the King, Edward VII. Their request was initially refused. The Swazi persisted. There were stormy meetings in which Labotsibeni, Malunge, and others spoke with passionate eloquence. Eventually, and reluctantly, Lord Selborne agreed and arranged with Coryndon that one of his officials accompany them. A.G. Marwick was selected. The Swazi delegates were Princes Malunge and Logcogco, Manikiniki Nkambule (Governor of the capital), and the brothers Josiah and Nehemiah Vilakati, as secretaries.

Superficially it was an auspicious time for obtaining concessions from the British. The Boer War had proved unpopular and was one of the issues which had contributed to the fall of the Conservative Balfour government and to the victory, in the general elections of 1906, of the Campbell-Bannerman Liberals. Important reforms in health and labour conditions had been introduced in England, and several associations were interested in and prepared to champion the rights of oppressed people overseas. Foremost among these was the long established Aborigines Protection Society.

The deputation, which arrived in England in November 1907 and remained there until February 1908, sought interviews enlisting support where possible, and received a sympathetic press. They were granted a royal interview with King Edward, and were invited to many stately homes, but their most significant meeting, a meeting which would have important consequences much later in Sobhuza's life, was with Lord Elgin, then Secretary of State, on 21 November 1907. According to the record of the interview and subsequent interpretation elicited by A.G. Marwick, promises of additional land were made to the Swazi. At the time, however, this made no difference

[12] Report signed by J. Smuts, President, W.H. Gilfillan, J.F. Rubie, W. Scott, Secretary, Pretoria 30/4/1906.

to the situation. The concessions were treated as legally valid. Before the Proclamation was enforced all western weapons – mainly gifts by concessionaires – were taken from the Swazi.

The rulers acquiesced; but acquiescence is not acceptance. Throughout Southern Africa indigenous peoples who had resisted white rule by force had been punished with greater force. The Swazi were not isolated from events in neighbouring countries, and were watching very closely events in Zululand, original home of Lomawa's people. In January 1908, Dinizulu, son of Cetshwayo, was exiled to St. Helena, and the great Zulu Kingdom, despite brave efforts, was crushed and divided.

Labotsibeni realized the military impotence of the Swazi, and the weakness of her own position as a Regent and as a woman. Pointing to the young Sobhuza she said, 'This child will fight for the nation and bring us back our land.'

CHAPTER IV
Education in Two Worlds

Generally speaking the education of a king's son is conservative, but paradoxically the education that the leaders of the nation required for Sobhuza was such as to equip him to challenge both the overriding authority of the British King, and later, the peculiarly British system of government.

It was essential that he be taught to read and write so that he would be able to deal with the complicated documents by which whites claimed their right to rule. This was the bitter lesson learnt from the concessions. Labotsibeni, who regretted that she had not insisted on Bhunu acquiring this skill, had brought (1904) a special tutor, Robert Grandon (Longamu), a coloured man from Cape Town, to tutor her. younger sons, Malunge and Lomvazi. According to Grandon, she put to him the question, 'In what does the power of the whites lie?' and before he could reply, gave her own answer, 'It lies in money and in books.' Describing those early days he said, 'My schoolroom was a storehut, my blackboard the hearth. There I taught geometry.' There were no local government schools, and though by 1905, several missionaries were in the country and eager to educate the young King, conversion was their primary aim. The Ndlovukazi-in-Council, while appreciative of their dedication and zeal, did not wish the young King to be exposed to mission influences which would draw him away from Swazi tradition, and Edgar Mzoli, educated in Natal, was brought to the capital, Zombodze, as Sobhuza's first teacher.

Sobhuza tells with much mirth how when he started school he had no idea that the signs written on the board had any relation to the sounds that the teacher made them pronounce.

The old man (Edgar Mzoli) would wave his stick about and make us say 'AA BB CC', but only after a long time did I see their connection. I never took notice of what was there on the board. I took it just as a song and as we were singing A B C, I used to watch a wasp build its nest in the classroom. Then one day the teacher came and took out one boy and said, 'Point out H,' and then he pointed it out. 'Will you point out M?' He pointed it out. Then I began to realise that I was required to know all those cold marks. Then I began studying, as boys and girls were being asked before he came to me.

He passed, and felt 'very pleased and proud', especially because he had done better than an elderly married man who was in the same class.

The question of what the King should be taught in school and hence of who should be his teachers, was a matter of general concern and later controversy. Local British officials were unimpressed by Mzoli and they were suspicious of Grandon. When Mzoli retired, they chose Joseph James Xaba, a Xhosa, trained at Willowvale in the Cape, an elderly man with experience as a teacher (1877-89), policeman, postmaster, registrar of births and marriages, and interpreter. He took up his position on 1 January 1907, the year the Land Partition was proclaimed, and Coryndon became Resident Commissioner.

At the end of two years, Joseph James Xaba's appointment was reviewed, and found 'entirely satisfactory',[1] whereupon the Resident Commissioner requested his 'permanent employment', and the following telegram was sent to his former employer in the Cape:

Lord Selborne asks for absolutely trustworthy Native to educate Chief son and others near Mbabane in Swaziland. A tactful man is needed whose presence at great place would tend to combat advice of certain half enlightened natives whose influence is believed to be harmful. Would you recommend and could you spare Joseph James (Xaba) otherwise can you suggest someone suitable. Salary offered £150 but believe £200 might be made available if necessary. (14 August 1909, R.C. to Resident Magistrate, Willowvale).

The Secretary, Native Affairs Department, South Africa, telegraphed: 'No objection to James' transfer.'

In 1908 the first official school, a large single room and a small office, had been built by the government, and opened by de Symon Honey. It was equipped with benches, a blackboard, and table and chair for the teacher; public funds could not extend to desks for the pupils, and they supplied their own slates. Most of them were children of princes, chiefs and councillors, and roughly twenty pupils attended daily. Every morning Ntjwebe Hlophe would marshal them with the encouraging shout 'Eheleni' (in line!) and lead them off in single file. Xaba, nicknamed by the students Majotane (little melon), required that they wear western clothing – shorts for the boys, dresses for the girls; gratefully shoes were not required.

Fortunately for Sobhuza the hours shut in the schoolroom were but part of a long full day which began with the rising of the sun and ended after his companions had fallen asleep. From as long as he can remember he required only a few hours' sleep. The night was a quiet time for thought. He did not take book learning particularly seriously and preferred the wonders of nature and the excitement of the world outside. He recalls the joy of riding his first horse, Mpompi, a piebald given to him by a Dutchman (Mathys Grobler), a friend of his father,

[1] Letter from Resident Commissioner to Secretary, Native Affairs Department, 25 June 1909.

and as he trotted along, his playmates, children of princes, governors and councillors,[2] ran behind him.

Sobhuza remembers the feeling of pride when he brought down a guinea fowl the first time he used an air gun (also a gift from Mathys Grobler), and the beauty as well as the thrill of hunting with the warriors. Then there was the terrible day when he and Mbangamadze Sukati, a son of Lomadokola, and Mzululeki Ndwandwe, his young 'uncle', were playing with a shotgun, and it suddenly went off, shattering Mzululeki's shinbone. The hospital doctor at Mbabane wanted to amputate but Labotsibeni refused and called in Mphabayi Jele, who came from a family well known for their skill in treating fractured bones of men and cattle. He put on poultices of ancient herbs, kept the limb in place with traditional splints, and when he removed the medicines bits of bone came out, and the skin had grown over the wound. Mzululeki was left with his own leg and a slight limp. More than fifty years later Sobhuza still remembered the details, including the names of the doctors.

After school he spent time with the men, parading in the *sibaya*, taking part in the excitement of the periodic stabbing of cattle for sacrifice and occasionally for food, helping in the flaying and enjoying the roasted tidbits, reward of the younger helpers.[3] There were, he recalls, many men in the barracks, and they would gather in the clubhouse, and smoke hemp (it did not matter that it was forbidden; then it was a white man's law). They sucked in turn on the long horn pipe and they spat thick white saliva in elaborate patterns on the ground, and to some the smoke brought inspiration of great praise poetry.

The court of Zombodze was a school of rich experience. There were always people coming and going, and under the large fig tree outside the byre the elders sat and debated, and eloquence and skill were applauded. Sobhuza heard Swazi history not in neat chronological sequence but episodically, often dramatically, listening to people who were living records of unwritten events. In cases of clan disputes, they would refer to early migrations and ancient settlements, and when dealing with rival claimants for succession and inheritance old and intricate family connections would be recounted, genealogies and marriage alliances traced in detail. Memory was an asset, and he remembered well; this served him in later years when many of the cases came before him under new disputants.

His education in national politics had begun by the time he entered the schoolroom. Following Coryndon's instructions to Labotsibeni, he was brought by his grandmother and mother to meetings in Mbabane

---

[2] Prince Mshede, Bholojane Nxumalo Ndwandwe, Mzululeki Nxumalo Ndwandwe, Makweleni Vilakati, Dzingabaleni Sukati, Nguye Sukati, Bhili Dlamini, Lomngeletjane Dlamini, Mgebiseni Dlamini. Many of these would be sent with him to high school.

[3] The herds were slowly being built up after the devastation of an epidemic of East Coast Fever in 1902.

and Zombodze, and though he took no part in public discussions, nor in the private meetings of the *liqoqo* (inner council) presided over by Prince Logcogco, he heard of the issues and was told of decisions.

On 31 May, 1910, the South Africa Act of Union was passed. In spite of strong opposition by African leaders and white liberals, the racist policies of the Boer republics prevailed. The Act provided *inter alia* for the transfer of the High Commission Territories at some future date, subject to consultation with, but not specifically the consent of, the inhabitants. Its implications were discussed by the Council and the government, and became an issue which would engage the attention of the King for many years.

It was not, however, the Act of Union but a fire at Zombodze that same year which had its direct impact on the young Sobhuza. It was a terrifying experience. Sobhuza recalls that in the winter (August), the hunting season, he was at Lobamba in the *lusasa*. Everyone was sleeping, and suddenly there was tumult. The mountain of Chakijane, creature of fables, was in flames; the whole valley was ablaze.[4] The fire rushed towards the capital of Zombodze. The cry for help rang out. Women and children fled. Warriors tried to remove the national records from the office of the Secretary, Josiah Vilakati, and the sacred rain medicines and heirlooms from the shrine hut. They rescued some of the most precious possessions, but many treasures were burnt and irreplaceable documents 'lost'.[5] The homestead was in ashes: only the harvest, kept in underground granaries, was saved. There were wild rumours and speculations as to the cause. Some said that it was the deliberate act of the people of Mantiweni, Sotho spies who lived in the mountain and to whom were attributed many evil and strange actions.[6] Officially, however, it was reported that the fire had been started accidentally by Phumphununu, son of one Sikhwama Dlamini, who had gone hunting and made a fire to smoke out rock rabbits. When he went home he thought the fire was out. But it was rekindled by the wind.

The nation rallied to the call for help. Labotsibeni and her close attendants moved temporarily to the old royal village of Ludzidzini; custom prohibited her from sharing the *lusasa* of Lobamba with Lomawa and the young King. Zombodze *wemagugu* (Zombodze of

---

[4] Chakijane is the miraculous hare and animal hero of Swazi fables, able to transform himself into any shape.

[5] One large trunk with major official documents was stolen. It was brought back in 1921 when the thief learnt that the case against the concessions was being prepared. He said that he 'had heard the papers were so valuable that he had taken the box for safekeeping', and he asked £1,000 for his trouble! Dr Seme refused to pay, explaining to Sobhuza that the necessary papers had since been officially published. This story was told me in 1974 after my trunk filled with most precious material was stolen from the car of an agent who had asked me what value I put on the contents. I had answered, 'They are invaluable.' Sobhuza commented that the theft was therefore my own fault!

[6] One version given for the execution of Mbhabha Sibandze, Governor of Zombodze, was that he, backed by Labotsibeni, was in collusion with the people of Mantiweni, sending them meat of sacrificial cattle to endanger the life of Bhunu.

Precious Things) was rebuilt, close to its former site, and similar to it in external essentials. The Council requested copies of all official material from the government; Coryndon replied they could be seen when necessary at Mbabane.

The following year, 1911, Labotsibeni imposed a levy on her people, primarily to promote the development of education. This fund formed a precedent for subsequent efforts by Sobhuza.

The number of pupils at Zombodze steadily increased, but highly qualified teachers were not prepared to go to a small school in a strange place on low pay. There is the story that when Labotsibeni saw how little the teachers received from Government she brought out an old hat full of coins, and said, 'Take a handful.'

It was about this time that a brilliant young barrister, Pixley Ka Seme,[7] a Zulu from Natal, educated first by the American Board Mission and subsequently at universities in England and America, became an important influence in Swazi life. He was introduced to Labotsibeni through Richard Msimang,[8] a lawyer with Swazi connection; Seme and Msimang were two of the founders, in 1912, of the South African Native National Congress (later the African National Congress). Seme became a friend of Prince Malunge, a protege of Labotsibeni, and an advisor to Sobhuza. From Swazi national resources over which Government had no control, Labotsibeni financed Seme's paper, *Abantu Batho* (first published in 1912). In it he gave *inter alia* publicity to the Swazi grievances against concessionaires and steadily helped build up the case which Sobhuza would eventually present before the courts.

By 1913 the 'five years of grace' under the Land Partition Proclamation (of 1907) were over, and concessionaires were now legally entitled to evict Swazi living on concession lands. Whites no longer considered themselves indebted to a Swazi king but settlers of a country under a British sovereign. They had no compunction in ejecting the former owners. The pressure of population intensified on the drastically reduced area of land available to the Swazi. There were major disputes over boundaries, not only between White and Swazi but between chiefs themselves no longer able to provide their followers with enough land for cultivation. Malunge headed another deputation

[7] P. Ka Seme was born at Inanda in Natal and named after his teacher, Rev. Pixley, of the American Board Mission. Seme's first wife, a Xhosa, married by Christian rites, died; his second wife was a daughter of Dinizulu (sister of Gatsha Buthelezi's mother), and he later took as third wife Lozinja, daughter of Mbandzeni. He had sons by his second and third wives, and had homes at Mhlambanyatsi in Swaziland and Ladysmith in Natal.

[8] Among the early converts who fled with Rev. Allison, the first missionary in Swaziland (in the reign of Mswati), were Daniel Msimang and Stephen Mini Mzoli. With permission of Mbandzeni, Daniel Msimang returned and reopened the station in the area henceforth named Mahamba (the runaways). Stephen Mini remained in Natal on Edendale Mission land where he was recognised as a chief in a community of educated families which included Msimangs, Vilakatis, Kunenes, Msomis, Masukus etc – members of an emerging western-oriented mission-trained African middle class. Labotsibeni was in close touch with these people, and Richard Msimang was welcomed by her as 'a son of Daniel'.

to Lord Gladstone (successor to Lord Selborne) at Barberton, requesting additional land and also asking for title deeds as the only unalterable security on which they could rely. Gladstone said the request for more land might be considered, but refused to grant title deeds.

On 27 February 1914, Malunge attended the 'Kimberley Conference', called by the South African Native National Congress and presided over by John Dube to protest against the South African Land Act of 1913. One of the organizers was Sol T. Plaatje, eloquent speaker and writer, who declared that the act 'made the South African native not actually a slave but a pariah in the land of his birth'.[9] Malunge reported the discussions on his return, and Sobhuza listened and remembered.

At the outbreak of the First World War, the Queen Regent and Chiefs sent a message of loyalty to the British, and, on their own initiative, raised £3,000 as a contribution, which was spent buying two planes for the RAF. Sixty-seven Swazi joined up, but were not allowed to carry arms. They were attached to a 'native labour contingent' and served in Flanders.

In the meantime, Lord Buxton had been appointed High Commissioner (8 September) and in an address of welcome, the Swazi repeated the requests made to his predecessor, Gladstone. In a written reply (21/10/15) Lord Buxton announced that the British government approved the addition of 14,000 morgen, but stated that it was not prepared to make any further additions. Insofar as title deeds remained, he asserted that the Proclamation fully secured the Swazi in the occupation of Native Area and that a title deed, if it were possible to issue one, would give no greater security.

The war did not immediately impinge on the personal life of the young King or most of his people. He was 15 years old and Robert Coryndon, backed by Honey and Marwick, suggested that he be sent to boarding school outside Swaziland. Labotsibeni replied that she herself favoured this, but it required the sanction of the nation. She called together the princes, chiefs and other councillors. There was tension at court. There had been a series of mysterious events. Mgudlula Mtsetfwa, chief councillor and Governor of Zombodze, had died (1914) while still in his prime; Mandanda, his son, had not yet been appointed as his replacement; a fire, less serious than the fire of Zombodze, but more inexplicable, had burnt part of Lobamba itself; and perhaps most disturbing of all was the health of the beloved Malunge. He was in his early 40s when he took ill and the best doctors in the nation could not save him. Old people recount that when Malunge died the rains fell without ceasing for a week, and the rivers flooded the gardens, and all was desolation.

The idea of sending Sobhuza out of the country for his education

[9] Plaatje, Solomon Tshekisho, *Native Life in South Africa*, 1916, p.17.

was hotly debated; many were opposed to western schooling, and some who favoured the principle wondered which place was suitable – or safe. At one meeting Prince Logcogco asked Labotsibeni bitterly, 'Do you want to kill the King?' But she was adamant, and eloquent, and backing her strongly was Lomadokola Sukati, the influential and respected Governor of Zabeni, born in the reign of Mswati. Lomadokola and Labotsibeni had both grown up at Ludzidzini; he had later served her husband Mbandzeni, and was experienced in diplomacy. The matter was discussed for days, until eventually Logcogco said, 'Let the Child speak for himself.' When Sobhuza was called, he said, 'I will always bear a grudge against anyone who refuses to allow me to go to school.' 'And who,' asked my informant, 'would like a king to bear a grudge against him?' (Phica Magagula, taped interview 24/2/73).

Finally it was agreed to send Prince Logcogco, Prince Lomvazi, Lomadokola Sukati and Josiah Vilakati, with A.G. Marwick escorting them, to inspect Lovedale, a high school in the Cape Province, and to report if there were good people at that place or if the King would really be in danger.[10] Lovedale, a mission station of the United Free Church of Scotland, founded in 1820, had a fine reputation for its academic quality, its practical training in agriculture and industrial skills, and the liberal racial policy of its founders. The headmaster at that time was Rev. James Henderson, a strict upright man who answered the questions put to him with care and honesty, showed the men around the entire mission, and, while making it clear that Sobhuza would not be publicly favoured, recognized the special position he held. Later, his wife came in and spoke of the education in home economics which was available for girls. The deputation reported on its return that it was 'quite satisfied'. In Lomadokolo's absence one of his wives gave birth to a boy, whom he named Mfundza (Education). It was he who became Swaziland's first deputy Prime Minister.

The Queen Regent, in an address to Lord Buxton, asked that eight lads be allowed to accompany Sobhuza 'wherever he may be sent for his education so that on his return to Swaziland he may have around him during his term of office men of ability to assist him in furthering the development of his country as well as the welfare of his people' (Swaziland Archives File 222, 21-8-1915). The Council decided that three girls go with the boys, to receive education in their own right, and also to do things, 'like sewing buttons, washing and ironing shirts,

[10] At the last moment Logcogco and Josiah were not able to go, and with Labotsibeni's consent the government appointed S. Sangweni in their place. Each of the three Swazi was also accompanied by an attendant. T.A. Steward, Government Secretary, wrote to the traffic manager of the South African Railways (Swaziland Archives, 30/11/1915) to reserve the following accommodations: 'First-class seat – A.G. Marwick; one second-class compartment for three Swazi chiefs; one third-class compartment for three Swazi attendants.' He asked that the second- and third-class compartments be as near together as possible.

which men were not expected to know'.[11] Most of the pupils were children of princes and chiefs who were his school friends at Zombodze, but two boys, Shwapha Mdluli and Ngolotjeni Motsa, were fetched for special duties as his personal attendants; they were his future *tinsila* (ritual blood brothers). One of the girls was his sister Sengcabaphi, who was instructed to see that Sobhuza's clothes were always washed, well pressed and in good repair.

As the time for their departure approached, Labotsibeni wrote to Honey that some of the chiefs and governors still argued that it was not wise to send the youngsters away when the war was still on, but that she, Lomawa and Prince Lomvazi (who had taken over the duties of Malunge) 'don't agree; we decided that he and his companions must go next month under any cost to school. I told them that if any trouble should arise about the war the Resident Commissioner would see that he is looked after and protected' (Swaziland Archives, 22 January 1916).

Labotsibeni wanted education for as many of her people as possible and, besides those who went with the King to Lovedale, a number of others were educated by the nation. Chiefs were requested to send children to Zombodze where the selection was made. Though many elders were uncertain of the advantages of school education (which took boys from the more manly and traditional outdoor tasks, and which conservatives interpreted as throwing away their customs for those of foreigners), eventually 'a regiment of children' were educated in well-known schools in South Africa – Ohlange, Tigerkloof and Amanzimtoti as well as Lovedale. The expenses were borne by the nation, not the government, and in addition to full fees and uniforms, each child received *umdvonso* (pull along, i.e. pocket money).

Sobhuza and his fellow students left for Lovedale in February of 1916, in the charge of Major C.H. Gilson, D.S.O., Chief of the Police. This was Sobhuza's first trip outside Swaziland, and it had been arranged that he spend two days in Johannesburg. Cleopas Kunene, who had acted as interpreter to the first delegation to London in 1894 and who was then living in Sophiatown, Johannesburg, received the

---

[11] Twelve students were finally chosen to be with him:
1.   Shwapha Mdluli, age 13, son of Chief Mbilini of the southern section of the Mdluli;
2.   Dunguzela (Solomon) Dlamini, age 18, 'son' of King Mbandzeni;
3.   Ncindi Dlamini, age 15, son of Bhunu;
4.   Mncele Dlamini, age 18, son of Chief Mboziswa, son of Ndwandwa, son of Sobhuza I;
5.   Mgebiseni (Gibson) Dlamini, age 16, son of Chief Mhubhe (son of Mswati), of Ngculwini;
6.   Lomngeletjane (David) Dlamini, age 18, son of Chief Lomngeletjane of Sikombeni (son of Msukusuku, son of Sobhuza I);
7.   Magaqela (Harvey) Mkhatjwa Ndwandwe, age 18, son of Chief Vanyane of Elwandle;
8.   Mzululeki Vezi Nxumalo Ndwandwe of Zikhotheni;
9.   Sengcabaphi (Maria) Dlamini, age 15, daughter of Bhunu;
10.   Lobulawa (Margaret) Dlamini, age 16, daughter of Prince Mhubhe of Ngculwini;
11.   Mvundla (Emily) Maseko, age 16, daughter of Chief Kubonye of Sandlane;
12.   Ngolotjeni Motsa, age 15, son of Nkhukhuma of Zulwini.
                                                    Swaziland Archives, File RCS 222/1915.

visitors with honour. He drove them around the city and hired a hall and band for their entertainment. When the Acting Resident Commissioner wrote that he 'was extremely surprised at the expense (£385.5.2d) and never anticipated that it was Kunene's intention to hold public receptions at the expense of the Government' (11/3/16), Kunene explained:

There was a high expenditure on cabs, for a number of Swazi came to meet their chief. They were anxious to accompany him to where he went and could not be chased away; but, of course, we could take only five of the principal ones in cabs. The chiefs accompanying Sobhuza did not want him to occupy the same vehicle with other people. So besides the wagon, one first-class cab had to be engaged for Sobhuza and three girls, one for the other chiefs by themselves, and a second-class cab for the two policemen sent to look after the young chief by the Native Affairs Department and two from Robinson Gold Mine and two cabs to carry luggage. Vehicles were engaged by the day to cut down expenses. I took the occasion to be most important as it afforded an opportunity to introduce the future Paramount Chief of the Swazi people to the various members of the other native tribes Johannesburg draws together ... as a Swazi I could view Sobhuza in no other light than that of my chief – young as he is – to whom I should give the greatest honour. I may have been over-enthusiastic, I grant that, but when a wave of enthusiasm envelops a man he sometimes loses equanimity and almost exceeds proper bounds in what he does, only to regret it (as I do) afterwards. (Cleopas Kunene to Government Secretary 23/3/1916)

Sobhuza was also taken by de Symon Honey to visit Lord Buxton and his entire family in their lovely home, Arcadia, in Pretoria. Honey records that after an exchange of formal greetings and the delivery of a message of loyalty from the Swazi chiefs and people, Lord Buxton 'addressed Sobhuza and gave him advice. The ceremony concluded with the presentation of a bicycle by the High Commissioner to the young Paramount Chief' (Swaziland Archives, File RCS 222/1915). The next day he and his companions caught the train to Lovedale.

The journeys to and from school were always exciting adventures. A government official (A.G. Marwick or Major Gilson) would drive Sobhuza to Breyten, where the rest of the scholars would meet him. In the train he and his companions travelled together, second-class, the government official, first-class.

We can find no letters to his family but he kept up a sporadic correspondence with officials, reporting on his progress. In very copybook handwriting, he wrote on 11 May, 1916 to 'His Honour, the Acting Resident Commissioner' (Mr Honey) –

Dear Sir, I thank you heartily for your letter I received yesterday from Rev. Mr. Henderson. It interested me very much to learn that you are remembering us, as we do you. As you perhaps know, I am in the sixth standard and I am enjoying my work and I think doing well. I hope I will pass the standard at the end of the year and that my people will be pleased with my work here in Lovedale. I have joined the 'Flying Stars' football club and I like the game very much.

The holidays will be soon here and I had been wondering what I can do during that time. It is too far to go to Swaziland for so short a time and I do not want to stay here.

Will you, Sir, advise me please what to do. I think I'll also speak to Mr. Henderson.

I hope all things are doing well in Swaziland and again thanking you for your kindness.

I have the honour to be Sir,

Your Obd' Servant,

Sobhuza Nkosi.

Swaziland Archives, File 270/1916

Partly in response to this letter Coryndon arranged with the Headmaster that the King and two of his friends, Hophia Nxumalo and Shwapha Mdluli, be taken on a trip to Kingwilliamstown and East London. The Rev. J. Martin Dower of the Church of Scotland showed them round Kingwilliamstown, and took them to a 'bioscope' where they saw 'good and instructive pictures ... and they heartily enjoyed the entertainment'. In East London they were met by the District Surgeon, Dr Anderson, and the party drove to the beach. According to the record they 'were deeply impressed by the sight of the sea but were singularly quiet and gave no expression to their evident astonishment'. Later they went to a concert at Westbank and 'were taken all round the town on trams' (Swaziland Archives, File 270/16, 26/6/1916).

The following day they went to the railway works and yard where an engineer explained the various activities and gave them the prices of engines and rolling stock. On leaving the yard Sobhuza remarked, 'The English are a rich and wonderful people. I do not think there is enough money in all Swaziland to buy this place.' Then they were taken for a trip in a motor launch up the Buffalo River which they 'evidently enjoyed'. The next day they paid their respects to the Resident Magistrate, spent some time in the courtroom, saw over the Post Office, a large business house, and the two offices, and then did some shopping 'under *my* [Dower's] supervision'. Later, after a visit to the West Bank, to see works connected with the building of the Pier, they were taken on a tug over the bar and out to sea beyond the three-mile limit. 'I think they enjoyed this trip more than anything during their holiday. The Chief Sobhuza took the keenest interest in the machinery and has remarked several times since that he would like to go back to his home via Durban so as to have the pleasure of a sea trip. They also visited the Electric Power Station and the Docks' (Swaziland Archives, File 270/16, Martin Dower, 26.6.16).

Back at school, the Swazi students made good progress and Mr Henderson wrote to Mr Honey who had succeeded Sir Robert Coryndon as Resident Commissioner:

The Swazi lads and girls are shaping well. Sobhuza has adapted himself wonderfully to the new conditions and has been in earnest in seeking to improve his education. There has been a good deal of leeway to make up in his knowledge of English and in the class tests he has not stood very high but he has always been ready to try in oral examinations and has been quite ready to try again at once when he has made a shot very wide of the mark. ... He has shown a pleasant spirit always. He has taken fairly well to the round of duties in connection with manual training. He was for a time working with the tree planting and nursery company and for another period with a party at the experimental plots. He has not yet, however, sufficiently grasped the importance of agriculture and I shall have to do a good deal to try to interest him in it.

(Swaziland Archives, Letter 2/6/16, File 270/16.)

In the examinations the Swazi pupils 'did quite creditably. I am greatly pleased to find Sobhuza ninth in a class between 30 and 40. It is a higher place than I thought he would have been able to take' (Swaziland Archives, Letter 20.6.1916).

Lovedale entailed a range of new experiences, which to the orthodox Swazi contrasted somewhat unfavourably with life 'at home'. The mission presented more open, less family-oriented, religious practices, a narrower morality, a more specific individualism.

For most pupils a redefinition of names was the first landmark on an imaginary path of progress; the names of prophets, apostles and saints were deemed singularly appropriate as 'Christian names' for new pupils; others assumed, or received, names of white benefactors or officials.[12] A few of the Swazi students followed the pattern of adopting 'English names' – Dunguzela became Solomon, Lomngeletjana – David, Sengcabaphi – Maria. For a brief spell Sobhuza II was Benjamin. Once again Marwick intervened, and Sobhuza recalls a letter in which he, Marwick, advised him not to change his Swazi name, a name of honour among his people, for any ordinary and common borrowed name. 'I reflected on this, and never again called myself Benjamin or let anyone else do so, and I also always addressed those who had come with me by their home names.'

There were many other little ways in which he and his companions kept their Swazi identity; at the same time that they mingled with the rest of the students, they formed a Swazi clique. They learnt basic western modes of greeting, eating, dressing, sleeping, talking, but still retained their own standards when alone together. Some mannerisms were easier to acquire than others – it was easy enough to stand up to show respect to a teacher in the schoolroom (it 'never occurred' to Sobhuza to behave in this manner to an elder at home); it was more difficult when talking to an elder to stare at him directly and boldly, instead of averting the eyes 'with proper decency'. Other traits were simply added to their cultural repertoire; hymns were new songs of prayer and praise; football a good new game; the two worlds overlapped.

From a western middle-class viewpoint, life at Lovedale was disciplined and austere, but Swazi pupils had little difficulty adjusting to discipline or austerity. They had been trained to obedience in the regiments, and the living conditions in their own homes were simple. But some of the rules seemed unreasonable – the prohibition on

---

[12] The rationale, unpronounceability.

traditional clothing, the disapproval of traditional dance-songs, the secretiveness imposed on sex; and living conditions in boarding school were strange – sleeping on a narrow bed instead of a mat, the rigorous time schedule, food which though adequate was different and less palatable than at home.[13]

Sobhuza's Swazi companions did not want him to do the more menial chores of sweeping the classroom and cleaning the dormitories, and arranged amongst themselves to take his turn. When the headmaster discovered this, he called Sobhuza to him and said, 'You must feel with your subjects.' Sobhuza readily agreed, and thereafter did his share cheerfully enough.

The school was an opportunity for him to meet with students from other countries and he was a good and easy mixer.[14] While English was the language of the schoolroom, students spoke various African languages among themselves. Sobhuza was at ease in Zulu, which was his mother's language, and he had been introduced to Xhosa through his teacher Xaba at Zombodze. Communicating with fellow students was no problem. But his closest companions were the 'regiment from home'; with them he spoke that deep and subtle siSwati his grandmother Labotsibeni had insisted he acquire. Probably because of their closeness Sobhuza managed to keep an inner balance, looking outward with interest and tolerance, less torn between the two worlds than many other Africans, rulers or ruled.

Sobhuza's education at Lovedale was interrupted in June 1918 by the death of Princess Tongotongo on her visit to her mother. Tongotongo had been given in marriage to Chief Dinane Ndwandwe, descended through Madzanga, brother of laZidze, and she was bringing to her family the cattle contributed by his people confirming her position as main wife. She left no heir, and later it would be necessary to find a substitute; it was this obligation that Sengcabaphi would later fulfill at Sobhuza's request. In a letter to the Resident Commissioner in which Labotsibeni expressed her thanks for his sympathy in the 'sad and irreparable loss of my beloved and only daughter', she said, 'This has affected my health to a very great extent', and she requested that all the children return for the mourning ceremony (Swaziland Archives, 24/6/1918, RCS 321/18). It was also the year of the Great Influenza Epidemic, and the Regent wrote that people all round were dying, and that she could not run the risk of Sobhuza dying away from home.

When he left Lovedale he said he hoped to return and later be able to go to university overseas. But in January 1919 Labotsibeni informed the Resident Commissioner that she and the chiefs desired

---

[13] Henderson explained when he received a complaint, this was not surprising since the cost of education was so low. Sobhuza's food was separate from others, and cost slightly more; but it was essentially the same as that of all boarders.

[14] Among his schoolmates were the young Chief Bathoen of Bechuanaland, Z.K. Mathews, A.B. Xuma, all of whom later played important roles in public politics in Southern Africa.

that Sobhuza be 'formally installed this year', and that they had decided that he should not go back to Lovedale as it would be necessary for him to go through [ritual] medical treatment (Swaziland Archives, 22/1/1919). The Resident Commissioner replied that her wishes were a matter of surprise to him because he had hoped the young chief would have spent two or three years more at school and college and so have better fitted himself for the responsible position he would occupy (Swaziland Archives, 25/1/19). Labotsibeni explained that during the year he would be trained in the necessary rituals and continue his education at home, and suggested that he could then be sent to study overseas 'in accord with the young king's own wishes'. The Resident Commissioner did not think it would be necessary to consider this at present. But she repeated the request that Sobhuza remain in Swaziland since she was 'in failing health' and might die in his absence, and that she was the only person who could communicate to him the sacred rites appertaining to the Chieftainship and the making of rain. Moreover, during his training it was necessary for him, from time to time, to undergo ceremonies involving short periods of isolation (Swaziland Archives. Report by D. Honey 9/3/19). The Resident Commissioner, who was genuinely interested in Sobhuza receiving a good British education, had no alternative but to agree.

As Sobhuza himself was eager to continue with his studies, a private tutor was a possible solution. However, the question of who would be suitable was a matter of controversy. Labotsibeni favoured Grandon (former tutor to Malunge and Lomvazi) and Sobhuza himself had gone so far as to make his own arrangements with Grandon 'on the grounds that he advances more quickly under his tuition' (Swaziland Archives. Letter from Labotsibeni to Resident Commissioner Honey, 8/8/1919). Moreover, Grandon taught not only school subjects but current Swazi history, pointing out that the education of a king is more than book learning.

Honey was hesitant, stating that he knew nothing about Grandon's qualifications. Labotsibeni persisted and so Honey agreed that Grandon could take over Sobhuza's tuition for the present. However, Rev. J.J. Xaba wrote in a confidential letter to the Resident Commissioner that in his opinion 'Grandon's appointment would be most disastrous both to the young chief and Swaziland at large', and urged that Sobhuza's education be continued in his 'old school where he would be under our supervision'. He added pointedly that he believed Grandon to be one of those 'whose aim is to spy out the country', and who neither 'admired nor loved' the government (Swaziland Archives. RCS 339/19, 23/3/19).

Honey then suggested that Mr Quinton Makhiwane be brought to Swaziland to teach the young King. Sobhuza again asserted his own views, stating that he had no wish to be taught by Mr Makhiwane since he had been under his tuition at Lovedale, in Standard VI, where Mr Makhiwane 'had taught him as much as he was able and so could not prepare him for matric' (Swaziland Archives, 9/7/19). The Queen Regent repeated her request that Grandon be allowed to tutor Sobhuza, and this time Honey replied that although he had attempted to see Grandon on a number of occasions, Grandon had refused to comply and that he was 'not prepared to agree that Grandon should act as tutor' (Swaziland Archives, 26/7/19).[15] Eventually the Resident Commissioner and Grandon met, but this only reinforced Honey's negative stand. Writing to Labotsibeni about this meeting, Honey said:

I have seen Grandon but as he takes up the attitude that he is under your instructions and will have nothing to do with the government ... I cannot agree that he is the proper person to be in charge of the young Chief's education for which I am responsible as well as you. I have also spoken privately to Sobhuza and have advised him to take lessons with Makhiwane for a while. If he finds he does not get on well perhaps you will send him up to me and we can consider some other arrangement. I hope you will agree that this is the best thing. I am sorry that Mr Grandon's own attitude makes it impossible for me to agree that he should be the young Chief's tutor.
(*Swaziland Archives, 4/9/19*)

When the Queen Regent still insisted, Honey sent back the message that he 'absolutely refused to appoint Grandon as tutor to the Paramount Chief and that if he took up the position he would have him removed from native area'. Honey also wrote to Labotsibeni:

I fear that he [Sobhuza] will not learn very much at Lobamba, whoever may teach him. It is the discipline of a school that is required for young men of his age. That is why the King's sons are sent to school instead of having tutors. My feeling is that the best thing for him would be to go to Fort Hare (near Lovedale) for about two years and that when he is finished there that he should be installed as Chief if you and the chiefs should wish that to be done then. I know that he is not anxious to go but it would be the best thing for himself, as he will recognise afterwards. He could always come back for holidays.
(*Swaziland Archives, File RCS 333/19/1154, 9/23/19*).

In the meantime the school at Zombodze had grown to over 100 pupils, with two teachers in two schoolrooms. One of the teachers was Lancelot Msomi,[16] a member of the well educated Edendale mission community, which included families of the first converts who had fled

---

[15] Rev. J.J. Xaba was a brother of Joseph James who had retired, in 1918, at the age of sixty-one.

[16] The Msomis were well known. Lancelot Msomi's mother, Jane Mloyi, was a sister of Cleopas Kunene; Evelyn's mother, Jane Masuku, was a daughter of Nicholas Masuku, interpreter for Sir Theophilus Shepstone at the coronation of Cetshwayo. Lancelot and Evelyn Msomi were trusted by Labotsibeni and used by her to check on official publications. The Msomis kept a warm open home, and made a number of converts in the district. Among them were the sons of Lomadokola Sukati. The Msomis kept up their friendship with the King and his people when, after seven years, they returned to Natal with their two daughters, Nomusa – Kindness, and Sibhimbi – a Celebration. Sibhimbi, christened Jane, was born on 28 September 1919 while her father was attending the great ceremony marking Sobhuza's coming of age – *sibhimbi sekutfomba*.

from Swaziland with Rev. Allison in the reign of Mswati. Labotsibeni was prepared to accept Msomi, whom Sobhuza already knew as a strict but serious teacher, and for whom he had much respect. A compromise was reached: Msomi was appointed as his tutor and Grandon remained in Swaziland. Sobhuza would benefit by the wisdom and knowledge of both.[17]

[17] When Malunge died Grandon wrote the following poem:

TO THEE SOBHUZA
(Future Paramount of the Swazi Nation)

An Extract (inserted here without explanatory notes) from R. Grandon's 'Tragedy of Malunge'.

Remoter Reasons for the Assassination of thine uncle Prince Malunge

Because of

1.

No greater love had he than this –
　No better off'ring could he give
Than to resign his life that thou
　O Bhuza, orphan Child mightst live,
And in the fulness of thy time
　The throne of Ngwaneland ascend –
To reign thereon a full-fledg'd King,
　Did destiny thus far intend.
But I am sway'd by doubts and fears,
　That thou wilt manhood fully see.
The fate, that overtook thy sires,
　Is verily pursuing thee!

2.

Malunge died for thee, frail Child!
　Believe me if thou wilt or not!
Thro' fifteen fleeting summers thrice
　The Devil tempted him to blot
Thee out, and seize the reins of pow'r!
　Three – thrice the Tempter fail'd – Defeat
And wounded pride arous'd in him!–
　Revenge implacable tho' sweet!–
Revenge impell'd him next to stretch
　Forth murd'rous hands to smite him down,
That he in his appointed time
　Might lure another with thy crown!–

3.

Malunge died for thee, frail Child!–
　His clay lies mould'ring in the tomb
His stalwart arm is impotent
　To save thee now from threat'ning doom!
Thou movest all alone amid
　Both secret and avowed foes!–
How thou from this day forth wilt fare,
　The Lord of Heaven only knows!–
Protection such as white men give
　Insur'd Malunge not from harm!
And Sorcery, which they deny
　Will smite thee too with unseen arm!

4.

Malunge died for thee, frail Child!–
　Didst thou his sacrifice for thee
Forget, then may the World declare
　Thee guilty of profanity!
Could sire for son severer tests
　Endure? To such as stoop to feed,–
Like beasts – on grass, Malunge's life
　A failure seems. To such as read
Him with their vision heav'nward set,
　Appeareth no obscurity!–
His failure view'd from higher planes,
　Suggesteth naught but victory!–

5.

Corporeal Nature profits naught!–
　Malunge's foes do rest content
That they have wip'd him out for aye!–
　How vain their energies were spent!–
The Spirit is the quick'ning pow'r–
　And this can never – never die!–
Hereafter shall his murderer
　Fling back upon himself the lie!–
Malunge therefore, is not dead!–
　This truth to many comfort gives;
And even Vilakazi now
　Takes up the strain – 'Malunge Lives!'

6.

The tenth, the sixth and eighth commands
　So far as these affected thee
And thy domain he strove by aid '
　Of Truth, that sway'd him visibly,
Inviolate to keep. His 'Man
　Internal' thus triumphant rose.
Tho' his 'External' fail'd amid
　The plots of his invet'rate foes.
Tho' thou and thy dead tribesmen have
　Forgotten him, his victory
Both echoes and re-echoes thro'–
　And Thro' – ka-Ngwane's perfidy!–

CHAPTER V
Celebrations of Maturity

In September 1919 Sobhuza reached manhood. The Queen Regent informed the Resident Commissioner by letter (dated 27/9/19), 'The young chief – Sobhuza – has this morning become of age (matured) and he has to be attended by doctors which will take a few days to complete the ceremony. The doctors are not here and we have to send for them which means time also' (Swaziland Archives, RCS 339/19).

Before dawn of that momentous day Sobhuza ceremoniously drove out the cattle from homesteads in the neighbourhood. The herdboys on discovering this followed after him and 'beat him', but not hard – they knew who he was. Then they returned the cattle to their owners, and accompanied him in triumph to Lobamba where the older regiments and royal women received him.

It was time to dance his *sibhimbi sekutfomba* (celebration of puberty) and show the grown youth to the nation. September, known as *Inyoni*, the Bird, is traditionally a good moon for celebrations. The sorghum – first staple of the nation – is ripe and harvested, the first rains begin, the earth is soft, ready for the planting of early crops of maize, legumes and pumpkins; cattle are taken to graze off the tender green, growing from the burnt stubbles of winter; the power of the ancestors has been recognized and their blessing sought through cattle taken to the royal graves and specified royal villages.

Princes, chiefs and warriors gathered at Zombodze, and playing a vital role were the royal women – princesses and wives of past kings. Holding a new place in the public eye was his own mother, Lomawa, who stood beside the grand old Ndlovukazi Labotsibeni. In the *sibaya* of Zombodze ancient dance-songs were reenacted, glorifying and inspiring the new King. The themes of these songs were beaten out repeatedly, rhythmically and solemnly, to haunting tunes, and when one song ended, another began, each deeply moving, with words heavy with symbolism, conveying the grandeur and the trials of full manhood, and Kingship. Then came *imigubho*, solemn chants rich in historical allusions and moral precepts, ending with *inqaba kanqofula* (the fortress of Nqofula), originally a hunting song composed in the reign of Bhunu and referring to the successful storming of a Sotho stronghold. For the *sibhimbi* of Independence, 1968, the same haunting songs were sung, and many would recall Sobhuza's first *sibhimbi* and the effect it had on all those present, and weep even as they rejoiced.

It was an intense emotional experience. The treatment was elaborate, part of it private, part public. The Regent had sent for Madlinkhomo of the Mabuza clan of Mafutseni, the only specialist with knowledge, inherited from his fathers, of the exact ritual. At one stage, the regiments went to the nearby Manzimnyama River where they dug up a huge stone on which the boy-king sat enthroned and underwent a symbolic circumcision – a solemn ordeal, imprinting in word and gesture the responsibilities of manhood. Actual physical circumcision – a custom probably borrowed from early contacts with the Sotho – had been stopped in the reign of Mswati.[1]

Supporting him through this (as they would at each subsequent stage of growth) were the two *tinsila*, Shwapha Mdluli and Ngolotjeni Motsa, his attendants from the days at Lovedale, united with him by a ritual transfusion of blood, the Mdluli being on his right hand, the Motsa on his left.[2]

At the end of that year, at the time of the summer solstice, the nation danced the *simema*. National priests of the Ndwandwe were sent from the capital with sacred calabashes to fill with water from the Mgwenya (Crocodile River), the Komati, the Umfuluzi and the Lusushwana,[3] the main Rivers that traverse Swaziland, and from the Lusaba (Sabie River), symbolic of the traditional boundaries of Mswati's kingdom.

Now the warriors were gathered at the capital when the priests returned. They wore elaborate costume – graceful capes of ox hair, long flowing tails tied to the right arm, kilts of leopard skin, and headgear of magnificent black plumes. They carried shields and sticks but no spears. The Child-of-the-Nation was treated with potions and medicines commensurate with his power. At Zikhotheni, when the first *simema* had been performed, his strength was but 'that of a calf'. Now, he was almost full grown. An ox, symbolically described as 'a bull', was caught by a regiment of pure youths and used in his treatment, which took place in a sanctuary covered in part by leaves of the *imbondvo*, a tough evergreen shrub. As yet he had no wives of his own. The regents were in charge, but he and his mother were being groomed for their own positions. On his face a half-moon was painted, and on her face a crescent. At the end of the ritual on the sixth day, a drenching rain extinguished a fire of burnt offerings and washed away the 'dirt' of the past year: the gods had given their blessing.

The elaborate symbolism of song and sacrifice moved with increasing clarity towards the final assumption of Kingship,

---

[1] In the last campaign sent by Mswati to the northern Transvaal the regiments, besides being ambushed, were also decimated by cold. Those who survived alleged that the cold entered the body through the circumcised penis.

[2] See Kuper, *An African Aristocracy*, especially pp. 78-9.

[3] At that period, the priests left on their pilgrimage as early as the new moon of October, since they went the long distance by foot. In the 30s, part of the journey was by motorcar, and their departure moved to November, but their return was controlled by the same symbols of time.

progressing each year. For two full years he and his mother would have to serve an intensive apprenticeship, learning the history and mysteries of the past and the knowledge of working the complexities of Kingship. Some, including the young King, felt the period long, but Labotsibeni insisted 'You have to go gradually into degrees of promotion' (RCS 756/1920).

He was twenty years of age. He had reached physical puberty rather late; most of his peers had already attained that desirable status, publicly announced in the more conservative families in the same way, on a smaller scale, as for the boy-king. His relatively late blooming had caused him some concern, but he was under treatment by the best *tinyanga* (ritual specialists) and assured that everything was all right. Puberty carried the privilege to court the girls publicly. Large groups of boys in the finery of Swazi costume, the princes with red feathers in their hair, toured the country, teasing and provoking; once a maiden favoured a particular boy she in turn gathered her bevy of companions and paraded to his quarters. The whole affair was public, henceforth they were *tingani*, lovers; the girl was committed to her chosen, and his age mates had to refrain from trying to steal her favours, and were entrusted to keep a careful watch on outsiders, rivals. The boy was free to win more girls; success was an encouragement to further efforts. But a lover was not a wife; and for the girl to become pregnant was a disgrace to both; techniques were taught to prevent defloration.

The case of the King was different. Marriage, carrying with it the right and obligation to bear children, was recognized as a matter of national policy. The right to marry was accorded to an entire age group only when the ruler gave permission. This was signalled by *kutfunga sidlodlo* – sewing of the waxed headring on each member of that regiment. Marriage was a formidable responsibility after the gallant days of freedom, and Sobhuza tells of men who had to be restrained by force from running away from the 'sewing' with all its implications. In the case of Sobhuza, the *sibhimbi sekutfunga* (celebration of sewing) followed soon after his puberty. The actual physical sewing was omitted; once again tradition was adapted to changed historic circumstances, the *sibhimbi sekutfunga* being performed symbolically, with appropriate songs and advice. The reason for this change was that his late father, Bhunu, had given instructions to Lomadokola before he sought asylum with the British that his son should not wear the headring, and Labotsibeni's advisors agreed that it would be awkward for him in his western contacts. Sobhuza added, 'Uncomfortable under a hat.'

He had grown accustomed to wearing hats as well as suits, ties, socks, and shoes at Lovedale, and was very fastidious in his selection and prided himself on being well dressed. But he still preferred to wear Swazi clothing at home, enjoying the greater freedom of movement. Because he did not wear the headring his men were also freed from it, but the age of marriage was still controlled by regimental affiliation.

Sobhuza had grown into a fine strapping youth, quick of wit, a beautiful dancer with a ready laugh, a generous heart and a mind of his own. The country was rich in beautiful girls among whom he had the right to choose his lovers. Once he had made his selection no one else was permitted to touch them; they were *emaphovela* (the King's betrothed), not ordinary *tingani* (sweethearts). His first betrothed was Lomabhunu, daughter of Ceme Shongwe, faithful attendant of his grandfather, King Mbandzeni. She made for him a decorative ornament tied at the waist and known as *umntfwana* (the child), which every young man in the past wore with pride as a gift from his sweetheart. When after some time Lomabhunu bore Sobhuza a child – her first, his seventh – he was named Makhungu (from the verb *kukhunga* – to present, to bestow), and his mother (who still has the vestige of past beauty, a pure singing voice and a remarkable memory) is known as NaboMakhungu.[4]

Sobhuza's first child, born on 29 February 1920, was a girl, whom Labotsibeni named Betfusile (She-Surprised-Them). The mother, Zintombi Zwane, was a daughter of Chief Mangetse Zwane of Mpuluzi. Soon after the birth of Betfusile, Lomacala, daughter of Chief Mgunundvu[5] of Nkuzweni in the Hhohho area, gave birth to Sobhuza's first son, whom Lomawa named Senzangakhona (Done-For-a-Purpose). The Inner Council knew the significance of this name. Sobhuza was indeed a man. In the intimate family circle the child was known affectionately as Sikhova (the Owl), and his mother, Lomacala, as NaboSikhova.

The King's betrothed (*emaphovela*) could not be recognized as queens (*emakhosikati*) until he had married two official wives, the first from the Matsebula, the second from the Motsa – two clans historically linked to royalty. He had no say in their selection; they were the choice of the nation, and neither could bear the heir. Described as his *tesulamsiti* (wipers away of dangers of youth), their role was in some ways the counterpart of the two main male *tinsila* from the Mdluli and Motsa clans; they too were ritual partners and protectors of Kingship rather than of any individual King. At this stage the quarters of his youth were transformed to the *sigodlo* for his wives (derived from the verb *kugodla*, to keep, to protect, to cherish).

[4] Makhungu was born at the time of the *Ncwala* in 1921 and attended school at Lobamba and Matsapha. When he left school he went to work at Havelock Mine, and from there was appointed a junior clerk in the registry of the Swazi Land Settlement Scheme Offices in Mbabane. With the approach of Independence he left the Government because of many national duties and other job opportunities. He is now on numerous committees and has shown himself to be a most enterprising and competent businessman. He buys cattle for a butchery which has, in spite of competition, obtained some of the larger contracts in the country. He is impressing on his own children the value of both traditional and western education.

[5] Mgunundvu was originally an Nkosi Dlamini (i.e., of the royal clan), but when Sobhuza, in accord with his privileges, married Chief Mgunundvu's daughter, the clan became distinct from the Dlamini and known as Nkosi Mgunundvu.

Marriages first to laMatsebula and soon after to laMotsa, both in
the winter of 1921, were essential to the complex installation ritual.
The Inner Council had requested a suitable girl from a section of the
Matsebula clan that lived at Mjindini. This had been a royal military
outpost established by Mswati, but because of the way in which the
border was drawn by the British and Boers, it now lay near the town
of Barberton in the Eastern Transvaal. From the time of their
incorporation into the Swazi nation in a distant past, the Matsebula
had contributed sacred and powerful medicines to the Dlamini rulers.
The root of their name, *tsebula*, means to overcome an enemy by specific
magical techniques, and their success is alluded to in their praises.
The section of Matsebula now living at Mjindini are famed for their
help in Mswati's victories.

Royal envoys, led by Longidi Dludlu, trusted councillor from the
south, brought back Lozindaba, virgin daughter of Mashila
Matsebula; she and her mother had given their consent. It was
essential that she come willingly; had she wept or resisted, another
girl of the same clan would have been sent in her place. But
Lozindaba came bravely; reserved, sedate, graceful, gracious, she was
regarded as a suitable choice for her office. Her face was serene, her
features fine, her skin a deep copper. There was no fear that Sobhuza
might reject her; he knew the care with which she had been selected,
and the points that had been considered – pedigree, age, character,
beauty. She was taken to his mother, and he did not see her until the
marriage ceremony. But what he heard was most pleasing.

Brides of ordinary men are accompanied by their girlfriends,
sympathetic women and affectionate brothers, but Lozindaba's party
was drawn from the royal regiments, dressed and armed as if for
battle. Not for her the songs and dances, the weeping and the wailing,
the demonstration of reluctance by a family to part with a daughter to
strange in-laws. She walked slowly, dry-eyed, showing to all that she
was 'a man', a ruler, proud to fulfil her duty, a fit partner for a King.
Leading councillors held her by the arms and took her to the *sigodlo*.
The 'mothers' and regiments remained outside, dancing and
chanting. The King-husband was brought to her by his priests. With
an ancient sharp-edged iron knife the head priest made tiny incisions
on the right side of each of the couple and mixed their blood – their life
– and gave Sobhuza potent medicines of fertility to spit through tiny
holes pierced through the grass thatch of laMatsebula's hut. He
followed the instructions, awed, unquestioning. It was the law of
Kingship. Suddenly the crowd was stilled by the shout – 'Silence' –
and then the words 'He stabs it', rang out. He was the victor, not as an
ordinary man but as King, the 'Sire of the herd'. Later, laMatsebula
was led once more into the *sibaya*, and the governors of the main royal
villages raised her above the ground, and the songs of the nation rang
forth.

A few weeks later, in a ritual not quite as elaborate but equally essential, Sobhuza married Fongofane, daughter of Mjoji Motsa, clan relative of Ngolotjeni Motsa, the young left-hand *insila*. Fongofane, whose home was Sitseni on the Mbuluzi River near Mbabane, had seen Sobhuza before; but he did not remember her until she came to him as a queen chosen by the councillors, a big dark beauty, laughing, voluptuous, warmhearted, with a zest for dance and song. She had been to a mission school for about a year where she had been given the Christian name of Leta. There she had worn western dress and had learnt to write and read a few words of Zulu; she would have liked to learn more but had no opportunity for further formal schooling.[6]

The traditional constitution dictated that Sobhuza could not enter the dangers and privileges of marriage on his own, and imposed on his *tinsila*, Shwapha Mdluli and Ngolotjeni Motsa, a parallel transformation and obligation. Their wives were not of specifically prescribed clans, but their marriage cattle were paid from public funds – the herds of Kingship. Shwapha's wife, Tfungo Zwane, was appointed as an attendant to Lozindaba Matsebula; Ngolotjeni's wife, Mqombo, daughter of Lomadokola Sukati, though related by marriage to Fongofane, was also affiliated to the Matsebula queen. Sobhuza, as their King, was the crucial factor in all their lives. So intimate was his identification with the two *tinsila* that if either, or both, should die before him their widows would be prohibited from weeping aloud or wearing the weeds of mourning.

When Sobhuza and his *tinsila* were married to their ritual wives, the girls previously betrothed to Sobhuza were recognized as Queens of the Nation, and brought into the *sigodlo*. It would be necessary for him to take many more wives, creating bonds with different clans, and keeping alive the royal villages of his predecessors. It was the duty of his mother to supervise them and help them look after his children in the way that Labotsibeni had looked after him and other children of Bhunu. No girl was picked at random, and there was no promiscuity; the King could have neither mistresses nor concubines, each was a girl respected as 'a mother of the nation', ranked in his lifetime by seniority in order of marriage.

Special huts were built for the *tinsila*, Shwapha's to the right of the Great Hut, Ngolotjeni's to the left. Surrounding this inner circle, the core of the nation, was a broad semicircle of huts occupied by notables and attendants, and at the tips the barracks of the warriors. The men of Sobhuza's regiment, the Balondolozi (from *kulondvolota*, to ward, guard, cherish), were more numerous than any other, and in their barracks was a platform for special black shields required in the ritual of Kingship.

[6] Her son, Mazini, born in 1931, was the first of all Sobhuza's children to be sent overseas, to England, for study. Unfortunately she died when he was on his way home; this affected him deeply. Then he had personal difficulties which the King, among others who loved the boy, tried to help him solve, but failed. He died in 1972.

At one level Sobhuza was part and parcel of the vast ongoing architectural plan designed in the remote past – at another he was himself the architect. Lobamba was his capital, the *sigodlo* was for his queens. 'The Child of the Nation' was being steadily inducted into the full responsibilities of Kingship; and the great priests of the nation were summoned to Lobamba to perform additional necessary rites. He and his mother were subjected to lustration and anointment with ancient potions, sanctifying their persons for the rest of their lives and preparing them for continuous battle against enemies, internal and external. For him the priests used the insignia of ancient kings, simple in material, complex in symbolism and association – a throne of buffalo horn, a sceptre of magical timber, a copper bangle, an ancient adze, and clothing of lionskin, the most powerful animal, praised as 'the one that devours men'. The coronation was a consecration, part of a traditional constitution of just rule. It gave the King the right to command obedience within the constraints of the total system. Hitherto he could only be addressed as Nkhosi; henceforth he was saluted as Ngwenyama (Lion). Before, his messengers summoned people to his presence with the words '*Phapha*' (fly) – fly like a bird; now he commanded '*Ngemandla*' – (with power).

On 6 December 1921 came the day for Sobhuza to be vested with full authority. For the first time in twenty-one years the *Ncwala*, the drama of full Kingship, was to be danced. Instructing the young King were the priests of the *simema*, headed by Vanyane, son of Nkamane of the Ndwandwe clan from the village Elwandle (at the sea), assisted by governors of all the royal villages, drawn from well-known clans (Mtsetfwa, Fakudze, Nkambule, Khumalo, Zwane, Nsibandze, Mdluli). The ritual had to be held at the correct time, and though the educated suggested this be calculated from the written calendar, the governors insisted that it be decided by observation of the position of the sun and the waxing and waning of the moon; nature was projected into Kingship and connected with the destiny of the King: 'The King races the sun', and 'the King is the sun', and 'the King grows with the moon'. The King had to be made sufficiently strong to face the approaching year and withstand rivals from within as well as kings of other nations.

On the day of the new moon of November, 'the Little Moon of the King', Sobhuza had sent out two groups of priests, each with a symbolic 'Princess' – a sacred decorated calabash. The Sea Priests would go to the ocean a little south of Lourenço Marques, and the River Priests to the great rivers. For the first time in twenty-one years the foaming waters of the sea as well as of the rivers would be used so that the 'waters of the world' would be brought for Sobhuza's sanctification.

It was necessary that the ancestors also witness the departure of the priests, who brought the vessels into the shrine hut, where the King, his mother, and leading councillors spoke to the dead and asked their blessings and protection. Snuff, traditional offering to the ancestors, was again shared by the Queen Mother, the Priests and senior members of the parties. Then, in slow single file, the priests taking the lead, they entered the great *sibaya*. The cattle had been driven in late in the afternoon. Before going eastward through the main gateway the priests sat on the ground to hear the last words of warning or instruction the King might wish to give before the two parties set out on their perilous journey, while the bards sang the praises of kings. Having seen the priests a short distance on their way, Sobhuza and his mother returned to the capital. It was the beginning of a long period of seclusion and isolation from active participation in their routine duties.

The priests returned to Lobamba the day 'of the blackness of the moon', bringing with them the sacred waters and ritual wild plants. The honour of opening *Ncwala* belonged to Mandanda Mtsetfwa, as *ndvuna* of Zombodze, village of the grandmother of the ruling king. Governors of previous capitals and members of the older regiments, dressed in the costume associated with the *simema*, began for the first time the first of the sacred dance-songs of the full *Ncwala*. A haunting refrain, 'They hate the child King', was repeated over and over again, as the men rushed into the *sibaya*, falling into the lines of a crescent under direction of their officers. Royal women entered through the upper gateway, each with a long thin wand of supple wood in her hand, and stood in rows according to their status.

They began a second sacred chant and hand song, describing how wizards and other evildoers, with treacherous and clandestine intrigue, contrive treason. In the sanctuary the priests were treating the King with appropriate fortifying ingredients and ancient medicines. As the sun set the dancers changed their formation from a crescent to a circle, from the partial to the full moon, and surrounding the sanctuary, again sang the *simema*. It was stilled abruptly by the command 'go out foreigners'; at the height of this ritual treatment the King must be surrounded only by loyal and unrelated supporters. All who did not owe him allegiance as well as members of the Dlamini clan had to leave. Those who remained awaited the order 'Silence' followed by the dramatic announcement, 'Eh, eh. He stabs it with both horns. Our Sire.' The King had symbolically broken the old year in preparation for the new.

The next morning, long before dawn, the people entered the *sibaya*, again singing and dancing the sacred songs. As the sun rose, the closing strengthening rituals of the preceding day were re-enacted. Later, beer and meat were distributed by the rulers and, when the feasting was over, the people returned home to wait until summoned for a new beginning, the second part of the ritual – the *Main Ncwala*. Every day during the interim, people in different royal villages of the nation learnt and rehearsed the sacred songs and dances of the *Small Ncwala* and prepared the full elaborate costumes. The dancing, the singing, and the clothing were not simply for entertainment; they were essential contributions to the strengthening of Kingship. Swazi from far beyond the arbitrary boundaries of modern Swaziland came to take part in the drama of Kingship, and joined their age-regiments at the capital.

The British local government had kept itself informed of the events. Senior officials recognized that traditionally the *Ncwala* had a military potential, and that in the pre-colonial period, the power of rival kings was manifested in great rituals at which warriors were assembled at central villages to fortify their leaders and to be fortified in turn by their mystical powers. In neighbouring Zululand chiefs had been prohibited since 1846 from summoning the regiments for their '*umkhosi*'. In Swaziland, the *Ncwala* had never been suppressed. The Zulu had been defeated in battle, the Swazi by Orders-in-Council; the Zulu nation had its origin in warfare, the Swazi of Sobhuza I owed its continuity to diplomacy. By 1921 British rule appeared sufficiently entrenched for its officials to view the *Ncwala* as 'a pageant' that did not threaten their supremacy, nor challenge their legitimacy. The Resident Commissioner accepted an invitation to come as a guest and make an official and formal appearance on the main day. Since there would be so large a crowd, and much celebration, he also instructed the head of the police to send a few men in case of trouble. Neither he nor the Swazi took much notice of objections raised by a few settlers who complained that labourers attended the summons to go to the capital at a time when they were most needed to work on the estates.

On the morning before the full moon, the capital was stirred by the shout:

Hear ye! Hear ye! Listen that I might tell you matters that come from him; he who wraps himself in the skin of a lion. Let such and such regiments go out! With all powers! At once! At once to the *Lusekwane!*

The King was sending forth young pure youths to bring in branches of the *lusekwane*, a magical tree, quick-growing with strong thorns and small leaves that remain green for many weeks. The branches were to cover the sanctuary in which he would be ritually reborn; they would overlay leaves collected since his *simema*. If a boy had secretly violated the code of purity and 'spilt his strength in children', or slept with a married woman, the leaves of his branch of the *lusekwane* would wither; and he would be disgraced, beaten, ostracized, his conduct judged less an ordinary offence than a defilement of the nation.

The warriors moved into the arena, and formed a semicircle, facing the royal women who entered in single file from their own quarters. Lomawa wore the regalia of the Ndlovukazi; in front of her were the Queens, laMatsebula, laMotsa, and then the other Queens in chronological order of marriage. The dancing began. The young King, escorted by a group of warriors, took his stand in the centre of the first row, among his own regiment. The men greeted him with the long shrill whistle, the salute reserved for Swazi Kings. The excitement was tremendous. 'Dance,' shouted the governors, 'Dance!' There were no spectators; everyone had to participate.

The governors signalled the end of that scene, and the youngsters left, accompanied by responsible men instructed to see that the laws were obeyed and there was no disturbance on the way. The journey tested endurance as well as purity. They walked barefoot some 40 miles, along rough and thorny paths and across two rivers swollen by the rains.[7] When they reached the valley of the *Lusekwane*, they rested briefly until the setting sun reddened the sky, and the moon began to rise. Beating their shields against their sides in a rocking soothing rhythm, they began a sacred lullaby. In the brightness of the full moon each youth hacked down a sturdy leafy branch.

On their return the rain, blessing of the ancestors, fell strongly, drenching the young knights, strong in virtue, who could not seek shelter but marched on steadily until they reached the place where they were told to rest. There the older regiments joined them, and the entire army went together to the outskirts of Lobamba to await the dawn, and the King.

The moon seemed to stand still as the sun rose, and the King, fetched from the *sigodlo*, came to greet the men whose cloaks he once described as glistening in the strange light 'like the wings of flying ants'. At his approach the warriors whistled and shouted praises, and the youths triumphantly raised their branches, and, singing the lullaby, danced through the main gateway of the *sibaya*, and dropped their branches in a high heap near the sanctuary. Everyone then gathered for another long session of dancing in the sun, the King in the midst of his men, the royal women facing him. Only when towards noon the regiments were dismissed did the youths realize their exhaustion, and most of them slept the rest of the day. Their strength would be required on the morrow, the day of *umdvutjulwa*, the sacrificial ox symbolically called 'the Bull'.

The day began for the King with the return of the priests carrying their vessels and token fines collected from anyone who had stepped in the path of 'the Princesses'. Ancient equipment was brought from the sacred huts of the nation, and the priests ministered to the King in the sanctuary. In the meantime the veterans opened the public ritual with the first sacred song, and the performance began afresh. Only the costumes conveyed subtly different messages. Lomawa and her co-wives wore special coronets in a design reserved for 'mothers-in-law', most feared and respected of women, and at the same time their leather aprons were not tied toga-wise, but under the armpits, a style indicative of the status of a young wife or married woman in first pregnancy. The older men wore tight-fitting caps of the black feathers

[7] Their route was along the slopes of Lancabane, across the Mtilane River, along the Manzini road, turning off on the rough and thorny path past Gunundvwini, royal village of Mbandzeni, below the Bulunga Hills.

of the ostrich, strange betwixt-and-between animal, and the youths were stripped of all decorations and wore only loin-coverings of leopard-skin.

When the governors herded a large pitch-black ox into the sanctuary, the women left the scene and went to their quarters for safety. The men continued their singing, the youths waited tense with expectation. Suddenly the animal rushed out 'strong and wild as a buffalo'. The King had struck it with a rod of concentrated power, carved of the same dark brown wood as the long beads in the crown of the Ndlovukazi and the necklace of Queens during the years they suckle their royal infants.

As the infuriated animal rushed out, the pure youths pursued. It turned. They withdrew. It escaped. They followed. An intrepid youth grabbed its tail. He was dragged along the ground. Others took hold. The beast slowed down. The rest caught up. They pulled it down, thumping it to the words and rhythm of the lullaby, imbuing it with the strength of their vigour and virtue. 'The-beast-that-is-thumped' (*umdvutjulwa*) lay still, bruised and beaten, not dead. They dragged it to the sanctuary and the priests killed it according to custom, and extracted from it those parts prescribed for medication. Another ox, also pure-black, was then driven in, but in sharp contrast to 'The-beast-that-is-thumped' this animal had never been, and must never be, beaten. It must never be killed; when it loses its strength a substitute is found, when it dies it is ritually burnt. This was a superb but docile creature; youths pushed it to the ground, the King sat on it and the right-hand *insila* bathed him on his right side and the left-hand *insila* on the left side with medicines twirled to produce foam, designed for personality, virility, and responsibility. The regiments chanted until late that evening, but long after they had dispersed, the priests remained with the King, preparing for the great climax.

On that day the King appeared in awesome splendour, at the same time that the dangers inherent in his position – rebellion from within and attack from outside – were publicly dramatized. It began with the praises and sacred songs, and the King in his sanctuary. Then at dawn the scene changed. Royal women and warriors lined the space between the arena and the Queens' quarters, and the King, flanked by his priests, appeared. He was dark, upright, strong, nude but for a glowing white penis sheath of ivory, and as he walked slowly through his kin and subjects, the women wept, and the song, with its theme of hate and danger, rang out with penetrating melancholy. Many years later his mother Lomawa explained to me: 'It is pain to see him a King. My child goes alone through the people', and a Queen said: 'We pity him. There is no other man who could walk naked in front of everybody'. An old man added: 'The work of a King is indeed heavy.'

More instruction, more doctoring at laMatsebula's hut and back to the sanctuary. There one of the rites was especially educative; among the medicines given him was the lobe of the liver, the *imphundvu*, which he had to conspicuously avoid eating. By Swazi tradition this part of an animal may never be eaten by young men, for it is believed it would make them lose their way, go astray, or become mentally deranged. The King, be he ever so old, would be bound by this restraint. When he came to this morsel, he called to the priests who exclaimed with simulated anger, 'Hau – he is eating *imphundvu.*' So having symbolically bitten into it, he did not chew or swallow it, but threw it away. At the same time he was made sufficiently strong to 'bite' the fruits of the new year – a green gourd, indigenous sweet cane, the tips of a gourd-vine, cooked and mixed with 'waters of the world'. After he had bitten the medicines, he ritually spat them to the east and to the west, and his people in different status groups performed their own protective rites. The Queens and the children of the capital were treated that same morning, others had to wait an allotted time.

Towards midday the people in full regalia were summoned to the *sibaya*. The costumes were more elaborate, and prescribed to the last detail. Lomawa wore the finest of leopard-skin cloaks, the claws left in. The young Queens were in traditional leather materials, no western cloth or ornament, their hair beautifully coiffeured, long black feathers of the widow-bird falling softly on their cheeks. The arena was filled with men in leopard-skin kilts, each regiment with its distinctive coronet under caps elaborately decorated with clusters of black plumes; brilliant red feathers of the lourie indicated young royals.

In the early afternoon, the Resident Commissioner and his wife, followed by a few officials, drove down from Mbabane. Labotsibeni, Lomawa and Sobhuza welcomed them and they were escorted to join other whites in a marquee erected for the occasion by the police. A large pot of Swazi beer was sent from the Great Hut for the official guests. In the meantime the Ngwenyama had rejoined the dancers and did not again interrupt his role in the ritual. After watching the sacred dance-songs for some time, the official guests took their departure; and thereafter other outsiders were asked to leave.

In the late afternoon the scene changed. The King moved forward surrounded by members of the blood royal. Behind them surged other warriors. The most solemn of all the songs rang forth, a melancholy song expressing the desire of the royal Dlamini clan to leave the country to non-Dlamini inhabitants.

The words and the tune were wild and sad, sounding to Sobhuza 'like the sea when the sea is angry and the birds of the sea are tossed on the waves'. The royal women moved backwards and forwards in small, desperate groups uttering their cry. Many wept. The men's feet stamped the ground vigorously and slowly, the black plumes waved and fluttered, the Princes came closer, driving the King in their midst. Nearer and nearer they brought him to his sanctuary. The crowd grew frenzied, the singing louder, the bodies swayed and pressed against the sides of the enclosure, and the King withdrew into his sanctuary. The priests followed; and the Princes moved back a little.[8] Then the song changed once again. The Princes lunged with their shields against the small doorway of the sanctuary, beat their shields in agitation, then drew back slowly and beseechingly, trying to lure him out, begging him with praises: 'Come from your sanctuary. The sun is leaving you, you the High One. Our Treasure.'

There emerged a figure impressive, awe-inspiring. A unique head-gear of black plumes of the widow bird covered his face and blew about his shoulders, revealing beneath it a coronet of lionskin. His body was covered in green grasses that trailed to the ground. In his left hand he held a shield, speckled with spots of brown and white. His right hand was for the time being empty. Fatty tissue of the beast-that-was-thumped, adorned with the blown-up gall bladder, was tied crosswise on his chest. Round his loins, he wore a kilt of silver monkey-skin.[9]

In this powerful costume the King appeared reluctant to return to the nation. He executed a wild, elusive dance with knees flexed and swaying body. The movements were an intuitive response to the rhythm and situation, a dance that no ordinary man knew and that the King was never taught. Old teachers who trained him in all his duties had explained: 'We do not know it; we are not kings; it will come to you at the time.'

Suddenly he crouched low and disappeared into his sanctuary. The Princes sprang forward, calling: 'Come out king of kings.' Everyone was urged to dance. The *tindvuna* brought down their batons; the people danced with vigour; here more than at any other stage they kept their King alive and healthy by their own movements. The mime continued with increasing tension, each appearance making a sudden startling and unforgettable impact. His eyes shone through the feathers as he tossed his head, his face gleamed with dark medicines, his legs and arms were streaked with black – he was terrifying and awe-inspiring, and as the knife-edged grass cut into his skin he tossed his body furiously.

During this scene the regiment of pure youths came in carrying

---

[8] What could it mean? I received two possible interpretations of this scene: First, The People of the Sun (Malangeni), the Blood Royals, want to migrate once again. They want their King to come with them; they want to leave the rest of the Swazi and the country in which they live. The second interpretation was that the Malangeni show hatred of the King. They denounce him and force him from their midst. The Committee advising me stressed the first interpretation.

[9] Each item of the costume had its meaning for him and its ritual association. From the special green grass (*umuzi*), technically *umhlahle*, razor-edged, strong, were made the mats of the shrine hut, kept from one reign to another, a symbol of the life and continuity of the nation. The sacred cattle, the *mfukwane*, have the tip of their tails cut off to brand them for work of Kingship. They are rarely killed and those who eat their meat lean cautiously forward so that no drop of fat touches the body lest it cause madness; their milk is said to be red, and to them are attributed human feelings. Only the King, his mother and the Matsebula queen, are powerful enough to smear themselves with the fat of the *mfukwane* and they are made more powerful by its use. The silver monkey has the power of life – 'no one has ever seen it die'. It was used for the sling in which Sobhuza, as heir to the throne, was carried as a baby.

large black shields, the distinctive shields of war. Pummelling them with clenched fists, like the beat of thunder, they started the final hymn. The drama was reaching its climax. Twice the King appeared and danced toward the regiments. In his right hand he held a wand daubed with black medicine. At his approach the warriors retreated. He retired and returned. Suddenly he emerged with nothing in his right hand. Aliens and royalty were told to leave. Then the King came out with a vivid green gourd in his right hand. It was *luselwa lwembo* – the wild gourd from 'Embo', the direction from which the Dlamini first migrated.[10] The Lion retreated into his lair, tantalizing the men. They placed their shields horizontally, waiting for the fruit that must not be allowed to fall to the ground. Finally, he lurched purposefully forward and threw the gourd lightly. As it fell on a shield, there was a wild stamping of feet and frantic whistling and hissing and thumping.[11] The dancers dispersed; the men with the black shields went to the river to bathe, and only the King remained in the sanctuary with a few councillors and priests who removed his elaborate costume.

When the warriors returned, the Ngwenyama, his face marked on both sides as a full moon, his bare body streaked with dark lotions, was seated on a traditional throne – a buffalo skull with its horns resting on a large ring woven of ritual grasses, pierced with four small arrows, marking the four cardinal points of the universe. The men greeted him with rich praises, containing the allusive phrase: 'When he sits on the skull of the buffalo the coward will run away.'[12] The buffalo is perceived as similar to and yet different from ordinary cattle, an animal in-between the wild and the domesticated, an animal that bellows like an ox, but is bigger, heavier and stronger. Its greatest defence is in its large curved horns, joined to the skull, that very important part of all living creatures, enclosing the brain – organ of knowledge and of thought.

According to custom the King spent that night with the Matsebula queen. The entire day following the throwing of the gourd, he remained secluded, sombre, in darkness, approachable only by his closest men and his two ritual queens. The population of the capital was symbolically identified with him; it was a day of seclusion and terrible quiet. There was no singing and dancing. The sacred songs were closed for an entire year. Ordinary activities – sitting on a mat, scratching, washing, any sexual contact – were prohibited. Emissaries of the priests saw that the taboos were not broken, and fined offenders, and the guilt was considered heavier if committed by an important person, and particularly a prince. The functionaries did not say 'You

[10] Two gourds are fetched year by year; the King 'plays' with one, and the other is kept till the following year and burnt.

[11] Some informants insisted that in olden days, had the recipient of the gourd gone to war he would have been the first killed. He had been selected to hold the powerful vessel symbolizing the past, and so became a national scapegoat, a sacrifice for the future.

[12] Mswati, the great fighting King, is praised as 'Buffalo with Rugged Horns.'

are scratching' or 'You are washing', but 'You scratch him (the King)' or 'You wash him', for the King must refrain from those activities on that day. He sat quietly in the sanctuary, forbidden to even discuss matters of state.

Lomawa and her co-wives stayed in the enclosure of the Great Hut. Priests of the Mkonta clan prepared for them their specific greens for biting the new year, and painted a half moon on the right side of the Ndlovukazi's face. It was a long day. The two rulers, each in their own quarters with their own attendants, remained separate, and quiet. This was described as *kufukama* – to sit like a hen on eggs, to incubate.

Before dawn and the breaking into the brightness of life, the nation had to be purified of sin and darkness. The regiments brought back from the Mdzimba Mountain wood without thorns, which they built into a pyre, at the upper end of the *sibaya*, and they laid on relics of the old year. It was the morning of the sixth day. When all was ready the cattle were driven in and Sobhuza set the offerings alight by making fire with ancient sticks, male and female. Then he walked round the flames and washed the medicines off his body. Towards noon everyone, now dressed in elegant traditional finery, gathered again in the *sibaya* and began a repertoire of solemn but not sacred national chants (*imigubho*). The fire blazed and crackled and the dancers knew that even though the sky was clear rain would fall, cleansing, purifying, fertilizing. It came in a deep steady downpour, and the dancing and singing continued, and the flames were quenched. The day ended with feasting and revelry. Huge platters of meat and pots of beer were sent from the great enclosure and from the quarters of the young Queens.

There remained a final national service – weeding of the nation's fields, ending with *imfabantfu*, the field near which Sobhuza had stayed on his return as an infant from his mother's people. The men weeded, jumping forward in regimental rows to the rhythm of special songs; the emphasis was on unity in action rather than efficiency in weeding. From the ritual garden they moved to work more seriously in other more secular national fields. When they had completed their tasks, the King rewarded them with cattle in recognition of their service to the nation and then dismissed them. But the full *Ncwala* period ended only on the dark of that moon, with a ritual burning of the *lusekwane* and leaves. Then only could the rulers resume the freedom of routine activities.

Every year since 1921 the *Ncwala* has been reenacted, a new production of an ancient and sacred script; minor additions and adaptations have been made, but the sacred, the essential, remains uniquely unalterable. In Sobhuza's words, '*Ncwala* is necessary for Kingship. When there is no King, there is no *Ncwala*.'

His first *Ncwala* gave him full command of the regiments, and the right to initiate war and attack enemies of the nation. In former times he would have been expected to demonstrate his new authority by military action, but now the prerogative of war was monopolized by the colonial government.

With this *Ncwala*, Labotsibeni's long regency was ended. On Thursday, 22 December 1921, she transferred full authority to Sobhuza in the presence of the Resident Commissioner and five of his officials, and leading representatives of the Swazi nation.[13] To the Resident Commissioner she presented the following moving address, read and translated by her secretary, Josiah Vilakati.

Honourable Sir,

This is the day I have always longed for. It has now come at last like a dream which has come true. King Mbandzeni died in October, 1889 (32 years ago). As from that day my life has been burdened by an awful responsibility and anxiety. It has been a life full of the deepest emotions that a woman has ever had.

The Swazi nation placed me in charge of all the affairs of the country as Queen in place of the dead King, and I have acted as Regent during the minority of two subsequent kings. Bhunu died after only a very short life, leaving me with the responsibility of bringing up his infant son and heir. I rejoice that I now present him to Your Honour in your capacity as head of the Administration of Swaziland. He is very young as Your Honour can see. He shall constantly require my advice. I and the Nation have every confidence in him. I have brought him up as a Swazi prince should be brought up. His spirit is in entire accord with the traditions and feelings and the aspirations of his countrymen and, what is more, I have given him the opportunity to obtain the very best training which any Native youth can obtain here in South Africa. I beg to thank Your Honour for all the help which you have given me in opening such facilities for the prince's education. His going away from me always gave me pain, which only stopped when I saw him return having grown greater in status and knowledge. In him I feel that I have done all that as his Grandmother and Queen I could possibly do.

I have asked your Highness to come here and bear me witness before him and the Council of the Nation to the effect that I have never sold even a single right of the Nation, I have never given away any of their land or people to others. I stand before them with clean hands. All my books are open for his inspection. Perhaps Your Highness is asking himself as to what my position is now to be and what relationship shall exist between the new Paramount Chief and myself. All this is governed by our ancient customs. I shall reply shortly. He will lead the Nation and deal with the Administration as King of his people, and I shall remain greater by the influence which my position holds over him and over the councils of the Nation. My duties towards him and the Nation will never cease until death. There is no truth in the fiction that old Swazi Queens are always killed or done away with. Look at our history. They all lived their natural life out except one who was killed through her own open rebellion.

In conclusion, I desire to introduce to your Highness, in your capacity as head of the Swaziland Administration, and local chiefs, representative of His Royal Highness the High Commissioner, this my grandson, Sobhuza II the Paramount Chief of Swaziland and King of the Swazi nation. In doing this I commend him to your friendly assistance and help. I cannot give him my experience. During my time I have had the friendly help of five noble High Commissioners and that of three honourable Resident Commissioners of this country. I thank your Highness and them all for all

[13] The Resident Commissioner was de Symon Honey; other British officials mentioned as present were Major Gilson, A.G. Marwick, Captain Roberts, J.B. Knowles and S.B. Williams. Swazi mentioned in the official records were Mandanda Mtsetfwa, Colo Nkambule, Princes Masumphe, Mhubhe, and Tigodze, and Ndabezimbi Fakudze.

assistance which you have always been ready and willing to give me. The Administration will henceforth address all its communications direct to him. Sobhuza II gets his name, title and position by the right of inheritance from his ancient house and kings who have ruled over the Swazi Nation from time immemorial.

     I bid Your Highness farewell,
       Most faithfully yours,
         Queen Regent Labotsibeni,
         Her X Mark.

Swaziland Archives, 22 December 1921

CHAPTER VI
The Struggle for the Land

As Ngwenyama, Sobhuza was confronted with the task of regaining the rights of his people to the land. This would be a long, hard, and at times bitter struggle, a contest with the powerful British and South African governments and with the white settlers. Violence was excluded, and Sobhuza II became a master of peaceful negotiation, adding to the wide range of traditional strategies new channels of appeal and pressure. The most obvious approach was through the courts of law, but this as we shall see was less effective than his persistence in maintaining the strength of Kingship by more subtle and indirect use of Swazi customs.

The groundwork had been laid by the Queen Regent-in-Council. Already in September 1920, when Prince Arthur of Connaught replaced Lord Buxton as High Commissioner, Labotsibeni, as Queen Regent, acting on the advice of Princes Logcogco and Lomvazi, and Josiah Vilakati, secretary to the nation, asked to send representatives to greet him and acquaint him with the problems of the country (letter dated 22-3-21). The High Commissioner consented, and at the beginning of June 1921, Sobhuza travelled to Cape Town with twelve Councillors on his first official deputation. Accompanying the deputation were the Resident Commissioner and the Assistant Commissioner of Police, representing the British government in Swaziland.

In Cape Town, Sobhuza and his men stayed for three days at the Stakesby Lewis Hostels, 10 Victoria Court. African friends came to greet him, and gave him news of local South African affairs. It was a month after the shooting by the police of the 'Israelites' – a group of Believers who, under the inspiration of their prophet, put up shacks on an open corner at Bulhoek, Queenstown. They prayed for deliverance from foreign rule, and refused to move from their chosen place. They ignored the warnings of more realistic African police, and threats from the State. When the police attacked with modern weapons, the Israelites raised their staves; 117 were killed, many were wounded. There was strong protest from whites as well as Africans, whose leaders were trying to gain acceptance into a single multi-racial society. Sobhuza, talking to me of this in later years, said his reaction was one of pity for the Believers. But he also condemned their leader as 'foolish not to know what guns can do; it does not help a cause if you are dead. Try other ways first.'

The interview with the High Commissioner took place at Government House on 6 June – the government representatives in uniform, the Swazi in western suits. Honey presented 'The Paramount Chief, Sobhuza' to 'His Royal Highness', who shook his hand (Reports of the interview are in the Swaziland Archives, RCS 181/21). Prince Arthur welcomed the deputation, and having enquired after the health of the Queen Regent and of the mother of Sobhuza, announced 'I shall now hear the message with which you have been entrusted.' Mandanda Mtsetfwa as main governor, since 1916, of the capital, Zombodze, and head of the delegation, responded. Benjamin Nxumalo, as secretary, read an official letter from the Swazi, combining a welcome to the High Commissioner and an introduction of the young King with subtle references to the problems lying ahead of him. Prince Arthur acknowledged the message in a rather patronizing speech, in which he said he could 'quite understand that many of the older chiefs did not like the new conditions', but that 'as things are today, especially owing to the great war, no people in the world can stand still'. He also remarked, 'it [was] a pleasure to learn how the Swazi had assisted the King [of England] in that great war.' Asked if the deputation had anything further to say, Mandanda replied:

I have got nothing to say, Your Royal Highness. Everything which was read by Benjamin Nxumalo is what the Chief Regent has said, but over and above that she would be very pleased to hear that you praise us as being men who helped His Majesty during the late war and for that you must remember our nation and remember that we are men. If a father treats his child in a cruel manner, of course the child does not like its father.

A man or a person may be so dissatisfied and displeased that he looks as if he is unwell, whereas he is quite well. Simply because he is ill-treated he looks as if he were not well.

According to the government records (RCS 181/21) a polite but stilted conversation then took place between Prince Arthur and Sobhuza, officially reported as 'a pleasant personal conversation … about Lovedale, shooting, and such things' (RCS 186/21, Report by Honey dated 28/7/21).

Two months after his return, Sobhuza signed a petition, drawn by Seme and dated 29-8-21, to be presented in person to the British government. It repeated the requests of his people for the withdrawal of the Swaziland Order-in-Council of 1903, for the repeal of the Proclamation cancelling the King's private revenue concession, and the amendment of the decisions of government in regard to other concessions. In addition to these old requests, he asked for control of the Swazi National Fund, joint control over revenue and expenditure, and recognition of his authority as King of Swaziland over Swazi both in and outside the Territory.

The High Commissioner replied at some length (in a letter dated 19 December 1921) that the requests could not be granted, nor did he think a personal interview 'would serve any useful end'. He closed with the comment:

There is one matter which I wish to mention. I notice that the Petition contains numerous references to the Paramount Chief as 'the King of Swaziland'. The word 'King' is not a correct translation of the word 'Nkosi' by which the Paramount Chief is addressed in the Swazi language, and the style 'King of Swaziland' is not one which I should be prepared to recognize. I do not think there could be a more dignified or a more appropriate title for the Chief of the Swazi than 'Paramount Chief'. It is a title which is only accorded to two other chiefs under my jurisdiction, namely the Paramount chiefs of Basutoland and Bechuanaland, neither of which territories is less important than Swaziland. A Native Chief, like an official of the Government gains more dignity by using a title which is appropriate to his position than by using one which people might regard as high-sounding and pretentious. I hope in the future the title 'Paramount Chief' will be used instead of the title 'King'.

Signed/ Arthur Frederick High Commissioner

To the Swazi this reply was irrelevant and insulting. Sobhuza was their only King and his Council considered that it would be necessary for him to go to England in person to hear officially the reasons for the actions of the British during his long minority and to express their opposition to the possibility of transfer of their country to South Africa. At the end of the First World War, the government of the Union of South Africa had again publicly expressed an interest in acquiring control of the three High Commission Territories; and when Swazi leaders tried to find out Britain's response, the British High Commissioner in South Africa (then Lord Buxton) had promised they would be permitted to send a deputation to England.

Sobhuza, accompanied by Benjamin Nxumalo and Seme, conveyed his people's reactions to Honey as Resident Commissioner; he was sympathetic, and undertook to advise the High Commissioner to accept the petition and give a hearing to a deputation whose spokesman would be a well-known South African barrister, Dr Manfred Nathan, K.C. The more the Swazi debated the matter, the more obvious it became that it was pointless to have any further interviews with the High Commissioner himself. And on 30 May 1922, Seme sent a further petition, together with a covering letter to the Resident Commissioner, pointing out that

the matters which form the subject of the petition have been pending for many years, that the future position of Swaziland is an active subject of discussion both so far as the Union Parliament and Government and the White Advisory Council are concerned, and that all these things are of vital import to my Clients, as representatives of the rights and interests of the Swazi Nation, the aboriginal inhabitants of the Country, and the overwhelming bulk of its population. (30/5/22, P.O. Box 94, Amersfoort, Transvaal).

He concluded with a request that permission be granted for a Deputation, which would include the 'Paramount Chief', Benjamin

Nxumalo, Prince Masumphe, and 'certain other Chiefs and Councillors of the Nation', to proceed to England together with their legal advisers – Dr Nathan, Mr Boshoff (a South African Solicitor) and himself. The letter ended with a flat statement: 'The non-European members of the Deputation, including myself, will require Passports. The object of this request is to avoid delay, in view of the possibility of a radical alteration of the affairs of Swaziland, as by its incorporation in the Union or otherwise.'

The 14-page-long petition repeated and elaborated the grievances of the Swazi Nation. In it Sobhuza is described as both King of the Swazis and Paramount Chief of Swaziland, and the argument begins: 'With reference to the year 1881, when Sir Evelyn Wood paid a visit to Mbandzeni for the purpose of obtaining from him and the Swazi Nation full military support against the powerful Pedi chief, Sikukuni ...' The document traces step by step the subsequent relations of British and Swazi, and concludes with specific requests 'in the interests of justice'. The document carried the signature of Sobhuza II and crosses for Chiefs Ndabezimbi Fakudze, Ntamo Dlamini, Maveletiveni Dlamini, Jabhane Dlamini, and Masumphe Dlamini; the witnesses were P. Ka. I. Seme and Benjamin Nxumalo.

Six weeks passed. Sobhuza, who had met with Seme and others at the Nkhaba royal village near the Transvaal border, sent a reminder and further request for passports. Nicholson, the government secretary, replied that the request for passports could not be considered until the Secretary of State informed the High Commissioner when he would be able to receive the deputation (letter 14 July 1922). Sobhuza said he desired the passports, even if the Secretary of State was not prepared to receive a deputation soon. Advocate Nathan was booked to leave on 29 July, and, as Seme informed Nicholson in confidence, one of the reasons for hastening the deputation was that there was a possibility that he would be appointed a judge, in which case he would not be able to be retained as counsel by the Swazi nation.

British officials did not wish the 'Swazi Question' to be raised by the opposition in Parliament or by friends of the Swazi outside of Parliament. From the 'persistent manner' in which both Sobhuza and Seme tried to get passports for 28 July, Nicholson concluded that some attempt might be made to send off Nxumalo and Masumphe without formal permission for the deputation being granted. He advised Sobhuza strongly not to depart from the recognized procedure in these matters.

Sobhuza and the rest of the deputation wanted to leave immediately after the last stage in the installation of his mother, Lomawa, who would finally take over the full duties of Ndlovukazi. The auspicious time for this ritual was regulated according to the moon and the sun – the day of the full moon in the month of *Ingci* (7 August) – and the young King had to be back for *Ncwala*.

On 17 August the Secretary of State cabled the High Commissioner in Pretoria to say that the deputation should not arrive until after the reassembly of the British Parliament on 14 November. The High Commissioner accordingly cabled the Resident Commissioner to postpone the sailing of the deputation indefinitely, owing to a change of Ministry in England. Nathan and Boshoff were already in England, waiting, and preparing the Swazi case.

On 6 September 1922, Prince Arthur paid his first visit to Swaziland. In his report he wrote:

On reaching the outskirts of Mbabane (6 September) I alighted in order to receive the welcome of Labotsibeni, the old Chief Regent who had come specially to greet me. She is quite blind and is becoming infirm physically, but her mental faculties show no sign of failing. She presented me with an address of which I attach a copy. The young Paramount Chief, his mother Lomawa and other Native Chiefs with their followers under the Assistant Commissioners were present, and one or two of Sobhuza's household Regiments were drawn under a guard of honour. Their appearance was picturesque. I thanked Labotsibeni for coming to meet me and for her address, and said that I would reserve any further remarks for the large meeting with the natives which had been arranged for the following day, Friday. I then inspected the native guard of honour. Owing to some mistake, due, I gather, partly to the lateness of the Paramount Chief's arrival and his consequent inability to give proper orders to his regiments, and partly to the fact that, being in plain clothes, I was not promptly recognized by the natives, the Royal Salute *Bayethe* was not given on that occasion (RCS 625/22).

It is clear that the High Commissioner did not appreciate the subtlety of the message of Swazi national pride and their rejection of domination. The Royal salute is reserved for their own Kings; Sobhuza had come late; the royal salute could not be given in his absence; the High Commissioner was not the King. The old Queen in her address of welcome described Prince Arthur as 'the grandson of the Most Gracious Sovereign, Queen Victoria, of Blessed Memory', and pointedly introduced Sobhuza as 'the son of Ngwane, the son of Mbandzeni, the son of Mswati, the son of Sobhuza, the son of Ndungunye, the son of Ngwane, the son of Dlamini, all Kings of Swaziland'.

On 8 September, the High Commissioner met chiefs and their followers at the Court House.

There was a very large attendance of Natives. The Paramount Chief was late in arriving and apologized for his unpunctuality. The Royal Salute was given to me repeatedly and with great vigour (Report of the High Commission, RCS 625/22).

The royal salute was in fact given to Sobhuza as Ngwenyama and not to the High Commissioner. Sobhuza, speaking on behalf of the Swazi Nation, his Chiefs and Councillors, greeted him as a 'blood relation of Queen Victoria' and said:

Your Royal Highness is already fully acquainted with the volume of the grievances of the Nation and that the Nation has decided to ask me to form a deputation to proceed

to England on appeal to the British Government. To this I have already given my
consent and I therefore pray that it may please Your Royal Highness to grant the
necessary facilities for passports for myself and the Chiefs who shall accompany me to
England on the Mission.

Prince Arthur replied that the Secretary of State

... will be prepared to receive the deputation and I hope, though I cannot promise,
that His Majesty the King, if his engagements should permit, may graciously be
pleased to command that the deputation should be presented to him. As you know
both His Majesty the King and the Secretary of State have very many engagements,
and the Secretary of State has asked me to tell you that it would not be convenient if
the deputation were to arrive before the middle of November. I suggest therefore that
the deputation should leave South Africa at the beginning of November, that is to say,
in about six or seven weeks' time, and I have asked the Resident Commissioner to
issue Passports to the deputation accordingly. I am also asking the Resident
Commissioner to send an officer of the Administration to England with the
deputation (RCS 625/22).

The paternal condescension of the High Commissioner's speech was not lost on the young King, who responded briefly, but courteously:

There is nothing very much to speak to Your Royal Highness about. I thank you very
much and am glad to hear that you will come down again to see us and that you will
bring the Princess and the Earl of MacDuff. I also thank you very much indeed that
our deputation is being allowed to proceed to England, and we are very pleased to
hear that His Majesty the King may be able to receive us. We appreciate that very
much.
    I regret Your Royal Highness that the present I intended giving you has been left
behind, but I will hand it to the Resident Commissioner to forward to you. The gift is
one that is used by our Royal Regiment. It is carried by the Regiment when they are
going out. I thank your Royal Highness very much for coming to see us (RCS
625/22).

The Swazi members of the deputation had been carefully selected
by the Council. In addition to Sobhuza, Benjamin Nxumalo and Chief
Mandanda Mtsetfwa as 'Governor of the Nation', the final list
included: Prince Msudvuka, son of Mswati, old in experience; Prince
Jaha, who, though younger than Msudvuka, traced his ancestry back
through Mancibane to Ndlaphu, son of Sobhuza I; Lozishina
Mndzebele Hlophe, trusted councillor and personal attendant from
the time of Sobhuza's boyhood; and Amos Zwane, as his private
physician. Pixley Ka Seme would accompany them, and the local
government would be represented by the Resident Commissioner and
the Assistant Commissioner of Police. Prince Lomvazi, Labotsibeni's
last surviving son, and Chief Lomadokola Sukati, who had been most
active in Swazi affairs, had died earlier in the year.
    At last the arrangements were completed. Bookings on the Windsor
Castle were confirmed and 'passports' could be issued. These were
not British passports, but a special certificate for each Swazi member,
given into the possession of Major Gilson, the Assistant Commissioner

of Police, described as 'in charge of the Deputation' (RCS 332/22, Nicholson, Government Secretary to Paramount Chief, Lobamba, 9/12/22).

On 13 December, two days before leaving, the princes and leading chiefs were called to Lobamba to bid their representatives a bright road, and over beer offered to the ancestors in the shrine hut of the nation, the royal family prayed for a successful visit and safe return. Sobhuza had previously travelled to Mjindini, near Barberton, an army outpost of Mswati, to say goodbye to his people over the border. In his absence the nation would be represented by Lomawa and by Prince Magongo,[1] Manikiniki Nkambule, first governor of Lobamba, and other councillors.

The preparations were involved! Elaborate planning of transport, hiring of cars to take the men to the train junction, last minute switching of trains, difficulties of bringing up the luggage, the making of connections. Throughout this hectic time Sobhuza was 'singularly unperturbed', and when Marwick came to say goodbye, discussed questions of appropriate behaviour, etiquette and clothing, as well as details of the case.

On the South African trains only whites were allowed to travel first class; so Honey and Major Gilson went first, and all the Swazi second. In Johannesburg, Sobhuza and his men stayed in Sophiatown in the home of Solomon ka Dinizulu, and in Cape Town he stopped the night with Rev. Msomi. Not only Swazi but Zulu, Xhosa and Tswana came to greet him and wish him well. There was a general feeling that the young King represented broad African interests; and that Seme was a wise choice as his lawyer.

They sailed from Cape Town on 22 December, on a bright summer's day, and many people crowded the docks to see them off. On the ship, a Union Castle liner, the colour bar was not imposed, and first-class cabins were reserved for Sobhuza and Mandanda and Seme, and second-class for the others, 'all close together and also adjacent to the cabin of Major Gilson'. Seme told Sobhuza of Gandhi's experience on a South African train and his reaction to the racial discrimination, making the point that it was not against discomfort but against discrimination that protest was necessary; 'once discrimination was removed, it did not matter how one travelled.'

On board they kept somewhat to themselves, a small group of Africans, distinguished, courteous, and rather remote from most of the white, pleasure-seeking passengers. Every day Honey and Gilson

---

[1] Prince Magongo was recognized as heir of Malunge by the royal family council, which had refused to accept a will drawn up by Seme at Malunge's request in favour of a son by another of Malunge's wives. Magongo's mother had been selected by Labotsibeni to look after Sobhuza as a child, and was of the same clan – Mdluli – as Labotsibeni. Magongo had received a western education at Zombodze, then at Ohlanga (in Natal), and finally at Lovedale.

would inquire after their comfort and well-being and chat with them a while. Mandanda and the two Princes spoke virtually no English, and there were recognised restraints on contacts permissible to the young King. He had his own food especially prepared; his companions also did not eat in the main dining room nor share in the nightly revelries. Though they enjoyed listening to the ship's band, Sobhuza never took part in the dancing; he said he felt a certain embarrassment watching couples holding each other close, as they waltzed in public. Much of the time they talked amongst themselves, but they did not find the journey long or lack for conversation. Sometimes they would sing songs from home. Prince Msudvuka would recount his daring exploits during the Boer War when he helped the British and was chased by Boers who put a price on his head. Prince Jaha of Lundzi, who had an excellent memory and was a fine speaker on any subject, would tell of other escapades of the Boer War, in one of which his father, Mancibane, was taken prisoner by a gang of English soldiers who thought he was helping the Boers. Lozishina could relate the perilous journey when the infant king was carried through the raging waters of the Mkhondvo. Amos Zwane had a fund of fascinating knowledge of African medicines. Seme told of Oxford and America and South African politics. 'Ben', wise, astute and kindly, had a great store of religious knowledge. And Sobhuza himself, the youngest of them all, would listen attentively, add his comments, put his questions, and recount his own already varied experience of life. He said he never tired of watching the ocean and listening to the deep roar of the waves, but he was glad when the days at sea were over and they finally sailed into Southampton. It was a grey wintry dawn. The Resident Commissioner had arranged with the Secretary of State that they be met, and the Swazi members were taken directly to 238 Portsdown Road, Maida Vale, a comfortably furnished house, but like all English houses, bitterly cold. It was hard to realize that it was summertime in Swaziland.

The deputation received a good press, largely through the efforts of members of the Labour Party and the Aborigines Protection Society (APS). The Swazi were widely entertained. They visited Sir Ashmead Bartlett (Chairman of the APS), Sir Robert Baden-Powell (who acknowledged that his idea for the Scout movement came from his knowledge of Swazi age regiments gleaned when he served as a young captain on the Joint Commission of 1889), Lord Buxton (formerly High Commissioner who remembered Sobhuza's grandmother with admiration), and other members of the British aristocracy.

On 22 January 1923 the Swazi accompanied by their legal advisors met British officials – Dr' W. Ormsby-Gore (Parliamentary Under-Secretary of State for the Colonies), C.T. Davis, C.M.G. (Assistant Under-Secretary of State), Sir John Risby (legal advisor to the Secretary of State), and J.F.N. Green (Assistant Secretary). The Resident Commissioner was present. The issues raised in the Swazi

1   Sobhuza, King of Swaziland, 1968

2. Sobhuza's father, Ngwane V, in whose brief reign Boer and British deprived the Swazi of their sovereignity. *c.* 1898

3. Sobhuza with his grandmother, the renowned Labotsibeni. *c.* 1903

4. Sobhuza with his own mother, Lomawa Nxumalo. *c.* 1907

petition were discussed and it was agreed that the deputation meet with the Duke of Devonshire to receive a considered reply.

In the meantime on 29 January they were granted an audience with King George at Buckingham Palace at which Sobhuza presented an address of loyalty. As on other occasions the young King's natural courtesy and appreciation of formal etiquette made for easy communication with the British. Commenting on this meeting in later years, Sobhuza said simply, 'The King of England follows English customs well. We and the English have much in common. Like us, they respect their tradition.'

But the official meeting, with the Duke of Devonshire at the Colonial Office at 11:30 a.m. on 31 January 1923, was deeply disappointing. The reply read by Mr Ormsby-Gore made it clear that the British were not prepared to change their stand. The King of the Swazi remained in their eyes 'the Paramount Chief of a British possession'. On the question of transfer, moreover, the Duke stated that 'the safeguards of the Schedule to the Act of Union were adequate' and he added that 'the Native Affairs Commission recently established by the Union has done excellent work for the natives ... its advice carries great weight with the Union government and Parliament. This circumstance, if fairly and reasonably considered, ought to go far towards reassuring you that the rights and interests of the natives of Swaziland could be protected as adequately under the Union Government of South Africa as they are now' (CO 417/697/4551). At the end of the interview the Duke presented Sobhuza and each of the chiefs with 'a small gift on behalf of the government to serve as a reminder of their visit to England', and also sent presents to the former Queen Regent and to the Queen Mother Lomawa.

On leaving London, Sobhuza remarked, 'The Duke of Devonshire did not give us what we asked for. He said he could not see sufficient reason for disturbing what had been done by his predecessor, but,' he continued, 'I have had a first-class time all the same. Your country is just – oh wonderful. It is so big and there are so many people in it – where do they all come from? What is the most wonderful thing I saw? Perhaps it was the theatre; I went to the Hippodrome – oh the fairies flying in the air were beautiful – I have never seen that before.' There had also been visits to the Colosseum and the Zoo and other amusements considered suitable for African dignitaries. He recalls how much he enjoyed the lights, the cars, the shops, the theatre – everything but the weather. He was more at ease in the modern world than most of his companions, and Seme with his previous knowledge of America and England was an excellent guide.

On the official photograph the young King looks calm and relaxed. His unaffected charm and sincerity had made a favourable impression on all who met him and it was typical of his warmth and generosity that despite the economic pressure, of which he was intensely

conscious, he befriended, during his stay in London, Sol T. Plaatje
whose money had run out. Plaatje was no stranger to the Swazi. He
and Seme had worked together in South Africa on the African
National Congress and for African rights – political, economic, and
social. Sobhuza had long admired him for his eloquent and
courageous writing exposing discrimination and injustice. When
Seme reported Plaatje's plight, Sobhuza, according to Mandanda,
replied, 'Of course, we must help him. He is one of us.'

The Swazi party left Southampton on the Armadale Castle on 3
February and were seen off by many friends and well-wishers and a
guard of honour provided by Baden-Powell's Boy Scouts. Seme
remained behind in London until the end of May continuing his
efforts to awaken English public opinion, consulting with the best
international and constitutional lawyers and briefing members of the
Labour Party who raised the case in the House of Commons. Honey
returned with the deputation. Gilson was given permission by the
High Commissioner to remain for a few weeks holiday.

There were a couple of days when the sea was rough, and despite
the good companionship the journey seemed long to Sobhuza. 'No
man is without fear and I was still young.' He recalls that one night he
drank very heavily of hard liquor and had terrible nightmares of
monsters and violence. After that he virtually stopped taking any
alcohol other than traditional beer. Using his own painful experience
as a moral, he has tried very hard, though not always successfully, to
persuade those close to him to refrain from excessive drinking.

February 19, 1923 – back in Africa. They were met officially at
Cape Town, caught the first train to Johannesburg, where they
stopped briefly, then trained to Breyten, where there were cars
waiting to rush them home. Following custom, Sobhuza made his first
visit to the former Ndlovukazi Labotsibeni, then Lomawa at
Lobamba. Before he could resume his normal routine he had to be
purified from the contaminations of the journey and strengthened by
priests of the nation.

The news of his return was carried through the country, and a
meeting of all his people was called to welcome him and his
companions and hear their report. Mandanda was the first to speak,
the King the last. They made it clear that while the Secretary of State
was negative, they had received encouragement from other sources,
and their legal advisers were confident of the ultimate triumph and
the justice of their cause. Those present then agreed that the young
King, acting on behalf of the nation, take the case to court. This was a
bold step made with full realization of all it implied. The financial
costs as well as the political stakes were high in relation to the limited
resources of the people. Sobhuza was being pressed by his lawyers,
apart from Seme, for payment of their fees, and, in 1923 when money
was very badly needed, the Standard Bank of South Africa brought a
lawsuit against him for payment of monies owing on his house in

Sophiatown. His lawyers argued that the court had no jurisdiction over him since 'sovereignty vested in the Swazi nation and the native ruler was the sovereign', but the Bank contended that the King of England was the only sovereign in Swaziland, hence a court recognized by him exercised the necessary authority. Sobhuza obtained conditional leave to appeal to the Privy Council but in the end decided not to appeal, and to raise the issue of sovereignty in relation to the more fundamental issue of the land.

The particular document on which the Swazi focused was the Unallotted Lands Concession granted by King Mbandzeni on 26 July, 1889,[2] at a time when he was already seriously ill and Allister Miller was Adviser to the Swazi nation. The concession allegedly gave to John Thorburn and Frank Watkins (for a period of 50 years with the option of extension for another 50 years in consideration of a yearly payment of £50), the sole and exclusive farming rights over the whole of Swaziland south of the Komati River, save for parts already granted for farming and agriculture. The concession contained the usual clause inserted by King Mbandzeni in which the concessionaires agreed to respect all prior rights of his subjects. The Concession Court, at which the Swazi were represented by Theophilus Shepstone, confirmed this concession in 1890. The rights under it were later transferred to the Swaziland Corporation Ltd. In 1908, the High Commissioner expropriated these rights, and in 1917, his successor granted the Swaziland Corporation Ltd. a farm named Dalriach No. 188 as part compensation. In 1921 the Corporation transferred part of the farm to Miller, who had married Thorburn's daughter.

The land comprising the farm was inhabited by Chief Mbabane Kunene and his people, and in it were mountain strongholds of the nation and graves of Swazi royalty. Miller had evicted some of the people under Chief Maloyi Kunene, the successor of Chief Mbabane. In the eyes of the Swazi he had interfered with the rights and liberty of Sobhuza's subjects and in land over which the concessionaires had no just claim. In the affidavit of Chief Maloyi, Miller was described as a European residing in the area and constantly molesting him and his people by trespassing on lands they had ploughed and occupied from time immemorial. He also charged that Miller had wrongfully and unlawfully ejected a number of his subjects, in spite of their rights, and without his consent, and contrary to Swazi law.

The case was prepared with immense thoroughness, and the King immersed himself in the essential historical documents. Working on the issue of the land sharpened his mind, trained and disciplined his memory, and taught him the practical importance of mastering both principles and details of history. He studied the numerous conventions, proclamations, official correspondence, and concessions;

[2] Details of the case are to be found in the Record of the Privy Council, No. 158 of 1924.

it is to these documents that he has referred on many subsequent occasions. He also summoned chiefs and elders to obtain their views of the facts, and to receive their advice. Seme, whose practice was in the Transvaal, came periodically to Lobamba to discuss the progress that was being made, and to report on his meetings with Dr Manfred Nathan, who was retained as counsel.

By the end of 1923 the papers were ready and in January, 1924, soon after another *Ncwala*, Sobhuza II, as 'King of the Swazis and Paramount Chief of Swaziland', with members of his Council, petitioned the Special Court of Swaziland to take action against Allister Miller. Joined with the King as petitioners were the Councillors Makhambane Fakudze, Ndabezimbi Fakudze, and Benjamin Nxumalo.[3] Seme signed as interpreter.

Seme represented Sobhuza and the Swazi. A local European attorney, A. Millin, represented Miller. Affidavits for the Swazi were submitted by Sobhuza, his grandmother, Chief Maloyi and others. The first exhibit went back to 1880 and related to the delimitation of the boundary of Swaziland, and quoted the written words of the British representative, 'While it is desirable to re-establish the old Boer boundary in Komati Valley, it is still more desirable that the Swazi should look upon us as firm and honest friends' (St. Leger Herbert to Major Alleyne, Victoria, January 3, 1880). The Swazi claimed that in Swazi law no King has the right to alienate any portion of his country, and that Mbandzeni had specifically reserved the rights of his subjects to the land in question. Miller, in his affidavit, denied that Sobhuza was 'the King of Swaziland', claiming that he was only the Paramount Chief, and also that the petition was not presented by the entire Council but merely by two chiefs. He further asserted that in terms of Swaziland Proclamation 240/1913, he had the right to eject any people 'irrespective of how long they had been there, if they refused to work for him as owner'.

The case was heard before a court presided over by Advocate S.T. Morice, K.C. of South Africa, assisted by two officials of the Swaziland government, and working with two white assistant commissioners.[4] It was considered belittling for Sobhuza to attend the hearing in person, but his representatives crowded the courthouse, listening, taking mental notes, and on their return, reporting each

---

[3] Links between the Fakudze and Swazi kings could be traced back to the days of Shiselweni, when Mngayi Fakudze led the armies of Mswati to victory against the Zulu in the battle of Lubuya, 1854. Mngayi's son, Mbovane, had served loyally as governor to the Ndlovukazi, laMngangeni Khumalo, and had done his best to prevent the tragic conflict between her and the King Mbandzeni which culminated in her death. Makhambane was a son of Mbovane and Ndabezimbi was a son of his brother Masiphula.

[4] Two assistant commissioners were B.W. Warner (Mahaha) of Mbabane and T.A. Steward (Ngisane) of Lubombo. The Resident Commissioner, Mr Honey, had requested not to be approached 'since he had personally dealt in his administrative capacity over many years with the questions that were involved'.

detail. During the trial the Swaziland Corporation Ltd. was added as a second respondent and it was clear that while Sobhuza put forward the interests of the Swazi, Miller represented the interests of the white settlers.

The judgment, given on 24 May 1924, declared that the British Crown had not exceeded its powers, and that the Land Partition Proclamation of 1907 had extinguished Swazi rights to the land in dispute. The application was dismissed with costs. Sobhuza and his people, astonished, dismayed and angry, decided to continue their struggle. Their last legal recourse was appeal to the Privy Council in London. Permission had to be obtained from the High Commissioner; this was granted, reluctantly, on 30 June, after £500 had been deposited in cash; the Swazi agreed that they would meet their own costs, including costs of the record. The feeling of outrage and injustice was aggravated by the fact that costs for the respondents were borne by the government!

The King had no alternative but to fall back on the support of his loyal subjects both inside and outside Swaziland for the raising of necessary legal funds. The collectors were carefully chosen and their job was neither easy nor pleasant.[5] No one would directly refuse a request made by the King, but there were some complaints to the government that donations made in cattle, as well as cash, did not reach him. The complainants did not appreciate, as the King himself did, that the collectors incurred expenses during their stay away from home and that it was not easy to market the cattle at a correct price. Sobhuza trusted his men, but when he found some had mishandled funds, he dismissed them. When the Resident Commissioner wanted the Administration to take control, he replied, 'The Council as well as the ex-Queen Regent desire that Your Honour shall exercise no Official Authority over the Fund as they desire that this Fund should ever remain under the control of this Council. I associate myself with this view. Yours faithfully.' This note was stamped with the seal of 'The King and Paramount Chief', and signed 'Sobhuza II' (9/9/24).

The application to the Privy Council had to be rephrased to incorporate the arguments made in the judgment and to present further documentation. Seme went to England with Prince Jaha of Lundzi, the young shrewd chief who had been on the deputation with Sobhuza in 1922. When the Resident Commissioner had questioned the utility of sending a man who could neither read nor write, Sobhuza explained that 'according to custom, in any proceedings affecting the nation, one of our own people should be present, who would personally report on his return so that there could be no

[5] His old school fellows Harvey Mgacela Nxumalo and Msimula Ndlela went to the collieries in the Witbank district; Philemon Nxumalo representing Chief Velebantu Dlamini went to Piet Retief, Wakkerstroom, Bethal, Standerton and Ermelo; Gija Nkosi and Prince Jabhane, son of King Mbandzeni, to Barberton, Lydenburg and Carolina, and Arthur Ndawombili Nxumalo and Chief Ntamo Dlamini to the rich gold mine area of Johannesburg and Pretoria.

misunderstanding'. In place of Nathan, Seme worked with a well-known English solicitor, E.F. Hunt, and two astute barristers, A.C. Clauson, K.C., and Horace Douglas of London. When it was known that Miller and the Swaziland Corporation would be represented by the Attorney General of Britain, Sir Douglas Hogg, K.C., and H.M. Giveen, instructed by the Treasury Solicitor, it became even more obvious that the case, though ostensibly against the holders of the concession, was in fact against the British Government.

After all the preparations, the hearing was set unexpectedly earlier and Clauson, the senior barrister for the Swazi, was 'unable to be present'. It is doubtful, however, if his presentation, however eloquent and persuasive, would have influenced the final verdict. This the Swazi did not know when they placed their trust in the judicial system of the foreign imperial government and challenged the validity of the Orders-in-Council issued by that government.

While the case was still pending, Edward, Prince of Wales, toured southern Africa. He arrived in Swaziland in the middle of June, 1925. According to a communiqué from the Resident Commissioner, Honey, to the Earl of Athlone, who had the previous year succeeded Prince Arthur of Connaught as High Commissioner, Prince Edward 'received a most loyal and enthusiastic reception ... from all classes of the community' (RCS 216/25. Letter dated 16 June 1925). But behind this bland statement lay an unrevealed truth. Sobhuza and his people were glad to welcome the heir to the British throne as an honoured visitor, but they were not prepared to recognize him as their future sovereign. On this, as on previous and subsequent occasions, they expressed their sole allegiance to their own hereditary ruler with skill and with subtlety.

To Honey and the British settlers this visit was a singularly significant occasion, a demonstration of identification with the Empire under the British Crown. Telegrams flew between the Resident Commissioner at Mbabane, the High Commissioner in Cape Town, and the Secretary of State in London. The preparations were most elaborate. Among other things was the difficult question of gifts, the Resident Commissioner proposing for the 'Paramount Chief' a sporting rifle, for his mother a pendant and a red or maroon cloak with tassels, for the ex-Queen Regent a large silver pendant with chains, and for the chiefs medals suitably inscribed, though the Resident Commissioner was doubtful that most chiefs would appreciate them. However, since the Prince of Wales would probably receive presents from them, it was necessary to reciprocate somehow. In addition, the Administration would supply cattle for His Royal Highness to present to the Swazi for feasts. This communication ended, 'Please telegraph if you think proposals unreasonable but important maintain prestige of future King and if necessary Administration could contribute.'

The reply from the Secretary of State was slightly cool: 'It had not been contemplated that HRH, Prince of Wales, would be called upon to give presents on scale suggested ... it would be preferable if chiefs could be induced to refrain from giving presents to Prince so that HRH would be relieved of necessity of making reciprocal gifts. But if this is not thought suitable, it is hoped that it can be arranged that any gift to be interchanged will be of as simple character as possible' (Date of Resident Commissioner's message 13 March 1925; from Secretary of State to High Commissioner, Cape Town, 18 March 1925). It was eventually decided that the pendants for the women would be omitted, the cost of the rifle be limited to £10 or £12, and that further presents be postponed and given subsequently only to such chiefs as may make presents to HRH and could be obtained locally (High Commisioner to Secretary of State, 12 March 1925).

The Resident Commissioner worked out the arrangements and details of the programme in separate consultation with a reception committee, appointed by a public meeting of European residents, and with Sobhuza who in turn consulted with his people. The whites took for granted that they would play the most prominent part, and that the Resident Commissioner would take precedence in all events. According to the official programme, he and his entourage would meet Prince Edward at Oshoek on the Swaziland side of the border, a mounted police escort would meet them two miles outside Mbabane, and at a slightly lesser distance, the Paramount Chief, with his chiefs and his Regiment of Guards, would be lined up on each side of the road, under the charge of Assistant Commissioners. On His Royal Highness' approach the Royal salute – *Bayethe* – would be given. His Royal Highness would halt for a few minutes, shake hands with the Paramount Chief and his mother, exchange a few words of greeting, and spend a short time inspecting the native regiments ('there will be a platform for HRH upon stepping from his car'). Thereafter, accompanied by the police escort, the party would proceed to the Residency, where in the evening there would be a dinner to which a few local guests of standing (all whites) would be invited, and that night there would be a dance in the Courthouse.

The following day would be the great public welcome. Starting at 10 a.m. the Prince would meet with Europeans, receive an address on behalf of the European inhabitants, another on behalf of the Girl Guides, and a third on behalf of the officers and men of the Hlatikulu Rifle Club. The Prince would then read a reply prepared by the Resident Commissioner. Following some light refreshment, individual Europeans would be presented to the Prince. At 11 a.m. he would be motored about half a mile away to find the Paramount Chief and his people expectantly waiting. The Paramount Chief would then present an address to which His Royal Highness would reply. Then the Paramount Chief and his mother, as well as the ex-Regent if she were able to appear, 'would be presented and shaken hands with'. This would be followed by a feast for the Swazi and a short informal consultation with the Paramount Chief and 'especially with the ex-Chief Regent, if she should be there'. There would then be 'a cursory inspection of native school children and a few words to them'. This would be followed by a dance by the regiments. At 12:00 noon His Royal Highness would return to the Residency for lunch, and at 1 p.m. leave for Carolina in the Transvaal.

On 30 April the Resident Commissioner had written to Sobhuza:

My Friend, the arrangement for the entertainments to be given by the Europeans in honour of the visit of HRH the Prince of Wales are in the hands of a committee elected at a public meeting. The committee proposes to erect 3 arches, including one to be for the Natives of Swaziland. For this purpose they require the following: about 400 shields, 100 spears, 200 knobkerries, and 200 ordinary sticks, a number of wooden pillows, milk buckets and platters and all kinds of articles of this nature used by the Natives. These are to decorate the arch. Care will be taken of these articles and they will be available for return to the owners as soon as HRH's visit is over. Please do your best to collect as many of these articles as possible and send them up at an early date, as it is desired to proceed with the building of the arches at once. I suggest that the words *Bayethe* be inscribed on the arch. I presume you concur in the suggestion.

The committee went ahead without waiting for a reply. In the meantime Sobhuza presented the letter to his own councillors, and on 10 June the following message with his signature came from the office of the Swazi Nation:

... the letter was placed before the Executive Council for reply. I beg to state that the Council unanimously agreed that the word 'Bayethe' should not be inscribed on the arch, but should be especially reserved for the Nation.

Posthaste came the exasperated response:

My Friend, I wrote to you some weeks ago about an inscription on the Arch for HRH. I received no reply until now at the last moment when all arrangements have been made.

You must tell your Executive Council that HRH the Prince of Wales is entitled to and receives the Royal Salute from all Europeans and Natives under the protection of HM. I trust I shall hear no more of any unwillingness to pay to HRH the proper compliments of his Station when he is coming here at great inconvenience as our Royal Guest. Had I thought for a moment that the Swazis or some of their Chiefs were going to be discourteous on the occasion of the Royal visit I should not have asked that HRH should come to Swaziland. You will remember that the Chiefs have been called up to come to Mbabane on Friday. I intend to have a rehearsal on Saturday at which you should attend to advise me. If you do not wish to come up on Friday night I have no objection but I shall expect you to be in Mbabane at the latest at 10 o'clock on Saturday morning. I must also request that after you have come here you shall not again leave Mbabane until after HRH has left.

You and your Chiefs must understand that HRH is paying a high compliment to us by coming here at great inconvenience to himself and I look to you and to them to assist me in giving a fitting reception as a sign of our appreciation.

I shall see you and your Executive Council at 10 o'clock on Sat. morning, before the rehearsal. Remember that I am looking to you for the assistance which I hope you will be only too glad to give on an occasion of this kind.

On 14 June the Prince of Wales arrived and superficially all went with full pomp and ceremony. The Resident Commissioner met him at the border, smart mounted police gave the salute and provided an escort. The King and his Mother, with a few senior councillors and a band of Swazi warriors, were waiting to meet him. The Resident Commissioner introduced 'His Royal Highness, Prince Edward' to 'The Paramount Chief'. The two young men, one questioning and mocking, the other steeped in sacred tradition and the responsibilities of Kingship, shook hands and spoke briefly. Since the Ngwenyama was present, the warriors boomed *Bayethe*, and court bards recited the great deeds of his (Sobhuza's) forebears. Sobhuza later described Edward as a very polite man.

The following day had been declared a Public Holiday, and school children were sent from all the (segregated) schools to chant their loyalty and wave small Union Jacks. Special arrangements had been made to bring up the children from the schools supported by Swazi nation funds. The Prince went first to meet the whites, who had flocked to pay homage. They gave him a great ovation. He received an address on behalf of the European inhabitants (signed by the Archdeacon of Swaziland, C.C. Watts and the Chairman of the European Advisory Council, I.H. Pearce), another by the Girl Guides and a third by the Hlatikulu Rifle Club, and he made a suitable reply. Leading settlers – among them Mr and Mrs Allister Miller and Mr and Mrs A. Millin – were presented to him. After light refreshments, the Resident Commissioner drove the Prince to the 'meeting of Natives'. The turnout of Swazi notables was significantly small, and the Resident Commissioner in his introduction explained this by saying, 'Some chiefs have not come personally to welcome Your Royal Highness to Swaziland but that is only because infirmity or old age has not enabled them to travel the distance between their homes and Mbabane.' He concluded his remarks with 'The Paramount Chief asks permission to present an address to Your Royal Highness'. It was somewhat restrained and distant, but still expressed loyalty and devotion.

MAY IT PLEASE YOUR ROYAL HIGHNESS,

We, the Paramount Chief, Chiefs and people of the Swazi Nation beg to extend to Your Royal Highness a most respectful and hearty welcome to our country.

We know that your programme necessitates constant travelling and we appreciate very much the fact that notwithstanding our long distance from a Railway, Your Royal Highness has not forgotten us. Our ex-Ndlovukazi has been unable to attend here to participate personally in the welcome to Your Royal Highness.

We pray that Your Royal Highness may take from Swaziland and from South Africa the most pleasant memories of your visit, which we on our part shall always remember with feelings of devotion to Your Royal Highness' person. May Your Royal Highness be pleased to accept our presents which we hope will serve as a remembrance of Your Royal Highness' visit to Swaziland.

In conclusion we beg that Your Royal Highness may carry to His Majesty the King

our protector, our most humble and respectful message of loyalty and devotion.
    Signed on behalf of the Chiefs and people of the Swazi nation.
        Paramount Chief of Swaziland

The Prince replied appropriately, but with unconscious patronage and superiority which rang in the memory of some Swazi listeners, particularly his reference to the benefits of agricultural training derived from 'working on the white men's farms'. He spoke a few encouraging words to the school children, and conveyed especial greetings to the old Regent (to whom he had sent a quilt which she graciously acknowledged). He and Sobhuza parted with mutual expressions of good will.

Six months later, on 15 December 1925, the great Labotsibeni died. To the end, despite a long and painful illness, her mind never weakened. She was buried at Zombodze, at the entrance to the cattle byre, not far from the grave of LaZidze, mother of Mswati. The whole nation mourned. Sobhuza underwent special purification and strengthening rites, but was prohibited by the rituals of his position from attending her funeral or giving public exhibition of grief. He had again to dance *Ncwala*, and when the flames of the final sacrificial offerings to the supreme power were at their brightest, the rains fell more heavily than in previous years, indeed too heavily.

On 15 April 1926, the judgment of the Privy Council was delivered by Lord Haldane. The Swazi appeal was rejected. This decision rested on the legal interpretation of the status of Swaziland. The moral issue, the justice of their cause, was not the point. As Lord Haldane stated with unconscious irony: 'This method of peacefully extending British Domain may well be as little generally understood, as it is, where it can operate, in law unquestionable.' The only concession made was with respect to costs: 'since the question involved is concerned with the constitutional issues and is of far reaching public interest,' the Lords decided, 'following precedents in other cases, that there should be no costs of appeal' (Privy Council Appeal 158. Judgment 15/4/26).

On 17 May, the Resident Commissioner called Sobhuza, his chiefs and Council to the courthouse in Mbabane to hear the judgment. When he finished reading the lengthy document, which had also been translated into siSwati, he added his explanation – 'It means this, that the laws of the King must be obeyed and cannot be questioned ... The case has now been dealt with by the King's highest court from which there can be no appeal and that judgment is final'. As to the question of costs, he stated that the levies imposed on the people had 'caused a great deal of dissatisfaction and must now cease'. He ended by asking: 'Would any of the chiefs like to address me?'

The first to speak was Governor Mandanda. He said he realized he could not challenge the judgment, but the burden of costs still lay ahead, and he wanted to know if any chief had come forward and said he had been compelled to pay, for 'Your Honour says that we must not collect any further but it is also said that each party has to pay its own costs. How can we do that? We have no money. How can we make both ends meet unless we collect amongst the natives?' Prince Masumphe pressed the moral issue, referring to the military assistance given by the Swazi to the British and the promises which had followed. The Resident Commissioner replied that he knew all Masumphe had to say. But when Masumphe sat down, old Prince Nkhundla, who had fought in the Sikhukhuni war, recounted the detailed negotiations of the past. He was followed by Benjamin Nxumalo who put the Swazi case again, clearly and firmly. The Resident Commissioner, who had interjected at many different points, said with some anger that

He [Benjamin Nxumalo] speaks as if England took the country ... It is owing to the protection of the English Government that the Zulus are not here today, and it is owing, as I have consistently got to tell you today, to the concessions which were granted by your own people that the settlement that you are complaining about had to be made. It is a settlement made by the English Government in your own interests.

The atmosphere was tense, but the Resident Commissioner agreed to continue discussions the following day. When the meeting was resumed, the Swazi view was again put by leading spokesmen including Chief Makhambane Fakudze and Princes Mnisi and Jabhane. Mnisi expressed in basic idiom what many Swazi felt:

We have always believed that the British people ruled others by freedom, and that the Kingdom protected those who are not powerful. Like others, the Swazi, who are a small nation, sought protection under them ... The milk that we sucked at the time of our grandmother, Queen Victoria, has now turned bitter like aloe. Sobhuza and his people sought to drink milk from their mother but they found that it was bitter ... The English people are changeable. It was very nice milk in the first place ... It was the milk that reared all the nations under the British flag ... We believe, Your Honour, that the English people should wash the teat from which we drank. Wash it and clean it so that we shall drink the same milk that we drank at the time of Queen Victoria.

The meeting went on and on, each Swazi speaker expressing disappointment and a feeling of betrayal. On the third and last day when the discussion seemed to have reached an impasse, Sobhuza himself spoke. It was a long speech, without notes but with frequent reference to official documents. In it he said:

I am standing up here just to speak to what the other Chiefs have said and to explain the origin of this case; how it started and until it came to its present stage. It started in this way ... our children and great-grandchildren will always say the British Government said, when the Swazis went to fight in the Sekukuniland War, they were going to be looked after by the Government; the British people guaranteed that we should have the right forever over this land. Sir Evelyn Wood came and gave us all these guarantees; he conferred with the King and he left leaving the King with a guarantee that this land was to be his sole property. The King of course was King over his own country, and some people came and said, 'We come with your permission; let us graze there.' One said, 'I would like to graze in that particular portion of land there.' They explained themselves and there was plainly trouble about the grazing of their stock and this and that, and the King said, 'I might just as well allow them to graze their stock.' When you give a white man anything at all he likes to have something in writing; a sort of document showing that a farmer has been given permission by the King to graze on such and such a portion, so that when any other man comes and interferes and wants to graze in the same area he can say, 'Well, I have got this document from the owner of the land.' That document is made for Europeans only. It is not necessary for a Swazi to have any document at all in connection with the grazing of his stock because the Swazi has a natural right over the land. That document to which I have referred serves as a letter to show another white man that on a particular place permission has been given to graze. Such documents started before the time of Mr Shepstone ... It was said that Mbandine had sold, well that is a wrong interpretation ...

Your Honour, the Resident Commissioner said Mbandine made a mistake by giving those people documents, and some of the speakers asked, 'Why did not the Government interfere and stop Mbandine from doing wrong?' Your Honour replied that if the Government had not interfered everything would have gone wrong ... What I want to be considered is this, did Mbandine do wrong in giving those people those documents?

... after Mr Shepstone arrived in Swaziland he spoke to the King and with the King. All the Concessionaires were called up – all the people who had been given concessions were called up. The Concessionaires appointed a Committee to act on their behalf. Then Mr Shepstone spoke to the Committee and said it was best that everything should come before him and be written down ... After that the King called up the Committee representing all those people who had been given documents. He then explained to these people that it must be understood that the land was not sold to them. He said, 'I only allow you people to graze and go away; I only hire the grazing rights to you and you must go away.' That is all. I would like to read what the King himself said. I am quoting from the record ... 'I wish it also to be known that nobody shall force kafirs to work on concessions, nor beat them if they refuse to do so. I have not sold you the ground, you have simply got a lease of it.'

Those are really Mbandine's words when he addressed that Committee ... 17th May, 1887 ... It is said that after the King had finished talking to the people there was applause from the Concessionaires. Why did not they then object and say to the King, 'You sold us land and we have only small grazing rights.' When applause is given it shows you are thankful and pleased at what has been done ...

What I say Sir it is not Mbandine who made the mistake but the Government did wrong too; it came here and did wrong. What I have explained Sir I think is quite clear to Your Honour, because the Attorney General says even if the Concessions were not granted the Government would have done what it wanted. Well, we are still in danger because the Government is liable to do anything it likes ... The guarantees have been altered many a time. We went to the Sekukuni War, fought there and were given a guarantee that we should remain on the land undisturbed; King Mbandine gave out Concessions and the Government turned round and altered the Concessions to whatever it liked. It is quite easy for a Government to do anything it likes; if it turns round and says, 'These Native Areas shall be turned into farms', it could be done quite easily.

Without our knowledge the British Government gave us to the South African Republic Government to look after us, to govern us; that is when the word Protectorate was introduced into this Country ... With regard to the guarantees, the South African Republic Government respected them all. When the British Government took over, there was not one that was kept right.

He then made his point in an allegory, a style which later became characteristic of his oratory.

I was just reading it in the Fairy Tales. It appears that a Princess was going to marry a Prince of a certain Nation. There was a hitch on the part of the Bridegroom ... On the day of the wedding when the Bride's party went to meet the Bridegroom's party there came a flying horse ridden by an Indian. It was said by the messenger on that flying horse, 'I am sent here by the Bridegroom's party to take the Bride on my flying horse.' The Princess rode on that horse very nicely. The horse started and the Indian let the horse go and it ascended; the horse flew a distance; the Princess became suspicious of where they were going, and after a time she came to know she was being taken away (kidnapped). It appeared there was no way of getting away from the horse so she thought she might just as well stick on the horse. After that the Indian descended and landed on the earth. When the Princess alighted she found there a hunting party – people were hunting.

After she dismounted, seeing the hunters knocking about, she started crying; where they alighted the Princess cried and the Prince of that particular territory hearing the noise came to the scene. The Indian said, 'Well, this is my wife.' The Princess denied all knowledge of this, contradicted him and explained how she had been taken from where she was originally, and how she came to be in that particular place. After the Prince heard what had happened and finding out that the Indian who had abducted the girl was of bad character, he ordered that the Indian should be killed straight away, and he was accordingly killed by the troops of the Prince.

The Princess thanked her lucky stars that she was safe. The horse was taken by the troops to the Prince's place. When they arrived at the Kraal, the Prince, looking at this Princess, loved her and said, 'She is now my wife.' The Princess again became sad because she did not love that Prince. The Princess had hoped that the Prince would be good enough to send her along with an escort back to her original place. The Prince said, 'You are here now; you cannot get away. The fact is you will be my wife.' To the Prince's surprise, she said, 'I have just got in the same corner again.' Well what the Princess did was to pretend to be mad. I cannot go any further with this story of mine, but she pretended to be mad. Your Honour, my explanation of this story of the Princess and Prince is just by way of illustration of what I have been explaining. First of all when the South African Republic was governing Swaziland we thought we were in torment. When the British Government came in it was worse.

It seemed as though nothing more could be done but to continue to demonstrate in ways that were their own that their attitude toward their King was unchanged. The time had come to build for Sobhuza as King of the Swazi a new and independent village which would serve as administrative headquarters of the Nation. Here he would have his own councillors and regiments, and establish some of his queens and their children. He chose a site with fresh breezes and a fine view, near the Mtilane River, from which the women and girls could draw their water, and in walking distance of good lands for cultivation and pasturage for the herds. It was less than 5 miles by footpath from the capital, Lobamba.

No money was needed for architects or materials; the plan was known and familiar; it followed an ancient imprint – a circular cattle byre at the centre; at the upper end a sanctuary for the King's private ritual; separate enclosures for the Great Hut and for the Queens; an outer semi-circle of citizens' quarters; and, on either side, barracks of the age regiments. It was like Lobamba, but subtly distinct. Though the *sibaya* (cattle byre) and the shrine hut were smaller, the *sigodlo* (Queens' quarters) were more centrally and conspicuously sited.

Subjects from different chiefdoms supplied the material and labour. Men brought lathes and poles and logs for building the strong palisade and the framework of the huts. Women carried grass for thatching and large coils of plaited rope, and young girls brought reeds, symbols of purity and fertility. All shared in the work and there was no distinction in the tasks of aristocrats and commoners. No fixed payment was demanded or expected, but periodically the workers received beer and meat as a reward which was distributed to them along lines of traditional protocol defined by pedigree, age and sex. The work was accompanied by singing and dancing and punctuated by the rites necessary for the security of the inhabitants.

Sobhuza moved from Lobamba in the winter of 1926, and with him came a few Queens with their children and attendants and some selected followers with their families. The village would grow with time but would never become so large that a stranger would not be observed, and he named it Lozithehlezi – (sitting surrounded by enemies), Lozitha or Zitheni for short.

CHAPTER VII

King at the Cross-Roads

There was the very real danger that the drama which had begun in the reign of Mswati, when Boers and Briton first entered into competition over his country, was reaching a close. The Union government was periodically pushing for the transfer of the High Commission Territories in terms of the schedule to the South Africa Act of 1910, with its equivocal clause of 'consultation', not consent, of the African inhabitants as a precondition. Sir Alan Pim, who had been sent to examine their economic and social conditions, reported their poverty and backwardness (Pim: 1932), and it was current talk that Swaziland, at the time the most neglected of the three territories, would be the first to be transferred. Britain was wavering.

Initially, the choice between Britain and South Africa was by no means clear to Sobhuza. Because of Swaziland's geographical position and history, and under the conditions of that period, there seemed to be no alternative to control from Britain other than domination by South Africa. The Swazi could have little faith in British promises. Their land had been reduced to one-third of the country, already limited by treaties drawn up without their consent,[1] and this land was scattered in 35 fragments between white farms and Crown lands.[2] Some of the Crown lands which Swazi anticipated would be made available for them, under their interpretation of statements by Lord Elgin to the Swazi deputation of 1907, had been sold to whites to cover costs of administration. The amount of money at the disposal of the King for national purposes had been drastically reduced when the Private Revenue Concession was converted into the government controlled Private Revenue Trust Fund from which Sobhuza and the Ndlovukazi received a small stipend.[3]

[1] For a neat discussion of the complicated boundary negotiations of Britain, South Africa and Portugal, see Matsebula 1976, pp. 87-114.

[2] The original apportionment of land, made by George Grey, was guided by two main principles: first, that as few Swazi should be moved as possible, and secondly, that they were entitled to a fair share of well-watered and fertile land. Thus people in some of the most densely populated areas remained undisturbed, but were without land for expanding cultivation, and though fertile land was included, the pressure of population on limited areas rapidly destroyed the fertility of the soil. Before the partition, the Swazi produced sufficient foods for their own needs; soon after, it became necessary to import food and by the 30s official records stated that foodstuffs grown by the people were only about one-fifth of their requirement (e.g. Colonial Report No. 1553 (1930), p. 7; No. 1654 (1931), p. 19; No. 1594 (1932), p. 19).

[3] The Private Revenue Concession amounted to £12,000 per annum; when converted to the Private Revenue Trust Fund, the government paid 4% interest, first to Labotsibeni, then Queen Regent, and subsequently to Sobhuza and Lomawa, as their total stipend.

Sobhuza was alarmed at the attempts that were being made to 'redefine' the powers of chiefs. In the early 1930s he had suggested to the Resident Commissioner that chiefs from the three territories meet to discuss common problems, but when this suggestion was put to the High Commissioner, he replied that he doubted if this would serve any purpose, and nothing had come of it. Sobhuza followed with particular interest the case brought (in 1936) by Chiefs Tshekedi and Bathoen of Bechuanaland (now Botswana) against the High Commissioner, a case in some respects equivalent to his own against the British government. The judgment, this time delivered by Malcolm MacDonald, Secretary of State, was essentially the same: 'His Majesty has unfettered and unlimited power to legislate for the government and administration of justice among the Native Tribes in the Bechuanaland Protectorate; and his power is not limited by treaty or Agreement' (HCT Law Reports 1926-1953).

Sobhuza realized increasingly that he and his people were kept outside the structure of power. All major decisions were made in Britain, and issued as Orders-in-Council under the signature – or its lithographed reproduction – of a Secretary of State, a member of a political party in power. Its local representative was the High Commissioner, but whereas the early appointees were powerful personalities with extensive authority granted by royal commission, later, more especially after 1931 when the position was separated from that of Governor General of the Union, the personality of individual High Commissioners had little influence compared with the direction of imperial interests, and the office itself became more formal and less effective. The British treasury held the master key and the Swazi nation received a pauper's share. Variations in expenditure on Swazi development could not be attributed to individual secretaries of state or individual high commissioners but rather to external factors – the trade demands of Britain, public opinion and political expediencies.

The record of the British and their ambivalence about retaining Swaziland forced Sobhuza to consider the possibilities of incorporation into the Union. The Boer administration during its brief period of control had honoured its obligations. Economic development in the Union was creating ties which might be advantageous to the Swazi. Moreover, there was the position of the South African Swazi to consider. Swazi chiefs in South Africa had petitioned to come under his control. Incorporation could mean the extension of his political authority to his people now under South African rule, and an addition to the land in communal usage. With the need to support a national increase in population as well as to respond to requests by South African Swazi wanting to return to Swaziland, the land shortage was increasingly critical.

Sobhuza made the point that if his people under South African jurisdiction were happy, he might not be unwilling to join them. But they were not happy, and eventually the choice became clear. In July

1926, shortly after Sobhuza had lost the case before the Privy Council, the South African Prime Minister, General J.B.M. Hertzog, introduced four bills which, as he explained to his supporters, would 'keep the native in his place, and secure for the whites permanent supremacy and control'. Economic privileges for whites were already entrenched in what was described as 'the civilized labour policy', passed during the government of General Smuts.

Hertzog defeated Smuts in 1929 by conjuring up fears of 'the Black Peril', but the fundamental interests of the two men were not dissimilar. They formed a coalition in 1933, and in 1935 two Hertzog Bills, the Representation of Natives Bill and the Native Land (Amendment) Bill, became law.[4] These laws struck both at African aspirations for integration into a western type society and at the possibility that the African people would ever be able to support themselves adequately from the land. Hertzog openly declared: 'The first duty of the white man is to himself. Whatever the right of the Natives may be, they have no right to call upon us to do anything which might jeopardise our supremacy' (Debate on second reading of Representation of Natives Bill, Parliament 4/3/36).

Racist colonialism was at no stage meekly accepted. The most consistent political resistance came from the African National Congress, but in the late '20s it was overshadowed by the Industrial and Commercial Workers Union (ICU), which at the height of its power claimed a membership of 250,000.[5] Sobhuza learnt of African reactions from relatives and friends working or living in the Union and actively engaged in the political struggle. Among them were the Nxumalos and the Msimangs[6] whom his grandmother Labotsibeni had consulted, as well as Seme, who replaced Josiah Gumede as President of the African National Congress in the early 1930s. Sobhuza was in accord with the views of Seme, who steered a path between the conservative and conciliatory approach of Tengo Jabavu

[4] The Representation of Natives Bill passed in 1935 removed from Africans in the Cape the right to register on a common voters' roll – a right granted in 1853 when Britain governed the Cape. Africans had pressed in vain for similar recognition as voters in the three other provinces of the Union. In lieu of a common voters' roll, all Africans were to be represented in Parliament by seven whites, four in the Senate, three in the House of Assembly. The Native Trust and Land Bill set aside additional land for Africans but still restricted the area of land available for African occupation to some 13%, and thereby continued and consolidated the hated oppressive Land Act of 1913.

[5] The ICU was started in 1919 by Clements Kadalie, born in Nyasaland (now Malawi). Sobhuza never met Kadalie, but many Swazi in the Union were influenced by him. When the ICU disintegrated the most active branch was that of Champion, a Zulu of Natal, whom Sobhuza knew and described as a man who 'struggled for African rights'. In 1928 a trained trade union organizer, William Ballinger, had come from England to assist Kadalie. Ballinger visited Swaziland and met Sobhuza, and, together with Margaret Hodgson (later Mrs Ballinger), wrote a report on Swaziland. Ballinger subsequently employed Norman Nxumalo (one of Sobhuza's maternal uncles) and they went together to the International Labour Organization, in Geneva, to urge improvements in the conditions of recruitment of African mine labourers from the High Commission Territories to the gold mines in South Africa.

[6] The Msimangs, who also visited Sobhuza in Swaziland, were Richard and Selby, sons of Rev. Joe Msimang, brother of Daniel Msimang of Mahamba mission in Swaziland.

(born in 1860), and the radicalism of Josiah Gumede.

Sobhuza was not kept officially informed of the discussions between South Africa and Britain affecting the future of Swaziland, but the vague and often contradictory rumours and reports he received made him suspicious. 'We hear what is said through whispers. We are not spoken to as men, but it is our life that is discussed. If England is going to throw us away, let them tell us so that we can be prepared. It should be done while we still have some bargaining power. Now both England and the Union (of South Africa) can oppress us.'

Swaziland was part of the South Africa Customs Union, but Swaziland's share of any benefits was minimal and when South African exports were threatened by Swazi productivity, Swaziland was treated as a foreign country. South Africa controlled the market by periodically restricting the sale of Swaziland's cattle (the main source of Swazi wealth) and also by regulating the price of maize, most of which the Swazi had now to import for their own consumption. The economic resources of the monarchy were possibly at their lowest; Sobhuza had little money himself; and at the same time, shortage of land, limited economic development and the necessity for at least enough money to pay a minimum of £1.10s. tax per annum, forced some 11,000 Swazi to sell their labour to the Union every year. The majority worked underground in the gold mines.

Sobhuza's attitude towards the mines and labour migration was complex. He was conscious that the recruiting process itself gave dangerous powers to unscrupulous men. The recruiters received capitation fees, and there were complaints of abuse – using cash and food as enticements, treating debts as labour commitments. But Sobhuza was legally impotent and when cases were brought to him he could do little more than speak to the recruiters or report them to the (British Government) officials. He had never been down a mine; the Nation would not allow it because 'it was too dangerous'. He considered migrant labour a necessary evil – there were few opportunities in Swaziland to earn the required – and desired – money. Moreover, work on the mines was considered to have replaced warfare; it certainly was almost as dangerous! Thus, the desire for excitement, freedom from parental and tribal control, the wish to prove their manhood and win the admiration of the girls also attracted young Swazi to the mines.

Sobhuza's position was difficult – what influence could he exercise at such a great distance? He was critical of the way in which individuals obtained leadership in Trade Unions and exercised their power. 'To whom are they responsible? They have grabbed power. It has not been given to them. They are not chiefs.' So Sobhuza, in cooperation with mine management, sent his personal represenatives – as *tindvuna* – to guard as best they could the interests of Swazi miners. Prince Ntamo was one of the first of these men, just and brave, as was his successor Prince Mhawu. But neither Sobhuza nor they could change the system; the men needed employment, and the threat of stopping labour recruitment was an added economic-political weapon of the Union government.

In 1921 Dr Seme had negotiated on Sobhuza's behalf the purchase of six stands in Sophiatown. On the corner lot was a five-roomed brick house formerly owned by Solomon Ka Dinizulu, King of the Zulu nation, and it was already well known as 'the house of a King'. A distant relative of Sobhuza who had lived and worked in the city for many years was appointed caretaker.

It was in the Sophiatown house in 1930 that Benjamin Nxumalo held the first meeting of the Swaziland branch of the African National Congress and where many of the educated African elite, Swazi and non-Swazi, came on different occasions. They included Sol Plaatje, who died in 1932; Selope Thema, journalist and editor, and Dr A.B. Xuma, later President of the African National Congress, as well as the Msimangs and the Nxumalos. But Sobhuza's main interest was in providing a centre for the Swazi, and in 1931 he inaugurated the Swazi National Royal Club, with the Sophiatown house as its headquarters. The aims of the club were to promote all aspects of Swazi welfare, encourage African cooperation, establish centres of discussion, help publish matters of African interest, obtain land for the purposes of the society, and raise funds for its support.

Sobhuza came there roughly once a year at the time of the Rand Agricultural Show, where he would spend a day seeing pedigree cattle, agricultural products, and new machinery. He would bring with him four or five senior men and sometimes two or three princesses and queens and their attendants. But he said Johannesburg was not a good place for women: 'There are too many *tingwadla* (prostitutes), too many *tsotsis* (thugs), too much fighting, too little *inhlonipho* (respect). It is good to visit, not to live there.' He conceded the advantages: 'There are better schools in the Union, and people (Africans) are able to learn trades and earn more money. We lose our educated because they are not given positions in our own country.' He recalls the struggle of individual Swazi, eager to receive education, and their disillusionment with their reception by government officials in Swaziland, and the tragedy that followed their frustrations. Before the Second World War there was in the whole of Swaziland no western qualified Swazi doctor, dentist, lawyer, accountant or engineer, and at the time of independence the few Swazi eligible for positions in a modern government had received their training mainly in schools and universities in the Union.

But the paradox was that those who worked in the Union did not want to be buried there. Although the opportunities for education and for earning money were greater in the Union, they were unable to establish cultural roots there; in Swaziland their identity was secure. Swaziland was not only their home but British rule was preferable to that of South Africa. The resistance to transfer came from men who had little education as well as from the lost intellectuals. Several meetings of protest against transfer were held in the Sophiatown house.

Leading Swazi in the Union were among the 400 delegates who on 16 December 1935 met in Bloemfontein, at a conference of all African organizations – the All African Convention – called to oppose the Hertzog legislation. The policy expressed by the Convention was directed to 'ensure the ultimate creation of a South African nation in which, while the various racial groups may develop on their own lines socially and culturally, they will be bound together by the pursuit of common political objectives'. (*Cape Times*, 18 December 1935.) Subsequently, Selby Msimang as Secretary of the Convention wrote: 'Let us now admit, both publicly and in our conscience, that Parliament and the white people of South Africa have disowned us, flirted and trifled with our loyalties ... Behind this brutal injustice is the reliance of the powers that be on the stupendous and murderous modern weapons of war and the advantages they have thereby against us defenceless people ...' (*The Crisis*, 1936, pp. 9, 11). He ended with a quotation from a speech by Smuts: 'To suppose that in the modern world you can dispense with freedom in human government, that you can govern without the free consent of the governed, is to fly in the face of decent human nature as well as of the facts of history' (p. 14).

When Sobhuza read his pamphlet, to which I had written a brief foreword, he commented: 'Men should always get together when confronted with problems. Even if we can't solve them it is good to discuss and share opinions. Msimang is right to speak of our troubles and then to point out that we must find solutions. A brave man is ready to die in war. But he should not start a fight simply to show his bravery.' While Sobhuza played no direct role in the politics of South Africa, he was well aware of what was happening on a wider political front. The fact that he was not actively involved in the power struggle in South Africa, and yet was kept informed of the different ambitions, goals and techniques, gave him a perspective which stood him in good stead in the years to come.

His resistance to transfer to the Union did not turn him into a servile admirer of the British, but helped him see more clearly the hardships and deprivations of the people in his own country.

In Swaziland itself Sobhuza faced the predicament of hereditary African rulers in a colonial situation. The Resident Commissioner exercised overriding authority and expected Sobhuza to implement colonial policy, but his own subjects saw him as their King and turned to him for protection against colonial demands. For Sobhuza the problem was that of maintaining his own integrity under these conflicting pressures.

In 1928 Resident Commissioner de Symon Honey was replaced by T. Ainsworth Dickson. Officials with long service and experience in Swaziland had summarily been passed over in favour of an outsider.

Dickson was a cultivated Englishman, 47 years of age, unmarried, with some twenty years' experience as an administrative officer in Kenya, and an observant traveller's knowledge of North Africa, Syria and Iraq. A few months after his arrival he sent Sobhuza a request for a memorandum on the 'forms and procedures of his councils, executive and general, since the notes available are not very full'. And added, 'This will be an interesting document to file with other papers connected with Native Custom' (Letter 18/6/29).

While Swazi culture was to him primarily 'Native Custom', he was actively interested in promoting Swazi education and in advancing Swazi in western culture. Sobhuza described him as an 'unusual man – complicated and reserved – a true Englishman'. Swazi nicknamed him Msunduza – one who pushes something forward, an innovator, or one who pushes something out, in reference to his promotion over the head of the unpopular government secretary.

It was Dickson who encouraged the formation of a Swaziland Progressive Association as a centre for the non-white intelligentsia with separate committees for Africans and for Coloureds in each of the districts to represent the interests of a new school-educated political elite. (The first meeting was held on 21 January 1929.) Sobhuza, prompted by A.G. Marwick, reacted with caution and suspicion: 'Why was it necessary to form separate associations? Might they not create a gulf between educated and uneducated? Wasn't it rather the duty of the educated, or of those who considered themselves educated, to influence others by mixing with them and by discussing matters with them, rather than by talking only amongst themselves?' It was not that he opposed the Association but he saw the danger of cutting off the educated who, because of special consideration from the government, might support the government against Swazi institutions. The matter was discussed in the Council, of which some of the most astute and highly respected members had little or no formal schooling, while others equally but not more important were well educated by current western standards.

Sobhuza agreed with the principles expressed in the first constitution of the Progressive Association affirming 'the essential dignity of every human being irrespective of race, colour, or creed' and the right to freedom of worship, expression, movement, assembly, and association, but he claimed that the rights of his people were adequately contained in the traditional Swazi constitution. In his memorandum on this subject, presented in response to Dickson's request, he showed the built-in checks on autocratic power, the balance between different offices in the government, and the rights of the Swazi nationals.

Sobhuza's doubts about the value of the Progressive Association were somewhat allayed by the support it received from Benjamin Nxumalo, whose loyalty could never be questioned and whose political skills had been developed in the hard school of South African politics. But for most positions requiring special knowledge the government recruited foreign Africans, mainly Zulu and Xhosa, and since the number of educated Swazi employed in Swaziland was small, Sobhuza feared that the Progressive Association could be taken over by non-Swazi with different loyalties and ideas. Benjamin Nxumalo was elected the first chairman of the Progressive Association, and F.F. Sepamla, a Hlubi who served as a clerk for the central administration, the Secretary.

The following year, January 1930, John J. Nquku, a Zulu from Natal, was brought to Swaziland as Supervisor of Native Education, and became an active member of the Association. Nquku, whose parents had been converted, baptized and confirmed by Bishop Colenso, was raised and educated by missionaries. He threw himself into his new job with immense dedication, travelling through the country on foot, horseback and motorcycle, encouraging and, when necessary, berating teachers and pupils alike. The national schools of Zombodze and Lobamba, as well as government subsidized mission schools, were under his scrutiny. One day Sobhuza told Benjamin Nxumalo to bring Nquku to meet him. He took a liking to the short, stocky teacher, with a big head, wide intent eyes and blunt manner. Sobhuza, who nicknamed him Madletjana (protruding ears), appreciated his sense of purpose and respected his fearlessness in stating his own opinion, and encouraged him to do research in Swazi history and customs. Nquku said that from the first meeting he realized that 'Here is a great man. He seeks the truth for himself and does not want to hear lies.' In 1940, when Nquku resigned his position with the government due to the racist ill treatment he received from a man appointed above him, Sobhuza gave him the position of a national advisor to the Swazi National Inner Council, with particular responsibilities for education and church affairs.

Sobhuza was deeply concerned with the quality of education given his people. All schools were legally segregated; for white children primary education up to standard six was free and compulsory; for Swazi children education was neither free nor compulsory and some 70% of Swazi children between 6 and 16 received no education at all; the government paid roughly £18 per annum for a white child, £1 per annum for an African child at school. Much of the money spent on Swazi education came from the National Fund started by Labotsibeni.

Most schools were run by missions, subsidized to some extent by government. Until the '30s there were only four (mission) schools that went as far as Std. VI, and government itself was uncertain of its priorities, wavering between spreading limited money as far as possible or concentrating on the raising up of a few promising pupils as 'capable and trustworthy leaders'. Dickson favoured the latter policy, and Sobhuza called it 'an important day for all the nation' when in 1931 he opened the first Swazi high school, Matsapha (The

Morning Star), as a non-denominational school supported from the Swazi National Fund. Sobhuza wanted it to be 'the best in the country, with the best teachers we can find. The thing we need is knowledge. Our children should go to England, France, America, everywhere, and then when they return they will be able to raise up the nation'. He encouraged princes, chiefs, and commoners to send their children and argued against those parents who said 'book education does not help'.

It was not only the intellectual standard that he wanted to raise; at a meeting in 1933 he criticized the social effects of the type of education which was being given. 'Children,' he said, 'no longer obey the law of the land, and when they throw away our customs they say they are following the laws of whites but really they don't understand these laws because they only get a little of the ways of the whites, who then say "these people know nothing" and criticise us.' He observed a breakdown in traditional courtesy, respect and obedience and an increase in immorality and illegitimacy. This he associated with a growing rift between Christians and non-Christians, educated and uneducated. As a remedy, he suggested the adaptation of the traditional regimental system (*emabutfo*) to the modern western school system. The regiments, which automatically included every Swazi male on the basis of age, were also the main educational institutions of the past, imposing and enforcing a national code of discipline, morality and unity. Boys were enrolled from an early age; no man could marry before his group received permission; breach of the sex code met with heavy punishment. In proposing to introduce the Swazi age system into schools, Sobhuza was already beginning to formulate the ideas which later became his explicit national policy: 'Choose the good from the customs of others and join it with the good which is in our own traditions. Only in that way can we go forward as a self-respecting nation. In order to do this you must know your own customs and start out from them. True education is more than book learning, wisdom is greater than knowledge.'

However, Sobhuza's suggestion evoked what he described as 'stirring a hornet's nest'. The initial reactions of most of the missionaries 'amazed and disappointed' him and showed the depth of their prejudices. They opposed just those Swazi customs specifically directed towards maintaining morality. They objected to young people publicly taking lovers before marriage, they objected to *ukujuma* (a natural method of birth control) and they objected to the prohibition against early marriage.

Sobhuza explained the courting custom of his people: 'When a girl agrees to accept a boy as a lover, she goes publicly with a group of girls in bright dance costume to the *lilawu* (barracks) of the boys and they call out the name of the boy she has chosen, and sing and dance. But mission children are afraid, and play with each other secretly, even when they are still young; sometimes you can see its effects – they do not glow, they are weak. The missionaries force this secrecy, and if they see two of their converts love each other, even if they are just children, try to force them to marry. If the boy doesn't want to, he runs away. The girls that are pregnant are disgraced.'

The missionaries, afraid that participation in the regimental system would threaten the foundations of their Christian teachings, requested that membership be voluntary. Sobhuza knew that for the experiment to be truly effective the entire nation should be involved but he attempted to compromise by assuring the missionaries that channels would be available through which any interested person could voice his complaints about the new organization. The missionaries still resisted, suggesting as a substitute the Pathfinder Organization – black Boy Scouts – in which membership would be voluntary and personal and, implicitly, control would be by the District Pathfinder and allegiance to an outside authority.

On the whole the administrative officials favoured Sobhuza's proposition. Marwick, who throughout was the strongest and most eloquent ally, wrote a memorandum, arguing that the regimental system, in comparison with the Pathfinders, was more of an 'integrating' influence since 'it is an indigenous institution motivated and controlled from within the tribe, capable of being operated efficiently by the natives themselves, without extraneous aids and with little or no training, fully understood by them and so extraordinarily efficient as to have itself provided the inspiration for the formation of the Boy Scout Movement.' Dickson was less enthusiastic and made it clear that he was not prepared to give it his blessing without fully examining the implications. Subsequently, with Sobhuza's approval, he invited two anthropologists, Professor I. Schapera and Winifred Hoernlé, to investigate the system and consider the feasibility of its application. Their report was favourable. Soon after, Dickson went on sick leave, and Marwick was appointed in his place, first as acting, and then in March 1935, as full Resident Commissioner. He was 58; in two years he would have to retire.

It was while Marwick was acting Resident Commissioner that I arrived and observed the restraint with which Sobhuza – then, as now – handled the different reactions, including the insults and attitudes of moral superiority adopted by many whites towards his people and their customs. He expressed himself generally with impressive self-control; only occasionally his face would darken and his eyes flash, and those who knew him trembled. Once, after a particularly humiliating experience he said to Ngolotjeni Motsa, 'They try to make us throw away our own way [of life] for a deception.' It hurt him particularly that some of his own people supported the missionary opposition.

But he would not be deterred, and while the dispute was on, went deliberately ahead and in September 1935 publicly inaugurated a new regiment. That this was permitted indicated both his weakness and his strength. On the one hand, it showed that his leadership presented no military threat – the making of war had become a British prerogative and his men were without modern weapons of destruction. On the other hand, he was able to keep the regimental organization alive, and mobilise followers for other national duties. By creating a new regiment he restated his position as Ngwenyama, head of the *emabutfo*.

It was a period of intense economic as well as political hardship. For two successive years (1934-1935) swarms of red locusts devastated the countryside, and no one who experienced this plague could forget it. Sobhuza named the new regiment *Sikhonyane*, the Locust, with a junior section, *Inkhasa*, the Hopper, which became better known as *Sukasambe*, Let us be on the move. All the men of the previous regiment, formed in 1923, were then free to marry (some of them had already taken wives without permission and were fined for this offence). Their ritual duties were taken over by the new regiment of youths whose courage and purity were necessary qualities for the part they would be required to play in the annual national ritual of Kingship. Sobhuza visualized the Sikhonyane as the first regiment of educated Swazi, and a leavening influence throughout the nation. In it would be his own oldest sons.

Eventually it was agreed that the experiment be tried, but limited to the Swazi National High School where the headmaster, G.E.P. Broderick, was enthusiastically supportive. Sobhuza realized sadly that in fact little had been achieved, since the strength of the age regiments was their national integrative effect; the numbers of boys at the national school were too few to make a real impact, and the opposition remained too vocal. But he also believed that if the system was once established it could be extended, and he and his allies decided to make it as effective as possible. He took an active interest in the committee appointed to control the school. He also sent along leading elders to speak to the boys on Swazi history, and arranged that a camp be organized at his residence. In August 1936 he appointed a special board to advise him in all matters affecting Swazi youth. The board was typical of his effort to get as wide a range of opinion as possible. Members included the volatile 'renegade minister' Solomon Madevu Nkosi as well as the very sedate Reverend Mdziniso; two teachers at the school, Mashiphisa Fakudze and Mzululeki Nxumalo; two chiefs, Princes Mhawu and Zece; and an outstanding councillor and poet, Lohhoko Mndzebele. They would work with Theo Keen, new principal of Matsapha and an expert in the Boy Scout Movement.

The first schoolboy appointed as Chief Officer was Mfundza, a junior son of Lomadokola Sukati who had spoken boldly against those who had opposed the education of the boy-king, Sobhuza. Mfundza – short, wiry, energetic, intelligent, hot-tempered, and enterprising – was well qualified by reason of his training in Swazi tradition. He was a strong leader; when some of the boys refused to do the manual work which was part of the regimental system, he ordered them to do extra on the weekend, and saw that the order was carried out by working with the offenders. Sobhuza recalled these qualities when in later years he appointed Mfundza First Deputy Prime Minister.

The school had girls as well as boys, and in charge of the girls in the hostel Sobhuza put Princess Silima and his own old nurse, Lambuli.[7] Complementary values to those of the *emabutfo* needed to be inculcated into the girls, the wives and mothers of the future, and soon after the Locust regiment was inaugurated, Sobhuza's sister, Sengcabaphi, suggested to the Ndlovukazi that an *umcwasho* be celebrated. This was a ceremony for girls who had reached or were near maturity, imposing a period of chastity and emphasizing the need for sexual restraint. When they spoke of this to Sobhuza, whose permission was necessary, he was delighted. The *umcwasho* was sporadically and sometimes locally performed, but now that five of his daughters were mature, it was appropriate that *umcwasho* be held on a national scale. Sobhuza sent runners to leading chiefs in the country and in March 1935 teams of maidens, each under a local princess or chief's daughter, arrived at Lobamba.[8] The leading princess was Sobhuza's oldest daughter, Betfusile, then sixteen years of age, and she was assisted by two girls, appointed as her *tindvuna*. When Sengcabaphi, as main advisor, introduced the three girls, she gave out the rules, the costume to be worn, the greetings to be used, and how they were to behave. The *umcwasho* was to last two years, and the most important rule prohibited an *umcwasho* girl from having physical relationship with any man, including the King. For this offence both parties would be punished by a fine, varying in amount with the seriousness and consequences, and demanded in a public dance accompanied by songs of ridicule. Nothing was more embarrassing and humiliating than the mockery chanted by a group of outraged maidens, throwing in front of the offender the decorative head ornament, the *umcwasho*, symbolizing their dedication to premarital restraint.

The *umcwasho* began, as it was to end, with national service, and the first task was to gather wood and subsequently to cut the long reeds required for fencing, and present them to the Ndlovukazi. The girls obviously enjoyed it all. It was great fun to sing and dance and wear short gay costumes that showed off their beauty, and to be admired for their performance. The tunes were catchy, the words pointed, and the movements subtle, and a few songs are still remembered: 'O those who argue. What will Nkosi say? He will beat us', and 'Nkosi looks

[7] Princess Silima, a daughter of Mbandzeni, was appointed as warden of the hostel, and Lambuli as her assistant. They had no academic training, but were chosen for their common sense. Co-education presented many problems!

[8] Sobhuza's oldest sister, Ladluli, was asked to assist Sengcabaphi, but the main responsibility rested with the younger girls, who called themselves the Lukhumbuntsetse. Ladluli, who was pregnant and not able to attend, commemorated the occasion by naming her child, a boy, Khumbuntsetse.

after his children together with orphans'.

The *umcwasho* soon came to the notice of missionaries, several of whom appealed to the Administration to prohibit it on the grounds that 'it was a reversal to heathendom', the costume was immodest, and that the ceremony 'would certainly end in a saturnalia'. Again the King had to defend his action; he pointed out that it did not contradict anything written in the Bible, that only girls without blemish could carry the *umcwasho* and that a ceremony which enforced restraint could hardly be termed immoral. However, recognising the hostility of missionaries, he agreed that it need not be compulsory and that neither parents nor chiefs should compel the attendance of their daughters, though many of them, he noticed, were very anxious that their daughters should receive such training. At two critical periods in the future, after the Second World War and after Independence, Sobhuza would again encourage the national *umcwasho* to remind the nation of its traditional morality.

Paradoxically it was the missions most dedicated to their system of education and their own puritanical concepts which presented the major obstacles to his efforts to introduce a national educational policy with its specific content expressed through age regiments of the boys and the *umcwasho* for the girls. In the '20s and '30s most missionaries were rigid in their approach and Sobhuza was frequently put on the defensive. These missionaries were conservative evangelicals or fundamentalists who, though drawn from England, America, Europe and the Scandinavian countries, shared a common religious background and generally negative attitude to Swazi traditional culture. Their objections differed, however, from mission to mission, and some allowed what others forbade. But all seemed to agree with a leading missionary who stated that 'sex is a torment and a temptation. It is the devil we must fight.' They could not understand the Swazi respect for sex, their recognition that the physical desires of the young were natural and healthy, and that fertility was the theme song of the universe; and together with this went the deep belief that because the power of sex was both creative and regenerative, it should be channelled by custom, associated with growth in ways that were good and beneficial to the nation.

Sobhuza decided that it did not help his people for him to quarrel with the missionaries or any other influential men in the country, and intuitively, rather than deliberately, he developed a wide range of tactics for expressing his own values without crude confrontation. He knew that the missionaries were divided among themselves, that Catholics did not ally with Protestants, and that among the latter there were numerous rival sects. He also realized that even those who were critical of him were interested in having his support, and that his strength lay in distributing his favours without committing himself to any single denomination. He was on personal friendly terms with a few individual white missionaries, and he never forbade even those who were most opposed to him from holding services in his villages, nor did he arbitrarily reject applications to build churches in Swazi areas. Almost every Sunday different congregations held prayer meetings at the capital which were attended by Lomawa and any of the queens and children who so desired.

Lomawa had at one stage contemplated being officially converted to the Methodist church with which she was familiar from her girlhood, but Labotsibeni had told her she could not serve two masters. The Swazi National Council, acting as a united body, finally dissuaded her on the grounds that this would conflict with her overarching obligation and ritual duties as Ndlovukazi of the entire nation. Nukwase, her sister, was baptised and other relatives were active in church affairs. Her brother Benjamin Nxumalo was a leading member of the African Methodist Episcopal Church, one of the earliest and most influential of the African independent churches, and one which was politically moderate, imbued with a vision of social, economic and political integration and racial equality.

There were also several smaller independent (Zionist) churches whose followers, in uniforms of shining white, deep blue, grass green, wandered over the countryside carrying symbolic staves, and praying and healing by faith. They responded with fervour to the name of Jehovah, and found in the Old Testament support for customs the missionaries condemned. Their preachers had the spirit of prophecy, and to many their King Sobhuza was one with the Kings of Judah.

Sobhuza was deeply interested in religious ideas and would spend long hours discussing the meaning of the Old Testament and trying to understand differences in dogma as well as in practice. He questioned the assumption that only Christians knew the way to *Nkulunkulu* (The Great Great Being) or *Mvelinchanti* (The Being who appeared before all else). One day a missionary had been to see the Queen Mother and offered a prayer for her soul and told her that by conversion she would attain salvation. Sobhuza arrived shortly after he had left, and Lomawa told him what the *umfundisi* (minister) had said. Sobhuza listened to her and then asked, 'Does he say a priest can give salvation? Isn't he a man like us? Can he save us from suffering? Or close off death? It troubles me to listen to someone who speaks with the voice of God. Is there a person on earth who has the truth to say he can forgive me my sins? Only God can do that. Has he seen God with his eyes, heard him with his ears? We too have God. We know he created us and we have seen his work.' His ally on the European front was again A.G. Marwick, who said publicly: 'A good man need not be a preacher and a preacher is not necessarily a good man.'

Sobhuza, critical of the disruptive effects of missionary competition, put the question: 'If there is one God whom we all believe in how do you know that my way of speaking to him is not as good as yours?' And once he asked with a touch of bitterness, 'Is religion a business that you must fight for God's customers?' So he was sympathetic to the idea of a national church, and when some of his own people (led by Prince Solomon Madevu, who had been excommunicated by the Wesleyans because he took a second wife and openly advocated polygyny) suggested this, Sobhuza responded favourably. However, he stressed the need for tolerance, saying that he left it to them to decide which customs should be recognised, and that when they reached agreement they should again bring the matter to him. It was inevitable with such a variety of churches and large number of priests that agreement could not easily be reached, and when different individuals appealed to him, saying, 'We want unity, the others do not', he would reply, 'Cool your hearts, quarrelling is not the right road to Heaven. Go back and pray, then get together again.' Eventually some common principles were found largely through the activities of Nukwase, and Sobhuza willingly granted a piece of land near Lobamba for the building of a national church. But the grass hut at the entrance of his mother's enclosure remained the heart of Swazi religion, the shrine of the nation.

Sobhuza had little authority to solve the many serious mundane problems affecting the peace and livelihood of his people. The delimitation of the boundaries under the Concessions Proclamation continued to give rise to recurrent and at times violent land disputes, some between chiefs and white farmers, and some between neighbouring chiefs. In several cases Swazi insisted that white farmers with vast tracts of land had moved the beacons, while the whites blamed the Swazi. Complaints would be lodged with the Assistant Commissioner and if he decided that the Swazi had trespassed, the only thing Sobhuza could do was to try to resettle the dispossessed.

Every year more people had to be accommodated on the limited area allocated for Swazi use, and many chiefs could not satisfy the requirements of their followers. The prestige of a chief rested on the size of his following ('People speak, the land does not speak'), and the more popular the chief, the more people he attracted and the less willing they were to transfer their allegiance elsewhere. He in turn would try to help them either by squeezing them into his restricted space, creating some tensions between his own followers, or by arranging for them to have their homes in his area but cultivate land lying idle under the jurisdiction of a neighbouring chief for whom they would perform certain services. This arrangement of chiefs borrowing land for needy followers who could then be called on for their labour frequently broke down, sometimes because the lending chief would demand too much and give too little, or because the clients, once established, would claim that the land was in the area of their more popular political patrons. The followers of both chiefs would express their allegiance by taking sides, and if no compromise could be reached there was the danger that fights would ensue, gardens be destroyed, and huts burned. Though the cases in which this occurred were relatively few they were deeply disturbing to Sobhuza, whom the people considered trustee of the land, and eulogized as 'the earth'.

Sobhuza contrasted his approach with that of the British government and white farmers. He and his people acted in these internal land disputes on the fundamental principle that every Swazi national was entitled to land for subsistence, and this principle, not any technicality, was a major consideration in settling cases. He would appoint a committee of trusted men familiar with the area to go and investigate the position on the spot, find out the history of the boundaries, and try to unravel the immensely complicated ramifications of conflicting claims. But even so, the root cause – shortage of land – remained; and it was in vain at times for him to declare:

The rule underlying all land disputes is that chiefs and their followers should be as friendly to one another as possible, as has been the case in the past. The chief awarded judgment should not spitefully interfere with the followers of the other chief, but should give them equal justice unless they prove to be still imbued with the spirit of dispute, when it becomes necessary that they should be removed to their original chief. (Undated letter by Sobhuza explaining the position to the Administration.)

Sobhuza did not appoint the chiefs but confirmed them in their appointment, which was the responsibility of the chief's own family council. Though it was the colonial government that secured Sobhuza's position he considered that he derived his enduring support from his chiefs, and when the British asked him to fill a vacancy and criticized him if an appointment was not made after a fairly long lapse of time, he would try to make it clear that he did not feel he had the right to interfere in an internal family matter, nor would he impose his own choice. All he could do was call some of the senior kinsmen, followers of the late chief, and put the position to them since they were responsible for carrying on the administration of the district until they agreed in their selection of the heir. He trusted them to go thoroughly into the claims of all contestants, guided by precedents which included principles governing hereditary succession. He appreciated that it was not possible to rule either effectively or peacefully through leaders backed by outsiders and rejected by the people.

If the individual who was finally chosen proved incompetent or too autocratic, his councillors, described as his 'owners', would not hesitate to rebuke him, and they also had the authority to fine him. If the situation worsened there was the right of appeal to the courts of Lobamba and Lozitha, which could order a recalcitrant chief 'to rest', and if necessary move him and his family to another site. In the past, of course, such a chief ran the risk of death or banishment, and failure to obey a judgment issued in the name of the Ngwenyama was treason. But, as Sobhuza was careful to inform me, even in the past one of the sons of the former chief would be chosen to succeed to the position. He concluded: 'If a chief does good it is because his people are good, if he does evil it is because the people let him. A chief must feel with his people and take his stand from their wishes, not from his own self interests. It is also to his advantage to draw people towards him, not drive them to seek the protection of another, not to ignore them but to recognize their *budvodza* (manly worth). He must not waste people or treat them brutally. They in turn must be loyal and trustworthy. If they criticize you let them speak in the open, then only can you respect them.'

In a report on one long dispute involving a chief who 'seems to take all power in his hands', Sobhuza wrote that 'he has been further warned that if he continues to misbehave himself, I shall be compelled to have him removed from that place without his followers, who won't be tossed up and down for his sake, or, in other words, that I shall not recognize them following him as a son of their chief' (RCS 989/33, 13 November 1934). Verbatim records of cases were never kept, but in the several hearings I attended, he persistently tried to reconcile the legitimacy of prior rights with the need to find land for the needy and displaced.

Though his basic ties were with the traditional chiefs he was sometimes compelled by the restrictions of his authority to turn to the Resident Commissioner or the Assistant Commissioners for help in enforcing decisions. His jurisdiction was limited to civil cases in Swazi law but if the messengers sent from his court failed in the execution of a judgement, they had to rely on the police over whom he had no control. The entire legal system was complicated by duality of courts and procedures. As he put it, 'The white man's court speaks the white man's law. A Swazi who wants to take his case there rather than before a chief generally has something to hide or is acting out of spite.' He hastened to explain that this was not because the Commissioner acting as Magistrate was 'a bad man', but because he did not understand Swazi law. To meet this difficulty the Administration appointed a Swazi as '*ndabazabantfu*' (literally, officer in affairs of the people) to each administrative court, thereby also facilitating inclusion of Swazi officials, chosen by the King-in-Council, in the lower levels of government bureaucracy.

He was acutely aware of the confusion created by conflicting systems of law and the need to reorganize the traditional courts so that they would be more efficient. It was difficult to know where to begin. Were there any procedures that he could follow? In 1935 he felt it necessary to summon old men of the Mgadlela Regiment living in the neighbourhood of royal villages to come to the capital so that he could find out which cases in the past went to the Queen Mother, which to the King, and which could be dealt with at lower levels without direct appeal. He also summoned the younger men concerned with this issue. His spokesmen were Councillors Alpheus Hlophe and Mabhuducapha Tfwala. The order of appeal from one court to the next was illustrated by cases and a general consensus emerged: The King decided only major cases – witchcraft, disputes in connection with land, conflicting claims to succession – and he should not be bothered with 'small cases'. This would avoid the piling up and long delay which was causing complaints among the people. At this meeting Mkukwane, Nukwase's younger son and Sobhuza's 'brother', stood up and declared, 'There is no sense in dealing with the old machinery without realizing that the country is changing. There are no men to help the *tindvuna* and no court to secure justice since all the men are away at work. The governors sit alone even as the King is alone. The land belongs to the whites. There is no longer discipline and even if the King calls, a man doesn't respond.' When this was reported to Sobhuza, he said sadly, 'I too see the faults but without knowing what was done in the past, I cannot see what should be done at the present.'

Swazi law was not written, nor was he sure that it should be since times were changing, and to write things down might make adaptations more difficult. Even more serious than the duality in civil cases were the fundamental conflicts between the Swazi outlook and that of the British in criminal cases. Over these Sobhuza had no authority. Cases went from the Assistant Commissioners to the Appeal Court, presided over by white judges, trained in Roman Dutch law, whose concepts of justice were often opposed to those of the Swazi. In no situation was this more evident than in their approach to the practice of so-called witchcraft. Swazi distinguish clearly between *batsakatsi* (evildoers) who destroy, and *tangoma* (diviners) ritual specialists trained to detect the evildoers. But to most Europeans this distinction was irrelevant and nonsensical; and under the Witchcraft Ordinance, the accusation as well as the practice of witchcraft was a punishable offence. Swazi argued that witchcraft was flourishing because by punishing the diviners the laws were in fact protecting the evildoers. At a meeting with government officials in 1931 a Swazi said, 'We regard the law of witchcraft with great displeasure. The wizards are doing us in on all sides.' And an official replied, 'You are talking nonsense. Illness and death occur amongst most families.'

Sobhuza believed that between the diviner and the evildoer there was perpetual battle. The evildoer killed his enemies; the diviner detected the evildoer and protected the community. Some people were believed to be born with the evil power transmitted through a mother who was a witch, others destroyed by obtaining poisons from a practising witch. A witch killed secretly for vile personal ends, and there were many ways of working witchcraft: *kuphosa* (to throw evil through the atmosphere), *kutsebula* (to work evil through contact), *kudlisa* (to poison through food). A witch killed from afar using the name of the victim, or a little piece of his clothing or a lock of his hair. There were also many ways by which diviners detected evildoers, the ultimate test being that of the poison ordeal.

Sobhuza, who knew that witchcraft was practised, did not accept all he heard about the powers attributed to witches and wanted to find

5. Sobhuza with some of his companions. Usually he too wore Swazi clothing. 1907

6. Lomawa, Sobhuza, Labotsibeni and Prince Malunge. *c.* 1911

7. Lomawa, Sobhuza, Labotsibeni, de Symon Honey (Resident Commissioner), Lord Buxton (High Commissioner), Mrs de Symon Honey and Lady Buxton at the visit of the High Commissioner to Swaziland, 13 September 1917

8. Sobhuza, not yet fully installed as King, in the uniform of the Simema ritual. *c.* 1920

out the limits of its reality. He had been told that in Portuguese territory there were witches who flew at night and stole the soul from their sleeping victims, leaving an empty husk. How true were these stories, he asked? He wanted proof before he accepted. In the early '30s he had sent Mnyakaza Gwebu, whom he later appointed as my assistant and companion, to Portuguese territory to research this issue. Mnyakaza had wandered through the country between Swaziland and Lourenço Marques, making contact with different specialists (he learned to speak Portuguese and ChiNdao) and after almost a year he returned to report that he had found one old man who claimed to possess those supernatural powers. The King sent for him. He came and stayed at Lozitha. He was very old, very wise. He and Sobhuza discussed this 'other reality' but when the King tried to pin him down to a demonstration, he was tantalizing evasive. He died shortly after and his secret was buried with him.

There were others who claimed to be able to raise the dead from their graves, in the form of tiny shadow men, to labour in the fields. One well-known doctor, Mgunquza Nkambule, who had a reputation for a wide range of cures and knowledge of nature's powers, boasted that he had at his command a special tiny creature, a *sipoko*, dwarf-like and hairy, which he could send to do his bidding. Sobhuza wanted objective proof of this claim, and in 1935 he sent me, together with Mnyakaza and Mkalimele Mhlanga, to investigate. We spent a week in Mgunquza's village, high in the Mdlaka hills, far from the main road, five hours by horseback from the nearest farm. It was a strange experience and insight into another world. Mgunquza was no fraud; and his medicines stretched the boundaries of the mind. On the fourth day he took us up the mountain, a long exhausting climb. At the top was a sheer fall of rock with huge cracks above a narrow ledge. There was about it an unforgettable fearfulness. He gave us medicines to chew for our safety. The wind blew and birds flew over our heads. The doctor talked more or less to himself: 'Perhaps he is there, I don't know. Can you see it?' At a certain point he stopped and said flatly, 'It is too dangerous for you to go further. I will try and make it appear so that you can see it clearly.' We tried to persuade him to let us accompany him. He was adamant. It was hot, and we were tired and the medicines were bitter. I do not know if what we saw in the end was real or hallucination – a small distorted body with a big head appeared to move across the rocky surface. Doubt is the limit of my disbelief. We reported to Sobhuza who expressed his disappointment. To this day Mgunquza Nkambule's claim remains unproven, not disproven.

Sobhuza tried on many occasions to have the government recognize the distinction between the practice of anti-social medicine (witchcraft) which according to Swazi law merited the death penalty, and the socially approved techniques of detecting evildoers. 'True Swazi', he insists, regard with horror and disgust the practice of killing people for medicine for personal ends, but punishment even by death of evildoers is the duty of those in charge of the well-being of the nation.

A crucial and tragic case brought to the fore the conflict that Sobhuza faced in this field of government. In 1936 Chief Fakisandla Nkambule, appointed by Sobhuza as court *ndvuna* to S.B. Williams, then Assistant Commissioner at Hlatikulu, was accused of a 'witchcraft murder'. Swazi could not credit this – Fakisandla, trusted and loyal counsellor, renowned for his integrity and national service, respected for his wisdom and sense of justice. All had been going well with him until for no apparent reason those dearest to him were struck down by death and mysterious illness. The first to die was his own mother (Princess Lomakhetfo, daughter of King Mswati), then a grown daughter, then other children 'were finished'; and his own health was affected. As Chief, Fakisandla called in many doctors, and eventually appealed to diviners. His fears and suspicions were confirmed. The dead were the victims of his enemies and if they were not stopped, he and those survivors close to him could be destroyed. Diviners gave him the names of the evildoers. He knew them all. He sent his local doctor to find someone who had the knowledge and skill necessary to make 'a rope' (also known as *luzeku* – revenge medicine) and put it on the graves of the deceased, so that by its agency the dreams troubling him might be turned from him and the evildoers responsible for the deaths discovered and destroyed through the inherent power of the medicines.

An attendant, Nyandeni, eventually found a doctor, Nhloko Hlatshwako, who undertook to perform the ceremony. In a letter written on Fakisandla's instructions, Nyandeni told him to come to the village on a certain day with his medicines; subsequently Fakisandla dictated two further letters, one addressed to Nyandeni and the other to Nhloko. Both were put in the same envelope; in the letter to Nyandeni were the names of four people. Nhloko, however, held a seance in the village and said he would find out who was guilty by submitting all those present to a test. But instead of administering the ordeal fairly, he had two pots; in one pot he had put arsenic, in the other a harmless potion. Three people died. Two were on the list. Nhloko and Fakisandla were charged with murder; Nhloko pleaded guilty, Fakisandla protested his innocence. In his confession Nhloko stated that he had acted in the belief that 'the Paramount Chief' knew that Fakisandla was consulting a diviner. The police subpoenaed Sobhuza for questioning. He raised the matter with the Resident Commissioner, informing him that he had no objection to attending Court to give evidence provided he had some knowledge of the case, but that it happened not infrequently that his name was mentioned in connection with some matter of a national character though it may have been one of his *indvuna* acting under his authority – and not he himself – who was concerned in the matter.

Both Fakisandla and Nhloko were found guilty in the Special Court of Swaziland and sentenced to death. Sobhuza was deeply distressed; Fakisandla was a good man. Also, Sobhuza felt an added responsibility to do all he could to help since Fakisandla's father, Mtilankhatsa, was brother to the late Chief Mutsimunye, who had responded to the appeal for help when Sobhuza as a baby had to be carried across the torrents of the crocodile-infested Mkhondvo river, and it was in his village of Buseleni that the entourage had rested in safety. So Sobhuza-in-Council had the case taken on appeal by Seme to the Privy Council Criminal Court. The appeal, argued primarily on grounds of procedure, was dismissed. On 25 June, 1940, after three years in prison, Fakisandla was hanged. He faced the gallows with dignity and courage, supported by the knowledge that his people believed in the righteousness of his action. He was no evildoer, no witch, no criminal. His case was seen by Sobhuza and his council as completely different from that of a murderer, or one who for personal greed or aggrandisement selects a victim to use in medicines. Such men are indeed judged by Swazi as guilty of witchcraft. This case, probably more than any other, undermined the traditional system of justice, and bolstered the current belief that under the white man's laws witches go free and good men are hanged.

CHAPTER VIII
A King Twice

So far we have seen Sobhuza mainly as a public figure, trained from childhood for the role of King, steadily acquiring a knowledge of government, learning to deal with the complexities of competing interests in a racist colonial system. Now it is time to look at him more closely and privately, more personally; for while the British treated him as a 'Paramount Chief' and Swazi recognized him as their King (Ngwenyama), his personal identity was rooted in the fertile soil of kinship. The Swazi say, *Inkosi kabili* (a king is king twice). He is King not only of the nation, but also of his own kin, the *Malangeni* (children of the sun); fhe two are interwoven.

The soil of the nation is rich, a compost of many elements of which the *Malangeni*, seed of the Dlamini, is but one. When Sobhuza's people talk of him as 'child of the nation' and also as 'father of the nation', they are not using meaningless metaphors. It is difficult to convey to a westerner, moulded by twentieth-century individualism, the realities of the ties and the obligations he has to a large variety of people. It is less subjection or clientage in a material sense than a complicated emotional relationship, imbued with mysticism. The closest parallel is that of the medieval theory of the King's Two Bodies: the body politic and the body natural. In the body politic were mysterious forces which reduced or even removed the imperfections of fragile human nature, the two together constituting an indivisible unit.

The King has two Capacities, for he has two Bodies, the one whereof is a Body natural, consisting of natural Members as every other Man has, and in this he is subject to Passions and Death as other Men are; the other is a Body politic, and the Members thereof are his Subjects; ... and he is incorporated with them, and they with him, and he is the Head, and they are the Members, and he has the sole Government of them; and this Body is not subject to Passions as the other is, nor to Death, for as to this Body the King never dies, and his natural Death is not called in our Law, the Death of the King, but the Demise of the King, not signifying by the Word (Demise) that the Body politic of the King is dead, but that there is a Separation of the two Bodies, and that the Body politic is transferred and conveyed over from the Body natural now dead, or now removed from the Dignity royal, to another Body natural. So that it signifies a Removal of the Body politic of the King of this Realm from one Body to another (Edmund Plowden, Commentaries or Reports, 233a (London: 1816), quoted in Ernst H. Kantorowicz, *The King's Two Bodies: A Study in Mediaeval Political Theology*, 1957).

In the course of English history the sacred-centred kingship was replaced by law-centered kingship, at the same time as legal separation was drawn between the King's Two Bodies; the Public Body was secularized so that by the twentieth-century in England the sovereign was subordinate to Parliament, and the Church was separate from State.

In modern Swazi Kingship the 'two bodies' are still joined in the one king though he works at different levels – the public, or formal, and the personal or natural. In the first he serves as Ngwenyama with the Ndlovukazi, two ritual Queens (laMatsebula and laMotsa) specially selected to mark his entry into official manhood, *tinsila* (Mdluli and Motsa) closer to him than his physical brothers, princes, chiefs and councils. But at a deeper personal level is a second network, interwoven yet of different thread, in which he is a natural son, husband, father, brother.

For his mother Lomawa, Sobhuza had the deepest respect and affection. This was indeed fortunate; the dangers of conflicts in previous reigns were well known, and the people believed that when there was friction nature itself reacted. It was interesting to watch how skilfully Sobhuza and Lomawa avoided disagreement. The fact that they lived mainly in separate villages made it easier to handle difficulties and differences of opinion. Sometimes both found it useful to employ diplomatic intermediaries, and let a few days slip by before any face-to-face discussion. Generally Sobhuza visited her frequently, not only to fulfill their joint duties but because he obviously enjoyed her company. They would sit together in her hut with a few attendants and some of the little children, and talk for hours, and laugh. Usually they spoke of routine things – visitors, tasks that had to be completed, the division of food; sometimes they talked of deeper matters of the heart. She always had a little pot of beer beside her and a carved horn snuffbox from which she would take delicate pinches and sneeze with obvious enjoyment, and she would give a little pinch with feigned reluctance to her old ladies-in-waiting while he looked on tolerantly. He did not take snuff, but enjoyed beer, for which he had a connoisseur's palate; and if she knew that he was coming she had beer brewed specially for him. It was against tradition for them to drink from the same bowl or for him to eat in her presence.

Both were aware that he knew more about western ways than she did, and also that the colonial administration placed greater responsibilities on him, disturbing the traditional balance of power, so he tried to keep her informed of all that was going on. On his way back from meetings at Mbabane he would stop at Lobamba, remove his shoes and go into the hut where she would be waiting, and report, appreciating the shrewdness of her comments. With her there were generally a number of older ladies including senior princesses, other 'mothers' (wives of his late father), and her own constant attendants. The women would not hesitate to contribute their opinions.

As Sobhuza's administrative duties increased, the Ndlovukazi was left to carry on the ritual and domestic arrangements, but he had always to be present to take part. He deferred to her in matters affecting his wives and children. It was she who was primarily responsible for deciding where his wives and children should stay. When he moved to Lozithehlezi, his ritual wives, Lozindaba Matsebula and Fongofani Motsa, were obliged by Swazi law to remain at Lobamba. With them stayed, in their own huts, other senior queens – Zintombi Zwane, daughter of Chief Mangetse and mother of Betfusile, his first daughter; Lomacala Mgunundvu, daughter of the Mgunundvu chief of Mkhuzweni and mother of Senzangakhona, Sobhuza's first son; Citsekile Nkambule, elegant daughter of Chief Mkhwankwa of Sigombeni, whose mother was the daughter of Msukusuku, son of Somhlolo; Zintombi Zibuko, daughter of a specialist also named Mkhwankwa, renowned for his skill in treating crops against marauding birds, and mother of Sehlephi, Sobhuza's ninth child, the first to be born at the present capital; Ncineleni Mngometfulu, daughter of Chief Mbikiza, son of Lubelo of Ngwavuma, some of whose people are in Swaziland and others in Zululand. Chief Lubelo had provided accommodation for Bhunu when he sought British protection at Eshowe from the Boers. Lubelo promised Bhunu a daughter as a queen but Bhunu died before a girl was sent. By the time Sobhuza was full grown, Lubelo had also died, but his heir, Zombizwe, sent his sister Ncineleni to fulfill his late grandfather's promise, and subsequently sent one of his own daughters, the lovely Khonjwa, born in 1942, to keep Ncineleni company; Khonjwa became one of Sobhuza's younger queens.

By Swazi law, Sobhuza was expected to place wives at different royal villages to 'revive the villages of his fathers', the great Kings of the past. Remaining at Nsuka, a residence of his father, Bhunu, were some of his first lovers: Lomabhunu Shongwe, daughter of Cheme, trusted attendant of King Mbandzeni; Ndlaleni Vilakati, daughter of Mdindane, a headman of Hhohho district; and Zihlathi Ndwandwe, daughter of Vanyane, principal priest of the *Ncwala*, of the same Ndwandwe clan, but of a different branch from that of the Ndlovukazi. No one could see the future and no one could know that Lomawa would die in 1938 and be replaced by Nukwase, her full sister, and that Nukwase would die in 1957 and that the King-in-Council would decide to choose Zihlathi to fill the ritual void, and that in 1975 Zihlathi would die and Seneleleni, her sister by the same father, would have to take the onerous position. But I am anticipating. In 1926 Zihlathi was but one of many queens.

Their dispersal at different centres was clear and once one knew the principles, logical and predictable. At Zombodze, capital of those Kings whose royal title was Ngwane, and identified for over twenty-five years with the indomitable Labotsibeni, Sobhuza's senior queen was Zimango, whose father Manzini was a Mabuza, the clan of

Labotsibeni's mother. For the King's new village of Lozitha the choice of senior wife was not difficult. Sidudu Fakudze, a girl of extraordinary beauty, serenity and generosity, was daughter of councillor Matsitsibala Fakudze of the old royal village of Nkanini. The King had noticed her and she had agreed to come to him; her daughter, Qondzaphi, born in 1921, was Sobhuza's fourth child. In later years three other Fakudze girls, Lomasontfo, daughter of Masiphula (former governor of old Lobamba), Lomntombana, daughter of Ndabezimbi (also a governor of old Lobamba), and in the '40s, Nanana, daughter of Mcimeti (son of Mbovane), came as co-wives. The Fakudze councillors of the past included Makhambane and Ndabezimbi, who had signed the petition against concessions presented by Sobhuza to the special court of Swaziland.

The Queens were ranked according to the chronological order of their marriage, with laMatsebula and laMotsa always recognised as his first official Queens. No matter how important the parentage of a girl might be, and irrespective of any feelings the King might have for her, her position in relation to all the other Queens was conspicuous and fixed. So at Lozitha, second to laFakudze was a charming Magagula girl, daughter of Chief Madlangapisi of Mzaceni. Then came Velephi Ndlela, daughter of Nganya, headman of Bufaneni and member of the clan of Lomawa's own mother, the maternal grandmother who had nursed Sobhuza as a baby. Others followed, including representatives of the Hlophe, Mdluli, Gwebu and Maziya clans.

Under each senior Queen of a royal village were women of different temperament and pedigree; and the harmony depended largely on the character of the senior Queen of the village. Sobhuza appreciated this, and though he was prohibited from any public demonstration of favouritism or even affection, it was clear to me from the way he spoke of laFakudze senior that he recognized and valued her exceptional goodness. It is perhaps wrong of me to single out laFakudze senior; in later life as the King established more homesteads, other Queens came more into the public eye, but the older women retained their privileged positions and the respect of their husband-King.

Over the years many other beautiful young women came to him and bore him children and were recognized as *emakhosikati* (Queens). He did not count them, that would have been improper, and he knew the family of each and the conditions under which she had been married. Almost every type of feminine beauty and charm could be found among them, and though Sobhuza had an eye for form and movement and an ear for the music of the voice, only a few of the Queens, known as 'mothers of the people', had been personally selected by him. Sobhuza knew well the dangers of awakening jealousy by showing preference, and avoided bestowing a gift on one without giving to others who were in the same group. Groups of wives and children appeared in public dressed in identical patterned cloths and blankets.

He had his own hut deep within the Queens' quarters at each royal village, and there his wives would come when invited through his messengers. The women respected his injunctions not to be indiscreet in their talk and to allow him to maintain a rich private life. From the western viewpoint it may appear impossible to keep harmony between a number of spirited women sharing a single man. Most Swazi men with whom I discussed this at some length shared the belief of the King that '*sitsembu* (polygamy) is the nature of man; women are fulfilled through children'. But I admit that initially I was surprised that many women favoured *sitsembu* though on somewhat different grounds – referring to the help and companionship often shown by co-wives, and the fact that a woman is not abandoned, nor need her husband deceive her, if he wants to take another wife. One of the Queens expressed a feeling quite generally shared by her 'sisters', that the success or failure depends on the man more than the woman, and that Sobhuza 'is the man who handles *sitsembu* best'.

There was remarkably little friction between the Queens, who spoke of Sobhuza with respect and warm affection – 'he treats us well, he rejoices us'. If and when they quarrelled, his mother or Lozindaba Matsebula were required to make the peace – 'The King does not enter such disputes'. He was sympathetic to the occasional woman who could not adjust to the restrictions of the position or suffered from the jealousies of co-wives, and argued against the claim made by some of the princes that they had the right to seize a woman by force. To two Queens dismissed for adultery – in the past they and their lovers would have been killed – he periodically sends money, and the children they bore him are well looked after.

In charge of the security of the Queens was a huge impressive man, Mkhalimele Mhlanga, who stopped the unauthorized – particularly adult men – entering the Queens' quarters, but since he had his own wife outside the *sigodlo* he relied a good deal on the alertness of the little valets whose duty it was to accompany the Queens and drive away those who approached too close. Sobhuza is not suspicious by nature, but he accepts human weaknesses and recognizes that all men may succumb to temptations.

While the King extended his personal contacts through his own marriages, he appreciated that the stability and security of the monarchy were also reinforced by marriages arranged for royal women; and his aunts and sisters – later it would be his own daughters – went as main wives to chiefs and men of substance. The marriage ceremonies of these princesses were more public and elaborate than for any of his own Queens, except for laMatsebula and laMotsa. None of his wives was married in such a way as to indicate that she would be main wife. Sobhuza says it is not the function of the King, but of his Council, to initiate such a marriage. All the girls who were brought to him had from his point of view the same chance of promotion after his death. And, as he said, the matter was outside of his control nor could it concern him during his lifetime.

Emphasis was placed on Sobhuza as father of the nation, not of any particular offspring, and when his own sons or daughters were asked, 'Who is your father', they were instructed by their elders as well as the Queens not to say 'Sobhuza', but, if pressed, to give the name of the mother. They were forbidden to boast of him or even claim him as their own father. He was restrained in his behaviour towards them, though he loved them dearly; and he would watch them at play and be with them and talk to them, and was deeply interested in their development. He and his mother agreed on how they should be brought up. The training of boys and girls was to be different in accordance with their rather separate but complementary roles. Special men were directed to guide the boys in their behaviour. Sobhuza had been brought up strictly himself, and he considered this necessary for his sons; he wanted them to learn what he himself had learnt. At Lobamba, Siteki Dlamini, son of Prince Hodvoba, a youngish man of admirable character, was charged with teaching them military duties and discipline. He did not excuse the princes from work in the barracks, where they had to sweep and treat the floor and go on errands for their elders. He also taught them how to fence with sticks – a sport which required agility and courage. Sobhuza instructed him to hit them if they did wrong. The herder woke the boys early in the morning, and they were taught how to milk the cows and deal with the calves; thus, they acquired a knowledge and an appreciation of pastoralism. The man in charge of the royal gardens took them with him to plough and they learnt to distinguish different types of soil and plants.

While Sobhuza was eager that they go through the traditional educational discipline he did not want it to interfere with their school attendance and he argued that the two could be combined. Work in the barracks and milking of the cows could be done throughout the year before the school-day started and when it was over; long 'holidays' were not part of the Swazi system of education and should not be spent in idleness which led to mischief. He admired the action of Chief Mnisi of Nkhaba, a strict disciplinarian and advocate of western education as well as a firm upholder of tradition. Mnisi had fenced in an area for pasturing the cattle so that children who would otherwise be responsible for looking after the family herds could be free to attend school; and Mnisi fined parents if their children played truant.

The education of Sobhuza's sons was primarily in the hands of non-relatives, but the education of his daughters was entrusted to their mothers, supervised by the Ndlovukazi. The girls worked with their mothers, learning how to grind grain and cook different foods, to gather firewood, draw water from the river, and cultivate the gardens, and at a very early age, they learned how to look after the babies and to carry them around snugly on the back. Dancing and singing were an essential part of the culture of girls and boys as well as of the adults, and Sobhuza encouraged these arts.

During a school holiday in 1935 he sent his four eldest daughters, Betfusile, Qondzaphi, Ntombane and Phetfwayini, together with some of their friends, to Ntfonjeni to have lessons in the *Ncwala* tunes from the old princesses, Lozinja and Myingili, daughters of King Mswati. 'The *emakhosikati*,' Sobhuza explained, 'have not grown up in the royal circle but had come there on marriage. The *Ncwala* is new to them.' The old women, openly contemptuous of the general ignorance of the 'schoolchildren', were highly exacting teachers, and occasionally Sobhuza would come and comment on the performance.

A year later he sent some forty schoolchildren, including his own older sons and daughters, to enjoy and learn from the celebration which was being held for the Fiftieth Jubilee in Johannesburg. The headmaster of the National School, Theo Keen, and I were asked to act as guides. One of the Ndlovukazi's brothers drove them down in a van and they stayed at the King's house in Sophiatown. The trip was full of excitement. The youngsters had never seen a train, a double story building, electric lights in the street, or such big shops, all stocked with novel things. The girls wore gay Swazi cloth, and their hair was neatly screwed in tight ringlets, the fashionable style of that time. They were charmingly unself-conscious, and reporting their visit to the King on their return, Betfusile explained that people stared at them a lot 'because', she said, 'they were admiring our beauty'.

It was a wonderful week rich in new experiences, marred somewhat at the end by an accident near the border of Oshoek, when the driver went straight for a white stone on the road, shouting 'There is a rabbit'. The tyre burst, the van skidded, lurched, and ended in a ditch. Not a child was hurt. Keen, Mashiphisa and I had driven ahead and were waiting with the Ngwenyama and the Ndlovukazi to welcome the children. At last they arrived. When asked what had happened, the driver said the van had simply skidded – 'You know the roads. Driving is always dangerous.' Lomawa expressed her sympathy for her brother who had nearly killed his own precious maternal nieces and nephews. Sobhuza listened in solemn silence and then said, 'The ancestors were with us.' But his oldest son, Senzangakhona, said the driver had drunk too much. The headmaster was furious. He was a puritan; drunken driving was a crime and since to him this was the obvious cause of the accident, he hoped Sobhuza would punish the driver. He did not believe that what appears on the surface is not always real, and that what needs to be sought is an underlying and fundamental cause. In this case the ancestors, mediators between man and God needed to be 'remembered' and placated, and before the driver returned to his employment in Johannesburg, special beer was brewed as their libation and an animal was sacrificed. Without making direct reference to the accident, Sobhuza in the driver's presence spoke of the dangers of alcohol particularly when driving.

Sobhuza himself lived simply, at a level basically no different from that of the ordinary peasant. As yet he had no western home in Swaziland and the royal villages were without electric light, running water, or other amenities provided by the colonial government for its own senior officials. But he did not envy these things nor did he desire them. He slept on finely woven mats laid on the floor, a wooden headrest as pillow, his cuisine was plain, his furnishings homemade. He appreciated the crafts of his people, the beautiful pots of clay, the large plaited baskets, the well-tanned hides, the carved bowls, the iron spears; and he encouraged fine workmanship. He did not, however, reject innovations and new goods, but incorporated them into his own style of living. One of his most treasured possessions was his car, which he usually drove himself at night, quickly, surely, enjoying the quietness and peace, accompanied by a councillor or a couple of his valets. He would arrive late at Lobamba, and most of the people there would only know of his presence in the morning when they heard the praiser reciting and saw his big black Buick outside the Queens' quarters.

He developed his own routine, regulating his daily activities more by the passage of the sun than the hands of the clock. As one educated man said almost fulsomely, 'He is the Sun; it takes a destined path.' He needed few hours of sleep and often got up when the evening star was still in the sky. At dawn (and at dusk) the ancestral spirits are closer to their human descendants, and without any ostentatious display of religiosity he would go into his sanctuary with his priests and special attendants to perform the sacred rituals of his people.

Once the sun was up his more public life began. The morning was the best time for paperwork and reading. Though he wrote and received few personal letters, he attended to a large official mail. Some of the issues were of considerable national importance, others were trifling; all received his personal attention. His secretary might pen the replies but he drafted them, and carefully scrutinized them before signing. In a single month matters raised in documents sent him by the Administration included land disputes, the sale of *dagga* (marijuana), the leasing of Swazi land to sheep grazers, the mode of acceptance of Swazi immigrants, illicit beer brewing, the use of hot springs, the appointment of court officials, the collection of fines, registration of marriages, regulations for burning grass, penalties for the hunting season, appointments of teachers, behaviour of chiefs, procedure in courts, and 'tax defaulters'. He received fairly regularly several newspapers and journals, some in Zulu, others in English[1]

[1] Among the newspapers that reached him were *Abantu Batho*, started by Dr Seme in 1912 as an organ of protest. It had changed hands in the 30s and Seme, in 1933 to 1935, partly with Sobhuza's assistance, started a new paper *Ikhwezi* – the Star. Other papers that reached him were *Ilanga laseNatal*, first edited by John Dube in the early 1900s; *The Bantu World*, started in 1932 with Selope Thema as African leader writer; and *Umteteli Wabantu* (Mouthpiece of the

and, occasionally, books, preferably on 'customs and history'. He read carefully and critically, laughing at some of the people who always believed the written word.

He refused to be interrupted until his paperwork was done. This was generally toward noon, when he ate his first meal, tea without milk or sugar, plain bread or buns, or a pumpkin dish or porridge – and occasionally grilled or boiled meat, brought and prepared by men and boys from well-known families, selected for their trustworthiness. When he had finished his rather frugal and solitary repast he would meet with his people. There were always a few councillors in residence, and generally a number of visitors from different parts of the country, discussing cases, talking, waiting expectantly for Ngwenyama to appear. He would join them, sitting on the ground under the trees near 'the office' or near the barracks, completely at ease, listening, laughing, skilfully directing the conversation. If he wanted to have a more private discussion he would send a trusted henchman – Mahhova Gwebu, Mgwangele Dlamini, Sigasini Maseko – to give the call *ngemandla* – with power – and the person summoned would hurry along. Sobhuza seldom saw anyone without the presence of 'a witness'.

Most afternoons were spent hearing the troubles and complaints of his people and doing what he could to alleviate them. The men who brought their cases to his court on appeal were accompanied by their local chief or representative. Chiefs were expected to attend council meetings and national celebrations. Sobhuza knew each chief personally, as well as his reputation as a leader. When the heir of a chief was presented by his family council for the first time, Sobhuza was frequently able to relate to him interesting incidents in their family history, and at the same time he took the opportunity of keeping abreast of recent developments in the chiefdom. His interest in the ordinary man was genuine and deep. He owed his position to his pedigree and did not claim that all men were born equal, but in his selection of men in whom he placed his confidence rank by birth was only one consideration; he himself paid little attention to wealth or occupation. It disturbed him that some of the most respected men in the nation were employed by whites as chauffeurs, gardeners, cattle-guards, police in charge of dipping tanks, or cooks, particularly when they were treated as menials and also poorly paid.

Being always surrounded by courtiers eager for his favour, he was constantly reminded that he was Ngwenyama yemaSwati. It did not matter that his clothing was almost identical with that of his most humble subjects, that his food appeared no different, that he lived in the same type of hut. He had a unique quality of dignity – the 'shadow

People), started in 1921 after a major African strike on the mines, as an organ of the Chamber of Mines; also occasional copies of the Communist party newspaper, *Umsebenzi* (the Worker), started in 1931. One of the journals he contributed to was *Africa*, journal of the International African Institute.

of Kingship', attributed to heredity developed by sacred treatment and recognized by his people who 'felt his presence'. A Swazi woman described to me how at an agricultural show in Johannesburg her heart suddenly beat quickly and her body trembled. She said to the friend with whom she was standing, 'Let us move, there is someone there too strong for me. I think he must be my King.' Later she learned it was Sobhuza who was approaching. Her friend, she said, was not affected, 'because she was a Mosotho and joined with other medicines.'

His position required that voices be respectfully stilled while he spoke and his remarks be punctuated by praises, for he is 'the lion', 'the sun', 'the milky way', 'obstacle to the enemy', 'child of the elements'. Even at that period when colonialism was so strongly entrenched he was recognized as a strong individual, worthy of the position and of the respect he received. He was not beguiled by subservience and flattery nor was he impressed by boasts of unproven deeds. Being himself somewhat reserved he respected the dignity of others. 'If a person feels shame,' he once said, 'it is not necessary to destroy him. He is a person you can teach. But since people are different some only learn the hard way. Even the children of one mother are different and need to be treated differently.'

The afternoon sessions generally ended towards sunset when he would return to his own quarters or drive to one of the royal villages. There were no theatres, no banquets, no expensive entertainments, but if the night was fine the children danced outside and when there were work parties and beer and meat provided, the different groups sang and danced. Sometimes he would watch or else join in with his own age regiment and perform in the barracks. Or, at Lobamba, he would dance and chant with a few age mates in the yard of his mother, graceful, dignified performances, and the women's voices would blend with those of the men. When the nights were dark and cold, inside the hut was cozy and intimate, lit by a single candle on the floor and the flickering flames of a twig fire crackling and smoking in the hearth, the centre of every hut. Conversation was lively and could go on for many hours but no one was offended if a listener fell asleep. The King himself retired late and often before sleeping would walk around the quarters of those closest to him to see that all was well, shining a long torch against physical intruders and evildoers who perform their nefarious deeds in darkness.

The winter nights were intensely still and the sky twinkled with a myriad of stars. The King, barefoot, wrapped in a blanket as coat, accompanied by a single attendant, finally entered the quarters of his Queens. In the summertime, when the rains poured down and the heavens were ripped by the lightning bird and thunder crashed applause, he still walked, undaunted and bareheaded, accepting the rain as a sign of blessing and benediction. His routine was adjusted to the rhythm of the seasons.

Hunting opened in the winter and he would go with his warriors to recognized hunting grounds in the districts of chiefs. Most of the big game – lions, elephants and leopards – had been destroyed by early professional hunters, but there were still some stretches of grassland and bush country where impala, wildebeest and kudu bred and roamed. There were different kinds of hunting parties – but the *butimba* was the most important. The hunting was on foot, the men armed with spears and clubs. Their dress was simple and entirely traditional, the men stripped to the waist, some with feathers of strange birds in their hair. Sobhuza found the hunt exciting and beautiful.

Apart from his hunting trips he would go on occasional visits to the old royal centres though the roads were poor and travelling was difficult. Almost every year he came with some of his court to the historic area of Hhohho in the north where he had his village, Ntfonjeni, looked after by a governor of the Mdluli clan, the clan of his grandmother. This was a meeting place for local princes – Mancibane, Pheme, Msudvuka, Mphikeleli, Gomba, Lodlakama, Madevu, Gija – and also for Swazi chiefs and headmen across the border of the Transvaal. News of the King's impending arrival would spread rapidly throughout the countryside, and during his stay he would receive a constant stream of visitors. Women would come in single file, carrying on their heads big pots of beer and golden pumpkins and baskets of food as tribute.

It was at Ntfonjeni that he established the *sibhaca*, a dance that he had seen performed by the Bhaca people in the Cape and in which he had taken part as a schoolboy; it has become one of the most popular entertainments throughout Swaziland. It is solely a man's dance, lively, energetic, with the rhythm beaten out on drums which in Swazi culture were limited to dances of exorcism and could not be brought inside royal enclosures. Each team created its own imaginative costume of cloth combined with animal skins, and the dancers improvised new steps, stamping and clowning until, at the climax, they ended with a leap and a fall, face flat to the ground. Sobhuza as Ngwenyama would watch and applaud, but bound by the restraints of custom and office, he could no longer take part. The *sibhaca* extended but did not replace the traditional dance songs prescribed for the more significant situations of Swazi life.

Lomawa died before dawn on Sunday 15 August 1938. I had received a telegram: 'Regret to Inform You Mother Passed Away Yesterday. Sobhuza.' The news was not altogether unexpected. She had been ailing for over a year, but it seemed hard to believe that the illness might be fatal. She seemed young to die. She was in her early fifties, and had only been installed as Ndlovukazi in 1925. During the last month Swazi specialists as well as European doctors had brought their medicines to her at Lobamba, and priests and prophets from different congregations had come to pray for her and laid on her their healing hands. But when I saw her in July she seemed to recognize the end was near and said, 'My child, I am now dead. We Swazi kill each other.' And her faithful old attendant, Lomakhala Shongwe, added mournfully, '*Vele, bamloyile. Ngematsambo nje*' (Indeed they have bewitched her. She is just bones.). Her sister, Nukwase, dressed somberly in western clothes, her face strained, her manner quiet and thoughtful, said sadly, 'It is the work of God.'

Daily bulletins were sent to Sobhuza who visited her frequently, concerned, solicitous, and at the same time very controlled. We as women were permitted to show our feelings. When I had said good-bye to her we both had wept quietly, and then she had pressed her lips to my wrist in the traditional greeting for a child after a long absence or on bidding it farewell on a long journey, and murmured, 'Farewell, my child. Do not forget us.' Forget her? Never. Not her nor her son nor the many others whose faces rose before me as I sat with the telegram in my hand. Then I realized that it was more than an announcement of her death; it was a call to take part in the mourning. So I drove to a township in Johannesburg to find her brother Mzululeki who had been to Lovedale with Sobhuza and who was then employed as a teacher. The sad news had not yet reached him, but by the time we left early the next morning all her close relatives in Johannesburg had been summoned. Most were already on their way, in hired or borrowed cars.

The King was secluded at Lozitha and could not come to Lobamba until her body had been removed, nor could he attend the funeral. With him were his 'fathers' – Msudvuka and Lasi – and other senior princes, Ngolotjeni Motsa and also the old Mbalo Motsa, *insila* of the late King Mbandzeni, bringing his specialist knowledge. Priests of the Mabuza clan, represented by Ngcatfo, who had been instructed by his father, the old Madlinkhomo, had been summoned from Mafutseni to perform the first of a series of purificatory sacraments. An entirely different set of priests and officials, including a number of senior women, were involved in the actual burial rites. The women had the heavy task of laying out the body of their 'Mother', 'the hearth of the nation'. They dressed her in her *Ncwala* skirt and apron, and sat her in the position of the dead and the newly born – knees bent, elbows close to sides, arms upwards. In her right hand the headwoman, the wife of the governor of Lobamba, Mshudvulwane Zwane, put a branch of the sacred and powerful *masweti*, the shrub from which are cut protective beads used in the necklace of queens when nursing their young, in the Ndlovukazi's unique crown, and in the wand used by the King in major crises. Early the next morning Mandanda, who had hurried over from Zombodze to take charge, supervised the sacrifice of a black ox and black sheep. The women wrapped the Ndlovukazi in the still wet oxskin, and then placed the blown-up bladder of the sheep on her forehead, as her *lusiba* (feather), as in the case of a bride departing from her home with the blessing of her kin.

Everything had to be exactly correct, and since there were no written holy scripts each step was debated and discussed, and the King kept informed. Mandanda, in consultation with the other governors of royal villages, decided that Lomawa be buried at Zabeni, the village started in the reign of Ngwane V, under the governorship of the trusted Lomadokola Sukati. Though Lomadokola had died many years back, Zabeni was continued by his kinsmen and had recently been rebuilt about a mile from Lobamba. The men carried her there on a wooden bier, and behind came the women carrying her few very personal possessions. They brought her into the main hut and sat her on the right-hand side; Nukwase and two other co-wives were among those who kept watch day and night, and spoke to her kin who had come from afar to mourn.

Zabeni was in process of being rebuilt. Bundles of golden grass for thatching were stacked high outside; they had been brought the week before by the women of Lobamba in tribute service. Then there had been dancing, eating, joy. Now the place though full of people was terribly silent. The bereaved were not allowed to cry aloud until 'the earth had closed over her'. Small clusters of men or women collected, whispering together. An occasional bellow of cattle from the small new byre was an additional painful reminder that on days of burial life was stopped. There was no milking, no grinding of food, no eating within the village that had the oppressive smell of death.

A specially designed coffin was constructed to accommodate the body according to custom. When it arrived, on the fourth day, a couple of old men protested that no wood should lie between their 'mother' and the earth of which she was part, and they recalled that when the old Queen Mother Labotsibeni had been buried, though 'a box' had been bought she was not put inside; it was placed beside her with personal possessions. But their protests were overridden, and Lomawa was buried in the coffin.

There was such concern that everything be done correctly, that nothing be omitted or committed that might offend the powerful ancestors and the one God, that everyone was afraid to make a decisive move. At almost the last hour of the long day, when the body was about to be taken from the hut, someone remembered that her 'tickets to Heaven', receipts of the church dues she paid monthly to the Methodist Church, were left at Lobamba. I drove to fetch them. Lobamba was almost totally deserted; only old Ntukubetane Makhanya remained on guard, with children who had been left behind.

For long hours the Inner Council had debated the question of her successor. Nukwase, already known as 'the little Ndlovukazi', was the logical choice, but she was converted, having been baptized in 1914, and was a devout churchgoer. She had to agree that once appointed Ndlovukazi she would identify herself with the position completely, in clothing and in action. The councillors reminded her that when she was converted Lomawa too had also been tempted but had been dissuaded by the wise Labotsibeni, who told her that she could not serve two masters, and had asked her what she was going to do with her son. The young mother replied, 'He is your child, I just brought him forth, and verily Swazi law gives the child of a King to learn wisdom from his grandmother.' The old Ndlovukazi had also said, 'Either you serve God or you serve the traditional gods, either you ask God to make rain or you make rain with His help.'[2]

The burial took place on the fourth day, Wednesday 18 August. Nukwase had made the decision. Grasping an ancient hoe in both hands she dug into the ground at the upper end of the byre – site of the last resting place for the head of a home. Then the men took over. The grave was long and deep, shaped to fit the coffin. All people in mourning for a person other than the Ndlovukazi were told to leave. She was going to her 'owners'; their message was for her. The men of the *libandla* brought out the dark wooden coffin, marked with a white cross. Immediately behind came Nukwase, dressed in deepest church mourning, her head bound in a black kerchief, holding in her right hand a long staff of dark wood.

The men rested the box at the graveside, and Mandanda opened the lid and told those close to look on their Mother and bid her farewell. At her head was a twig of the ancient tree of death – *impungahlolo* – sign of permission to enter the kingdom of the dead. Her acceptance was doubly sure. Her 'tickets to heaven' were next to her. All the time the mourners walked round, Mandanda spoke to her loudly and clearly, 'Here are your children. Care for them. They are still your children and you must not forget them. Don't forget your people or your work. You must help your children, you who are the spring of the country. You were not killed by us. You are with your mothers!' Nukwase stood at the grave, her big eyes heavy with unshed tears, but some less strong in character sobbed, and were rebuked, 'This is not the time to break down. Don't weep here.'

The coffin, looking like a huge cupboard, was then securely tied with rope and lowered into the hole where two women, who had to clamber down roughly-made ladders, received it and carefully, reverently, moved it into the correct position, facing east, the rising sun, the direction of Dlamini origin. The women clambered out; Nukwase threw the first sod. The sound fell hard; steadily the earth closed.

Among the crowd were priests and missionaries of a wide variety of denominations – Methodist, Catholic, Independent African Churches

---

[2] The question of conflicting interests was later again raised by the Ngwenyama when Lomawa wished to be baptized by the Methodists. Things were all set and the news that she was going to be baptized was published in the Methodist journal. The insecurity of her position were she to adopt Christianity to such an extent was explained to her and she abandoned her project.

of Zion – all anxious to contribute their own services at the graveside. The governors agreed to let them pray, but asked them not to interfere with the Swazi rites. Reverend John Duba, a Methodist, who lived near the capital and had been Lomawa's most frequent comforter, was asked to lead. He spoke directly to God, simply and movingly, reporting the greatness of their loss and asking Jehovah to take care of 'our girl' and wrap her in His Holy Spirit. Other preachers followed. Only old Father Bonaventuras of the nearby Catholic Mission of St. Mary's said nothing in public. He had followed her condition with concerned interest during the last weeks of her life, and on hearing the end was near he had rushed along the path separating his mission from the capital, his long white beard floating in the wind, and baptized her *sub-conditione*. At the graveside his finely chiseled face glowed white, and his grey-blue eyes shone happily. He had opened for her the gates of Heaven, and she would find peace.

No member of the Administration was present. The Resident Commissioner, C. Bruton, had not been officially informed or invited. He was nicknamed Mcindzeteli (the Oppressor); his relations with Sobhuza were strained. The Queen Mother belonged to the Swazi; they were the sufferers, her powers and her replacement were their concern alone. Bruton had heard the news, but did not know where the burial was to take place, and Marwick was kept in ignorance because, as one old man explained, 'It would have been hard for Ndlavela to have lied if he had been asked.'

The service over, the missionaries were asked to leave. The mourners needed to be purified and strengthened with potions and drugs appropriate to their station and relationships, and the sacrifices of animals to the ancestors had to be performed in peace without interference or questioning. The little children were the first to be brought back to normal life by the rite of cleansing with milk (*kudla lubisi*); the milk tasted bitter and they were glad to spit it out. All the elders, except for the Dlamini, bit of the flesh of the ox; the Dlamini ate alone of the flesh of the sheep, the animal taboo to them on all occasions except for royal death. The rest of the meat was eaten without joy, and what remained was burnt. The grave was enclosed with special wood cut by the warriors, and the village of Zabeni, which could never again be visited by any Swazi King, became another sacred center of Swazi history.

Nukwase was prepared with special potions and elaborate solemnity for her role as Ndlovukazi. The crown of her predecessor had been removed, and given in safekeeping to laMavimbela, one of her few surviving co-wives, fetched for the funeral from Mbelebeleni. The crown was with laMavimbela a few hours, a sad burden as well as a

---

[3] Among the preachers were Reverend J.V. Cantrell, Superintendent of the Methodist Church throughout Swaziland; Nkonyane, an Apostolic 'prophet' of the Church of Zion; Edith Owen of the South African General Mission; and Bishop Constantine Attilus Barneschi, head of the Catholic missions in Swaziland and close friend of Sobhuza.

deep honour. For, as she told us, 'I was asked to take care of the country by keeping the rain on my head. Ngwane's country is here', and she pointed to the sky. 'There is no rain when there is no Queen Mother' (interview 10/2/75).[4] The day after the funeral, with Nukwase installed, it had to rain. And it did – a heavy downpour lasting all the afternoon and evening, which washed off the first contagious darkness of death. There would be later rituals, until Lomawa's spirit was finally brought back to join all the royal ancestors addressed at the national shrine of Lobamba; the intense series of initial mortuary rites had made it possible for the King to carry on with his national duties.

When Sobhuza was again required to visit Lobamba, Nukwase was clothed as Ndlovukazi. It was a transformation. He had grown accustomed to see her in the sombre dress of conversion, her hair hidden by a kerchief. Now, in goatskin apron and dark hide skirt, a fresh bright feather of the rainbird in the crown worn at the base of her small but neatly shaped high bun, she looked elegant and regal. He had always called her 'mother', and her children, Mshengu, Mnengwase, Mkukwane and Lomusa, were his closest siblings; now they were even more free to move in and out of the Great House over which she presided.

Sobhuza and she spoke of what had happened, comforting each other. There had been some who considered it a bad omen that the mother had died before her son, comparing this to a pumpkin plant in which the fruit dies first and the plant expands, but Sobhuza had been told by one of his old councillors: 'If a pumpkin plant has a good early fruit, it shows that the whole plant is going to flourish, but if the fruit dies, then the whole plant is no good.' He knew that it had not been easy for Nukwase to commit herself, and he respected her sense of duty, and the sincerity of her convictions.

[4] LaMavimbela, it should be recalled, was the mother of Bhunu's posthumous son, Makhosikhosi, father of Princes Mfanasibili, Ncabaniso, et al. Though she was never appointed as Ndlovukazi, she was fetched to 'hold the crown' on the death of Lomawa and subsequently on the death of Nukwase. In 1975, she was the only surviving widow who had borne a son to Bhunu.

CHAPTER IX
Why Are We Fighting?

Sobhuza did not seriously consider that he and his people might become actively involved in conflicts in countries overseas. Europe seemed remote and very far away. Franco, Mussolini, Hitler, Chamberlain were unfamiliar names rather than real people; Fascism and Nazism were foreign doctrines. There were few people with whom Sobhuza could discuss world affairs. The complex nature of the conflict was covered over by descriptive details. The papers gave news of actions; and the first events that roused strong African interest were Mussolini's attack on Ethiopia, the fall of Addis Ababa (May 1936), and the flight of the Emperor, Haile Selassie, to England. Ethiopia was seen as part of Africa, a part free of white colonial rule; the Emperor, the Lion of Judah, an African King; Ethiopianism was a message of African Separatist churches.

Sobhuza and his Council were having their own political troubles; they were again caught in the dilemma of choice between South Africa and Britain. There were authoritative rumours that Hertzog, the South African Prime Minister, was trying to induce the Swazi to accept the transfer with the promise of favourable conditions, which included the uniting of the Swazi with their people across the border, and the land they occupied.

After 1937, when Bruton replaced A.G. Marwick as Resident Commissioner, Sobhuza had to play his hand very carefully. He knew that secret negotiations which related only in part to the transfer of the three territories were taking place between Hertzog and Malcolm McDonald, Secretary of State for Dominion Affairs. Sobhuza was informed by Marwick, not by Bruton, that a committee had been set up (in March 1938) to study openings for economic as well as political co-operation and to consider other matters of mutual concern. In a memorandum dated 7 September 1939, but discussed and drafted in August, Sobhuza wrote:

Indirect rule is an instrument which was devised by persons of unusual gifts among Europeans, and has indeed done a very great amount of good in the hands of understanding Administrators, but it unfortunately happens that when European Officers wish to discover the best means of administering natives they almost invariably consult other Europeans who are self-styled 'Native Experts', instead of consulting the natives themselves who are better qualified to understand the subject ... There are places where it can operate successfully and there are places where it cannot work with success. It is for this reason that Indirect Rule is applied where people welcome it ... To make the principle of Indirect Rule apply in order to preserve the Native Institutions where you find them still intact and in full operation, you do not necessarily have first to destroy them, and vest yourself with its authority, and give them back again to the same people. If that is the case it would be the most dangerous instrument and it would be incompatible with the statement that the white man is there as trustee who, in the course of time when the Africans shall have attained the knowledge of ruling themselves efficiently, would disappear.

He then elaborated Swazi objections to three main points in the 'Native Authority Proclamation'. He dealt first with the provisions in regard to the recognition and powers of the 'Paramount Chief':

Is the Paramount Chief after being fully installed under native law and custom, a policy strictly and constitutionally recognised under the Convention of 1894, not recognised? Does the Government or the natives themselves doubt his position? Undoubtedly not. We also note that his powers and functions are to be defined. Are his powers and functions new, or does he derive his powers from the High Commissioner, or from the native institutions? If his powers have to be defined by the High Commissioner or prescribed ... it means it is no recognition but creation of a new appointment, so that the Paramount Chief now can no longer be connected with his past long lineage, neither can he claim those rights his predecessors enjoyed as protected under the Convention of 1894 ... Instead of preserving and maintaining the rights of our people it goes to destroy them.

Then he criticized the regulations for the appointment of chiefs.

Now to be a Chief will depend on his personal efficiency, which is not our custom; efficiency is not expected from the Chief alone but from himself and his council ... in the long run we shall have no original chiefs, but only persons with required qualifications [required that is, by the administration] ... How can we be expected to accept to be made the basis of transition when we know that in course of time such appointment based on hereditary rights will soon disappear.

Finally, he argued against the requirement that Natives assist in carrying out the duties imposed upon the Paramount Chief:

In this are we following the European form and policy of Government or the native form of Government? Certainly not the former and still not the latter ... there is no provision in our constitution which imposes duties on the Paramount Chief etc. which may come from the High Commissioner, and the people know what duties they are expected to carry out as are required under their native law and custom. Where the High Commissioner expects any duties to be performed by the inhabitants of a protectorate it should not be discriminate but should affect both natives and whites. What is good for the whites is good for the natives and what is bad for the whites is bad for the natives ...

It must also be remembered that the assumption by the High Commissioner of the powers of the Councils entitles him to full sovereignty over native law and custom, and as such to all rights of land which is administered in accordance with the native law and custom, thus now having the effect of turning the native areas into Crown Lands. Secondly it would make our defence against transfer impracticable as no other rights under native institutions shall have been left to be considered, respected and protected.

In August 1939 Sobhuza asked Sir William Clark the crucial question: Did he as High Commissioner think the Swazi should in their own interests accept transfer and negotiate on their own terms, or continue in their opposition? Sir William's reply was noncommittal, evasive and unsatisfactory. He implied that since the Swazi were already geographically in the Union, they should 'understand the position that one day they would be [incorporated] in the Union' (interview with Sobhuza, 9 August 1972). It was clear to Sobhuza that Britain did not regard his people as an asset, but as a responsibility reluctantly accepted; and Clark's attitude made him feel that they could be 'handed over to the Union at any time'.

At the same time Bruton was pressing Sobhuza to accept a proposed Native Authority Proclamation as a necessary step in the application of the policy of 'Indirect Rule'. The British claimed that this would be advantageous to the Swazi. The Swazi considered it would jeopardise the traditional position of the King and his chiefs. Sobhuza felt himself threatened from both sides; he did not want to subject his people to the laws of the Union, but he could not accept basic principles of the proposed legislation.

On 1 September, Hitler invaded Poland. England and France came to Poland's aid. Swaziland was involved as a small part of a vast British empire. Suddenly and dramatically the whole world seemed changed. Sobhuza was in Johannesburg on a personal visit when the news broke. He rushed home. Sir William Clark had instructed the Resident Commissioners of the High Commission Territories to inform the chiefs and people. Bruton called Sobhuza urgently to Mbabane. Sobhuza came, bringing with him senior councillors. Bruton told him, 'Hitler is an evil man, trying to conquer the world, so Britain has been forced to intervene on behalf of the small countries and the rights of decent people.' Sobhuza expressed his loyalty to Britain, but made no definite commitment. Britain might have declared war, but the participation of the Swazi people did not automatically follow. They would ask many questions: Who is Hitler? What has he done? Why were we not told before war was declared?

The news had evoked different reactions among the Swazi. Prince Michel, who was in charge of the King's house in Johannesburg, was listened to with some approval when he argued, at a meeting in Johannesburg, that Hitler was right to try to 'win respect for his country' after its defeat in the last war, a war in which he (Hitler) had fought as a soldier. Even Sobhuza's initial attitude was tinged with some sympathy and he found it hard to believe that the terrors and horrors of the Nazi system were not being exaggerated. Otherwise why had Britain not done something before? Dispersing the regiments after the 1972 *Ncwala* he recalled this period.

But on general humanitarian grounds Sobhuza disagreed with those of his people who argued that 'This war is not our affair. Let the white men kill each other.' Any doubts that ran through his mind were over-ridden by his feeling of friendship for the British and by a growing realization of the threat of Nazi ambition and undisguised contempt for non-Nordic people. In 1938 some seventy German Jews, the largest single batch of white immigrants, had been accepted as refugees in Swaziland. Sobhuza wondered, almost naively, 'Why should God's chosen people be persecuted?' He did not accept or understand anti-Semitism any more than any other 'racism'. 'To me,' he said, 'there are good Jews and bad Jews; good Germans and bad Germans; good Italians and bad Italians. People's hearts are not alike. Look at so and so,' and he mentioned a few people we both knew. I pressed him by asking, 'Can you then ever justify a country going to war?' To which he replied without hesitation, 'The leaders of the country must decide; they must see if war is necessary; they must consider their people. But,' he added, 'once the war is declared (*kuyaliwa*) a real man does not know how to refuse to fight for his country.'

Though his loyalty to England was strong, his primary concern was for his own people. He had several options – maintaining diplomatic inactivity, indirectly discouraging his people from joining, or putting the full weight of his position behind the war effort. Before rushing into action, he first found out what was happening in neighbouring countries. In the Union of South Africa the decision to go to war on the side of England had been taken in an atmosphere tense with emotion and bitter memories. At the thirteen-man Cabinet meeting called urgently on the 2nd of September, when war was certain but not yet declared, Smuts had obtained a majority of one. The following day, a Sunday, Hertzog, ignoring the joint United Party Caucus, contacted Dr Malan, leader of the Afrikaner Nationalists with its pro-German members, and secured their support, and on the Monday morning Hertzog moved a motion for neutrality. In it he expressed his own sympathy as a Boer, whose people had been defeated by the British, for Hitler's efforts to remove the humiliation of Germany's defeat in the First World War. General Smuts with equal passion argued that the Union could not make a separate peace 'without forfeiting its honour and sacrificing its vital interests'.[1] Smuts, whose supporters included rabid English segregationists as well as the three liberal white Native Representatives, received 80 votes, Hertzog, 67. In the new (all white) government Smuts appointed Colonel Deneys Reitz as both Minister of Native Affairs and Deputy Prime Minister; he himself was in control of Defence. There was to be a voluntary army on a segregated basis; non-Europeans were to be enlisted in an unarmed Native Military Corps. He said he hoped Africans from the Territories would join it. The response of Africans in the Union of South Africa was one of qualified support; they were generally

---

[1] W.K. Hancock, *Smuts: The Fields of Force 1919-1950.* Cambridge: University Press, 1968, p. 337.

disillusioned, but Smuts was on the side of England, and English rule was recognized as preferable to the outright racism of the Nationalists.

Portugal, then colonial overlord of Swaziland's other neighbour, Mozambique, proclaimed a policy of neutrality, but allowed the Allies to use the harbours at Lisbon and Lourenço Marques. Basutoland, at the outbreak of war, was going through a crisis of succession to the paramountcy, but there was a strong tie to the British and a positive response to the request for recruits.

The chiefs of Bechuanaland had reacted by offering their resources to the Allies and expressing their willingness to put down, if necessary, any Afrikaner revolt in South Africa, demonstrating in this way both their loyalty to Britain and their continued resistance to transfer whether South Africa be under Hertzog or Smuts. It came as no surprise to Tshekedi Khama, who, throughout the '30s, had been the most active opponent of transfer, to hear that Smuts had raised with Sir William Clark the possibility of taking over at least Swaziland and possibly Bechuanaland while the thoughts of the British were focused on other issues, despite the fact that Colonel Deneys Reitz had agreed with Clark that for the time being the issue should not be pursued.

General Smuts' high international reputation, which was different from Africans' experiences of his actions on the home front, made it more difficult for the British to deny his requests. Sir William, however, pointed out that 'M.P.s interested in the Territories would more probably draw an uncomfortable contrast between our chivalrous attitude toward small nations in Europe and somewhat high-handed procedure apparently contemplated in respect of no doubt smaller nations in South Africa' (quoted in R. Hyam, 1972:164). The matter was dropped for the duration.

Sobhuza did not prevent any Swazi from joining the Union Native Military Corps, but refused to call up his Swazi regiments on a national basis. When the Chief of Staff wanted to recruit a labour contingent from the High Commission Territories, he replied, 'I'm afraid you would not succeed since our people take more pride in military activities than in ordinary labour.' The result was that only a few hundred Swazi responded to the South African army officials who came into the territory to recruit. However, Sobhuza agreed to appoint two Swazi representatives to see to their well-being; he sent a message for Mfundza Sukati, then employed at the Havelock Asbestos Mine as a clerk, and to Prince Dabede, employed by government as a cattle guard, to come and receive instructions and appointments from him. They joined the Swazi recruits in the Union and both were given the rank of Sergeant Major.

As the battlefront extended, and the Allies' difficulties in the Middle East increased, Sobhuza responded to the urgency of Britain's appeal for manpower. Colonel Herbert Johnson, representing the

British Military Mission, arrived in Swaziland and impressed Sobhuza by his sincerity and his honesty. He was sympathetic to Sobhuza's reluctance to draft his men as non-combatants in a labour battalion while at the same time emphasizing Swazi readiness to fight and their military record. Sobhuza informed Colonel Johnson of the help given by Mbandzeni to the British in the war against the Pedi, and of the promises of friendship given by Sir Evelyn Wood. He concluded by pointing out that, as Ngwenyama, King of the Swazi, he could only call up his men if they received both responsibility and recognition as fully armed soldiers. The Colonel agreed. On 18 April 1941, at a Conference called by Sir William and attended by Resident Commissioners of the three territories, representatives of the Union Defence Department and of General Headquarters for the Middle East, and members of the British Military Mission, it was decided to form a separate African Pioneer Corps for the three High Commission Territories. The Secretary of State cabled his approval and large-scale recruiting began. Sir William said he hoped three Companies would be raised in Swaziland, and this time Sobhuza replied that there would be no difficulty as 'the youth of the country was already impatient at not being allowed to assist in the war effort'. He suggested that he form a complete Swazi Pioneer Corps and make recruiting a national movement. At the same time he urged that the Swazi Company in the Union Native Military Corps be sent back to Swaziland, and he raised the question also of recruiting his people in the Transvaal for the Swazi Pioneer Corps.

Throughout the country special messengers armed with battle spear and shield shouted traditional war cry. Warriors mobilised at the headquarters of their local chiefs, many of whom led them in person to Lobamba. They gathered in the great arena, performing stirring traditional war dances while the praisers chanted the history of ancient Kings. Then they left for training in the camp of tents erected at the Agricultural Show ground in Bremersdorp (now Manzini). The response to the call was greater than the British first anticipated, and the camp, built for 1,000, was extended to accommodate over 2,000.

At Lobamba, they had been among the regiments controlled by old Lugodvolwendlovu Gamedze of the Magavu regiment. The new army, however, required new leaders. For the important position of *indvuna* (traditional commander) Sobhuza called back Mfundza Sukati from the Native Military Corps in the Union, and Sobhuza-in-Council appointed as royal representative (another traditional post) Prince Mshengu, the oldest son of the Ndlovukazi Nukwase. Early in the training period Mshengu fell ill and was replaced by Prince Dabede, son of Logcogco (brother of Mbandzeni and hence a 'father' to Sobhuza). The Swaziland government representative approved by Sobhuza was F.P. van Oudtshoorn, a capable policeman fluent in siSwati and already nicknamed Matatazela (one-who-achieves-things-quickly). The Commanding Officer was Colonel Johnson.

Training was rigorous, but the recruits were age mates and morale was high. It was not a case of transforming isolated peasants into an army; the Swazi peasant was a citizen and traditionally every citizen was a soldier; the new techniques and organization were seen as an extension, not an obliteration, of the past. But incorporation into the western system was not without difficulties; the majority had little western education or knowledge of western technology.

During the period of training, Sobhuza visited the camp and talked to the men, listening to their complaints, and responding as far as he could 'to make them feel happy'. Music and marching were pleasures of the life of warriors in the barracks at the royal villages; he encouraged each company to have its own brass band, at the same time urging them to remember their own rich anthems and chants. Mfundza suggested that the Swazi should have their own national flag (equivalent to the beads and other insignia which marked traditional royal age-regiments), and the King consulted with Jane Maclaren, a wonderfully gifted craftswoman and wife of the new headmaster of Matsapha, the National High School.[2] The flag was sewn in silk by four princesses – Sobhuza's sister Lomusa, daughter of Ndlovukazi Nukwase, and his daughters, Ntombane, Phetfwayini and Qondzaphi. Every stitch had to be perfect! Twenty-six years later, British officials decided to organize a competition for a flag for the Independent Kingdom of Swaziland and after many designs had been submitted, the King-in-Committee 'remembered' the flag of the regiments and said that was the accepted flag. It had been kept in safety at Lobamba, and was almost like new. Copies were quickly and easily printed.

On completion of the training, before going to fight, the soldiers assembled at the Showgrounds in Manzini and the King addressed them. He had not slept well the night before; he knew the dangers into which he was sending his men, and wondered how he could inspire them with purpose as well as courage. How could he talk of 'freedom' when they would be fighting alongside people who had taken their freedom from them? Up early, as usual, he went into the sanctuary. This was a time of seclusion and meditation. Later he was joined by his Inner Council. He had chosen his dress very deliberately – the traditional Swazi uniform. The recruits were already assembled. He searched their faces, his own face unusually solemn. They were his people, he was sending them to fight, far away. They had a military tradition. But who was the enemy? And what did they stand to win?

Then inspiration came. The exact words are not recorded, but all who heard remember the message. He said that by their actions they would remind the British of the help the Swazi gave them in the Sikhukhuni war and the promise that the British had made. He then

---

[2] The former headmaster, Theo Keen, had already enlisted.

commended the warriors to the care of their ancestors. Mfundza Sukati told me that the Ngwenyama spoke so eloquently that 'the elders wept that their age kept them from joining; those of the right age rejoiced to have their chance to repeat the deeds of heroes – Sandlane, Mbovane, Lomadokola. Those who were still too young to fight were envious and impatient'.

From the camp the men went again to Lobamba. It was necessary to have the traditional priests of war fortify them so that they would be able to resist and destroy the *lilumbo* (destructive power) of the enemy. Most of the old priests were dead but their clans and even personal names were remembered. The full ritual for a successful attack had been last performed in the reign of Mbandzeni.[3] The oldest surviving war priest, Mahiyane Nkambule of Buseleni, another son of Chief Mtilankhatsa, grandfather of the late Chief Fakisandla, directed the dramatic ritual of 'taking out the army'. A fierce black bull was sacrificed, the men ate of the offering, and were sprinkled with potent medicines as they rushed through the narrow gateway of the cattle byre, ready to fight for their King.

Sobhuza gave Prince Dabede the ritual baton of the army (*indvuku yempi*), a small hollowed stick filled with special power (*umtfumbu*), bound with the skin of a formidable animal. He was to guard it carefully and hold it aloft in times of crisis, and return it to the King when the men were safely home. There was no special chaplain for Christians but three ministers, Samuel Dlamini of the Nazarene Church, Jonathan Shongwe of the Scandinavian, and Augustine Phungwayo of the Anglican Church, had joined with their peers.[4]

Before the soldiers left Lobamba, they ate their fill of meat from cattle provided for them from the cattle-posts of Kingship. Sobhuza bade them farewell with the words: 'I give you God and Mswati. When you are in difficulties just remember these two. Go well and good luck.' Singing the war song 'Shisizwe', the men left en route to Durban. They did not know where they would go from there.

Between 22 November and 13 December 1941, six companies (1991-1996) comprising 24 white officers, 23 British other ranks, 2 Swazi sergeant-majors, and 2,262 Swazi left the camp at Bremersdorp. No sooner had they sailed from Durban than an urgent request for 5,000 more men from the High Commission Territories

---

[3] One of the priests was Mzala of the Gwebu clan; at Sobhuza's suggestion I interviewed Mzala (18 October 1935) who was in his 80s. His father, Mahamula, had served Mswati, his grandfather Ndlela had served Sobhuza I, and his great ancestor Dlamini had served Ndungunye. The Gwebus, who were living at Dumbe in the South, when the early Dlamini kings came there, have rites for a number of different situations; and the priests who could inspire the warriors with fierce courage could also work for peace. Thus after the death of Bhunu, when there was the danger of fighting between rival factions, Labotsibeni called Mzala to 'cool the blood'.

[4] Samuel Dlamini, who was still alive in 1976, was blinded in the war; Jonathan Shongwe died in the '60s but in 1973 when the government was seeking a suitable person to fill a new post of Officer in Charge of Celebrations, his son, David, was selected, his father's loyal service being an important credential.

came from Middle East Headquarters. Sobhuza agreed to raise three additional companies. It was again *Ncwala* time; national enthusiasm was at its peak; the King took the March Past, and the bands played, and later Col. Johnson was presented with a shield to take north. By April 1942 one more company was trained and two others were in the process of formation. But the situation was grim; and in May the call came for a further 15,000.

Sobhuza repeated his willingness and that of his people to do what they could. He once again made it clear that he desired the Swazi Companies to be kept together under the command of Col. Johnson and not be dispersed among other units. In a letter (10 May 1942) to Brigadier Mills, newly arrived in Swaziland, he had made this very explicit.

After conferring (on 13 May 1942) with the Resident Commissioners of the Territories, the High Commissioner informed the Secretary of State that little could be done unless recruiting for the mines was suspended; an intensive propaganda campaign should be launched and visits of chiefs arranged to the Middle East. He estimated that of the 15,000 men, 10,000 might be obtained from Basutoland, the remainder from Bechuanaland and Swaziland.

Recruiting was intensified. The Transvaal Chamber of Mines, financed largely by British capital, agreed to suspend recruiting for the mines for six months (from July 1942). General Sir Claude Auchinleck, Commander-in-Chief, Middle East, wrote official letters of appreciation and encouragement to the 'Paramount Chiefs of the Territories' and to the men on the front.[5] On 15 June 1942 the African Pioneer Corps was incorporated by Royal Warrant into the British Army, within which the Swazi Companies retained their distinctive identity as the Swazi Pioneer Corps.

Ironically, at the same time that Britain was asking help from the Swazi, Sobhuza was being subjected to further pressure to accept the legislation curtailing his traditional authority and that of the chiefs. He consulted his Council, his friends and his lawyers. The wise and trusted Benjamin Nxumalo had died in 1941, but Mgcobeya Nxumalo, Princes Mhawu, Keyi and Majozi, other chiefs and councillors including the governors of royal villages were always available.

Early in 1942 Sobhuza submitted an impressive petition, drawn up by Seme and H. Basner (a radical lawyer for whom Norman Nxumalo worked, and one of three Native Representatives in the South African House of Assembly). In the eyes of Sobhuza and his Inner Council the proposed laws 'would destroy the foundation of Swazi Kingship and

---

[5] In his field message he added, 'I look to you to serve your King and your country with loyalty and efficiency and so to demean yourselves that you may continue to obtain good reports from your officers, to keep the name of the Basuto, the Bechuana and Swazi in good repute among the units with whom you are serving and to deserve the praises of your people when you return to your homes.'

allow the will of the High Commissioner to be made the law of Swaziland so far as the Swazi are concerned'. In the preface to the petition, Sobhuza wrote:

From the time of my grandfather, King Umbandeni, Swaziland has never failed to respond to the call from Great Britain when her help was needed. Once again in the course of the present conflict, that call has come and has been responded to by the offer of men and material.

It might therefore appear inconsistent with this response that just when the British peoples are fully occupied with the defence of the realm and the need to bring the existing conflict to a successful conclusion, a Petition should be presented to the King-in-Parliament, setting forth the grievances of the Swazi nation and seeking redress therefor. Indeed it was not our desire to do this at the present stage but we were impelled thereto by the wishes of the Swaziland Administration, which in spite of our entreaties will not allow us to wait until the end of the war. The reason for this is that it is desired to have proclaimed the proposed laws regarding the appointment and powers of the Chiefs, against which the Swazi nation has objected. The nation sees in the proposed legislation not only the complete destruction of native customary law, particularly as regards the hereditary rights of chieftainship and the laws of succession pertaining thereto, but also the destruction of our present status and our constitutional relationship with the British Government.

The Swazi nation desires to develop the economic and social organization of its people in conformity with its needs, and those needs must inevitably be related to sufficiency of land and the protection of the rights of the nation in the land. Closely interwoven with these fundamental interests of the Swazis are the rights of Chieftainship.

The Swazi nation seriously fears that legislation which tends to undermine the basis of the Chieftainship of the nation, rights cherished from time immemorial, must ultimately also adversely affect their rights and interest in the land.

After a particularly lucid summary of past history, the arguments previously presented in his memorandum of 1939 were formally restated and addressed to 'The Sovereign Legislative Body of Great Britain' (see Appendix). This time the appeal was not to the judiciary, characterized by obedience to technicalities of law, but 'to the People of England through their chosen representatives'.

The petition received strong support from A.G. Marwick who, having retired (in 1937), was more free to express his opinions publicly. In a ten-page letter to Margery Perham (dated 25 August 1942), he wrote:

Sobhuza, Paramount Chief of Swaziland, has addressed a petition to the King in Parliament. It is a very long document and though it does refer to, it does not sufficiently focus upon, several instances of glaring injustice from which he and his people have had to suffer. I believe that the appeal to the King in Parliament is a good tactical move, but I think that it is not unlikely that the Government will try to prevent the matter coming before Parliament on the ground that, as the direction of the Administration of Swaziland has been entrusted by Order-in-Council to the Secretary of State for the Dominions, he can exercise those powers independently of Parliament. Consequently I advise him to get in touch, through the medium of the Aborigines Protection Society, with as many members of Parliament of both houses as possible, in order that they might be able to counter any evasive tactics to which the Government might resort, and I offered to write to you in the hope that you might be persuaded to bring your and your influential friends' powerful batteries also to bear. He accepted the offer.

He then discussed three main points. The first related to the draft Native Authority Proclamation:

He [Sobhuza] holds, and I believe is perfectly right in holding, that neither he nor his predecessors have ever given the Protecting power any reason to make any further inroads upon his sovereignty ... merely to take away power which we cannot demonstrate had been abused, only because it has been done with no apparent unfortunate consequences elsewhere, seems to me to be indefensible, particularly in the name of that 'blessed word' 'indirect rule' ... I am afraid that the tendency in our Colonial Service is easily and lightheartedly to conclude that because a particular brand of Native Authority Proclamation operated well with a certain tribe, it must succeed everywhere else. Local conditions and the history of our contact with the Swazis are very important, and I think that the latter-day High Commissioners have a very poor and superficial knowledge of them, nor do I think that any of them really understand how very democratic Swazi institutions are.

The second related to the non-fulfilment of Lord Elgin's promise that the Crown Land held by the British Government in 1907 would be available for the use and occupation of the Swazi. Quoting from the shorthand notes he took as interpreter for the interview, Marwick reiterated Lord Elgin's promise:

It is further provided that there shall be a deduction from every concession of one-third of its area. That is a very exceptional, and indeed, enormous deduction to be made from concessions granted by a chief, and I believe that taken in conjunction with lands belonging to the Crown it will make so ample a provision for the native occupation, that it is not too much to say that half the land will be in their occupation. Further still, if that does not make ample provision for native occupation, there is a power reserved to take even more land from the concessionaires, though, of course, in that case, compensation will be payable.

Marwick added that when he repeated this statement to Lord Selborne, pointing out that according to his (Marwick's) interpretation Lord Elgin had made 'an unconditional promise to keep the Crown Land for the Swazis', Lord Selborne replied that he had had no right to do so and

then authorized the sale of the greater part, including the choicest portions, of this Crown Land to Europeans, with the result that today only practically valueless and insignificantly small portions of such Crown Land remain in the hands of the Crown while Native Reserves are intensely overgrazed and are deteriorating badly from soil erosion.

The third point Marwick dealt with related to the cancellation of 'The King's Private Revenue Concession'. Explaining that this concession, which authorized the payment of £12,000 per annum (a percentage of the total rents, royalties, transfer fees, etc., collected from concessions) to 'King Umbandeni or his Successors', was cancelled in 1905 by Lord Milner, then High Commissioner, Marwick continued:

When the concession was cancelled the explanation given to the Swazis for this step was that the revenues collected were needed for the administration of the territory ... I think that the broadest and most generous view of the cancellation is that the revenues represented the very inadequate price given by concessionaires for the rights which they acquired from the natives, and that they could only be regarded as general revenue from the point of view of the natives, and if taken from the Paramount Chief should have been applied solely to Native Welfare and Development, and not appropriated to the general expenditure of administration as they were.

The pressure on Sobhuza to accept the Proclamation reached a climax in 1942. Lord Harlech, the new High Commissioner, intent on 'getting Swaziland into line with the other High Commission Territories', described Sobhuza as 'an obstacle to progress', and at a public meeting in the University of Witwatersrand, he compared unfavourably the resistance of the Swazi with the cooperation of the chiefs of Bechuanaland and Basutoland.

In 1972, at another critical period of Swazi history, when the second elections were planned under an 'Independence Constitution' formulated by the British, Sobhuza recalled this earlier crisis in the following words:

I once abdicated. Just open your ears. What was the cause for my abdication? There was once a law during the days of my friend Bruton. They introduced a law that for a King to be King, the Resident Commissioner must first give his consent, even chiefs, their installation must obtain government's consent before they became chiefs. Then they would be salaried by government, thereby the whole machinery would function and perform well with government permeating every aspect. I strongly objected to this. He disagreed with me. It was a prolonged battle and none of you at your homes knew about this. I am revealing a secret that you never heard of. We fought this battle until one day I went to a show at Hlatikulu, where we met again and he again brought up the issue, to which I replied that, 'I told you that I don't want this law.' 'Why do you reject it?' I asked him, 'Why should we discuss this matter at a show? Why don't we go and meet at your place?' Where? 'In Mbabane'. When? 'Today, this evening, when I get home, and will drive up to your place.'

When I got home, I didn't waste time, I hurried to unload the burden in my heart. We got there and the two of us met. He asked me my opinion and I told him that there was nothing more I would say than I had already told him. Again he asked me to reconsider the issue and I told him plainly that I had nothing to do with such a law ... Have you ever heard of a King being installed twice? I will never be installed twice. I don't even see why the government should interfere with the installation of chiefs. Whereupon he told me that all other African nations including the Basutos had agreed to this and I was the only one against this law. I still refused. He then busied himself looking at pages of a book, but I even refused that he open the book where this law was written. We argued at length and I finally told him, if you are in a hurry to initiate your law, let me abdicate. Then you will look for your own King to suit your purposes. As long as I am here, nothing of this nature will happen. Since you claim that you are going to help the country, let me abdicate. Let me abdicate, then you will help this country. He then beat about the bush and tried to persuade me to accept the law. I still told him, I don't care for Kingship, and you find your own King who will co-operate with you, I will never do that. Thereupon he said, I think it best for you to abdicate. Then I replied, I like to appreciate that word. That is the end – I have abdicated. You can now find your own King. He tried to speak and I told him I am now through.

Then he offered me tea and we drank, discussing other matters. Again he returned to this issue. Then I took leave of him and he said as we shook hands, 'Are we still friends?' I replied, 'What is there between us two? You are representing your people and I am representing my people.' Then I left, it being obvious to him now that there was nothing more he could do about this matter because I had told them to find their own King. (King's speech at Lobamba 25 March 1972)

In a memorandum submitted by Bruton to the High Commissioner, he stated:

My first impression of Sobhuza II was that of a pleasant but weak personality. I subsequently realized what an extremely difficult task he has. The question of possible transfer is ever before him (though the War has given him temporary respite in this respect), he has a reactionary and extremely difficult Council, there are the conflicting interests of the European Community and, furthermore, the past history of the Swazi Nation cannot be described as a happy one. The Queen Mother is an important factor in the Native Authority and I found both Sobhuza's own Mother and, on her death, her successor anxious to assist. It is greatly to be regretted that Sobhuza's Mother died in 1938 as her good influence with Sobhuza was greater than that of her sister.

During my service in Uganda I think I can claim a fairly wide experience of tribes in various stages of development (e.g., the Baganda, the Basoga, the Bagesu, the Bagwere, the Teso, the Lugbara, the Medi and the Alur) but the Swazi National Council is the most suspicious and unprogressive body it has ever been my lot to encounter. In the course of Native Administration one naturally expects to meet objections to innovations, the Native being exceedingly conservative, but with both Sobhuza and his Council suspicion is more deep-rooted than mere conservatism and the main reason for this is the feeling that they have not had a square deal over their land.

And he also wrote, 'I think it is a fact that the Military Authorities consider Swaziland's effort, comparatively speaking, to be the best in the High Commission Territories with regard to the Pioneer Corps' (Memorandum, C.O.R. C.L. Bruton Mss. P.R.O' Afr.s. 1366 (8) 1942:1).

Between 28 June 1942 and 17 April 1943 four more Swazi companies (1997-2001) left Swaziland, bringing the total number of Swazi troops to 3,836 men. Their participation was in response not to slogans of democracy, which had little relevance for Africans in a colonial situation dominated by racial discrimination, but to the call of Ngwenyama yemaSwati. As Mfundza said simply, 'He defined allies and enemies'. At the same time, approximately 20,000 Basotho and 10,000 Bechuana enlisted in the Pioneer Corps. The large number from Basutoland reflected the chronic economic poverty of that tiny country, and its dependence on outside employment; fighting for England was economically as well as politically more advantageous for the populace than working in the mines of South Africa.

Most of the men called up by Sobhuza were between 20 and 30, whose age regiments (*Emasotja* and *Sikhonyane*) had not yet been officially freed for marriage. They were the youths, strong and pure, essential for catching the wild black 'bull' required for the ritual of

9. Sobhuza, before leaving for London in December 1922, to present the case of the Swazi to the British

10. The Swazi delegation in London, January 1923. From left to right, seated: Benjamin Nxumalo, Mandanda Mtsetfwa, King Sobhuza, Prince Msudvuka, Dr P.Ka.I. Seme. Standing: Amos Zwane, Lozishina Hlophe, and Solomon Plaatje (author, not a member of the delegation)

11. King Sobhuza, Ngolotjeni Motsa and Lomawa, now fully installed as the Ndlovukazi, during the visit of Edward, then Prince of Wales, to Swaziland, June 1925

12. Queens of Sobhuza dancing the Ncwala. December 1935

Kingship; now they had become part of world-wide military manoeuvres, and to replace them at home Sobhuza formed a new national regiment of boys aged roughly 13-20. This unit he named *Malindane* (those who wait for another) or *Lindimpi* (those who wait for the return of the army), and they would take over the national duties required of unmarried youths in their own country.

Sobhuza felt his responsibility keenly; he had sent his men into unforeseeable danger. He would not let himself think what would be the fate of his people if the Allies were defeated, and concentrated on trying to provide for their return and forestall the disillusionment raised by the question – Why did we fight?

CHAPTER X
A Time of Waiting

The years of war dragged on. Although there was no local radio station broadcasts from the Union reached Swaziland. Sobhuza listened regularly to the news, following the movements of the troops in the different arenas of war – North Africa, Sicily, Italy, and the Middle East. The Swazi served as stevedores, worked on the docks, unloaded and carried supplies in battle areas and maintained essential communications. In Swaziland they had not been armed; overseas the position changed. Some were trained as infantrymen, and one company – the famous 'Smoke Company' – served as machine gunners with the Fifth Army in the crucial attack on Anzio. Reports were sent home of their cheerfulness in face of danger, their high standard of discipline, and their intelligence:

Anyone who watched the Swazis at the Docks during the critical months would have been struck with the care-free, joking manner in which they pulled, pushed and heaved sugar, mealie meal, machinery and bombs, from place to place; but it would have been a mistake to imagine, as you listened to the continuous rhythmic chant of six or seven men lifting a heavy load, that they were oblivious to the importance of their work. In Camp, in their odd leisure moments, they followed the progress of the war on maps, and listened to lectures as they worked. Their purpose and effort was as conscious as yours[1] (Swaziland Archives, File 606E, p. 3).

The British requested that Sobhuza visit the troops, pointing to the example set by the Chiefs Tshekedi and Bathoen, who accompanied their Resident Commissioner (A.D. Forsyth-Thompson) to the Middle East. The Council refused permission; the chiefs of other countries could go among the dead and dying but not their own King. As Prince Keyi asked rhetorically, 'What would we do if anything happened to Sobhuza when he was overseas? Never will we let him go to where fighting is. Our King must not look on corpses. He gives his *impi* strength by the work he does for them at home.'

In 1942, C.L. Bruton was replaced as Resident Commissioner by

---

[1] Soldiers mentioned in despatches: In recognition of gallant and disciplined service in the Middle East, or singled out for special recognition, were Mfundza Sukati, Mcimeli Mdluli, Sgt. Major J. Mkhwanazi, Sgt. Major M.P. Mtembu, Corp. M. Magagula, Sgt. Major Dabede Dlamini, Corp. J. Dlamini, M. Lukhele, Sgt. P. Hlatshwako. The port of Tripoli was almost entirely manned by Swazi, and five Swazi were killed at Anzio where the '1991' entered with the assault troops. Daniel Sikhova Mndzebele received the British Empire Medal for bravery.

E.P. Featherstone, a small dapper bachelor whose most obvious positive qualification was seen by the Swazi as unreasonable obstinacy, hence his nickname, Magandeyane (The Pounder, from *kugandzaya* – to pound or stamp down an earthen floor).

Sobhuza carried on the routine of ritual as well as administration. He spent many hours with his priests in the sanctuary and each year he performed the ancestral ceremonies. In August 1944, in addition to sending cattle to the royal graves in the country, he sent special men to Tzaneen, in the Eastern Transvaal, to bring back to Swaziland the spirits of ancestors who had died there in an expedition against Sikhukhuni.

The people at home had to show fortitude and avoid actions that might weaken the soldiers. If someone died, 'the weeds of mourning' were prohibited; children were not allowed to play guessing games or games of chance. Women whose men were away tied tightly around their waists a girdle indicative of fidelity. As in all wars, young girls thrilled to the uniform and bands; wives and mothers were heavyhearted. The women were called on to provide clothing and comforts for the troops, and Nukwase – energetic, reliable (she won for herself the nickname Macaphazela; pattering of raindrops, quick and refreshing) – was responsible for getting together Swazi women of different beliefs and standards of education to work together with the wives of white officials and soldiers.

It is important to emphasize that Sobhuza's petition of 1942 was not contingent on the support he gave to the Allies in the war. However, the timing was undoubtedly opportune. British public opinion was more receptive than ever before to the claims of colonial peoples. The Aborigines Protection Society (APS), armed with information obtained from Marwick, as well as others,[2] made strong representations to the Dominions Office, and canvassed members of Parliament. In an official acknowledgement to the APS, Clement R. Attlee, former leader of the British Labour Party, and now – in 1942 – Secretary of State for the Dominions in the Churchill government, repeated the reply conveyed by the Duke of Devonshire to the 1923 petition from 'the Paramount Chief', and also wrote that Lord Elgin's statement 'has never been interpreted in the sense suggested by Mr Marwick' (Letter signed by H.N. Tait, Dominions Office 28/12/42. C.O.R. No. Y184/19). Marwick was filled with anger at 'this breach of faith', and persisted in his efforts to persuade the British to admit the injustice they had committed and to rectify it.

While denying the correctness of Marwick's interpretation of Lord Elgin's 'promise', the Under-Secretary of State for the Dominions informed the Aborigines Protection Society that the British

---

[2] The Aborigines Protection Society received documentation from the South African Institute of Race Relations, headed by J.D. Rheinallt-Jones, and also independent evidence from others including the Ballingers, Margery Perham and myself.

government was 'prepared to consider sympathetically proposals for providing additional land for the Swazi'. Detailed evidence for this need was provided but Sobhuza's representatives at the same time repeated that the Swazi did not accept the contention that 'Mbandzeni had granted away' all the land in Swaziland; and they referred once more to the clause in which the grantees bound themselves to respect his (Mbandzeni's) position, and in no way to interfere with the rights of his subjects. To the British, this 'repetition grows wearisome'; to Sobhuza it was a demonstration of endurance and persistence in the affirmation of the rights of his people. Over the years British officials expressed themselves, according to their varying temperaments, with disappointment, indignation or anger, at the Swazi 'absence of gratitude' at Britain's approach to land for the use of the Swazi people. Few could understand that to Sobhuza grants of additional land were not a favour but a moral obligation.

The first Colonial Development and Welfare Act, passed in 1940, allocated £190,000 for an extensive Land Settlement Scheme to provide for some 4,000 landless Swazi families resident as squatters on European-owned farms and for those soldiers who, on demobilization, might wish to become full-time farmers on controlled allotments. When councillors asked – Would the land be vested in the High Commissioner or in their own King, trustee of the nation, Featherstone had replied that this was not land to be simply handed over to the chiefs and allowed 'to deteriorate like other Swazi areas through overstocking, overgrazing and poor agriculture'. This land, he said, would be used to develop a prosperous agricultural sector of the community under expert guidance, with special consideration being given to progressive soldiers. Many of the Council were suspicious and sceptical, but Sobhuza said, 'Let us make the most of the offer and not look a gift horse in the mouth. Also,' he added, 'to the British possession is nine-tenths of the law. They say this land will be given to our soldiers. Can the British ever claim it back?'

Plans were drawn up under the direction of officials in the agricultural and veterinary departments, in close cooperation with Brian Marwick, nephew of A.G. Marwick. Brian Marwick had the confidence of the people not only because of his bond with A.G. but through his own character. Nicknamed *Musawendvodza* (Son of a trusted man) he had become widely known through eleven years of arduous service (1925-36). When, after three years in Nigeria, he returned in 1941 to Swaziland to take up the post of District Commissioner, Sobhuza welcomed him as 'his friend', and trusted he would continue the role of 'his father, Ndlavela (A.G.)' who, though retired officially, had settled in Mbabane and 'would be there to advise us both'.

How many meetings were held to discuss the Native Land Settlement Scheme and how high were Sobhuza's initial hopes! 'I see it,' he said in 1943, 'as a joint effort, something in which we will have a direct say. It is the approach of Aggrey, who pointed out that a piano to produce harmony needs both black and white notes.' Plans were suggested for 'model' rural communities, with houses grouped in villages for greater sociability, and arable plots so spaced as to allow for maximum development and efficient cultivation. There were to be holding grounds for cattle, experiments to improve stock, cooperative buying, and roads for transporting produce.

While relations between Sobhuza-in-Council and the technical planners were good and contacts frequent, relations with Featherstone were often strained; personal confrontation was avoided as far as politeness permitted. When Bruton was still Resident Commissioner he had created a position, at meagre salary, for a Swazi, selected by Sobhuza as his representative, to act as intermediary and liaison officer. Sobhuza chose his brother, Mshengu; when Mshengu was designated for the post of Prince of the Army (the position later given Dabede) Sobhuza appointed Dunguzela, a son of Mbandzeni and hence a senior prince in the royal genealogy. Dunguzela, a man of little western education, interpreted his post very differently from Featherstone, who found him incompetent and dismissed him.

Sobhuza then looked for someone who would combine qualities of both cultures – someone who on the one hand had a western education and office experience, and on the other was well versed in the Swazi way of life, a man of good standing in Swazi society – not necessarily a prince – who understood and appreciated the richness of Swazi culture. Several names were considered,[3] and the final choice was Samuel Thornton Msindazwe Sukati, now Dr Sukati, son of Lomadokola, governor of Zabeni.[4] The government representative was at first reluctant to consider Sukati mainly because his salary of £144 per annum was higher than that proposed for the liaison officer at £120. As an excuse, the government representative pointed out that it would mean taking an experienced clerk from district work. The Council replied that Sukati's training and position fitted him for more

[3] Sobhuza first suggested David Dlamini 'or some other teacher; he considered that Chief Puhlapi Sibandze was too young – he had not yet addressed the Council'; Mashipisa Fakudze (a teacher) was unwilling; and Solomon Madevu, though suitable in many ways, was too hotheaded (Meeting of Director of Native Land Settlement Scheme, Sobhuza and Council, 4/7/44).

[4] Lomadokola had taken fifteen wives; most of them bore him one son and several daughters each. The mother of Msindazwe and of Mfundza were both of the Mavuso clan attached to the group of his first wife Mfongo Sibolile, mother of Mbangamadse, the boy involved in the dramatic shooting accident in Sobhuza's childhood. Lomadokola's main wife was a Dlamini; her son Magciba, the main heir, died in 1935. For a while Titjulo, by yet another Dlamini wife, acted as guardian for Magciba's young heir, Mafohla. The appointment to high offices of Msindazwe and Mfundza indicated the recognition of individual ability in the traditional system. Msindazwa was born at Zabeni in June 1910, brought up in royal villages, and educated at Zombodze, Lovedale and Fort Hare. He obtained by correspondence a B.A. degree, from the University of South Africa. In 1935 he had been employed by government at a salary of £5 per month and thereafter for nearly ten years he served as Revenue Clerk in Mankayane and Manzini at a salary of £12 a month.

useful work than that of a clerk in a district office, a post which could
be filled by any intelligent Swazi, and that his work would be so
important that the money should be found to employ him in the new
post (meeting of Director of Native Land Settlement Scheme,
Sobhuza and Council 4/7/44). Sukati accepted his promotion
philosophically; he knew that there would be some who would
criticize his selection since he was not a prince, but he was the son of
Lomadokola, and 'governors and princes may eat from one dish'. He
was officially designated *Lisolenkosi*, literally Eye of the King, and
generally translated into English as Senior Liaison Officer.

By July 1944 Sobhuza and his Council were voicing certain doubts
about the Native Land Settlement Scheme – the arable allotments
were on the small side (5-15 acres depending on soil and climate)
especially for men with more than one wife and grown sons; the
number of stock allowed each plotholder was too few; and there was
no provision for new developments. Too much money was being spent
on administration and on housing for white officials.

The officials of the Land Settlement Scheme tried to meet the
objections and arrive at a compromise. The Director said that
successful schemes were already operating in parts of the Union, and
it was agreed that three Swazi – Msindazwe Sukati, Chief Gija Nkosi
Mgunundvu, vigorous, forceful, intelligent and conservative, and
Stanley Nxumalo, a son of Benjamin, educated at Fort Cox
Agricultural College in the Cape – together with two officials visit
settlement schemes in the Cape. According to the Director, the men
expressed themselves as favourably impressed with what they saw and
he was nonplussed when on their return they stood up before the
National Council and condemned it utterly. Chief Gija was the most
vehement: 'It would ruin our country if we took home this poison.'
And he made the point that 'It might be good for those people, but not
for us. They don't have chiefs there.' Individual ownership, with its
stress on individual achievement, was foreign to the Swazi, and the
Council decided that the Cape system could not work in Swaziland
(File 7725, Swaziland Archives, 8/12/44).

Sobhuza was not surprised, but wondered if the scheme might not
appeal to the more westernized soldiers. He realized that the war had
propelled his warriors into a battlefield from which they might return
with new outlooks and expectations. Until then very few Swazi had
travelled beyond the borders of South Africa, where their experiences
had been those of peasants, manual workers, mine labourers. Now
some had been overseas, visited great cities and acquired other skills.

Sobhuza sent messages to find out what the men might like to do on
their return. He was very insistent that any project be discussed with
them and 'not just presented to them'. He said they must be asked for
suggestions, and that two things should be borne in mind to make
reabsorption effective – 'education and cooperation – they are the
bolsters required for the support of the whole structure'. He

complained that the Advisory Committee for the Reabsorption of Swazi Soldiers did not seem to be functioning adequately. What arrangements had been made to continue their education? To keep them together as a unit? He was distressed that those who had been disabled and were already back were not being cared for and were 'degenerating'. Some of the councillors raised the question of the reward the soldiers should expect. In the past men would bring back booty and display their prowess before their people; in this war who would realize their bravery and see their achievements? Would the African Pioneer Corps have nothing to show for what they had done? A fund, *iNyakato* (up North) had been started, and each soldier was expected to contribute £5. How would this be spent?

The Land Settlement Scheme was designed largely for the more progressive; for the 'former herdboys' Government suggested to Sobhuza-in-Council other, less intensive agricultural projects. Sobhuza replied that he was apprehensive of making any distinction between young soldiers and old soldiers, or educated and uneducated. 'They must learn to work together and respect each other.'

The land bought by the Government in 1942 and registered in the name of the British High Commissioner did not relieve the increasing pressure on Swazi areas, nor did it accommodate squatters who were being turned off European farms or Swazi from the Union requesting to *khonta* and return 'home'. So Sobhuza, continuing the policy inaugurated by Labotsibeni in 1913, decided to buy back land in the name of the nation. Purchase of land by any Swazi, irrespective of education, wealth or rank, still required the consent of the High Commissioner and there was a general feeling that Government, while recognizing the need of the Swazi for more land, did not want them to acquire it, individually or nationally. The first area selected for purchase was Thulwane, a large farm owned by Carl Todd, a lawyer who had come into the country in 1929 but had kept up his South African practice and company connections. He was to play an important part in the politics of Swaziland and eventually became a member of the first Swaziland Legislative Council and later Senator in the Swaziland Parliament. The price was negotiated by George Gordon-Bennett, a friend of Sobhuza from childhood days, who acted as Sobhuza's representative.[5] After some hesitation the High

[5] George Bennett was the son of Joseph Bennett, a British pioneer interested in trade, who had been befriended by Mbandzeni and whose wife, Elsie, had borne her first child, named Mantayi, at the capital of Nkhanini, residence of Ndlovukazi Tibati. During the Anglo-Boer War, Bennett was taken prisoner by the Boers, and his wife and child remained in the care of the Ndlovukazi Labotsibeni. After the war the Bennetts identified themselves with Swazi life and were close to the Swazi royal family. The oldest son, Mantayi, stayed for some time in the barracks of the capital. George, the second of the five Bennett children and the most western educated, was the only one of the four boys to marry a white wife; his sister married Prince Matsafeni Dlamini. George became a successful trader and recruiter for the gold mines. Sobhuza frequently visited him at his home and did much of his buying from his shop in Manzini. George died in 1972 and was buried, as he had requested, at the foot of the Mdzimba mountains, the place of his happy boyhood memories.

Commissioner agreed, but insisted that any land purchased be paid for in cash (Meeting of Resident Commissioner, Director of Settlement Scheme, Sobhuza and Council at Lobamba 3/11/44). Norman Nxumalo, who likened his job to that of 'Chancellor of the Exchequer, but more difficult', was responsible for collecting cattle for sale. In August 1944 he claimed that 800 head had been contributed but more were needed; records were vague; some cattle disappeared; an extension of time for collection was requested and transfer delayed. The sale only went through in 1948, and Thulwane was registered in the name of the Ngwenyama in Trust for the Swazi Nation. The title deeds were placed in the Deeds Office in Pretoria, South Africa, where all transfers (and concessions) were kept.

At a farewell in Bremersdorp on 8 February 1945 for men of the African Pioneer Corps who had been on home leave and were unexpectedly recalled, the District Commissioner addressed the gathering on the Native Land Settlement policy. Sobhuza was present, and invited the men to discuss their situation. Several men related, with deep emotion, personal grievances and disappointments – the branding of cattle, eviction of kin from farms, payment of grazing fees. Then, according to a report submitted by Msindazwe Sukati: 'The Paramount Chief, seeing that the African Pioneer Corps were getting "heated up", stood up to speak':

Warriors! I notice that the texture of your complaints here today is the same matter for which I went to England to complain about. It is true, and it is quite natural that you should complain about these things, not so much that you complain as the fact that you are just continuing our requests for the fulfillment of those promises that were made to your fathers and grandfathers when they came back after the Mshadza wars. As I told you when I sent you out that you were not being sent out by me, but you are just another detachment of that regiment which went out to Mshadza and I told you that the young men of any nation are its atonement, its burnt offering sacrificed for the well being of that nation; it was with that understanding that I sent you out and I told you that you were not being sent by me to the Army but it was my grandfather, Mbandzeni, who chose the British Government. I am thankful that you have shown some of those people who do not like us that you are a nation amongst others and several reports have been written about you – I have them at my Office. These are very good reports, but it is not the time yet to praise and thank you for the work you have done there. I shall have my time for that after the war when you come back and narrate stories of how you did all these performances, at Lobamba in the kraal. At present even if I hear something good about you I dare not laugh out, I just smile to the side and hide my smile because the time is not yet ... So I ask you once again to go back and finish the work that has been entrusted to you.

The successful purchase of Thulwane stimulated further effort; over 27,000 Swazi were still virtual serfs on European farms, and the soldiers were returning. The settler farmers, hearing that the Swazi were striving to buy back more land, raised the price, and simultaneously some began evicting families who had been there many years. Moreover, there was an increasing interest in land in Swaziland among Europeans. 'Areas which had not been worked or occupied were now being worked by Europeans or were sold to other Europeans who would work them. The great fear was that because of this increasing interest the opportunity for acquiring more land for the Swazi Nation would be lost forever if it was not taken soon' (Meeting of Government Secretary accompanied by the Director of the Land Settlement Scheme, Sobhuza and Council, 24 July 1945).

The government, though sympathizing with the Swazi, made it clear that with the burden of war Britain could make no further grant for land purchase. A suggestion by the Government Secretary, G.J. Armstrong, that soldiers might be willing to contribute part of their deferred pay 'especially if they might have a chance of occupying some of the land' (*ibid.*) was rejected by some of the Council. Sobhuza agreed that this money belonged to the fighting men, and that they should be helped to use this money wisely. Some might want to go into business, others to take new employment, others to go into professions. He also pointed out that land was 'not a machine for making money', and he asked that Government make a law to control the price of land in different areas. In regard to the question of Swazi from one district contributing towards the purchase of land in another district, Sobhuza commented that it was Swazi custom that a man could move for a variety of reasons from one part of the territory to another. He was not bound to stay in one area. The whole area belonged to the whole nation and therefore if one contributed towards buying land anywhere one was in effect buying that land for oneself.

It was at this point that Sobhuza conceived a plan to deal with both land shortage and overstocking. Instead of periodic levies, there would be a new national *Lifa Fund* (treasury of the Swazi nation), to which every owner of more than ten head of cattle would contribute one head; the animals thus acquired would be auctioned, and a levy on the proceeds credited to the fund. The *Lifa* was officially registered in 1946 and it was hoped that collections would not be too difficult and the records accurate. Councillor Joshua Lukhele, who had served for many years as clerk in the office of the District Commissioner at Manzini, was appointed first treasurer and Prince Magolwane was made his assistant. Magolwane, a son of Sobhuza by Ntfombitodvwa Mgunundvu, was a bright young man (born in 1925) who had left School in Standard V.

In conversations with his Council as well as at meetings with government officials, Sobhuza linked the Swazi war effort, the reacquisition of land and the need for improved education, with the continuation of the traditional system of chieftainship and kingship. He was eager that the nation be more directly involved in the administration and policy of schools, so that the young would be more appreciative of their own culture and institutions: 'Western schools are a new thing, but learning is old. Now the world is turning round, and the knowledge that is brought together must be sifted. Why should our children be taught to despise our customs and disobey their elders?'

His critical attitude towards mission 'interference' with Swazi custom expressed by him in the earlier period of his reign had been reinforced by several recent incidents – the building of church schools without consultation with the chiefs in whose areas they were to operate; the claim by a missionary of 'ownership' of church land; a missionary's punishment of children in the Hhohho area for drawing water for their mothers to brew the traditional beer; a condemnation of Swazi foods; the continued denigration and misrepresentation of Swazi customs and beliefs. At the same time he repeated his appreciation of the contribution of those who 'stuck to teaching', and recognized that missionaries had pioneered African school education. 'To point only to the bad does not help, either. Weeds grow quickly.'

The position of the churches was not altogether easy. Some of the most hardworking missionaries were German and Italian, and the government, alert to the possibility of espionage, allowed them to continue with their services but kept a close watch on their movements. It came as a great shock when a transmitter and other equipment were discovered in the house of a highly respected German couple in Mbabane. The man was a Lutheran minister, his wife a qualified and skilful doctor, devoted to her work, who, in her small hospital, treated patients with deep understanding.

There were more Italians than Germans, but they stuck to preaching and teaching. A deep personal friendship had grown up between Sobhuza and Bishop Barneschi, then head of the local Catholics, a man of erudition, kindness and courage, who had been wounded in the First World War, and had lost the use of his right arm. He came to Swaziland in 1922, learned the language, and moved easily among the people. The Swazi nicknamed him *Lungcwazi* (the big one) and Sobhuza introduced him to me affectionately as 'my Bishop'. The two made a fascinating pair, engaged in animated ecclesiastical discussion – Barneschi, his blue eyes sparkling, punctuating his points with graphic gestures, bursting into jolly laughter; Sobhuza questioning, drawing analogies, enjoying the stimulus of other ideas, but measuring them by his own values. It seemed to me that Bishop Barneschi, more than any other missionary, understood – and sympathized with – Sobhuza's eclectic tolerance.[6]

Sobhuza was also in touch with leaders of independent African churches in Swaziland and in Zululand, as well as with ministers of the more orthodox and conservative religions. 'All,' he said, 'are looking for what is right.' He regretted the 'ever-splitting irresponsible formations' of small sects (letter to Resident Commissioner 16/11/40), and supported the effort by prestigious Swazi to

---

[6] Sobhuza's initial introduction to Catholicism was during the period (1913-1933) when Monsignor Peregrini Belleze was Prefect Apostolic of the Order of Servites of Mary. Belleze, Italian and humanist, was active in advancing Swazi education; he also showed respect for Swazi religion and supported Swazi custom (e.g., *lobola* – bride wealth) and never insisted – as did most of the Protestants – on Swazi wearing western dress.

amalgamate the independent African churches into a single church. With his sanction this was discussed with the Resident Commissioner by councillors Solomon Madevu, of the United Swazi Christian Church in Zion in South Africa, and Benjamin Nxumalo, of the African Methodist Episcopalian Church; and Sobhuza asked that the church be registered.

Ndlovukazi Nukwase aided him in this approach. From the time she was installed, in 1938, Good Friday became a major religious occasion. Preachers of different sects gathered with their congregations at Lobamba and prayed and sang hymns. Sobhuza as well as Nukwase attended and spoke to them. Among the more influential prelates were the Revs. Stephen Nkonyane and Stephen Mavimbela of the Church in Zion. Both were followers of Stephen Nkonyane's father, Daniel Nkonyane, whose main centre was at Charlestown in Natal, but who had frequently visited Swaziland and prayed for the sick, including the late Ndlovukazi Lomawa, at Lobamba. On Daniel's death in 1935, the leadership was split, and Sobhuza urged them to reunite. He invited them to attend the *Ncwala*, which they did for the first time in 1938. Subsequently Stephen Nkonyane married Princess Thembi, one of Sobhuza's daughters, and set up another homestead near Lobamba. Mavimbela, who lived near Zombodze, was often consulted by Nukwase; he helped organize Good Friday (which he described as 'the *Ncwala* of the Christians') and to build up the 'Swazi National Church'.

Nukwase had the idea of building a great and beautiful church, centrally placed, non-denominational, where 'all could worship and praise God'. Sobhuza approved. It would all take time, but by 1948 plans drawn up by an imaginative architect, living in the Union of South Africa, were passed by the Swazi National Council. A site close to the capital was allotted by Sobhuza, and the Resident Commissioner was informed by the Swazi National Council that it had decided to build a Royal Church with funds raised both inside and outside Swaziland. The Ndlovukazi was appointed Hon. Treasurer, assisted by an organizing committee (Lobamba minutes 18/9/48).

Mavimbela came from a family renowned for visions and powers of divination, and he himself had a dream in which 'the Holy Spirit' ordered him to design a 'shining rod' to use as a symbol, '*Umlamuli*' (Saviour or Peacemaker) to 'keep peace and support kingship'. Mavimbela had the rod made by a silversmith in Johannesburg, and since then it has been used at a certain stage in the *Ncwala* and also at major national events, including each celebration of Independence, and in situations of crisis. The power is not in the rod itself: 'It is a reminder that we must ask the help of God to make the world be stable' and 'to keep peace'. Mavimbela died in 1949; the stick is in the care of a man of the sect, trusted by the King.

Sobhuza placed much faith in the national school, for which special legislation was being designed. He tried to work out a satisfactory solution to problems of control and direction. It was necessary to define the relative positions of the Swazi National Council, the Resident Commissioner, the Superintendent of Education, and parents. Again there were differences of opinion, openly and at times heatedly expressed, and he would intervene at critical moments, defusing hostility, recognizing arguments on both sides, then indicating his own opinion. 'When I think one of the councillors wrong, I must say so, just as when I think Government is wrong.' At one crucial meeting, Featherstone spoke with authoritarian anger at opposition voiced by Mgcobeya Nxumalo and Amos Zwane against the proposal that policy be controlled by a government body. Mgcobeya was furious. Sobhuza, who sympathized with his feelings, explained that 'the Council would be surprised to find that the Resident Commissioner and the Superintendent of Education were discussing important matters with the governing body first. The Council was like a householder who employed a builder to work for him. It was the householder who decided what had to be built and not the builder. Matters of principle should be discussed in the Council. The Council should say what should go to the Board but it could not say what matters should not come before it.' Mgcobeya accepted this, and rebuked the Resident Commissioner, who 'should not accuse members of the Council of fighting. This would cause them to fear to express their own views even if they could be helpful' (Swaziland Archives, Meeting with the Resident Commissioner, Government Secretary, Director of the Native Land Settlement Scheme, Superintendent of Education, Sobhuza and Council, 14/11/44).

The Constitution giving the Swazi additional control over national schools was passed, but negotiations over the proposed political legislation had dragged on for so many years that there was an apparent stalemate. According to Lord Hailey (1953:388), the Swazi leaders showed themselves 'unusually tenacious in regard to the wording of those clauses which appeared to curtail in any way the authority exercised by the Paramount Chief and his Council, and insisted on reading into the terms of the Order-in-Council of 1903 a binding agreement that their assent was necessary to any legislation which might affect Native law and custom'. But the Swazi remained adamant, anticipating that the British would now be more ready to respond to their legitimate claims (phrased by the British as 'making concessions').

In his speech of welcome to Sir Evelyn Baring, appointed High Commissioner in October 1944, Sobhuza took the opportunity to inform him, in very typical fashion, of the main concerns of his people:

Your name Sir Evelyn reminds us of Sir Evelyn Wood who was sent into Swaziland by the British Government after the distinguished services of the Swazi Regiments during some of the South African Wars in 1881. Through him the British pledges and guarantees ... were given us ... May I add that recently there has been another such calling on our young men as was the case in 1881. These brave young men, whom we gave to serve with His Majesty's Armed Forces in the great World War, are the flower of our regiments in Swaziland and they are the hope of our Nation, and through them we desire to show His Majesty and the British Government that we are worthy of their continued trust and protection.

He continued pointedly,

Matsapha our National School, and the Native Authorities Proclamation are two great issues that need not only great statesmanship, but a friend to wield them, and we trust you will fill this role so that we may look upon your term of office with satisfaction and pride ... Matsapha, the Swazi National School, is one of our greatest prides – a 'Morning Star' as it were – not only as a national institution, but also because it is the big cauldron in which to mould and shape the minds and morals of our young men and young women in the preparation for life and good citizenship. Here lies our treasure and it is in this respect that I say we cherish Matsapha with great pride.

Dealing with the Native Authorities Proclamation and the problems it raised he mused,

Possibly you have heard that we are backward, unprogressive and difficult to deal with because we did not readily accept the Proclamation. We may even have been misrepresented as having repudiated the Crown's powers to make certain laws in Swaziland. This of course is not true. Our contention has been that the Crown pledged to us certain rights which it undertook to respect. We feel sure that you will agree with us that we should not be doing justice to the British Government, our country or ourselves if we accepted blindly any proposals put before us merely with intent to please, or out of fear of being thought unprogressive only to find ourselves full of dissatisfaction and suspicion and the disastrous consequences they might entail.

Sir Evelyn Baring was more sympathetic than his predecessor to Sobhuza and the reports he sent to the Secretary of State were more favourable. Far from considering him averse to new ideas, Sir Evelyn found him actively interested in promoting the welfare of his people. 'Naturally he is cautious.'

By the end of April 1945, Allied victory was in sight. For many Swazi it was a personified war, with the fate of the world identified with the fate of the two leaders, Mussolini and Hitler. In the words of Mfundza Sukati: 'With the execution of Mussolini and the disappearance of Hitler the enemy strength collapsed. It is hard to describe the joy of the soldiers when they heard they would be sent home with victory. Some wept tears, others said prayers, others could just talk nonsense.'

Demobilization took several months, and the troops were shipped home in batches. They had been sent out by Sobhuza as the army of the Swazi nation; and he had impressed on Colonel Johnson that they should stay together and come home as a single unit. Johnson willingly agreed, and promised that he would do all he could to retain their sense of national unity and pride. They might be freed from the army regulations of the British but they remained on as warriors in the age-regiments of the Swazi King. Any official 'Stand Down Parade' was but a preliminary to national ceremonies which reaffirmed their position in the traditional Swazi system. When Colonel Johnson was transferred (against his will) to other duties, his replacement, F.P. van Oudtshoorn, who had been made a Lieutenant-Colonel, did his best to carry out Sobhuza's plan, and though the men were eager to rejoin their families and return to normal life, the majority agreed to wait in the camp until all were ready for demobilization.

Dabede and Mfundza, summoned to Lozitha to report to the King-in-Council, described with graphic detail the ordeals and achievements of the warriors. Truly a magnificent record of courage, discipline and heroism, equal to that of the great regiments of the past. Dabede recounted that 'When there had been danger, the Swazi and the whites who were with us would shout, 'Take out the stick, Dabede. Take out the stick, Dabede,' for they knew help rested with me to protect them from the bombs' (interview 9/8/73). Mfundza reported on the courage of the 'Smoke Company' in the grim battle of Anzio. Sobhuza listened, impressed, then questioned them on 'everything' – strategy, the planning of attack, the different weapons, the strength of the enemy, acts of individual courage, and he commented on how warfare had changed from what he had heard of the First World War. The time passed by. Beer was brought and drunk and, as Mfundza said, 'It was good, and we saw we were home.'

Traditional rituals were performed at the capital. The Ngwenyama was in full command. The war priest, the venerable Mahiyane Nkambule, was again in the arena. In a superficially simple ritual, but one of utmost meaning to the warriors, he had purified them from the contamination of death, curbed their readiness to kill, and in general removed the misfortunes of war.

The more formal public official welcome was called for 13 July 1946, and the announcement went forth through the chiefs and district offices. The site was chosen by the Swazi; it was not the Bremersdorp Showground or the playing field at Mbabane, but an open plain near Lobamba backed by the majestic Mdzimba mountains. (In 1966, at an historic meeting of the House of Assembly, Swazi insisted that their first House of Parliament be built on this tradition-sanctified ground and not at Mbabane, then headquarters of the colonial administration.) All members of the public of Swaziland were invited to the spectacular occasion, described in the *Times of Swaziland* (18/7/46):

The Saturday scene was unique and its setting majestic. On the west Rider Haggard's 'Sheba's breasts' framed the plain and the grim pinnacle of the 'Jumping-off place', Nyonyane, rose aggressively from the valley of the rugged Mdimba peaks to the east completing the perimeter: a great discovery for mass concourse quite overshadowing our dainty Oval at Mbabane, hitherto the scene of many historic gatherings. There was room for everyone, thousands of Swazi men and women, and for the troops forming three sides of a square, with the dais, and flag-staff and a concourse of European residents and many visitors, and the Paramount Chief's bodyguard in their Native habiliments completing the quadrangle. The whole scheme was admirably organised by Lieut.-Colonel F. van Oudtshoorn, M.B.E. (Military) commanding his men on parade.

Shortly before eleven o'clock, the Paramount Chief and Ndlovukazi arrived. A party with the regimental band was drawn up, and as the Paramount Chief ascended the dais the bugles sounded a greeting. At eleven o'clock the High Commissioner, accompanied by His Honour the Resident Commissioner, reached the parade and were welcomed by the Paramount Chief and Government Secretary and Mrs Armstrong, and as His Excellency stepped onto the dais the Colour Party with fixed bayonets presented arms, the Band sounded the royal salute.

Sobhuza began his speech by expressing the nation's pleasure at having with them Sir Evelyn Baring 'who represented the eyes and mouth of the English King'. Then, turning towards the troops (with loudspeakers echoing his words) he continued (according to the *Times* report):

'You see the hills and valleys watching you. Today they are smiling. When you went away they were dark.' He then referred to their departure when he addressed them at Manzini. He had told them to work together, and help one another. He was quite right. They had come back with honour through their behaviour and faith in themselves. All of them should now understand that if they obeyed their leaders and worked together they would succeed. If they did not respect their leaders then they would not get results. When in Manzini he handed them over to their officers, he told them to obey. They had done so and they had not spoilt their good name.

What they had learnt during the war he hoped was good. They had seen Europe and other countries, and customs good and bad. He hoped that they would abide by the good customs they had seen. They had both friends and enemies. If they followed the good customs they would be happy, but if the bad, it would be their enemies who would be happy. Above all things they had learned to work together as one company.

The warriors punctuated his speech with the royal whistle and shouted *Bayethe*! The salute of the troops in the march past was taken by the High Commissioner.

Dabede formally returned the *indvuku yemphi* (the stick of the army), that sacred and powerful weapon, kept in peace time in the fragile arsenal of a hut in the enclosure of the Ndlovukazi. Traditionally, the stick had to be returned with cattle, and Dabede presented the rulers with a lump sum of roughly £400 to purchase animals as replacements for those brought by the Ndlavela regiment from the Mshadza war: 'The King slaughtered many cattle for us [as food] when we left and when we returned, and these were cattle brought back in previous wars. We had to bring back our own cattle for we ate our fathers' cattle. Our cattle will be used for the next war [!], for the army that is now being conscripted' (Dabede 9/8/73).

In a vividly remembered past, war was a recognized means of increasing national revenue; cattle were raided and brought to the

King to distribute as he wished, some he slaughtered to feast the fighters, others he gave as rewards to heroes, others were herded in cattle posts of the nation. The Luhhumane, Ludlambedlu, Lukwati marked the victories of Maswati, the Shiyabanye, Incamu and Impholonja the victories of Mbandzeni. Now it, was the turn of Sobhuza II. But times were changing, and whereas before conservatives claimed, 'Cattle are our bank; they should not be sold,' after the Second World War when soldiers received their pay in cash, they transposed the axiom saying, 'Our cattle are money and banks our cattle posts.'

In August 1946, soon after the men had returned home, Featherstone's term of office was terminated. Sobhuza's speech bidding him farewell is worth quoting at some length:

Your short term of office as Resident Commissioner for this Territory has been characterised by several events of great importance. Your task has been heavier than that of your predecessors as one can see from the notable events which will always be associated with your name and actions, namely,

(i) the Matsapha Constitution;

(ii) The Native Land Settlement Work and laws therefor;

(iii) The Native Administration Proclamation; and

(iv) the putting into effect of the Grants from the Colonial Development and Welfare Act.

All these are said to be for our ultimate benefit, but in actual fact so far Matsapha is the most outstanding because of its Constitution which was so prepared that it does not absorb our rights as a nation but places the Government in a position of Guardianship. We are fully alive to the fact that if we as a nation sit still, like a hen which broods on her eggs and never shuffles them about with the result that they rot, we cannot hope to survive. In everything we do, including the Proclamation already referred to, we hope for success on the lines you have so often promised, i.e.,

(a) That these Proclamations are not intended as a means best calculated to bring about our ultimate absorption, but that they turn to safeguard our traditional laws and customs in a modernised form.

(b) In our participation in the preparation of these Proclamations we have always maintained that they should be such laws as will not bring about any disintegration of our institutions and customs which might cause friction between the people and their hereditary leaders.

(c) That we should not in future find ourselves so oppressed through these Proclamations that we are not able to rise as a nation.

We have always been made to understand that the policy of the British Government is to help young nations all over the Empire to grow up to a stage where they can be able to stand on their own feet. However this year we have read from newspapers with great concern that the established policy of the Government of the Union of South Africa is not to develop the Natives for their ultimate growth. These are conflicting policies which keep us greatly concerned so that nothing should be done which might prejudice our position in the event of whatever changes may take place.

Another great event has been the return of our Swazi troops from the Army. These young we sacrificed as a nation for the freedom of the world in general and Swaziland in particular, in the same manner as those who served in the Sekukuni War during the reign of my grandfather. Our hope is that through the victory achieved by the great powers with our participation the promises given to the King Mbandzeni may · be strengthened so that we may enjoy the same freedom as other races of the world for which we have fought and conquered. Your term of office has been the most difficult one for you have been burdened with the task of laying the foundation for the big events which will be remembered for generations to come whether for good or evil (*Times of Swaziland*, August 8, 1946).

In the Honours List of 1945 Sobhuza was awarded the O.B.E. in recognition of his services *to* the nation; in his speech of acceptance he said it was a recognition of the services *of* the nation. He and his Council were still working on the Proclamation, knowing well that it could only be effective with their cooperation; they could not be forced and they would make their own decisions in their own time. He felt hopeful; his men had acquitted themselves with great honour; on his own battlefront he and his 'peace force' had achieved important gains – a more promising educational policy, additional land for his people, a firmer toehold in the total money economy of the country, and more conscious powers of negotiation.

CHAPTER XI
A Time of Promise

Edward B. Beetham, Featherstone's successor, came to Swaziland with a background of administrative experience in Kenya and Sierra Leone. A strong, energetic man in his early forties, married, approachable, enterprising, he soon won the support of both the Swazi and the whites. The Swazi named him *Hlangabeza* (meaning 'He met them half-way in solving their problems').

In the four years of his office two major social events were celebrated – one very western, the other very Swazi. The first, the visit by King George VI and Queen Elizabeth of England, and their two daughters, Princesses Elizabeth and Margaret; the second, a national *umcwasho*, with the unmarried girls represented by one of Sobhuza's daughters, Princess Pholile. The first was given publicity in the major official government publications; the second, to many Swazi the more important, was not mentioned.

According to the Annual Government Report for 1946, 'This gracious act [the promise of the Royal visit] delighted the whole community ... who had feared that the remoteness of the territory from the railway might have made the visit impossible.' The officials did not know that the initial reaction of many leading Swazi to the news was one of deep concern. At a meeting of the Council of Princes, the leader, Magongo, son of Malunge, quoted the proverb: 'Kings [Rulers] do not look at one another.' There was a deep belief that such a meeting, a meeting of two men each imbued with the ritual potions of his high office, would be fundamentally and automatically a dangerous confrontation, and without any conscious or deliberate act, the stronger would survive and the weaker be destroyed.

On hearing that on this account King Sobhuza II might be restrained from meeting King George VI, the intrepid Mgcobeya Nxumalo went to Lozitha. On arrival, he began to chant praises of the Lion of the Swazi, and at the same time he used the acceptable technique of inserting into his oration subtle criticisms, spontaneously composed, alluding to the decision of the Council of Princes. The King heard, and called Mgcobeya to him and asked him what he meant. Mgcobeya gave his opinion – King George was King of the British, not of the Swazi. Further, he washed and bathed with plain water, whereas the King of the Swazi was washed with *tintseleti* of ancient power. And had not Sobhuza been sent overseas in 1922 to put the case of the Swazi personally to King George V, who had died in '36? Sobhuza himself recalled how his great-great-grandfather, Somhlolo, Sobhuza I, the Wonder, Creator of Miracles, had had the courage to accept the invitation of Shaka, the Zulu King, then at the height of his military power. Shaka had welcomed him, and they had looked at each other. The 'beauty of Somhlolo' (a beauty more than physical) was his protection, and he had returned safely; his subjects had greeted him with pride and given him cattle, *tinkhomo takaqoza*, which he placed in the royal homestead of Ludvondvolwcni, in the south. (In later years Sobhuza II would merit his own 'cattle of achievement'. Somhlolo outlived Shaka by many years; and when George VI died, in 1952, Mgcobeya was 'shown to have been right': Sobhuza, though older than the English King, was the King who survived.)

The celebration was to take place at Goedgegun, renamed after independence Nhlangano (the Meeting Place). It was the centre of a predominantly Afrikaans-speaking farming community and had been selected instead of Mbabane since it was nearer to a railhead in the Union of South Africa and, particularly in the heavy rains, more accessible by car.

Having once committed himself, Sobhuza participated enthusiastically and generously. He ordered from a well-known firm of jewellers in Johannesburg a stick engraved with a lion, and three cups to present to the royal guests, and he sent word to the chiefs to attend with their followers.

Sobhuza and Nukwase drove in cavalcade with the Resident Commissioner and Mrs Beetham and other notables to greet the British royal family at the border of Mahamba, and then escorted them to the arena.

Goedgegun was transformed to a vast encampment of many hundreds of Europeans and tens of thousands of the Swazi people who came from all parts of the Territory. The Europeans had travelled by car during the previous days and the Swazis had walked in their thousands over the hills. Many people of all races also came across the border from the Union. (Swaziland Annual Report for 1947. London HMSO, 1949:3.)

In front of the audience, facing a dais reserved for the royal visitors and VIPs, were Swazi soldiers of the Swazi Pioneer Corps in battledress, flanked on either side by school children, and behind them rows of warriors in traditional costume, with spears, shields and knobkerries. The Royal party drove slowly round in big black cars for all to see – Sobhuza dressed in a blue tailored uniform with a white helmet and plumes, Nukwase in traditional Swazi regalia, King George in naval white and many medals, the British Queen and Princesses in formal dress, hat and gloves.

Speeches were read by Sir Evelyn Baring, the Ngwenyama, and Allister Miller as 'the oldest surviving European settler in Swaziland'.

King George expressed thanks and appreciation, and bestowed medals and other honours accompanied in each case by a Royal British handshake. Sobhuza was presented with a medallion, Nukwase with the King's Medal for African Chiefs and a medallion, Sergeant Daniel Sikhova Mndzebele of the Swazi Pioneer Corps with the British Empire Medal, and Brian Marwick, then first Assistant Commissioner, with the O.B.E. King George took the salute of the soldiers led by their own band, but when he and his family walked with Sobhuza along the lines of warriors, it was to Sobhuza as their king that they gave royal greeting. It had been previously agreed that the English King be hailed as 'Nkhosi', which the Colonial Administration misunderstood as the equivalent of the true Royal salute, but that the high-pitched whistle be reserved for the Ngwenyama of the Swazi. The warriors' performance ended with the solemn chant, 'Here is the Fortress', the hunting song composed after their victory against Sikhukhuni. It was a fine occasion, 'a really first class show'.

The *umcwasho* of Pholile was inaugurated with the dual purpose of celebrating the homecoming of the soldiers, and bringing the people back to their customs. It was part of the attempt by Swazi leaders to deal in a traditional manner with new social problems. The discipline of the soldiers overseas had been excellent, their crime rate low, drunkenness no more excessive than in many other units. But they had all been deprived of women, 'whose influence can check the evil in men'. How would they, particularly those who had left as unmarried youths, or had lost their wives in the long absence abroad, behave on their return? What solace had they found for loneliness and fear? What bad habits might they have acquired? What passions and frustrations might be loosed? The heroes of war could be criminals in time of peace. That was why in the past the bravest warriors, rewarded with cattle and widely renowned, had also to be specially doctored to cool the lust to kill, and to protect them from the vengeance of those whose blood they had spilt. The Nation as well as the family and the individual had to be protected.

War was also hard on the women, in some ways even harder than on the fighting men. There was the danger that when the soldiers came back the girls who were not yet married might abandon all restraint. Sobhuza shuddered at the thought of a 'generation of children without fathers or self-respecting mothers'. Quick marriage was no solution; divorce a foreign concept.

The *umcwasho* had not been performed since 1935; Betfusile and the girls of her age had long since been married; some of them were called to instruct the new group. Its Princess was Pholile, who was attending high school at Matsapha; her mother, Nkotsase Ntjalintjali, was one of Sobhuza's senior queens.[1] The organization and procedures were

---

[1] Pholile, who considered the *umcwasho* a valuable experience, went on to lead an unusually productive and active life. She completed Standard VII (at Matsapha), studied Home

based on the '*umcwasho* of Betfusile'. The girls were distinguished by their costumes, and followed special rules of conduct. The same penalties for sexual contact were laid down, and much the same objections were raised as before. Some of the girls – not many – married by civil or Christian rites during the period of the *umcwasho*, knowing that neither they nor their husbands could be legally penalized. The *umcwasho* ended with great feasting and dancing; and though it is impossible to know whether or not it succeeded in reinforcing morality, it certainly did not increase immorality. Some of the girls fell by the wayside, most went through the year with restraint. The government had appointed one Welfare Officer but Sobhuza asked, 'What could he do? He comes in when the person is already in trouble!' Sobhuza viewed the *umcwasho* as a reminder of traditional moral values which needed constant reiteration and reinforcement. It was obviously not a solution to immorality, nor did it operate in isolation.

As a pragmatist who recognized the harsh necessities of daily existence, Sobhuza considered that virtues of righteous living should be embedded in the fulfilment, not the denial, of the flesh. 'A man with nothing is open to crime; a man with too much grows greedy.' Swazi religion does not idealize celibacy or asceticism, or value suffering as a means to salvation, nor does it advocate hedonism and encourage licence: it sanctions enjoyment of the good things life can offer, but this enjoyment must be contained within boundaries of self-discipline. The *umcwasho* could not be divorced from the broader context of living.

The soldiers whose return was being celebrated were entitled to receive economic security and recognition. Until 1946 the outlook of the government towards economic development was summed up in the typical statement that 'Swaziland is poor and every major development has been due to the generosity of the United Kingdom' (Annual Report for 1946:3,5). Sobhuza had protested, 'Swaziland is not poor. The government servants are not poor. The settlers are not poor. We Swazi are poor.'

After the war was over things looked more promising. Important new economic enterprises were planned. A 'Ten Year Plan' (1945-55) based on the promise of generous funding under a second Colonial Welfare and Development Act had extended the possibilities for Swazi education, welfare, and economic advancement. To implement the Act the British government created a special body – the Colonial Development Corporation, later in 1957 called the Commonwealth Development Corporation (CDC) – which would provide technical assistance and underwrite major large-scale economic enterprises.

Economics, married, with full Swazi ritual, a well-educated man, and bore him fourteen healthy children. She also worked as a matron at the Libby's Canning Factory in Malkerns, served as appointed member of the Mbabane Town Management Board, worked in a factory at Sidwashini in Mbabane, and is active in the women's national organization.

The Land Settlement Scheme, the main investment in African development, had been formally instituted in 1944, and land for three settlements was being surveyed and serviced. Final details for the Lifa Fund had been settled. Unfortunately, the Ten Year Plan had to be revised for financial reasons, and as a result of recommendations by V. Liversage, an agricultural economist commissioned to make a study of Swaziland, it was decided – against the wishes of both the Swazi and the local officials more directly concerned – 'to curtail considerably the Native Land Settlement Scheme as originally contemplated' (Annual Report for 1948:16).

A new Eight Year Plan placed greater emphasis on 'development as opposed to welfare' (Annual Report for 1949:5). Sobhuza then gave a lead in rural development, which became more than a postwar slogan. In Swazi areas as well as on Land Settlements grass stripping and consolidation of scattered plots were effectively introduced against erosion, and Sobhuza firmly established a Rural Development Board. He saw this as an opportune time to rouse the people to work for improvements and not simply accept the plans produced by experts.

One of the first major economic developments initiated by the government was a vast afforestation scheme, originally suggested by Sir Evelyn Baring. It would bring in much needed revenue and open employment for several hundred Swazi. But there would be major obstacles to overcome – options had to be obtained over land held in freehold, land exchanges would have to be negotiated, finances arranged, conflicting claims adjusted, and many Swazi families would have to be moved. Sir Evelyn got full support from Beetham. The idea was exciting and challenging but both men realized that unless they were able to convince Sobhuza that the scheme would be of the greatest ultimate benefit to the Swazi as a nation as well as the country as a whole, nothing could be done. In the end they succeeded; Sobhuza had still to convince his people.[2]

In Swazi customary law indigenous trees were free goods (like water and grass), open to all the people in the area. But over the years the country had been virtually denuded of its rich covering, the land was increasingly scarred by erosion, and the people were suffering from shortage of timber for building and firewood. As far back as 1909, Prince Malunge had suggested that trees be planted to mark the boundaries between Swazi and European areas, but the surveyors had rejected this in favour of beacons. Later, Sobhuza and his mother accepted an offer by the Agricultural Department to plant a grove of wattles at the outskirts of Lobamba. Some of his councillors feared this was yet another technique of acquiring control over Swazi owned land.

---

[2] At a meeting in 1973 Sobhuza requested that a report by Sir Evelyn Baring (now Lord Howick) on the development of the afforestation scheme be included in this biography. It is, however, too long to be published here; we trust that we have incorporated the essential points.

For any new scheme, Sobhuza's backing was crucial, and on one well-known occasion he was placed in a particularly difficult position. Land already acquired by the Native Land Settlement Department was required by Peak Timbers, Ltd., a company with a South African Board but controlled from London, prepared to invest in commercial afforestation. In exchange, it offered a large area elsewhere, better suited for mixed farming and settlement. Sobhuza was involved in discussions with government on one side, and the Swazi National Council on the other. He trusted Sir Evelyn and Mr Beetham, who 'had nothing to gain for themselves'. They assured him that his people would not suffer from the exchange, and that they would see that the company provided the workers with adequate pay and decent living conditions.

When the matter was brought to the Swazi National Council the debate was heated. The land had been bought for the Swazi, there were Swazi families already in occupation and others expecting to join them. The new entrepreneurs were not Swazi, nor even Government. Objections were strongly expressed. Sobhuza responded that he recognized the love a person had for his 'home', and the strength of neighbourhood and kinship ties, and the wish to live in a place he chose for himself. It was hard to compel a man to move without good reason but there were times when the good of the nation and of posterity ought to be given priority over self-interest. The sacrifice of those who would be uprooted would always be remembered.

In the end, according to the Government Annual Report, negotiations between the government and the company were 'successfully concluded ... and the Native Land Settlement Department surrendered to the Company 14,555 morgen of land for approximately 20,000 morgen elsewhere' (Annual Report for 1947:23). The company would give employment to some 750 Africans, and twenty Europeans, and accepted 'certain conditions for the welfare of employees' laid down by government (*ibid.*:8).

A second vast area of 100,000 acres – the Usutu Forest – was financed by the Colonial Development Corporation. Again complicated negotiations were involved, and again some Swazi families had to move; but acting on Sir Evelyn Baring's initiative the Corporation agreed to plant on behalf of the Swazi nation some 3,500 acres on land adjacent to Swazi area, and, once the Corporation had recovered the costs of planting, to credit all profits to the Swazi. For the first time the nation received, in addition to employment opportunities, a direct share in a major economic enterprise.

But the majority of uneducated Swazi still worked in the gold mines and coal mines of South Africa, which paid higher wages than almost all the local enterprises. The result was that an increase in demand for local unskilled labour was met in part by Africans from Mozambique (whom Lomawa once described as 'the thinnest men she had ever seen') and from Nyasaland (now Malawi). The largest single employer of African labour in Swaziland was the Havelock Mine, where many of the workers were non-Swazi.[3]

It had become an established practice for Sobhuza to have an official representative at the mines, with instructions to report grievances of Swazi workers to the managers, and to himself. Trade Unions provided for by British legislation in 1942 were not familiar or acceptable.[4] The Swazi system of expressing the workers' views had been introduced at the Havelock Mines; Prince Mhawu was his responsible nominee. He did his best for the men, but conditions were bad, and in 1948, when he was away for a short period, there was a strike – the first strike by African workers in Swaziland. It was quickly ended by the dismissal of its leaders, who were not Swazi. Sobhuza expressed his opposition to the strike as a technique of redress, but wanted to know if the complaints were legitimate.

With the approach of Independence the presence of 'foreign Africans' who retained their separateness from Swazi custom and did not offer allegiance to the Swazi rulers or receive land from them would become a major political issue, but during the immediate post-war period of 'new economic growth' encouraged by the colonial government this was not considered a serious problem. Although Sobhuza had frequently protested against non-Swazi Africans remaining in Swaziland without following the procedures of traditional Swazi citizenship, it is doubtful if even he realized the full political implications for the future.

The issue was raised in the Council in relation to the request by a farmer to import labourers. Leading councillors argued that foreigners as competitors in the labour market kept wages low, and brought in different (bad) customs and ideas. Sobhuza agreed, but his response was – What would the Council do? If applications to employ foreigners were refused, would the Council agree to force Swazi to do the work? The interests of European farmers as well as Swazi had to be considered and since the Council could not guarantee Swazi workers, it could not object to 'foreign natives' coming in. At the same time he argued that permission be given for foreign women to be with their husbands, and to leave when their husbands terminated their contracts (Meeting at Lobamba 4/10/46). Some officials agreed in principle but since the suggestion would obviously have been uneconomic for employers seeking cheap labour, it was not made part of the government labour policy.

[3] The rate of pay in 1948 for African unskilled labour was a little over 2/- per shift, plus free quarters, food and medical attention. For Europeans it ranged from £100 per month for medical officers and resident engineers to £30 per month for nursing and clerical staff. Foremen and storekeepers received £45-50 per month and daily paid employees received from 17/6 to 27/6 per 8-hour day according to qualifications. Overtime was paid at time and a half and free unfurnished quarters and medical benefits were provided (Swaziland Annual Report 1948:23).

[4] As early as 1938 Sobhuza had contemplated erecting 'The Swazi Labour Institute' to help people find employment, and help maintain good relations between the employer and his people, and generally 'to open up, provide work, develop and promote industrial activities' to meet the needs of the members.

In 1946 Sobhuza predicted that the Swazi would realize that it was not necessary for everyone to be a farmer sometime in the future and suggested more and better opportunities be given Swazi in the civil service, in commerce and in the professions. After the war a deliberate effort was indeed made to employ more Swazi, with preference being given to ex-soldiers, as clerks, police, cattle guards, artisans, agricultural demonstrators and health assistants. But the civil service was small; all top posts were automatically given to whites; some of the senior posts open to educated Africans were still held by Zulu or Xhosa. The appointment of Msindazwe Sukati, as Senior Liaison Officer, marked the first real breakthrough in terms of a prestigious post specifically for a Swazi. Other Swazi, who served in the offices of District Commissioners and District Officers sorting out cases and helping with judgments, were very poorly paid.

Lucrative trade was in the hands of whites. Those few Swazi who had obtained licences as general dealers were struggling, partly because of inexperience but partly because they lacked capital, and no matter how intelligent they were, they were not able to get credit from either banks or South African wholesalers with whom whites were able to establish connections. The situation was exemplified in the case of Sobhuza's 'blood brother', Ngolotjeni Motsa, who died in 1946. He had worked hard all his life, and had tried vegetable farming, shopkeeping and even running a small hotel; but when he died he left nothing but debts. The care of his widow (a daughter of Lomadokola) and the education of his children inevitably became the King's responsibility.

Less typical was the success story of Duma Dlamini, born in 1913, who, at the age of sixteen, started work underground in the gold mines, and by 1934 had saved sufficient to buy a hand-driven sewing machine and a second-hand car to use as a taxi. When the latter did not pay he sold the car and bought more sewing machines, building up a small tailoring business. With his profits he bought a few goods for sale and opened a small shop in Mankayane. By 1949 he had sufficient capital to take over a slightly larger shop at Ngwempisi. Asian storekeepers in Piet Retief in the Transvaal helped him with credit and for a short time Duma was their front-man, but gradually he was able to pay them back. In 1967 Duma Dlamini was one of the King's nominees to Swaziland's first Parliament to represent interests not adequately represented.

It was around this immediate post-war period that Sobhuza began to formulate in his own mind the policy which he would encourage when Swaziland finally became independent. But at that time there was little that he could do except offer encouragement and request greater participation in the more diversified economy of the country by individuals with special skills and interests. Specialization, particularly in medicines and crafts, was an accepted part of traditional life, but seldom on a full-time basis, and specialists did not form a class apart from ordinary workers.

One of the few post-war ventures opening to Africans in South Africa, and one which required relatively little capital, was the running of 'taxis'. Prince Dabede, on his return from the Army, approached Sobhuza and asked to be helped to go into the transport business: 'The King liked the idea.' However, the South African Railway (SAR) had a virtual monopoly of transport and the matter of granting licenses to Africans required negotiations at all levels. It was discussed by the King-in-Council at Lobamba, the Resident Commissioner was involved, and the managers of the SAR were then approached, Princes Dabede and Mhawu serving as Sobhuza's representatives. Finally, a schedule was worked out so that there would be no conflict between the SAR buses and the new Swazi entrepreneurs. Later Dabede introduced other taxi owners to the King, and there are now many Swazi taxis and buses, each owner with his own copyrighted fleet.

Such enterprises absorbed relatively few people; most educated Swazi worked in the Union where they had been trained and where employment opportunities were slightly more favourable. In the 1950s Sobhuza, however, was beginning to bring qualified people 'home'. There was also a deliberate effort on his part to promote a new organization, the Commercial Amadoda, designed to help Swazi in trade and protect those in Swazi areas from foreign competition.

In Beetham, Sobhuza felt he had a genuine friend and a strong advocate of Swazi interests, economic and political, who was prepared to admit mistakes of the past and to attempt to remedy them.[5] Beetham soon accepted that the Swazi were determined to maintain their own constitutional system of chieftainship at the same time that they were eager to take an active part in the development of the country. Sobhuza presented him with an African model of an integrated government under an inclusive kingship.

While Featherstone was in control Sobhuza had proposed that a small permanent committee be set up to facilitate negotiations between the 'central authority' and the nation. The idea had been welcomed, but got bogged down in bureaucratic detail. Beetham had pushed ahead and provided for an official Standing Committee, appointed by Sobhuza-in-Council:[6] any member of the Inner Council who happened to be at headquarters was fully entitled to participate in its deliberations.

[5] At a meeting with Sobhuza and his entire Council at Lobamba on 18 October 1948, Beetham stated that 'he had received from the Paramount Chief a list of undertakings which had been given to the Swazi Nation by Government and which had not been fully honoured by Government; he had asked that this list which had been mentioned at the General Council Meeting in July should be forwarded to him. He explained that he would do all that he could to remedy the position where he could but there were obviously some past actions which he could not undo' (Swaziland Archives, ST 128, no. 772/v).

[6] In 1947 the members of the Committee were: Princes Magongo and Mhawu, Ndvuna Mandanda Mtsetfwa, Chief Phuhlaphi Nsibandze, Alpheus Hlophe, Benjamin Simelane, Mgcobeya Nxumalo, John J. Nquku, Mfundza Sukati.

Beetham realized that it was essential to amend the Native Authorities Proclamation of 1944 before going ahead with establishing 'Native Courts' or a 'Native Treasury' – the other prerequisites of what the British considered essentials for an acceptable 'Native Administration'. Beetham and Sobhuza worked together towards a satisfactory reformulation of the authority to be accorded Swazi government. Both men appreciated the difficulties of the other side. Sobhuza, who had mastered the arts of negotiation as well as the strategy of delaying unacceptable decisions, would not be rushed. Beetham was eager to move more quickly but appreciated the necessity of Sobhuza's support, and knew that he could not give it without the sanction of his councillors. The ground for the final stages of the new Native Authorities Proclamation was well prepared; similar preparations were necessary before the Swazi would accept the Native Courts Act, or the Native Treasury.

Swazi suspicions and fears could not be allayed by vague promises. There were deep conflicts of procedures and assumptions underlying the two different legal systems. The appointment of court officials, their legal standing, the power of chiefs to enforce decisions, the recognition of Swazi courts, the definition of crime, the type of penalty that could be imposed – these and other matters were discussed at meetings of the Swazi Council with government officials.

Sobhuza was always involved, not as a silent observer but as the active leader and spokesman of his people. Yet it cannot be too often repeated that none of the decisions expressed by him was taken without long consultation with his main councillors. He argued that Swazi courts could be made still more efficient in dealing with cases of his people than could the courts presided over by District Officers administering 'western law'. Sir Walter Harragin, C.M.G., K.C., was brought in at one stage to help in the drafting. Sobhuza led the discussion. The clauses he and his Council found most difficult to accept involved the words 'incompatible', 'consultation' and 'concurrence'; he pointed out that these words had created many difficulties in the Union of South Africa, Nigeria and elsewhere.

The law in its original draft form had laid down that the Resident Commissioner would 'consult' the Native Authority in various matters. Therefore the Resident Commissioner might dismiss Native Court Officers after mere consultation with the Native Authority. The Council was dissatisfied with this formula as it did not imply that the Resident Commissioner would necessarily reach full agreement before taking action and felt that a law with such a provision would not in fact be giving the Nation control over its own Courts ... The next difficulty was that when the word 'concurrence' was inserted in the draft it was accompanied by a proviso. This proviso had been included because it was the view of Government that if the Resident Commissioner could not appoint a Court, where necessary without the concurrence of Council, it would be incompatible with the due exercise of His Majesty's jurisdiction. The Council did not understand how this was the case and he was very glad that the Judge had visited them to explain to them how it came about. The Council could understand how a native law or custom could be described as bad and therefore incompatible with the due exercise of His Majesty's jurisdiction but it could not understand how failure to agree for instance, to appointments or dismissals could be said to be incompatible (Swaziland Archives, Minutes of meeting, S.T. no. 128; no. 772/v, p. 795).

The dialogue continued, but in the end conditions more acceptable to the Swazi were agreed upon, together with 'essential controls' by the British Government. The Swazi accepted drastic limitations on the number of courts, and they agreed to the maintenance of written records, a more fixed procedure, and more control over Swazi legal officials who would receive pay.

Paying Swazi officials appointed for specific Swazi matters was linked by government with the establishment of a separate Swazi National Treasury, a matter broached cautiously by Beetham only in 1947. It was a sensitive issue, opening the festering sore of resentment against the British for arbitrarily discontinuing in 1905 payment of the Private Revenue Concession. The so-called Swazi National Fund (established by Proclamation in 1910) was under the control of the High Commissioner; its resources were limited mainly to two shillings deducted from the tax (of £1.15s to £4.10s according to the number of wives) paid by every Swazi male over eighteen years old. The remaining amount of 'Native Tax' was credited to General Revenue. Sobhuza received 'subsidies from Government funds' amounting to £1,400 per annum, and the Ndlovukazi £100 per annum; they were without the money necessary either to fulfil traditional obligations or to finance modern developments.

No one, least of all Swazi spokesmen, seriously believed the argument that the National Treasury would serve as a valuable training school in modern finance – such training could obviously be given more quickly and efficiently by more direct methods – but the terms agreed upon for the establishment of a National Treasury gave the Swazi a greater share in the national economy.

On every major issue Sobhuza adhered to the principle that the *liqoqo* (Inner Council) should arrive at a consensus before he could make a commitment. These issues had also to be put before the *libandla* (General Council) open to all, which met less frequently, and though it was highly unlikely that it would reverse the decisions of the Inner Council, anyone present could express his personal opinion. Sobhuza had the final say. He, as King, was 'The mouth that speaks no lies' – which means, in Swazi interpretation, that the King must speak the truth for the nation. It does not mean that the King dictates what the people should say; he is their 'mouthpiece', he could not speak lies.

Sobhuza said one day with an infectious chuckle, 'Of course I respect the English, they follow their own traditions. But that does not mean that I must follow them too. When we agree on one end we can still reach it by our different roads.' On a basis of mutual respect, though by very different roads, Sobhuza and Beetham had managed to reach agreement. The Proclamations which were promulgated on 22 December 1950 conformed more closely than any previous legislation to a Swazi model. The three-legged stool of indirect rule had been modified to their own posture.

Beetham had also won strong support from settlers by introducing a new note of optimism, envisaging 'development which might make Swaziland the envy of South Africa'. In 1949 the European Advisory Council had received statutory recognition, giving members the legal right to consultation (but not legislative authority) on all matters affecting their interests.

Discussions over the Proclamations were set in a much broader economic and political context than the arena of Lobamba or the courthouse of Mbabane. Sobhuza took into account events in the Union and the two other High Commission Territories, Basutoland and Bechuanaland.

In June 1948, the white electorate of the Union had voted into power the Afrikaner Nationalist Party. General Smuts had been defeated. Dr D.F. Malan was the new leader. 'Apartheid' was the new slogan for which the Swazi created their own word – *lubandlululu* – separation, isolation. What, they wondered, would this do to Africans?

Sobhuza maintained active personal contact with his people in the Union. Usually he stopped in Johannesburg but occasionally he visited chiefs across the border. In between his visits, delegates of the Swazi National Royal Club, which had become formally reconstituted as the Swazi National Royal Society, came to report to him and the Inner Council at Lozitha. They dealt with a wide range of subjects – employment opportunities, the clash of marriage customs, housing difficulties, education and sports – and he generally welcomed recommendations submitted to him. Sometimes he expressed his disappointment in the failure of his representatives to carry out duties with which they had been charged; sometimes he congratulated them on work well done. Inevitably their discussions focussed on the future of the Swazi.

Nor was it only Swazi he saw when in Johannesburg, and who came to pay their respects. The urban townships, though racially segregated, were frequented by workers from many parts of southern Africa. News travelled fast, and the Swazi were interested in events in neighbouring countries.

Dr Xuma, elected President of the African National Congress in 1940, had a home near Sobhuza's in Sophiatown and would come when he heard that Sobhuza was there, to pay his respects and inform him of the latest happenings. Dr Xuma had initially been optimistic about the possibility of Congress's efforts at breaking down discrimination, and had the support of even the more militant younger men. But by 1949, after a year of Nationalist Afrikaner rule, there was increased frustration, and disputes over leadership. In the

ANC elections, held in December 1949, Sobhuza's old friends had lost their lead. Dr Xuma was defeated by his former ally and colleague Dr James Moroka, the nominee of the Youth League.

Sobhuza did not take any part in these internal quarrels. His concern was on a different level. Dissension weakened the effect of those who claimed to speak for the Africans. How could a section that called itself the Youth League represent the interests of all the people? Yet he agreed with many of the things that these people were saying and knew them by name even though he had met few in person. They included dedicated and responsible young men and women – Anton Muziwakhe Lembede, who in 1943 was articled to Dr Seme, and who expressed with greater passion but less polish many of the ideas that had influenced Sobhuza as a young boy; Jordan Ngubane, a teacher and a journalist; Nelson Mandela, son of a Chief, studying law, who usually visited Sophiatown when the King was there. Some of the young men advocated more radical action – boycotts and strikes – than the deputations and compromises and petitions of Congress under Xuma, and their internal disputes weakened their organizations and their opposition to exploitation. 'Africans in the Union,' Sobhuza said, 'are not singing!'

In Basutoland, since the death of Chief Griffith in 1939 and then of his recognised successor Seeiso in 1941, there had been a pathological eruption of murders of innocent people whose bodies were mutilated for medicines. The guilty included leading men, and the situation could be linked with the legislation that had limited the number of chiefs recognised by government and given effective power.[7] The case of Chief Bereng, a son of Griffith, was particularly disturbing. Bereng considered himself the rightful heir and, after the death of his brother Seeiso, challenged in the courts the appointment of Seeiso's widow Mantsebo as Regent. He lost the case in 1949, was found guilty of complicity in a medicine murder and executed.

Sobhuza wondered: What is this terrible thing that is happening among the Basotho? These people have more children at school than we have (Bereng, too, had attended school and was a nominal Catholic), they have been under the British administration for a longer time, higher officials have drawn unfavourable comparisons between our reluctance to accept the Native Authorities Act and the willing cooperation of the Basotho in innovation. Sobhuza knew that the guilty were not irrational men, nor were they fundamentally evil. Yet they were capable of destroying the most important of all creations – the human being – for their own ambitious purposes. When such murders were committed in Swaziland Sobhuza emphasized that they were 'a terrible foreign custom'.

In a letter to Sobhuza, Dr Seme, who had acted for Bereng, wrote that his argument had been directed to 'the purpose of awakening the

[7] See Report by G.I. Jones (Cmd. 8209, HMSO, 1951).

public conscience of all the Basotho people to realise that ritual murders must stop' (Swaziland Archives, 1949). Such acts were in a totally different category from the action of the good Chief Fakisandla whose aim was to exterminate evildoers. And it was also different from wars in which brave men were killed and mutilated for a noble cause even though the leaders were sometimes cynical men lusting for power or misled by false dogmas or beliefs.

In Bechuanaland there was conflict over chieftainship at quite another level. In October 1948 Seretse Khama, Chief Designate of the Bamangwato and nephew of Tshekedi, married an English girl, Ruth Williams.[8] Initially the Regent Tshekedi and the Council of his people had opposed the marriage, but by 1949 the majority of the chiefs and people supported Seretse and recognized his wife: Tshekedi went into self-imposed exile. Sobhuza respected Tshekedi and knew well that he was not anti-white and that his attitude was not based on racial prejudice but expressed his concern that in a matter of major importance young Seretse had acted without consulting his own advisors. Tshekedi also feared that the South African government would do its utmost to use the situation to further its claims for incorporation.

The British appointed a commission under Sir Walter Harragin, the same learned judge who had explained to Sobhuza and his *libandla* the subtleties of the English terms – consultation, concurrence, incompatibility. The commission ended without announcing any decision, but early in the new year Seretse was flown to London at the request of the Secretary of State for Commonwealth Relations. He left Ruth behind in Serowe. The next thing that Sobhuza heard was that there had been a reconciliation between Tshekedi and Seretse, but the British had ordered that Seretse and his wife live outside Bechuanaland and Tshekedi was banished to an area outside of the Bamangwato reserve while the chieftainship was 'in suspension'.

A new thread was being woven into the complex traditional pattern of Sobhuza's own life, and the marriage of Seretse and Ruth may have had for him a particular significance. He had met a very beautiful girl – Pauline Fikelephi Masuku. He saw her singing in a choir of senior girls, the graduates of Matsapha. Tall, graceful, honey coloured, radiantly lovely. His daughter Pholile was in the same class. He told Pholile to bring her friend to him. She came reluctantly and afraid. He spoke to her and found her as intelligent as she was beautiful. She responded to his kindness, his unaggressive charm; she told him of her family, and her own ambitions. She was the daughter of Elias Masuku, subject of Chief Luvuno Dlamini of the Kupheleni area. She was keen on studying and was going to be a hospital nurse. Sobhuza did not touch her. She came again. He sent letters by Pholile. He was not behaving as a King; he was wooing her as an ordinary suitor. She

---

[8] This dramatic story is well recounted in *Tshekedi Khama*, Mary Benson (Faber: 1960).

was deeply attracted, but also disturbed. Her parents were devout members of the evangelical South Africa General Mission (SAGM) Church that condemned as 'heathen' traditional customs Sobhuza upheld. She had not taken part in the *umcwasho*, polygamy was a cardinal sin. She did not easily tolerate the thought of being one of many wives, even though all were queens; and she had worked hard at her studies. So, with her parents' connivance, she disappeared. But she had fallen in love with him, and for all her show of resistance was glad that he sought her out and sent messages and letters to follow her where she hid herself, first in Durban, then in Johannesburg.

In the meantime Sobhuza carried on with his many duties. The opinion he had expressed in 1936 when first informed that King Edward had abdicated on account of his love for Mrs Simpson remained unchanged – 'A King's duty is to all the people. A King should not put his love for a woman above his love for the country.' Sobhuza, as King of the Swazi, would never abandon the Queens he had already taken or foreswear the taking of future wives.

One day, as he was driving from Lobamba to Lozitha, a beautiful buck appeared and ran along the road at the side of his car. Buck had become rare in this part of the country, and its behaviour was unusual. What might it mean? So he stopped at the village of Guvela Mkhabela, a famous doctor. Mkhabela read the sign – a girl he had desired would return to his side. In 1949 Mfundza Sukati, who was also related to the Masukus, brought Fikelephi home.

On Sobhuza's instructions Mfundza left Fikelephi at the royal village of Nkhaba in the charge of Prince Mnisi, who publicly accepted her on behalf of the royal family as one of Sobhuza's queens.[9] There Sobhuza visited her, and after a few weeks she was brought to Lobamba. Nukwase received her and put her into the house of laMatsebula. The initial period with in-laws and co-wives is known to be hard for any newlywed. For a girl brought up in a strict Protestant mission atmosphere it was undoubtedly an ordeal, and though many of the queens, more especially laMatsebula, were patient and understanding, instructing her in the ways of tradition, a few showed their jealousy in barbed taunts and spiteful tricks. Sobhuza appreciated her difficulties and decided to move her temporarily to a place of her own.

The nation had bought with Lifa funds a fine estate rich in grass and timber and wild game, with a large farmhouse built by the original concessionaire, David Forbes, a robust character, known to the Swazi as *Mahleka* (Laughing Man). Sobhuza had always liked the place and after Mahleka's death his widow agreed to sell it back on

[9] Mnisi, grandson of Malunge, brother to Subhuza I, was recognized by Sobhuza II as progressive and responsible. His village, in which I had stayed in the summer of 1935, attracted people from a wide area. He himself was never idle; his court cases dealt with, he would go to work in the fields or inspect his herds; and he had the reputation of being strict but just in all his dealings.

13. Royal children in traditional ritual dress. December 1935

14. Sobhuza with the British Royal family at Nhlangano in 1947

15. King Sobhuza in London for the Coronation of Queen Elizabeth II, 1953. From left to right: Paramount Chief Designate, King Moshoeshoe II of Lesotho (then Basutoland); Professor M.O.M. Seboni, attendant to Paramount Chief Kgari Sechele of the Bakwena of Botswana (Bechuanaland); Paramount Chief Kgari Sechele; Chief Griffiths, uncle of King Moshoeshoe II; Princess Gcinaphi, daughter of King Sobhuza; Chief Majara, grand-uncle of King Moshoeshoe II, whose daughter was subsequently married to King Moshoeshoe; Mr Mackenzie, guide to the group; Prince Magongo, Chairman of the Swazi National Council and senior Prince in Swaziland; Queen Lomakholwa; King Sobhuza II; and Msindazwe Sukati, A.D.C. to King Sobhuza.

16. Harold Macmillan, British Prime Minister, with Sobhuza and Brian Marwick (Resident Commissioner) – Swazi warriors in the background – visiting Swaziland at the time of his historic 'Wind of Change' speech in South Africa. 30 January 1960

relatively fair terms. It became Sobhuza's first western-style residence in Swaziland and he called it *Ehlane* (At the wilderness, the Bush). He had it furnished with beds and chairs and tables and drapes, bought in Piet Retief and brought across the border by lorries. LaMasuku, who was consulted about the details, was established in the house with a co-wife, the charming warmhearted Funani Hlophe, who helped laMasuku acquire the skills of traditional Swazi women, and had her little son Mahlaba with her. The year was 1950. LaMasuku was twenty-two years old. The two Queens lived there with a few attendants until 1953 when the King bought a larger house, his second western residence, Masundvwini (the Place of Palms).

The King came to Ehlane in the wintertime during the hunting season, when the aloes were in flower and the bougainvillea covered the veranda in brilliant crimson. He would bring with him some of his other Queens, and laMasuku was accustoming herself to co-wives. Industrious, artistic, an imaginative craftswoman, she kept herself busy in his absence crocheting, sewing, embroidering, doing beautiful beadwork, and cultivating a vegetable garden. In summer visitors were few and the heat intense; and sometimes the King would send his car to fetch her and her companion to Lobamba or Lozitha. When laMasuku bore her first child, Sobhuza named him Phikanebenkhosi (complete with royalty).

Beetham, having accomplished much in Swaziland, was transferred in November 1950 to the position of Resident Commissioner of Bechuanaland to be confronted with the unresolved crisis of Seretse and Tshekedi. Sobhuza said goodbye to him with genuine regret. They exchanged gifts on parting. A beautiful silver bowl, suitably inscribed, that Beetham gave Sobhuza, is used when guests come to Masundvwini. Appreciating the difficulties Beetham would experience in Bechuanaland, Sobhuza said he could call on him in need. Beetham, who availed himself of this offer, told me Sobhuza's advice was excellent, but that unfortunately he, Beetham, also had the colonial office to deal with!

CHAPTER XII
The Quiet Years

The British considered that they had at last introduced machinery essential for efficient and enlightened administration; they did not question their right or, on the whole, their ability, to control its direction. Though Indirect Rule was originally formulated to develop African political institutions, in countries with white settler populations such as Swaziland, or Kenya, parallelism or dualism seemed the wisest course to the British with strict vigilance at all intersections. If the possibility of independence had been suggested it would have been dismissed as absurd; it is unlikely that the Swazi themselves envisaged that within Sobhuza's lifetime he would rule not only their own affairs but those of the settlers, and with their support.

Beetham's successor, David Loftus Morgan, an Englishman with a Cambridge education, was friendly, active, sensitive, and eager to please. The Swazi named him Mazithulele, derived from the verb *kuthula* – to be quiet, at peace. He had served 25 years in Kenya; he respected the knowledge of men with local experience and was prepared to delegate authority to them. His right-hand man, the Secretary for Swazi Nation Affairs, was Dan Fitzpatrick, nicknamed by the Swazi, Malamba (The Lean One), born and educated in Swaziland, fluent in siSwati, and in the service since 1928.

The transfer of senior expatriate officials, particularly Resident Commissioners and Government Secretaries, from one colony to another contrasted with the traditional Swazi system of permanent and often hereditary appointment to high office. Sobhuza and his Council found it hard to understand the rationale for frequent moving of senior officials in the civil service.[1]

There was the feeling that the British tended to treat all colonies, more especially the three High Commission Territories, as identical without appreciating that each had a different history and its own

[1] Brian Marwick had been transferred to Basutoland (in 1949) when an equivalent position, which had fallen vacant in Swaziland, was given to J. Stebbing, who had been transferred from Bechuanaland. When Beetham had been on overseas leave from May to July, 1950, G.J. Armstrong, C.B.E., Finance Secretary in Basutoland, had been seconded to serve as Acting Resident Commissioner for Swaziland. The Deputy Resident Commissioner and Government Secretary of Swaziland, W.F. MacKenzie, O.B.E., had been seconded for special duty to Bechuanaland in April. He returned to Swaziland in November when Beetham was transferred as Resident Commissioner to Bechuanaland.

problems.[2] Men conversant with one territory were not necessarily able to deal with situations in others: when Sobhuza sought information about what was happening elsewhere it was not necessarily to imitate or replicate but to learn and select.

Sobhuza and his Council continued to recruit by their own criteria personnel required to run the adjusted model of 'Indirect Rule'. Committees for specialized tasks were no innovation; the essential battle had been to maintain the historical hierarchy of authority, and in this they had succeeded. The fluidity and at the same time the extensiveness of the Swazi monarchical system was summed up in a statement by old Prince Mshoshi, 'a son' of Mswati, still alive in 1973: 'Kingship is the blood in the body of the nation; it runs in all the parts. The body is one but the blood runs throughout.' The Members selected for the Standing Committee of the National Council, presidents and scribes in the Swazi courts, treasurer and secretary-clerk of the Swazi National Treasury were chosen in the same way as officials had been in the traditional system. They were nominated by Sobhuza, in consultation with members of his Council: the pool from which he drew was historically defined by clanship and service, but within these limits individuals qualified on their own merits.

For the new posts natural intelligence and loyalty were not enough – there were many in the Council with those essential basic qualifications; it was more difficult to find men with the requisite administrative and technical knowledge. Facilities for education, practical or academic, in Swaziland were still sadly limited;[3] but every year a few Swazi were sent on government scholarships, for both higher and specialized education, to the Union. However, in 1950 the High Commissioner was informed that no students from the High Commission Territories would be allowed into educational institutions in the Union after 1957; those already attending would be permitted to complete their courses. For this reason some of the secondary schools were upgraded to high school status. In 1951 Matsapha and the Mahamba Methodist School (in the south) became full secondary schools opening the opportunity for Swazi to matriculate in their own country. A Trade School, giving training in such practical fields as building and mechanics, had been started in

[2] In November 1950 the Secretary of State, the Hon. Patrick Gordon-Walker, visited Swaziland as part of a tour of the three High Commission Territories. This was the first visit of a Secretary of State since Lord Amery's visit in 1927. Gordon-Walker congratulated the Swazi on having reached a successful conclusion in the lengthy negotiations over the Proclamations, which brought the Swazi into line with other British territories in Africa. In Bechuanaland, which he also visited, Seretse was in exile in London and Tshekedi out of favour with the government and told not to attend the meeting addressed by Gordon-Walker, who was welcomed by a government-appointed representative (for details see Benson, 1960, pp. 211-14).
[3] For European children education up to the age of 16 (or successful completion of Standard VIII – Junior Certificate) was free and compulsory; for African children it was neither. Enrolment figures for the period 1949-52 show a slight increase but by 1952 still represented less than 20% of the school-age African population (though 100% of the corresponding European population) (figures derived from Swaziland Annual Reports, 1949, 1950, 1952)

1947; and at the end of 1950 the first apprentices were ready for employment. In urging practical training Sobhuza had asked rhetorically, 'Is working with your hands less important than with your eyes and mouth only?' And he answered himself, 'It depends on the needs of the country.' He urged however that students should not be mere 'tool-boys', but fully qualified builders and mechanics.

The core of the first Standing Committee was recruited from men whose families had contributed toward the building of a unified Swazi nation but who were forceful personalities in their own right, critical and independent in their thought, respectful of tradition and forward looking. Sobhuza also selected a number of members purely on the basis of personal ability and without reference to clan affiliation. Over the years additional men were recruited to the committee but the qualifications remained the same.

As President of the Higher Court of Appeal (1950) Sobhuza selected Prince Mhawu, who was well versed in Swazi law and custom and generally respected by the workers for his sense of justice. The presidents for lower courts were mainly elderly men, some of whom had been sent to schools as youths by Labotsibeni. There was no qualified accountant, or well-trained bookkeeper, to serve as Treasurer for the Swazi National Treasury. The first to be appointed was Joshua Lukhele, an able clerk retired from the administration.

A full-time, officially recognized and paid 'Secretary for the Swazi National Council' was required to deal with increasing correspondence at the office at Lobamba, and Sobhuza eventually selected a young man, Polycarp Mafeletiveni Dlamini. From the time of Mbandzeni educated Africans had served as scribes and translators,[4] but recognition of a secretary by the colonial government was new and conferred high formal status and responsibilities. Like Msindazwe Sukati, whose position and career ran rather parallel, Polycarp had the qualifications of family credentials and school certificates, but again the final consideration was his strength of character and sense of purpose.[5] Sometimes Sobhuza addressed him as Polycarp, but when he really wanted to honour him he addressed him by the name of his famous hero-ancestor, the great warrior Ndlaludzaka. Polycarp's own Swazi name, Mafeletiveni – he-who-would-die-in-a-foreign-place – refers to the fact that he was born after his father Cishakubamude (Nearly Tall) had been badly maimed in a

[4] For example, Labotsibeni had employed Alpheus Hlophe and Josiah and Nehemiah Vilakati; Sobhuza had employed Makweleni Raymond Vilakati as his private secretary at Lozitha.

[5] Born in 1918 to Cishakubamude, son of Ndlaludzaka, Polycarp had a good record at the Matsapha National School, and from there had gone (in 1942) to work in South Africa, first as a clerk-interpreter in Barberton and then as a mail-order clerk in Durban, during which time he studied privately and matriculated by correspondence. In 1952 he was employed during the day as a social welfare and probation officer paid by the South African government; in the evenings he attended classes at the University of Natal. Solid, hardworking, with a keen sense of family and national duty, he 'could not refuse' to return home, though in the middle of his B.A. Social Studies course, when the King called him.

mine disaster in which many of his fellow workers were killed. The English teacher at Matsapha found Mafeletiveni unpronounceable and christened him Polycarp, which his kin accepted as 'nice sounding'.

Msindazwe Sukati and Polycarp Dlamini were the two Swazi officials most in the public eye at that period. They were the most western educated and their English was perfect. But there were others, also educated and with new positions in government, who had equal access to the King. The nucleus was the cadre of Rural Development Officers (originally titled Land Utilization Officers) who had been appointed in 1949 to implement plans at the grass root levels. They would work in close cooperation with Swazi as well as with the appropriate government technicians, and report personally to the King.[6] Could one have predicted that in twenty years' time most of these men would hold important political positions and that one of the Rural Development Officers, Prince Makhosini Dlamini, would be the first Prime Minister of the Independent Kingdom of Swaziland?

Makhosini, son of Prince Majozi, was educated at the Franson Christian Memorial School at Mhlosheni and the National School at Matsapha, and trained as a teacher (1938-40) in Natal. He taught in schools in Swaziland, but resigned in 1947 – on a matter of principle against prejudice – from the headmastership of the Swazi National School at Lobamba. He then turned his knowledge and energies to farming his father's fields at Nkhungwini in the Hlatikulu area, and to serving on the Swazi National Council. When Majozi died (in 1950) Makhosini was appointed Chief, but still continued to fulfil various national obligations including that of Rural Development Officer. It was a hard time; he recalled with a bitter smile, that when he requested transport from the government to move between Hlatlikulu and Lobamba, not only was it refused but he was told by a supervisor that he 'was incapable of driving a car'. But Sobhuza appreciated him and trusted his judgment, and the experience he gained in the civil service has stood him in good stead. His first diplomatic visit was in

---

[6] They included Prince Makhosini, Mfundza Sukati, Prince Mkhatjwa (a son of Sobhuza by laFakudze senior), B.B. Shongwe (son of Mbhuduya, late governor of the burial village of Sobhuza's father), Humphrey Dladla, George Mabuza, Joseph Mkhwanazi, Madibhi Dlamini (son of Prince Mnisi), and Esau Magumede Dlamini (Swaziland Archives, ST 150/49, no. 772/v, p. 856).

[7] Among them were Lutfo of Siphocosini, son of Jabhane, a senior son of Mbandzeni, wise, quiet, very thoughtful and always worth listening to; Jaha, son of Mancibane of Lundzi, who had gone with the King overseas and was still alive; Mnisi of Nkhaba; Chief Gija of Mkhuzweni, who had been sent to see land settlement experiments in Griqualand East and had returned convinced that communal development not individual ownership was best for his own people; Sifuba of Velezizweni, heir of Dalada, whose great grandfather, Ndwandwa, had been, for a brief time, Senior Prince for the young King Ludvonga; Sozisa of Ngunundwini, heir of Logcogco – brother of Mbandzeni and, for a brief period, Senior Prince for Bhunu; Magongo of Nhlantleni, heir of Malunge, Senior Prince in Sobhuza's minority; Makhosikhosi of Mbelebeleni, one of Sobhuza's surviving brothers.

1952 as spokesman for a ten-man deputation to Basutoland to observe techniques of soil conservation and study the working of the Basuto courts and treasury; the following year he was in charge of the Swazi party to the Rhodes Centenary Exhibition in Bulawayo, Rhodesia.

These 'new men' did not oust the chiefs or other members of the royal coterie; on the contrary, the fact that some were princes and others were chiefs reinforced the foundations of the traditional system. Princes also maintained their positions according to seniority in the royal genealogy. Some of them were relatively young in years, others, older in years, were lower in rank.[7] The influence of the highest princes, the Malangeni, the Children of the Sun, was strong. But Sobhuza did not belong to them alone, he and his mother were symbols of the nation as a totality, a nation greater than the Dlamini or any separate clan or family.

Of 171 'chiefs' in a list supplied by Sobhuza-in-Council to the central administration for purposes of tax collecting, more than half were of non-Dlamini clans. Their appointment had been either recognized or made by Sobhuza.[8] Non-Dlamini, whether identified with their own ancient local areas or not, were not expected to put forward their clan viewpoint but to represent the interests of all their followers. The same of course applied to princes and to governors of the royal villages. Mandanda Mtsetfwa as governor of the old capital of Zombodze continued to be recognized as main Governor of the Nation (*Ndvunankhulu*), entitled to the honour of performing the opening song of the *Ncwala* each year at Lobamba.

While most of the intermediaries between the Swazi Authority and the Central (Colonial) Administration were picked by Sobhuza because of their knowledge of the western idiom, some of those appointed to posts in the traditional structure included in their qualifications knowledge derived from western experience. Thus at the head of the traditional regiments Sobhuza appointed Logwazela Bhembe, who, after a very traditional education in the barracks of royal villages, had served with distinction in the Second World War.[9]

[8] See Hilda Kuper, *The Swazi*. Ethnographic Survey. International African Institute. London, 1952, pp. 59-81.

[9] His qualities had been noticed by his predecessor, Lugodvolwendlovu Gamedze, who had pointed out the tall lean young man to the King. The Bhembe had a long history of loyal service. A clansman, Somntsewu Bhembe, was a chief in charge of one of the King's cattle posts in the south. His son Vusumuzi had married Princess Mzamose, daughter of King Mbandzeni. Somntsewu had been selected by Sobhuza to take the marriage cattle of his mother, the Ndlovukazi Lomawa, to her guardian at Zikotheni. These cattle had been contributed by the chiefs and headmen of the whole nation, thereby demonstrating Sobhuza's position as Child of the Nation. In 1976 Vusumuzi was appointed governor of Lobamba.

In the same category was Maboya, kinsman of Ndabezimbi and son of Makhambane, the Fakudze selected by the Council to put their crosses on the documents presented by Sobhuza in his fight before the Privy Council for the land of the nation. In 1950 both Ndabezimbi and Makhambane were dead; and Ndala, a brother of Ndabezimi, was acting for Ndabezimbi's heir Mathendeka, who was installed in 1955; Makhambane's heir, Gebuza, died soon after being installed and his brother Malangatonkhe, another son of Makhambane, was acting as guardian for Gebuza's heir, Lusentfo; then Malangatonkhe died and Maboya, as son of Makhambane, took over the guardianship of Lusentfo.

There were many elders who spent months at Lozitha or Lobamba. They did not constitute a fixed civil service, nor could they be described as bureaucrats; unpaid (though periodically rewarded), they were a circle of advisors whom the rulers selected because of personal character or intelligence. Virtually every clan that constituted the complex nation of Ngwane had members visiting the court; and each individual was personally known to Sobhuza and each had his own fascinating story of service.

Fairly soon after the Proclamations had been accepted it had become evident that the existing hierarchy of authority needed reorganization and reinforcement at the local level. District Commissioners, all of whom were still white, were effective enough as 'chiefs of office' administering areas defined by government, but with changing circumstances the traditional Swazi system had become less effective. There was a need to develop a Swazi system of regional government.

In 1953, after much discussion with senior government officials and with his own Council, Sobhuza came forward with a suggestion to decentralize Swazi administration through the formation of *tinkhundla*. *Tinkhundla* (regional committees), he explained in a memorandum of 1955, were royal villages which according to Swazi law and custom a Swazi King could establish wherever and whenever he wished, and to which chiefs were attached as *emakhanza* (local contingents). The word *inkhundla* refers to the space outside the cattle byre where men gather to talk cases and local affairs. These royal villages would be strategically sited to serve administrative purposes and as mobilization centres for 'exploiting the natural resources of the area to the full, in the way of agriculture and animal husbandry', and so be involved in national development of schools, afforestation, and other developments suitable for the environment.

Each *inkhundla* would have its own cadre of officials, again combining traditional with modern qualities, at the head of which would be an *indvuna*, appointed by the King-in-Council, who would act as 'chairman' at meetings. Assisting him would be executives titled 'the Brains' (*bucopho*) constituted by the chiefs, ex officio, and members nominated by them, responsible for maintaining liaison with the corresponding government departments. The *tindvuna* would be ex-servicemen who had held the rank of senior non-commissioned officers; Sobhuza believed that their army training and experience together with their initial qualifications would make them the most suitable candidates.

Appointment to a national position was no sinecure. High office carried heavy risks, and this was impressed on each new incumbent. So when J.S. Mkhulunyelwa Matsebula[10] was appointed Senior Liaison Officer the King said:

[10] Making the announcement public at Masundwini, Msindazwe Sukati said:
'Bayethe! Silosikhulu, here is Mkhulunyelwa Matsebula, son of Langa Matsebula of

According to western custom you would be congratulated but in siSwati we sympathize with a person and feel sorry for him when he is given such a great task which is between the grinder and the grinding stone. He will be criticized and insulted by Africans on this side and by Europeans on the other (Meeting with King's Liaison Officer and Council at Emasundwini. Lobamba Archives, File 453, 9/9/59).

Sobhuza saw a great difference between the position of a traditional Swazi official and an official in the western bureaucracy:

There is nothing so hard to get rid of as a redundant public servant who always sticks closer than a brother. Also it is the usual experience that a department originally too big has an exceptional temptation, if not closely employed with really useful business, pompously and industriously to engage in the task of spinning cocoons of regulations and ritual around itself (Comments by the Ngwenyama on the Report of the Mineral Development Commission, 1954).

In 1953 there was a happy interlude; Sobhuza went to England for the second time. This visit was quite different from his mission in 1922. Then he had been a young man seeking clarification of his own position and petitioning against wrongs inflicted on his people. This time he was going as a royal guest to the Coronation of young Queen Elizabeth II. He had outlived her father and her grandfather; and he remembered her vividly as a young unmarried girl to whom he had spoken briefly when she came to Goedgegun (now Nhlangano) with her parents and sister. Now there were no problems of passport and transport. The Resident Commissioner and his wife did all they could to assist, and they gave Sobhuza a farewell dinner at the Ezulwini Hotel.

Sobhuza had been invited to England in 1951 to attend the Festival of Britain, but had politely declined – 'There was much to do at home. The time was not right.' Msindazwe Sukati had been sent in his stead. The Coronation of Elizabeth, however, required his presence in person. During his absence, the Ndlovukazi would be assisted by Prince Lutfo of Siphocosini.

The Council agreed that Sobhuza be accompanied by a party of five: three men, Prince Magongo, in his capacity as Guardian Prince; Msindazwe Sukati as *indvuna* and aide de camp; Mgwangele Dlamini of the house of Ndlaludzaka, as special retainer; and two women, one Queen, Lomakholwa,[11] and one Princess, Gcinaphi. Travelling with them as far as Cape Town were Princess Mnengwase, Sobhuza's

eMaphalaleni ... He studied at Matsapha where he became the *indvuna* of *libutfo* (head of the regiment) after Mfundza left. He qualified as a teacher, and by correspondence obtained his matric and finally a B.A. degree. He has taught for 18 years and ended up as the principal of Mjindini secondary school from where the King recalled him' (Lobamba Archives, File 453, 9/9/59).

[11] Lomakholwa was a daughter of Chief Gija Mgunundvu of Mkhuzweni. Gija's sister Lomacala had borne Sobhuza his first son, Senzangakhona. Several of her sisters had subsequently joined her as recognized Queens; Lomakholwa was the latest. Princess Gcinaphi, a schoolgirl of sixteen, intelligent, charming and fluent in English, was the daughter of Queen Ncineleni Mngometulu, the daughter of Chief Mbikiza of Ngwavuma.

sister, Queen laMasuku, Prince Mancibane and Reubin Mchoza Sibandze (Liaison Officer).

It was a happy party that left by car for Johannesburg. There they would catch the boat train to Cape Town after having tea with the new High Commissioner, Sir John leRougetel, in Pretoria. Sobhuza was in excellent mood, there was none of the anxiety of preparing himself with knowledge of history, and his companions were there to share his pleasure. A few anxious moments beset them. They were held up by traffic and nearly missed their train. Urged by Sukati to run, Sobhuza replied calmly that 'when the King runs, the earth runs' (i.e., the country gets out of control). Their luggage had not arrived, but Purcell, of the Swaziland Government, who was with them, managed to have the stationmaster keep the train waiting, for which courtesy Sobhuza sent a special personal message of thanks to the South African Railways (Swaziland Archives, 14 May 1953). In Cape Town they spent a day with another of Lomadokola's sons, who was working there and who arranged a reception for them.

Sobhuza and his retinue were not the only Africans from the south invited to the Coronation. Among his fellow passengers were Chiefs Kgari and Bathoen of Bechuanaland, and Bereng Seeiso, fifteen year old Paramount Designate of Basutoland with two senior chiefs, Majara and Griffith. A large crowd of followers from the different High Commission Territories, as well as from the Union, came to the docks to see them off. There was great shouting and praising and performance, and the band played as the Winchester Castle steamed regally out of the harbour.

In a letter to the Resident Commissioner dated May 14th from the boat, Sobhuza wrote:

We have had a beautiful sailing since we started out from Cape Town on the 1st May. We crossed the equator a little after midnight on Wednesday the 6th and then the sea, which up to that point had been somewhat rough, was beautifully calm. The following morning we had the pleasure of seeing my daughter Gcinaphi and Sukati going through Neptune's initiation ceremony before they were presented with the certificates of the King of the Deep. After so many days of voyage we were all very happy on the morning of the 9th to see Africa again as we passed Dakar and then landed for a short time at a Spanish island, Las Palmas, early in the morning on the 11th. Then we saw Spain as we passed and the French coast at noon today. The voyage has been so enjoyable that we think we shall now object to return to Swaziland.

Sobhuza and Chief Kgari had a great deal to talk about and shared many interests. Chief Kgari was widely travelled, having served in the Second World War as Regimental Sergeant-Major, the same position that Mfundza had held in the Swazi regiments, and the highest given an African in the South. In Bechuanaland his section, the Bakwena, were traditionally senior even to the Bamangwato, and when Tshekedi had gone into self-imposed exile it was Chief Kgari who had invited him to live in his area. In the negotiations towards a peaceful settlement of the painful dispute between Tshekedi and Seretse, Kgari had played a most constructive role. Kgari agreed on the substance of a long letter that Sobhuza had written to the Resident Commissioner of Swaziland in 1952, in which he had pointed out that if the Administration made its own nomination of a chief, any man who accepted it would 'be regarded in the African mind as a traitor or Government chief. Even if Tshekedi himself were asked or nominated as a candidate by the tribe as a whole I doubt if he would accept such nomination unless he was asked or nominated by Seretse himself' (Swaziland Archives, 27/3/52).

The boat trip was also the beginning of a personal friendship between Sobhuza and the royal house of Moshoeshoe, and Gcinaphi and Bereng were much the same age. Sobhuza enjoyed talking to the Basotho about their customs and history (some of the first clans in his country were of Sotho origin), and at the same time he acquainted himself with recent political events.

Sobhuza was relaxed, enjoying the company and the beauty of the trip. Msindazwe described him as being 'very popular', and whenever he appeared people would want to talk to him. But, he added, 'he was clearly a King whom everyone also respected, and when there was too much noise he would remove himself, politely of course, and all of us followed his example.' He had come prepared with his own home food and drink since, as he said, this time he was 'not going to take any chances'. He brought with him two casks of beer and the necessary ingredients to make more, and an adequate supply of mealie meal for both the voyage and later at the hotel.

They were met at Southampton by John Stebbing, Government Secretary, and Dan Fitzpatrick, also of the Swaziland Administration, who took them to the Selston Park Hotel in Sanderstead, Surrey. In a personal letter to A.G. Marwick, Sobhuza wrote, 'Having got here in the winter months during my last visit to the U.K. it never occurred to me that the grass could be so soft and green as I see it now' (Swaziland Archives, 5/6/53).

London itself was dazzling with lights and decorations. A great crowd from all parts of the globe, representatives of all the countries of the Commonwealth, had gathered to rejoice and to honour the new Queen of England. As Sobhuza recounted his recollections of the uniforms, the pageantry, the music, the colours, the lights, he kept on saying 'Most wonderful!' He attended all the great occasions, the invitations to which carried instructions on correct dress. Some of the people came proudly in traditional costume, and though Sobhuza was not as yet sufficiently emancipated to appear in the costume of his people, and was not prepared to expose his Queen to possibly embarrassing comments, he encouraged Gcinaphi to wear the bright cloths and beads and feathers of home. One amusing incident occurred when – as the voluble Msindazwe tells it – Sobhuza, who sometimes enjoyed going around unrecognized and inconspicuous, visited a West End tailor. The salesman, mistaking the aide for the master, urged persuasively, 'Come on, Your Majesty, tell your secretary to buy this for you.' Before Msindazwe could explain, Sobhuza interposed in siSwati, 'Don't you dare tell him I am the King.'

At the royal garden party at Buckingham Palace, Sobhuza was described in London newspapers as 'bearded and elegant in morning dress, top hat, wing collar and bow tie'. He was also described as a 'fine figure of a man, with lively shrewd eyes, a stub of black beard and finely shaped hands, a likeable fellow with a robust sense of humour and acknowledged as a skilled administrator'. Queen Lomakholwa wore a well-tailored suit, a trim hat, gloves and bag, and matching shoes. Gcinaphi 'walked barefooted with yellow bead bracelets bobbing on her ankles and a headdress of radiant feathers, and round her a gaily striped blanket of yellow, scarlet and black' (London *Daily Mail* 29/5/53).

At the hotel Sobhuza had his dishes prepared from his own supplies and ate apart from the rest, stating simply: 'The head of our people must never drink pure water. The customs of different countries are not the same and we must respect our own as well as those of others. We can't throw off customs simply because they are hard to follow but only if they are harmful.' He was in fact faced with a major dilemma at the Coronation itself. It took place in Westminster Abbey amidst a scene of unforgettable splendour. Suddenly he realized that he, the King of the Swazi, was on a grave and surrounded by graves. There was nothing he could do but remain seated with dignity and composure. As a child he had walked unwittingly on such a polluting site and his survival at that vulnerable age is recorded in one of his praises. Since then he had overcome many misfortunes and dangers, but he admitted he was relieved that the superb and solemn thanksgiving service was held in St. Paul's Cathedral! The Swazi had not been provided with a chariot in the cavalcade and had some difficulty in finding cabs. When Msindazwe enquired why the Queen of the Tonga travelled by chariot, he was officially informed that the reason was that Swaziland did not enjoy equal status – that of a protected state. (This issue would be taken up with the approach of independence.)

A very full programme had been arranged around the great official functions. The party went to visit some of the more beautiful parts of the English countryside, historic sites – old cathedrals, fine castles, the Houses of Parliament – as well as experimental farms and agricultural shows. In between these organized tours he met various old friends and people interested in what was happening in Southern Africa, including Reverend Michael Scott, Director of the Africa Bureau, and his devoted helpers, and Margery Perham and other members of the Aborigines Protection Society. He also visited the Colonial Development Corporation.

While serious and controversial matters were studiously avoided at social gatherings, Sobhuza arranged to have an interview with Viscount Swinton, Secretary of State for Commonwealth Affairs. This interview was part of his general approach to try to understand and grapple with major issues of policy. From Viscount Swinton he inquired *inter alia* about new developments in the Chieftainship of the Bamangwato. He went to see Seretse Khama and Ruth in a house in Cheapside in which they were living, and one of his first acts on his return was to write to Tshekedi, informing him that he had seen his nephew and found him to be in good health with his family.

The party sailed back on the Pretoria Castle, which left Southampton on 18 June, and they were met at Cape Town by Mfundza Sukati, Mchoza Nsibandze and Prince Mancibane. Sobhuza was anxious to return to Swaziland as quickly as possible, but he agreed to visit Johannesburg early in July for a reception by the Swazi National Royal Club. It was first necessary, however, for him to report to the Ndlovukazi, and Prince Lutfo, and the rest of his Council, and also see to his personal affairs.

His people were delighted to see him and hear about the Queen of England. They gathered at Lobamba and presented him with *tinkhomo takaqoza*, Cattle of Achievement, welcoming him back from a dangerous journey, repeating the tribute given the dauntless Sobhuza I on his safe return from a visit to Shaka. The praise songs reaffirmed him as 'King of Kings who crossed the waters twice'.

The reception for Sobhuza by the Swazi National Royal Club took place on Sunday 5 July. He had arrived in Johannesburg a few days earlier, accompanied by councillors and by his sister Mnengwase and two of his daughters, Buyisiwe and Phetsani, girls slightly younger than Gcinaphi, who were being given the treat of a first visit to the big city. As usual it was a trip which combined business with pleasure. In fact, he once said that he could not imagine the idea of a holiday in which he had nothing to do except enjoy himself! This was not because he was unable to relax and give himself to pleasure, but rather because of his intense zest for life, his immense curiosity and his need for involvement – 'To do nothing but rest would make me very tired.'

In Johannesburg there were many people whom he wanted to see as well as others who wanted to see him. He acquainted himself again with recent developments in the Union. In 1950 Dr Verwoerd had become Minister of Native Affairs in the Malan government, and the policy and philosophy of apartheid was moving on with ruthless logic. While geared to the maintenance of white domination, Verwoerd justified apartheid by promises of an ideal of total territorial separation on racial and tribal lines. But full autonomy (independence) with economic and political control by Africans in the Bantustans was not envisaged. A series of laws were being passed to cut off the sharing of meaningful relationships – physical, emotional, intellectual. Beginning with the Population Registration Act which classified every man, woman and child into one of three 'races', the laws ranged from the Immorality (Amendment) Act penalizing intimacy between Africans and whites, to the Bantu Education Act, providing a distinctive and inferior education for Africans. Underpinning apartheid was rigid living segregation embodied in the Group Areas Act of 1950, which was introduced despite strong protests by African and Indian organizations and by radical and liberal whites, and later necessitated the removal, and expropriation, of hundreds of thousands of people. In Johannesburg, 10,000 Africans were to be removed from the western areas alone, part of which was declared white and part coloured. It was in this area that Sobhuza held freehold property on behalf of his people, and though the order of expropriation had not yet been issued, the threat and uncertainty were there.

Separation continued discrimination, and in urban areas pass laws and 'influx control' were rigidly and brutally enforced. At the same time cheap labour supplied by migrant Africans continued to bolster the basic economy of the country.

In 1952 peaceful protests culminated in a Nonviolent Resistance Movement (the Defiance of Unjust Laws), in which 8,577 volunteers, both African and Indian with a handful of whites, deliberately courted arrest by committing technical offences against the pass laws, curfew and other apartheid regulations.

Sobhuza had sent word, through Msindazwe, to his people in the Union not to take part in the Defiance Campaign. When I asked him why, he stated that it was clear to him that such a movement could not succeed at that time and could only result in further oppression and even loss of life. 'It was an act which would not change the hearts of those who are oppressing us.' And he put the question – what would his people do when confronted by police fully armed who had on previous occasions indicated that they would not hesitate to shoot? He recognized the moral courage of the resisters but considered their actions futile. He did not want his people put into South African jails for nothing.[12]

The government had in fact reacted by introducing the Criminal Laws (Amendment) Act, imposing *inter alia* fines of up to £500 or five years' imprisonment or whipping for advising, inciting or encouraging people to break the law. Confronted with overwhelming force the campaign fizzled out, leaving in many of those who had participated sadness and frustration and bitterness and, at the same time, a determination not to be crushed by defeat but to continue to seek ways to promote African freedom within a common society. It was to this situation in the Union of South Africa – existing laws and

[12] For a full account of the movement, see Leo Kuper, *Passive Resistance in South Africa.* New Haven: Yale University Press, 1957.

regulations being tightened, new restrictions being imposed on those who protested or resisted – that Sobhuza returned from the Coronation of Elizabeth II.

The Swazi National Royal Club planned that Sobhuza be welcomed not only by Swazi working and living in and around 'Goli'; they invited representatives of the Federation of Swazi, Basothos and Bechuana, the African National Congress and Transvaal Indian Congress, Advisory Boards, the Swazi Women's Council, Dingaka (herbalist) Associations, as well as the Mayor of Johannesburg and members of the City Council. The mayor excused himself and sent a Councillor in his place.

The core was Swazi; and the reception began with Sobhuza's subjects from the mines and townships assembling in vast numbers at his home in Sophiatown. From there they moved in chanting convoy along a carefully planned route to Orlando, the huge all-black township on the outskirts of the city. At the entrance, marked by a gate in the high encircling fence, Sobhuza was greeted by the stirring trumpeting of an African band. A special praiser recited the greatness of Swazi kings, and Sobhuza met the invited dignitaries.

Finally everyone gathered on the large ground set aside in the township for special functions. The speeches made on this occasion are not recorded, but I was told that though the speakers avoided direct criticism of the political situation in South Africa, much was said by implication. Sobhuza, in his reply to the speech of welcome given by Councillor Hurd, representing the Mayor, first thanked all those who had come to greet him, then said that they came from different places and were of different groups, but all had come together as his friends and therefore friends of the African people. It was because of the services of the Swazi that he had been invited to England where he had received good treatment. He would convey the good wishes of the people of Johannesburg to the Ndlovukazi and people at home. His speech was followed by the giving of tribute, dancing and refreshments; and the afternoon ended with the singing of the African national anthem – *Nkosi Sikelela Afrika* – (Lord Bless Africa).

It was situations such as this which reaffirmed Sobhuza's fundamental optimism and his belief that people of different races and tribes could keep their own identity and at the same time, and despite opposition, cooperate on a friendly basis with one another.

Soon after his return to Swaziland he bought his second western house which he named Masundvwini – the place of palms – an impressive home with a wide porch, big bay windows, large rooms with high ceilings, furnished with red velvet curtains, a thick carpet and comfortable armchairs. It was off the main road to Manzini, set in the grassy midlands, and when the King saw it, he liked it and bought it. It became his main residence in Swaziland though of course he kept up and continued to stay at different times at the older established royal villages – at Lobamba for the necessary rituals, at Lozitha for administration, at Ntfonjeni for the *sibhaca*, at Ehlane for hunting. The Queens of Masundvwini included a few of the older as well as the younger wives.

At Masundvwini Sobhuza fused Swazi and western culture under a single roof. It did not happen in a single moment and possibly much of it was not planned deliberately but occurred spontaneously with the precedent of principle rather than of detail as his guideline. He retained the heavy drapes and solid furniture of the original white owners in the front room and there he served hard liquor and tea from bone china cups. Since no Swazi may stand upright when the King is seated, the girls, usually his daughters, who served the tea balanced the tray very skilfully as they shuffled forward on their knees with the grace of dancers. The rooms at the back acquired a more traditional atmosphere. Here privileged Swazi guests sat on mats on the floor with the Queens, and the utensils and general style of life continued the older Swazi culture. But there was no sharp break between the front and the back. The doors between were not locked and the same people crossed their thresholds and moved freely between the sections.

The front verandah faced a fine open stretch of garden, a natural public meeting place, encircled by a broad driveway. The cars of the King and his guests were parked under the trees which also gave shade for the men waiting for an audience. The big yard at the back was used by the Queens and the children, and there they would sit in small clusters, talking, weaving beads, sewing skin skirts, or engaged in the usual activities of women as wives and mothers. Some food was generally being cooked out-of-doors and there were always children playing. A few chickens and ducks enhanced the bucolic quality and a couple of peacocks strutted around proudly. The first peacocks had been given him by an old settler when Sobhuza was a youth at Nsuka, and strangely, when he moved to Lozitha and then to Masundvwini, a few of these great birds subsequently appeared. He admired the beauty of their feathers but never wore them. Unlike the plumes of the royal bird, the red lourie, he said the feathers of the peacock were 'more beautiful on the bird than on man. Peacocks adorn nature, and they are as good as watchdogs – they give warning with their shrill cries'. Later, pigeons joined the birds, cooing in the trees outside and occasionally fluttering into the rooms. And people vow that they have seen snakes which, no matter how poisonous by nature, are friendly and harmless at Masundvwini.

Close attendants and councillors built their traditional huts around the back of the estate, so that from the road only the green painted iron roof of the house is visible above the cluster of beehive-shaped thatched-roofed huts. A small cattle byre was built at one side of the entrance and on the other, a couple of rooms for guards of the traditional age regiments; but until the 60s there were no gates and no guards conspicuously on duty.

The successful purchase of Thulwane had started a crusade by Sobhuza and his people to increase the land available for the nation; and after his return from Britain their efforts were accelerated in a policy of consolidating into larger blocks the scattered areas allocated the Swazi in 1907. Sometimes the request was initiated by a chief or group of chiefs whose subjects were suffering from shortage of land or involved in a dispute with a neighbouring farmer. Sometimes the white farmers made the first move. Several owned huge tracts of land – 10,000 morgen and more, much of which was undeveloped; and for the undeveloped land some £8-£10 per morgen was asked, with a down payment in cash and the balance to be paid over a period of usually one year at $6\frac{1}{2}\%$ interest. The price put by government evaluators was nearly always less than that deman('d by the owners, but the government did nothing to stop the actual speculatioi, except to suggest in certain cases that the people refuse to buy at the price demanded by the holders.

The white population was increasing rapidly, and by 1956 numbered nearly 6,000, an increase between 1946 and 1956 of 87.4% as compared with 16.8% in the previous decade[13] (Annual Report for 1956:6). Many of them were immigrants from South Africa, attracted to the new developments in industry and commerce as well as farming.[14]

The major land deals in which Sobhuza and his Council were involved continued to be complicated by the different systems of ownership and land usage laid down in a series of laws which had never been clearly coordinated. Any African, irrespective of education, had still to obtain the consent of the High Commissioner before he could acquire land. Europeans, on the other hand, were free to purchase on the open market. Native areas, set aside for the sole and exclusive use and occupation of the Swazi by Proclamation No. 39 of 1910, were vested in the High Commissioner. Land acquired by the Swazi Nation – Swazi Nation Land – was vested in Sobhuza as 'Paramount Chief in trust for the Swazi Nation'. Native Land Settlement land was vested in the Swaziland Government, and farms purchased by individual Swazi were registered in their own names.[15]

The considerable sums of money required by the Swazi for the purchase of Swazi Nation Land were obtained by the sale of cattle

[13] According to the 1956 census figures there were 5,919 whites, 229,744 Africans, and 1,378 mixed or coloureds. Between 1946 and 1956 there was an increase of 26.7% (as compared with 18.3% in the previous decade) in the African population, and of 84.9% (as compared with 5.6% in the previous decade) in the coloured population. The large increase in the coloured population was attributed to faulty enumeration in the 1946 census and not any large-scale immigration or high birthrate. In actual fact, that was the year when the coloureds were finally removed from the Voters Roll in South Africa and many entered Swaziland.

[14] By 1953 the main canal of a vast irrigation scheme in the fertile Malkerns Valley had been completed; new Colonial Development and Welfare schemes were initiated; and a pineapple factory was started at Malkerns.

[15] For a concise description, see Swaziland Annual Report for 1956:18.

collected through the Lifa Fund and sold at auctions at which the prime animals were frequently bought by whites who were developing large ranches in the country. The rounding up of animals, the borrowing and investment of the money, and the relative priority of different farms, involved a series of complicated deliberations; and Sobhuza increasingly familiarized himself with the legal complexities of large financial transactions. He missed the advice of Seme (who had died in 1951) as he struggled to grasp the nature and the legal implications of an entirely different financial system. Very few of the transactions were straightforward. Sometimes the sellers showed consideration when they realized the difficulties with which he was confronted; others simply withdrew their offer. Not all the areas had been accurately surveyed and there was also a widespread belief that white landowners frequently moved beacons and that surveyors employed by them tended to find in their favour.

At a meeting of Sobhuza and his Council with Dan Fitzpatrick, Secretary for African Affairs, Sobhuza said, 'This matter of beacons is puzzling. In fact there is a general feeling that we are not treated fairly.' And he urged that 'an effort be made to trace the map in which the original survey is reflected. Then we can discover the various beacons that were shown to the people' (Minutes of meeting, Lobamba Archives, 4/9/53). At many of the meetings that he had with his people they expressed their resentment at having to pay money to 'buy back our own land which had never been given or sold to whites'. But every additional purchase was recognized as an achievement and Sobhuza went ahead, supported by the more progressive of his chiefs, and advised by officials in the Department of Agriculture and Animal Husbandry.

A somewhat new factor had entered into his economic calculations, or rather, an old factor in new disguise. This was the renewal of interest by whites in the extraction of mineral wealth. Sobhuza said, 'We always knew that the country was rich in precious stones and different ores.' Quite how rich was being revealed through the findings of an official geological survey department started in 1945. Apart from asbestos, the most valuable and important export,[16] there was evidence of iron, gold, tin, tinstone, barytes, diamonds, kaolin and coal. Whites claimed that all mineral rights (which were separate from surface rights) had been given by Mbandzeni to concessionaires.[17] Some claims had subsequently been validated by the British government, others denied; in 1953 the mineral concessions held by private persons or companies covered 51.7% of Swaziland, and Crown Mineral areas, in which the colonial government controlled all rights, extended over the remaining 48.3%.

[16] The total value of mineral production was approximately £2,000,000 and royalties payable within the territory were 2½% on base metals and 2% on asbestos.

[17] The late David Forbes claimed in fact that his father and uncle had originally been granted all mineral rights. (See *My Life in South Africa*, 1938:89).

No specific rights were vested in the Swazi Nation. Prospecting or mining on 'Crown Mineral Areas' was not permitted without special authority from a Mining Advisory Board, established in 1950 and consisting of the Director of Geological Survey as Chairman and the Treasurer of the Central Government and First Assistant Secretary as members.

White investors were urging government to reduce controls and open the country, including Swazi areas, for prospecting. In 1954 a government-appointed Mineral Development Commission sat in Mbabane and later issued a report which, after being put before the European Advisory Council, was released to the public for comment. The Ngwenyama and the Swazi National Council submitted a written response, which indicated clearly the relative weight they placed on agriculture and on mining in terms of the interests of their own people:

Mining even under ideal conditions represents in essence the extraction of capital from the good earth, and it leaves it that much the poorer in addition to the destruction involved particularly in alluvial and open-cast working, and to a lesser extent in subterranean mining ...

Agriculture, wisely practised, is an ever appreciating asset and the one thing in respect of which you can have your cake and eat it, in other words, it can give those practising it a good living and can be steadily improving in value while doing so ...

It is clearly of more importance to preserve the soil than to realize the value of the minerals, however valuable. If mining cannot be realized without reducing the soil's food production value and without endangering its preservation, then the minerals are costing too much to the country at large ...

In dealing with applications to mine on Native Area, our policy would be to exclude from prospecting or mining all Swazi residences, burial gardens, cultivation, grazing or hunting grounds, forests, hot springs, beds of reed, beds of rushes of the *incoboza, likhwane* or *indvuli* kinds, areas grassed with *umuzi, lucungwa, luhlonga* and *lutindzi* grasses, and any places reverenced or needed by the Swazi (Comments by Ngwenyama and the Swazi National Council on the Report of the Mineral Development Commission 1954, Swaziland Archives).

Sobhuza's involvement in mining developments intensified as he saw the natural wealth of the country depleted and the profits going to foreign investors. He was about to enter a long and bitter legal struggle, which would continue for the next fifteen years – until Independence – to regain for his people the reversionary rights of grants allegedly made by Mbandzeni, and ultimately to control mineral development. He backed his arguments by reference to the familiar documents which he had used originally in pressing for the rights of the Swazi to surface land.

In 1956 he presented yet another petition dated 28 August to the High Commissioner, Sir Percivale Liesching, who had succeeded Sir John leRougetel, and to the new Secretary of State for Commonwealth Relations, Lord Home. In this important petition appears a note of greater bitterness and more open condemnation of

British policy than in most previous documents. The Order-in-Council of 1903 is described 'not as an instrument to extend justice but to deprive the protected peoples of their property and other rights ... By means of an Order-in-Council in a Protectorate the British Crown can break agreements, promises, guarantees, pledges and assurances, can confiscate and extinguish rights in property and possess itself with its protected people's properties or do anything it pleases irrespective of whether it be moral or immoral without fear of any court of law.' He described the process of control over Swaziland as 'the law of quiet conquest over helpless protected peoples', and he stated that he was 'painfully aware' of the better treatment meted by the British to Basutoland and Uganda where full mineral rights were reserved to the original owners.

Again Sobhuza stressed the controls that Mbandzeni had inserted in all the documents for the protection of his people. In an early letter (undated) he had written: 'Thank God to the Foolish King who left a clear record in which he clarified the true position about the concessions and in which the British Government, South African Republic and the concessionaires are his principal witnesses.' Underlying his protest was a criticism of the British for their role in taking over mineral rights to the total exclusion of Swazi claims, and, more particularly, their arbitrary assumption of royalties which should have been paid to him, as the Boers had paid them to his father, under the Private Revenue Concession. But this criticism did not imply willingness on his part to accept South African control. The issue of incorporation had been raised again by J.G. Strydom, successor to Malan, in a widely publicized speech at his opening of the Free State Congress of the Nationalist Party (13/9/55). Sobhuza knew that in the Union, Africans could no longer buy land, that the maximum area available to them 'to develop their national homes' was totally inadequate,[18] and that the Group Areas Act was being implemented. But the fact that conditions in Swaziland were more promising than in the Union did not mean that he should submit to what he and his people considered injustice and did not deter him from seeking to obtain redress by peaceful means.

The more publicized activities of land and mineral negotiations took up less of his time than his diversified tradition-based duties. To consider some of these duties as mundane or secular and others as religious introduces a false dichotomy. They were all part of his

---

[18] The area available to Africans was some 13% of the country. A Commission reporting in 1955 found that the 'Reserves' consisted of some 260 separate areas which 'save for a few blocks like the Transkei were generally so fragmented and scattered that they formed no foundation for community growth'. The proportion of Africans living there was put by the Commission as some 40%, the remaining 60% living and working in the so-called white areas and entirely dependent on them for their homes and occupations. The 'Reserves' themselves were generally undeveloped with a high population density. (Socio-economic Commission, UG 61/1955 – the so-called Tomlinson Report.) In this Report all three High Commission Territories were theoretically included in the proposed Bantustan system.

obligations as Ngwenyama of the Swazi. The calendar of all activities was marked by national rituals, but these themselves related to the regularities of a seasonal economic cycle. Within this framework he conducted his meetings with chiefs and government officials, the handling of disputes and the complexities of extensive kinship obligations. Few situations revealed the added ambivalences of his position more clearly than in his dealing with cases. As Ngwenyama he was appealed to in all difficult and major legal disputes. The separation of courts did not resolve the clash of laws, though the issues could be more clearly focussed. His opinions and his judgments were providing a corpus of law based on principles different from Roman-Dutch law, but not necessarily identical with traditional laws. In cases of disputed succession the approach was clear, though the investigations were often difficult: he based his decisions on history and variations of custom according to clan and locality, and evidence as to the relative rating of widows, the proof of paternity, unravelling innumerable threads of kinship ties over several generations.[19]

In some cases, however, conflict between different types of law had to be resolved. Many of these cases related to marriage laws and the disposition of property. Did any honourable Swazi have the right to make a will benefiting his favourite wife in disregard of Swazi custom? What were the relative claims of a woman married by Christian law whose husband subsequently took additional wives by Swazi law and custom?

The Proclamations had given Sobhuza greater executive authority than any of the other chiefs, but to enforce his orders he had still to rely on the Administration and sometimes on the police (who were under the Central Administration, attached more directly to District Commissioners). The majority of chiefs and subjects accepted his leadership and his judgments, but there were two major cases affecting chiefs – Prince Solomon Madevu and Chief Saphaza Maziya – in which he was forced to turn to the Administration for assistance. Whether he wanted to or not he was unable to act independently, and inevitably was criticized as a puppet of the government by those who would not accept his orders.

Prince Solomon Madevu, preacher and teacher, erratic and religious, son of King Mbandzeni by the daughter of a former Prime

---

[19] A typical case was the dispute over the Chieftainship of the Ndlangamandla in which the contestants were Nqanqothi, a son of Zombode, and Nkulane, son of Manuka, Zombode's brother. Nqanqothi claimed that his father was buried at the *nshungushu* – the upper entrance of the cattle byre. Nkulane argued that all headmen were buried at that site. The King had to send investigators to the villages to gather evidence. Finally, on the basis of the evidence of eyewitnesses, he decided in favour of Nqanqòthi because only his father, Zombode, had been buried in the site recognized by the Ndlangamandla as reserved for the rightful successor and heir. (Lozithehlezi Archives, 1955.) Cases came to him not only from Swaziland but from Swazi outside of the borders. One of the more interesting was the case of the Mlambo chieftainship in New Ermelo, a suburban township in the Eastern Transvaal, when in 1954 Sobhuza's intervention was requested by the mother of one of the disputants.

Minister, Sandlane Zwane, claimed the area of Timbutini which the King had given in 1885 to his mother as her *liphakelo* – 'the wife's allotment' (a principality given in form of land or cattle). Prince Solomon himself came to the area in 1925. There were conflicting claims about the boundaries and, correspondingly, the allegiances of many of the people in the area. He levelled accusations of corruption against some of the most important of the King's representatives and complained of threats, and actions, against his person. It was a long drawn-out dispute which lasted until his death in 1963 and, punctuated by recriminations on all sides, involved Resident Commissioners and Government Secretaries as well as the King-in-Council. At the same time Prince Solomon Madevu continued to work with ardour to build up a single united Swazi church, with the Ngwenyama as its head, and in this capacity he was occasionally sent by the Council he criticized to interview the officials of government.

Less complicated was the case of Saphaza Maziya, a chief in the area of Maphungwane near Siteki. Saphaza, ambitious and obstinate, considered himself diminished by the Proclamations and refused to present himself before the Swazi National Council when summoned by the King. In the past the issue would have been settled in open combat. As it was, Sobhuza inflicted a fine and when Saphaza refused to pay, he asked the District Commissioner to see that it be paid, and that Saphaza be suspended from exercising 'undue authority'.

It is important to point out that the opposition expressed in both these cases was not on principle, not a challenge to hereditary chieftainship, but a bid for greater personal privileges. Not until later was opposition expressed in the competing ideology of political parties.

Both Morgan and Dan Fitzpatrick were due to retire at the end of 1957, and both had decided to spend the rest of their lives in Swaziland. Sobhuza welcomed the idea of white officials retiring in the country where they worked – 'that would show if they had a true love of the people'. For Fitzpatrick it was his home. He would buy a shop in Hlatikhulu and continue to work with the Swazi.

Morgan had been away from England for so many years that it was no longer his home, and Kenya, where he had served for almost twenty-five years, had been torn by the crisis of Mau-Mau – a situation the complexities of which Sobhuza understood, and described as 'horrible'. After a short visit to Kenya, Morgan and his wife returned to Swaziland where they felt secure and welcome. They bought a small farm at Malkerns, the fertile valley which, with irrigation, was becoming a centre for progressive farmers, white and black, growing citrus, pineapple and rice in place of more traditional subsistence crops.[20]

---

[20] The growing of pineapples by Africans had been stimulated by J.W. Allen, a philanthropically oriented American who built a pineapple canning factory in 1954; settled with his family on the Malagwane hill; was one of the first white settlers openly to entertain Swazi in

The new Resident Commissioner was Brian Marwick, and Sobhuza and all the Council welcomed him and his wife Riva 'home'. Brian had been away for eight years, seven in Basutoland and one in the High Commissioner's office in Pretoria. He was remembered as Musawendvodza, son of a trusted or brave man, abbreviated to Musa, and literally interpreted as 'Kindness' by those who did not know the origin. No one could foresee the turbulent period that lay ahead and the dramatic and tragic conflict that would develop between him and Sobhuza, two men who respected each other deeply.

---

his home, and started the Bahai Faith in Swaziland. He and his family were accepted as friends by Sobhuza and members of his family. Hitherto the only Americans had been missionaries.

CHAPTER XIII

New Directions

The atmosphere at Lobamba was tense. The Ndlovukazi Nukwase was critically ill, and there were bad omens. One evening in July, towards dark, when the girls who had taken part in Umhlanga (the annual reed ceremony) brought the reeds to Lobamba, the hut behind laMatsebula's in the *sigodlo* burst into flame, and then that of laZwane and several others before the fires could be extinguished. There was no one whom one could blame, no obvious cause, but there are some evildoers with power to perform *lubane* – the throwing of fire at a distance, and of *umbane*, lightning. There was no fire engine in the vicinity and there was no piped water at the capital. It was a dry winter; and it was a miracle that the whole village was not razed. People murmured – was it accident or arson? Sobhuza-in-Council appointed a committee to investigate quietly.

Then, during the *Ncwala* there was terrible lightning, thunder and rain, especially on the day of the catching of the bull. But the King showed his bravery. He never tried to hide; he took part in the dancing with the men; he knew that he was the King and could not show fear. Nukwase forced herself to make a brief appearance on the main day but she could not take part in the dance. There had been friction in the royal family and in the inner circle, and too many unaccountable deaths. Nukwase herself had lost both her sons, Mkukwane the younger in 1939, and recently, in 1955, Mshengu.

Among many doctors called to treat her in her long illness was Ambrose Phesheya (Across the Seas) Zwane, the first Swazi to qualify as a medical doctor, son of Amos Zwane, the ritual specialist who had accompanied Sobhuza to England in 1922. Sobhuza also sent his son, Nqaba, by car to Zululand to fetch Konzinja Mbatha, a relative and renowned *inyanga* (traditional specialist) who had stayed at Lobamba in the period of Lomawa and performed amazing cures. But when Konzinja saw Nukwase, he realized he could do nothing. The will to live was gone, the spirit wanted to be free from the burden of the flesh, and when Nukwase sent Maboya Fakudze to appeal to Sobhuza with the message – 'I ask you to set me free,' he agreed sadly. 'Indeed, we let her go, we too now set her free.' Then members of her family came to say goodbye. 'The spirit left the body' on 15 September 1957.

The question of Nukwase's successor was not easy. There was no other Ndwandwe queen of Bhunu, and his surviving widows had been given to his kin under the custom of the levirate. However, Sobhuza had three Ndwandwe women among his own queens,[1] and from them the Malangeni chose the oldest, Zihlathi, of Elwandle. She would no longer be accessible to the King as a wife; she would hereafter be deemed his mother, the Ndlovukazi. She was a kind, unaggressive woman, intelligent without schooling and totally without ambition. Sobhuza knew that it was a position that none of his queens had anticipated or desired. When Zihlathi was fetched from the rather isolated village of Nsuka where she was living peacefully, and told of her appointment, she was overwhelmed by dread, feeling herself unprepared, and she wept bitterly. Sobhuza sympathized with her but the choice was for the national good, and so she accepted this duty albeit with a heavy heart.

Mourners carried Nukwase's wooden coffin first to Zabeni, site of Lomawa's grave, where the insignia of sovereignty were transferred to Zihlathi. The mourners then moved on to Nukwase's own burial site in the homestead of an old retainer, Magcugcumela Magongo. National priests and governors of royal villages performed the rites, and Zihlathi was given the hoe with which to cut the first sod, signifying her new status. Nukwase had been baptised a Methodist, but had moved closer to the Catholics, and Sobhuza's friend, Bishop Barneschi, was the main officiant in the Christian service, though preachers of different evangelical churches also offered prayers. A government official represented the Resident Commissioner, Brian Marwick, with whom the King was, at that time, on very cordial terms. Sobhuza, who by custom remained at Lozithehlezi, was treated against the contagion of death, and strengthened to face the hazards of life.

A few days after the funeral he came to Lobamba where the princes and governors and councillors were waiting, and they all gathered in the clearing between the *sibaya* and the Great Hut. The new Ndlovukazi sat with the senior princes and the governors of royal villages, separated from the other queens, her former co-wives. Mandanda as chief governor presented her, 'Here is your Mother, *Nine Bekunene* (you people of the right hand).' And she wept. The people acclaimed her *Bayethe*. She would be given less administrative responsibility than her predecessors, but would perform the necessary rituals and domestic duties. Lozindaba Matsebula, Sobhuza's first official Queen, would do all she could to help the new Ndlovukazi.

Sobhuza himself was heavy hearted but could not show the nation either sadness or fear. On Good Friday, which had become the main gathering of Christians in the nation, crowds of mourners flocked to

---

[1] The three Ndwandwe Queens were Zihlathi, daughter of Vanyane, principal priest of the *Ncwala*, Seneleleni, another of Vanyane's daughters, and Lomzoyi, daughter of Makanandela, brother of Lomawa. Zihlati had two grown up daughters; Seneleleni, a grown son; Lomzoyi was childless.

Lobamba. Nukwase's dream of a national church in which all could worship a single God was not yet fulfilled; the building itself was unfinished, roofless. The King spoke briefly, saying she had belonged to the nation, not to him alone, and then he asked an old priest, Reverend Andrew Zwane of the Zionist Church, to speak for him. 'Someone helps by speaking on behalf of another.' He explained that he considered Reverend Zwane his father since he had been present during the reign of Mbandzeni and Bhunu, and so could speak better than he, Sobhuza, about such sorrows. Reverend Zwane spoke of past Swazi rulers and 'it was like listening to our own Bible'. Many people showed their grief by bringing offerings of money[2] and these he distributed to old women, 'the grandmothers and mothers' for whom he was responsible.[3]

Bad luck continued for the first years of Zihlathi's office. In 1958 the spring rains were late, followed by a brief dry spell. In the summer, torrents washed away soil and crops, flooding the river banks. Then came another period of withering heat. The Annual Report described it as 'a trying year for those engaged in agricultural, forestry, and veterinary pursuits ... Grazing and water supplies for stock deteriorated so much that a large number of animals died from starvation and thirst ... A further effect of the dry winter was to increase the fire hazard throughout the territory and in fact large areas were devastated by fires' (Annual Report for Swaziland 1958:1).

More fires broke out in royal villages. The matter was discussed with the Government at a Council meeting, and precautionary measures, including the installation of a piped water supply and the appointment of guards, were agreed upon. Suspicions and rumours grew. The governor of Lobamba was dismissed. Sobhuza was under considerable strain and there were many days when his health troubled him. I visited him briefly in 1958. He looked thin and tired; he spoke of Nukwase, her courage, her idealism, her vitality, and then expressed the faith that enabled him to go through these constant personal losses. 'Death is the end of the flesh alone. Those down below stay well.' And then he told me the story of an old man, whose name I cannot recall, who had told him that he had gone to the place of the dead and had been turned back for his time to rest had not yet come. The dead, he said, are not troubled. It is we on the earth who have troubles. He quoted a Swazi proverb, 'People die, their work goes on.'

The struggle to reacquire land for the nation continued. Permission for any African to purchase land had still to be obtained from the British High Commissioner. For unaccountable reasons this was often

[2] This money is known as *ligqolo* from the bitter wattle bark used in purification from death.

[3] For example, he sent some to NaboLakhiza, sister of Labotsibeni, and to NaboKhopitale, the real sister of his own mother, and to the remaining widows of his father. The number whom he was helping to support was constantly increasing and he is reputed never to have turned away any genuine appeal for help that reached him.

long delayed. If the farm was good there was the risk of its going to any white buyer and the nation lost a number of chances to buy farms at auctions. Letters, in Sobhuza's name, were sent to 'sellers' asking for patience, and, when consideration was shown, expressing appreciation. At a meeting held at Lobamba offices on 15 July 1958 which both he and the Resident Commissioner attended by invitation, he urged that the restrictions be lifted. He added that this law, though designed to protect the Swazi, could be used against them 'presumably in cases of pressure from the European public ... all he [the administrative officer] needs do is to use delaying tactics until our deal falls through or just tell us that the High Commissioner has refused our application and that is the end of it.'

At the same time he claimed that 'individual African buyers should of necessity receive the consent of the Swazi authority to guard against land hunters who with pockets full of money may flood the country with a lot of undesirable characters – men who often have prohibited immigrants as sleeping partners'. The idea of individual tenure for Africans was itself a moot question; the concept of personal freehold ownership was contrary to Swazi traditional tenets, and a major issue in the interpretation of the validity of concessions. The majority of Swazi were still opposed to individual freehold. However, experts in the Department of Agriculture advocated it as the best incentive for progressive farming, as well as the only real guarantee against eviction by a 'backward or vindictive chief'. Sobhuza accepted the first reason as 'perhaps true and necessary for modern times'.

The Lifa Fund, in which Sobhuza had placed great hopes, was running into serious difficulties. Payments for farms could not be met, collectors were accused of mishandling funds; they denied it, but admitted that the books – complicated by entries of sporadic cattle sales – were in a muddle. After fifteen years of immense effort, the Swazi had managed to buy back only 268,093 acres, bringing the total land held by the King in trust for the nation to 1,907,780 acres (a little over 50% of the country). The area bought by individual Africans was 22,384 acres; and that owned by Europeans and Eurafricans totalled 1,847,680 acres (Swaziland Annual Report for 1961:27-8). Swazi 'squatters' on white farms still numbered several thousands.

Sobhuza openly confronted the difficult question of how much land should be set aside for Europeans, and how much for Swazi, and restated that the Swazi had a right to claim the whole country. 'But,' he continued, 'seeing that things in land ownership had got so mixed up and Europeans had come to stay, it would be advisable to forget the old wounds and deal with the situation as it presented itself today.' As a compromise he suggested that 50% of the total area of Swaziland be reserved for exclusive Swazi occupation, and he clearly indicated that this 50% should not include land already purchased by the Nation. Of the remaining 50%, 25% would be opened for purchase by individual Swazi and 25% for European acquisition and occupation.

Sobhuza and his Council did not want to obstruct development; they wanted to share in its benefits. The interest in technology he had shown since a young boy had never diminished; he was fascinated, impressed and constantly surprised by the power of industrial machinery – sawmills, tractors, printing presses, dynamos, engines of all sorts. He applauded and welcomed the great feats of irrigation, and at the same time continued to perform ancient rituals for rain. The two to him were not incompatible. When he opened the dam that would irrigate some 30,000 acres of land in the lowveld, he named the area *Mhlume* – Growth, Progress – and interpreted it as meaning 'the promise of good things to come'. However, the impersonal distribution of water, using a strange measure, *cusecs*, raised serious problems, and for the Swazi it was important that the waters should not be diverted solely to the large estates.

Of more immediate concern were the effects of new concessions on the mineral resources of the people. By 1957 the basic geological mapping of the country was completed. Of special significance was the award by the British administration of an exclusive prospecting licence over the rich iron ore deposits in the mountains west of Mbabane, bordering the Transvaal, and the granting of permits for prospecting the rich coal deposits in the bushveld.[4] The Swazi had known of the iron deposits for many years. Indeed it was they who had called the ridge Bomvu (the Red) and there were many legends of the powerful spirit that needed to be placated when the deep red pigment (haematite) used in marriage and other rituals throughout centuries was dug out from that mountain.

A conflict between Swazi and European interests crystallized when the Resident Commissioner sanctioned the agreement of the Swaziland Iron Ore Development Company to supply two Japanese steel companies with twelve million tons of high grade ore over a period of ten years. Sobhuza-in-Council argued that not only were minerals a wasting asset, but even the royalties to which he and the Swazi nation were entitled under the Private Revenue Concession were merged with general revenue. Brian Marwick pointed out that the project was associated with the building of a railway, the first within the country, which would link Swaziland with the railhead at Goba on the Mozambique border, and so give access to the port of Lourenço Marques, now Maputo, and to the outside world.[5] Sobhuza agreed that improved communication was essential for economic

[4] The licence for prospecting iron ore was awarded to the Swaziland Iron Ore Development Company, a subsidiary of the Anglo-American Corporation in joint holding with a British firm (Guest, Keane and Nettlefold). The permits for coal prospecting were granted to two major Johannesburg companies, Central Mining Finance Ltd. and Johannesburg Consolidated Investment Company Ltd.

[5] There had been several suggested projects for a railway in the past and access to the port of Kosi Bay had been an important reason for the Boers of the early Republic wanting to control Swaziland. The Swazi claimed that most of the area around Lourenço Marques was inhabited by Swazi.

development,[6] and was excited at possibilities opened by the railway, but he was disturbed that the Resident Commissioner should have given the green light without waiting for the approval of the Swazi.

Marwick, though sensitive to Swazi reaction, replied that he had waited for months, that the opportunity was not one to be missed and that the time was ripe for rapid development. He tried to convince Sobhuza that he would negotiate terms to the best advantage of the Swazi. Sobhuza expressed his appreciation, but made it clear that to be kept informed and even to be consulted was not the same as taking part in the final decision. Again he found himself protesting on behalf of the nation: land, trees, water, minerals, each gift of 'earth', the world of nature, created its own disputes.

In spite of spectacular developments, the country still did not produce sufficient maize, the staple food of the Swazi. The deficit was purchased from South Africa, involving the government with its small staff in complex problems of price regulation, transport and distribution. In 1959, after much deliberation, the Resident Commissioner had granted a monopoly over the purchase and distribution of maize with acceptable price control, to an astute South African, Natie Kirsh, newly arrived in Swaziland, who foresaw Swaziland's 'glowing future'. Sobhuza-in-Council, as well as some of the settlers, expressed misgivings when they realized the powers of the new company – the Swaziland Milling Company – which steadily extended its interests. But the government expressed its confidence in Kirsh.

To Sobhuza both capitalism and socialism were foreign economic concepts; his economic policy was not guided by any set theories. In the traditional system, rooted in communal use of land, free individual enterprise was possible, and inequalities of wealth accepted as natural. A rich man was respected if he distributed wealth, if he accumulated it he was despised. Sobhuza encouraged his people to go into 'business', at the same time cautioning them not to overreach themselves or to expect large profits quickly. At a meeting at Lozitha (3/5/59), he congratulated members of the Commercial Amadoda[7] on the progress they were making, and he emphasized that 'trade was in currency brought to the country by the Europeans and known to them'; in his opinion their success lay in their 'careful accounting of expenditure and revenue'. The Swazi had much to learn about the 'conduct of business', and he advised his listeners not to rush into ventures beyond their resources.

---

[6] The Colonial Development Corporation offered to lend some four and a quarter million pounds for the building of a railway and the purchase of rolling stock. In April 1961 the first all-weather airfield was opened at Matsapha, not far from Masundwini. In August 1962, following a visit from the Swaziland Secretary for Finance and Development and the Director of Public Works, the World Bank agreed to lend Swaziland two million rand for road construction.

[7] The Commercial Amadoda was started to protect the small Swazi trader from competition with non-Swazi in Swazi areas.

This was the time to be careful. Which of you has ever heard of a person being killed while learning to ride a bicycle? Danger is not present at that stage, but comes at the time when the rider starts swanking and putting his feet on the handle bars as he rides. The expert swimmer dies in the water as the Swazi proverb says. I would not wish that the appreciation of your work which I have expressed should so stimulate you traders as to make you forget proper business caution.

The struggle for an equal share in economic development became part of a wider political struggle in which Sobhuza again played a crucial role. When the Gold Coast became the independent state of Ghana, under the leadership of Kwame Nkrumah, in 1957, the process of African decolonization accelerated. Superficially Swaziland appeared unaffected, but Sobhuza was alert to major changes, reported in the papers he read and by people who came to see him.

In 1957 John J. Nquku went overseas, acting more or less as a self-appointed ambassador for Swaziland. He was an active member of the Swazi National Council, President of the Swaziland Progressive Association, organizer for the United Christian Church of Africa, and editor of the Swaziland newspaper (*Izwi LamaSwazi*). He left with Sobhuza's blessings, letters of credentials from both Protestant and Catholic missionaries, and a British passport. When he returned from a long journey, which took him to England, America and Europe, at each place meeting people of different creeds and political opinions, he was full of enthusiasm for 'democracy and progress'. Sobhuza listened to what he had to say with much interest and agreed with some, not all, of his ideas.

Western democracy, permitting organized opposition between competing political parties, was presented by the government as the ideal; if there was a monarch he would be subordinate to an elected parliament. The idea of democracy in a one-party state had not yet been openly formulated, and the possibility of democracy under a traditional African monarch was not contemplated. Sobhuza pointed to the absence of democracy under a parliamentary system in which a nation was governed by Orders-in-Council issued by a foreign power, and noted that though he had succeeded in retaining some authority his people had no control over legislation affecting the country as a whole.

In 1960 the British Prime Minister Harold Macmillan visited southern Africa, and on 3 February made his historic speech on 'The Winds of Change' before the South African Parliament. He also came briefly to Goedgegun (Nhlangano) to meet with the Resident Commissioner, Sobhuza, and other notables. Sobhuza had summoned warriors to pay their respects and Harold Macmillan danced with them. Sobhuza spoke to him privately, but was not given the opportunity to make a public address. A confidential minute, which found its way into the hands of the Swazi National Council, stated that Sobhuza was of low education, had many wives and had a speech impediment. The Council resented this as an insulting description; the author of the letter, the Secretary for Swazi Affairs, who had failed his matriculation, explained that this document was intended only to inform the Prime Minister of the King's 'particulars', and that 'there was nothing derogatory about the description' – after all, 'was it not true that the King had reached low academic education, that he had a slight impediment in his speech (and the Prime Minister had to be advised lest he be surprised) and that anyone who had many wives was ... [considered] a source of pride among the Swazi?' (Minutes of meeting of the Swazi National Council Standing Committee and the Secretary for Swazi Affairs 25/2/60).

In an informal meeting with the Resident Commissioner, Sobhuza, omitting any reference to his personal insult, 'thanked Government for having made it possible for the Prime Minister to visit Swaziland even though the time was short'. He pointed out that what was reassuring about Macmillan's speech was his contention that the rights of the people would be respected, and that 'developments in whatever sphere would not be done in isolation but that every advance would be taken with and not without the people. The Protectorates have reason to be happy,' he continued, because Macmillan had 'stood by' Churchill's statement that no change would be made in their status until the inhabitants had been consulted.

In South Africa Verwoerd, having succeeded Strydom in September of 1958, put the appeal of apartheid as 'separate development' to the Protectorates. As the government speeded its implementation of apartheid, African frustration intensified; peaceful protests and campaigns were not only ignored, but evoked at times violent reprisals.[8] Not impressed by Macmillan's ideas, Verwoerd pursued the policy of racial separation and white hegemony. His Cabinet included members of the Broederbond – once a secret Afrikaner racial nationalist body, now openly in power. Among the members was Balthazar John Vorster, who had been interned during the war for pro-Hitler activities.

Wary of both British and South African politics, Sobhuza tried to find his own path between them and to bring together black and white in Swaziland in a new and harmonious system, in which both could retain their cultural identity. In the 50s Lord Hailey, recognized by the British as their leading authority on colonial administration, had proposed that a legislative council be established in each of the High Commission Territories as a preliminary stage towards more

[8] The culmination on 21 March, 1960 was Sharpeville, forty miles from Johannesburg, when police in armoured cars fired on defenceless non-violent demonstrators against the pass laws. Following the shootings at Sharpeville and at Langa, Chief Luthuli, President-General of the African National Congress, proclaimed 28 March a national day of mourning and appealed to all Africans to stay away from work. The government responded by declaring a State of Emergency on March 30, 1960, and soon after both the ANC and the Pan-Africanist Congress, a more militant and racially oriented group that had seceded in 1958 from the ANC, were banned. Increasing numbers of political refugees, white and black, were seeking asylum in Swaziland as well as other High Commission Territories and overseas.

responsible participation in government. For Swaziland, however, he suggested as an initial step, the formation of a Native Advisory Council 'which can take part in joint sittings with the European Advisory Council, followed by the establishment of a representative legislature in which the position of the Paramount Chief and his Council would be that of agencies, recognized for the conduct of certain aspects of Native Affairs' (1953:429). To him the strength of the traditional Swazi system appeared as a barrier to progress.

Sobhuza had met Hailey on his two visits to the country, and read his publications with critical interest. Sobhuza had also read without enthusiasm his recommendations for Swaziland. Marwick was more impressed and was also at that time influenced in his thinking by Sir John Maud, appointed High Commissioner in 1959. Sir John, a highly cultivated, charming, twentieth-century English aristocrat, was eloquent in his belief that the destinies of all individuals could be best protected and directed by the British and their system of government.

Sobhuza was confronting the new constitutional challenge. Having established separate African and European bases in the 50s, the British were contemplating a way of bringing the two closer together along the lines suggested by Hailey in 1953. The need for such a move had been reiterated in another official report by Professor Chandler Morse, proposing that to achieve economic advance 'the present occasional opportunities for informal consultation between the groups be developed into a regular and less informal association, and that a channel be established along which joint advice will flow toward the government' (Report of the Economic Survey Commission, 1959:422).

The findings of the Morse Report were not new; 'Experts', Sobhuza said, 'often spend a long time first finding out and then telling us what we already know, but then they put forward their own solutions without consulting us.'[9] Probably no one was more sensitive than he to the dangers of the cleavages growing between Africans and Europeans. In May of 1959, he submitted a memorandum to Marwick in which he related the political awareness of his people to the land and mineral situation. The European Advisory Council heard of this and, at a special meeting held in January, submitted its own memorandum to the Resident Commissioner to forward to the Secretary of State, advocating a multi-racial legislative council in which both European and Swazi interests would be represented through their separate organizations.

Before the European Advisory Council received a reply from the Secretary of State, Sobhuza took the initiative and invited the Resident Commissioner and one of his staff, and two members of the

[9] When I put this to a senior government official in 1966 he replied, 'Why on earth should we consult with them? They aren't economists or political scientists.' Marwick, however, made a point of discussing each project that affected the Swazi with Sobhuza and his Council.

white community, to meet with him and his Council at Masundvwini.
This meeting, held on 23 April 1960, was a landmark in Swaziland
political history, comparable to that of the meeting between
Mbandzeni and the concessionaires. The Resident Commissioner was
out of Swaziland but the Acting Resident Commissioner, R.
Armstrong (*Mathendele* – the partridge) and the Secretary for Swazi
Affairs, Purcell (*Sigwili* – the swank) attended; the whites he invited
were Dr David Hynd (medical missionary in Swaziland since 1925
and educator) and William G. Lewis (a self-educated man and
successful cattle farmer who had opened the first creamery in
Swaziland).[10] In Sobhuza's view Hynd and Lewis complemented each
other. Also present were Princes Magongo, Madevu, Masitsela and
Matsafeni, Councillors Sifunti Matsebula, Benjamin Simelane,
Samuel A. Sibiya, Mfundza Sukati, Msindazwe Sukati, Abednigo
Khuseni Hlophe, Mabalizandla Nhlabatsi, Polycarp Dlamini and
Mkhulunyelwa Matsebula.

The company met in the early afternoon in the big front room of his
house. The Ngwenyama was in traditional Swazi dress; a few
councillors and all the guests were in formal western suits. The
Ngwenyama, the government officials and the two whites sat on the
chairs; the Swazi, in accordance with tradition, sat on the carpet
facing him. After an informal exchange of pleasantries the meeting
began. The King spoke for about two hours in siSwati, without notes;
Msindazwe Sukati stood up and translated. The speech at this
meeting is so important and so typical of his approach that I quote the
taped translation almost in full.

ST. 280/60

Your Honour and Gentlemen,

We are met here to consider and talk about what is happening in the world today.
We have seen from reading newspapers and hearing radio reports that there is quite
an unrest and a number of things happening around us. I am sorry that the day has
proved unsuitable in that we find that the weather is inclement and that therefore the
roads are not very nice to drive on; but I hope that that is an omen of something good
that may come from what we are trying to do here today. [Rain is an auspicious omen.]
The unrest and many disturbances that I have mentioned just now alarm us and
cause us to wonder where the world is leading to, and in particular Africa. The Prime
Minister of the United Kingdom in his speech at Cape Town mentioned something to
the effect that Africa is on the crossroads – they did not know which side they might
have to choose of the two worlds, East or West; he was convinced that the only way to
solve the problem would be by treating the African people in a humane way, and in a
way that would so satisfy them that they would not join in the struggle that is at
present taking place between the East and the West. But as we see the day to day
events taking place we feel unhappy about what is happening in Africa, so much so
that we cannot pride ourselves in Swaziland that we are not included in the struggles
that are taking place elsewhere; nor can we say that we are better off in any way. I

---

[10] Lewis came to Swaziland in 1938 from Rhodesia, and gave allegiance by *khonta* to Chief
Mandanda.

17. King Sobhuza toasting his daughter Gcinaphi at her marriage. On the right is Queen Fikelephi Masuku. 1963

18. King Sobhuza with Sir Francis Loyd (Queen's Commissioner) on the main day of the Ncwala, 5 January 1966

19. Taking the oath as King of Swaziland, 25 April 1967, administered by the Chief Justice, Victor Elyan

20. On 6 September 1968, King Sobhuza in the uniform of the main day of the Ncwala receives the 'instruments of Independence' from George Thomson, Secretary of State, representing the British government

personally think that we are utterly in the midst of the trouble. There is no room for complacency.

The most disturbing factor which I think is the source of all trouble in Africa is fear. If only we could get rid of that fear complex we would have solved all our problems. Let us consider what the source of fear is. Now let me explain it in this way – a human being is an animal like other animals; then in this analogy consider what animals do when they are in fear, and I come to certain conclusions. I have observed that an animal such as a lion will kill a male cub when it is still young, kill it, because once it grows to maturity it may be a danger to it. So is the case with a human being; it has also got that instinct, with this exception only – that a human being has got the power of thinking ahead on any proposition before him. One finds two types of human beings. There is one type that will bring up his children in such a way that they will become very cruel and inhuman because they have been brought up in a rough way at home, and another type of person will bring up his children in the spirit that they are his children, his responsibility and the future prop of his declining years. Even if he beats the child he only does so in order to teach him or give him a training of some kind, and when he is grown the child will say, 'Oh how my father did beat me'; but the father will be in the position to say that 'I wanted you to be a man and by my discipline I have brought you to what you are now'. And in his own private talks the child will be able to tell his comrades and friends: 'You know, I was brought up by my father, under hard discipline, but that was good for me and has made me what I am today.' The other child who has been brought up in a brutal manner in a cruel way, when grown will try to do what was done to him by his father. We have come to the conclusion therefore that the difference between human beings and animals is that in the case of human beings where the child has been brought up in a reasonable, humane way the child will develop to be a good citizen but when the child has been brought up in a brutal and unreasonable way he may develop to be something unruly, difficult and a bad man generally.

Next we come to consider what happens in the case of the treatment of races be they white or black. Let us take for instance the case of Europeans and place them in the position of parents who have to bring up their child and we watch how they bring up the child. We find that what actually happens today is that the Europeans will so handle the African that they would not like to see him grow and try to be something to contend with. The treatment the African receives is such that it aims at keeping him just at that level so that he does not achieve complete independence. In a way you could say that the European is defending himself, is protecting his interests. Can anyone tell me if it is a good state of affairs that the European must seek to protect his interest in this way? What will be the position if the white man acts thus? The African too will seek to do that at some stage. There are many ways of stifling the development of a person so that he does not grow or does not thrive.

One way would be the elder man will not give full rights to the younger one. Another way is so to apply economic pressure that the African has no incentive to develop. In certain cases you will find that there are many obstructions that are in the way of the development of the younger man. Yet another way is to deny him a full, and fundamental *education* that will enable him to stand on his own, as a man. All those are ways and means of trying to debar the progress of the junior man to develop to the stage where he compares with his senior.

I read the other day something that was said by the leader of the Opposition in the Union, Sir de Villiers Graaff, where he said that he did 'not think that the people overseas who thought that there should be equality even in the economic world were genuine in what they said'. He thought that that would never obtain. He thought they merely meant that there should be equality in a shallow way because no African can hope to be on the same level with the European at the present moment. When I read the article I wondered what Sir de Villiers really meant, what sort of equality was he referring to, that of stature, or what? I could hardly appreciate his idea, because as an African together with many others we are looking for fair play and justice only. All that the African people seek to achieve is to be able to face their own problems themselves rather than have things done for them by some other person. The type of equality and fair play that we are referring to is not such as to demand that even though someone has his own property here we will try to oust him from that property of his or show off in any way. All we need is fair play in every sphere of life, that's all that we are asking for. Having read that article I felt I wasn't at all convinced that Sir de Villiers had grasped what type of equality we are striving for. I thought of what's happening up in North Africa.

In casting my thoughts over this and wondering what actually it was that was worrying the whole of Africa, and looking around in my predicament, I read one article from a man in East Africa, in Kenya, who says: 'No, we are not actually trying to deprive some other person of his own right, we want rights of our own.' And another one came out from Nyasaland who says: 'We are not out to fight, against Europeans – we realise that we must live together with the Europeans.' I said: 'This is exactly what we have been thinking ourselves, because, when someone says "We don't want Europeans here, we don't want Europeans with us" I just wonder really if those people are saying so genuinely from the bottom of their hearts. Truly speaking one wonders if there is anything at all in that type of talk.'

Personally I feel that no man with all his senses and a good citizen could ever think of depriving one of his own property and still remain complacent with somebody else's property. People who try to do such things are those who have had ill-treatment like a child that has been ill-treated from its earlier stages, which usually thinks: 'If one day I grow I will pay back to this person.' That type of person I am referring to now, is such as we have read about in papers who say: 'Let the Europeans go back overseas' and speak in an unreasonable way like that. But I would like to give an assurance to this house here and now that personally I feel that no true African would think in terms of trying to oust a person from his house or think that he can just chase his neighbours out.

I have often wondered what it is really that these people are struggling for or are striving for when they say that they are trying to establish white protectorates and things of that nature which don't seem to make any sense to me. And I think that's where the danger of the whole thing is. It is a danger that I think is threatening us even in this country Swaziland. I have read that we are trying to get more and more immigrants into Swaziland and I have read also that even though the Union did not want to have immigrants from elsewhere they are now trying to open their doors to get as many people from outside as possible. I think that they will go wrong. That's where the conflagration is going to start which will lay waste the whole countryside.

Let me take for example what is happening in the Union. I'm sure that they haven't got a proper solution of the problem how to settle the Africans in that country. Now they are seeking to bring in more and more Europeans. What will the Indians do? The Indians will wonder why they should be debarred from entering the Union, they are human beings like anybody else, and so will the Chinese and other Asians, they also have a right to live. Everybody else will demand: 'Why am I precluded from entering the Union if these other countries have a right to send their people as immigrants into South Africa?' And then there is also the position in which one finds there are Africans who are not allowed to go out into other countries – they are in South Africa all the time and are refused permits or passports for going out. They will join the other people that are struggling against what is happening in South Africa and they will join hands with those to whom Mr Macmillan was referring when he pointed out, 'Let us beware of trying to work the situation in such a way that will estrange ourselves from the Africans and make them join the East instead of going with us.'

To drive my point home let me make an illustration of what happens among the Swazi. When a man has to reprimand his wife, often there will be found an ill-intentioned man who will come to the wife and say: 'How sorry I feel for you because your husband always scolds you and treats you badly and I would do something better for you.' Such a man is a bad man. And we feel that such a man in the political world is Russia and others like her. Now if you try to stop the Africans from doing what they would like to achieve by way of entering Territories outside the Union or the Asians and others from entering into South Africa, you are really setting against each other the East and West. Personally I think that among the Africans there's no need whatsoever, nothing required by way of immigration laws and things of that nature to regulate the migration of the people.

All that type of legislation emanates from the fear complex that is there all the time and each man wants to protect himself. Each side fears that if there are more and more people of the other section coming in they must protect their rights so that these people that come in will not eventually swallow them up. Actually what I mean is that by bringing in more and more Europeans the country's Government is trying to equalise the position so that some day when it is needed to vote the Europeans should not be found to be in the minority or have lesser numbers. There I feel personally that there is nothing to fear, 'they fear leopards in the dark where they do not exist'.

In the protection that they are seeking in this manner they are getting themselves into worse positions than they would otherwise have been in. Let us take for instance the example in the Union or Rhodesia; if, say, people were to be told that they are now placed on equal footing or equal rights in all respects, how many educated persons would be found with adequate education to supply all commodities that are necessary in modern life, how many years would it take them to get to that stage? Or let us take a hypothetical case where by some miracle we would suddenly find that Europeans had all disappeared and left the country and we are left in Africa without any Europeans at all. What could we do? Where would we get trains? Where would we have the electricity, power, or the commodities that we have learnt to use with comfort nowadays? ...

Now seeing that each of us is seeking to find a proper protection as to his rights in future, in what way shall we have this assurance that the European is not going to be ousted from any country and the African is assured of a proper place for his posterity. It is for that reason then, gentlemen, that I have asked for this meeting to take place here today so that we can consider, confer together and find out a way which will make us have a common understanding and how we can remain in peace knowing that we are here settled and going to live together. Now even if one may deceive oneself by saying that it is only the Europeans that are seeking security for their future, the truth is that also the Africans would like to get assurance of what is going to happen with them in future. I say so because it is common practice among the Europeans that when he lends out money he must have security, a surety for what will happen in the event of the client failing to pay the money. In Africa we have also got to look into the practices of the Africans as to whether the practice used to obtain whereby when one borrowed money it was necessary to have some sort of surety. This one thing I know among the Africans, that if you marry a woman and you pay cattle as lobolo, those cattle are there as security – you are buying the right to have the children and your wife is also bound at her husband's kraal because she feels that she cannot leave the children there. She knows that if she were to leave her husband's people, she would have forsaken her children, have abandoned any right to her children because the children were actually bought by her husband's people by the lobolo that they paid. And if she were to decide to desert her husband's kraal she would have to leave the children behind. So far I have been trying to deal with the situation of the whole world but now I'd like to come nearer home and refer to Swaziland in particular.

We find that what is the source of trouble elsewhere obtains even in Swaziland. Indeed I have read from the newspapers, that this country too seeks to bring in a lot of people from outside, and somebody else mentioned on a certain occasion that we need to have people from outside, for the development of the country. And that has caused me much concern – I feel this is the source of all problems that are going to come.

Our practice and indeed what we uphold in Swaziland, is a position where people will come into the Territory of their own free will, when they feel that there is something for which they want to come into the Territory, not because they have been invited or told to come in numbers into the country. I wonder how this house feels about that, whether they think that is the way in which we are going to solve our problems.

I draw attention to the policy of the Government overseas, a glimpse into their policy will show what their aim is about the whole of Africa. You will find that the policy now is to let go. They feel that to be sitting on a people, in that old Imperialist and Colonialist fashion when they are unhappy and all that, is not a healthy state of affairs. Give them independence and let them carry on their own – just in the way that Mr Harold Macmillan mentioned in Parliament in Cape Town. And you will realise that the West as a whole – England, America and others that are grouped together as the West – their ideas, their policy now is that people should look after their own affairs. The white people should have nothing to complain about. The black people should not find cause to complain either. If that would come to pass, that state of affairs where there will be peace, between the white and the black – these Western countries would be very happy – they will sing 'Halleluja'.

And it is for that reason that even in Swaziland one has heard a number of people here and there coming out with views and ideas that we should come together and work together for the well-being of our country. We have this one great fortune in Swaziland that we live together as one – there is no underdog – we just live as a community. And this lack of equality elsewhere does not exist in Swaziland – we are all equal.

We should now look for a way which will make us feel at home, feel that we are quite secure in this country, but how shall we go about getting this security that we seek? Even if there are difficulties I don't think that they are insurmountable. Many a difficulty has had to be surmounted. We can have difficulties of whatsoever a nature, but we should find ways and means of trying to fight against those difficulties and live together in peace. I have already mentioned that the metropolitan Government has already expressed a desire that we should manage our own affairs. A number of men have been to consult me about whether it wouldn't be a good idea to meet together and join in the Advisory Council as one Council.

I have decided to place my dreams before you here present. At first I thought I would hold back my views and leave the matter in the hands of my Council and those men who were desirous to discuss it, and await their views. I thought that my Council would confer together and discuss these matters with the European Council or Government and with ordinary members of the public to find out ways and means of how to come together and develop something that would be of help to the country. But because of the turn of events that have been taking place in North Africa, in East Africa, in Central Africa and elsewhere, I began to realise that probably I was making a mistake by sitting quiet – now I am convinced I must say my mind, however wrong it may be – a number of people may not agree with me but I think I'd better express my mind now. And even though perhaps what I am going to say now may probably prejudice the position in that some people may try to follow what I have already said without reasoning it out, I am now going to say out what my feelings are on the subject.

I think it would not be a good idea to join with the Advisory Council, for these two reasons: Firstly, we are a Protectorate and the set-up of a Protectorate is such that the people are an entity on their own, a people that have their own institutions, have got to carry on in the way that they have been wont to do, but they go to someone to protect them who has got to bring them up, teach them certain things in which they feel they are deficient until such time as they feel they are fully developed. And then he hands over.

And you find that the protecting power, as we have heard is the practice among the Germans, when they are protecting a certain state, instead of developing that state to a stage of being able to stand on its own feet, they begin to absorb that particular state. And that causes ill feeling from that state which was expecting to be brought up and which was being nursed until it was able to stand on its own feet. They feel that they have now been deprived of their rights.

Now I will ask His Honour the Resident Commissioner and the Secretary for Swazi Affairs now to listen intently. What I am going to say will probably be somewhat sore to them but I would ask them to bear with me and just listen to what I am saying. It may help them because sometimes to speak the truth even though it may be painful, does help. The members of the Council may probably think that I am spoiling their chances by saying much too much and more than I should have said but, well, let them bear with me. A man who always has bad ideas sometimes has also got to be listened to, so please listen to this.

I believe at the present moment there is quite a lot of talk in Council sessions with Government on matters concerning immigration laws and deportation laws, so much so that decision on one law has been withheld for an inordinately long time and the Government feels that the Council is so delaying matters that now the High Commissioner's Office is becoming very impatient on these things, and the Council feels 'What is Government trying to do with us? They're probably leading us into something that we've never heard of or are going to ruin our country' and things of that nature.

I did not like to participate in these discussions because even though I am a man, a member of the Council, they have the chance to discuss matters among themselves and convince one another on these matters before I come in. But now I begin to feel that I should really come out with the truth and ask the Council 'Why don't you say so and so', which will make the position quite clear to the Government, and why doesn't Government do so and so and so and so, so that this matter may be cleared up.

I am of opinion that the mind of the Council is working on these lines: 'That instead of Government protecting us they are now taking away some of our powers – they are now suppressing us.' Take for instance the deportation draft Proclamation. The Swazis wonder why it should be the Government that has got to deport people rather than that people should be deported by the Swazis if they have to be. It is felt that Government should be in a position to deport Europeans but the African people who have come into the Territory should only be deported by the National Administration – the Swazi Authority.

A number of these members of the Council here present, have got relations of some kind in the Union somewhere. Chief Comfi here with us, has his senior brother in the Lydenburg district. Councillor Nhlabatsi has always told us that when the boundaries were first set up his home was on the Swaziland side of the line but the boundary has shifted time and again and now they don't know how they got to be in the Union. Mnt. Madevu's physical father used to live in the Carolina district. The Secretary to the Nation has got some of his people living in the Transvaal and others living in Swaziland. A number of Royal kraals, some of them in the Barberton district, others in the Carolina district, are under my direct control in the same way as other Royal kraals of past reigns are under my care today.

Now if these people were to come back to Swaziland and we accept them to come back to Swaziland and should there be something wrong because they were born outside the country, they become deported by Government. What does that bring up in the minds of the Swazis? That is what is really causing a lot of difficulty among the members of the Council on this draft Proclamation, that we are doing something that is not known among the Swazi. They fear that when the whole Libandla is called upon, they will censure them rather severely, they will tell them that they have exceeded their powers in accepting this thing because it has got great repercussions, great difficulties behind it, if it is going to bring about dismissal or deportation of Africans in Swaziland without the authority of the Swazi – it is something unheard of.

I don't know if this has been explained to Government by the Council but this that

I am explaining is the reason why they have been so very adamant about it, and that they also feel that our rights are being whittled off. Instead of being brought up properly we are now being swallowed up. In all this I have been trying to explain how a protecting Government can help to protect and develop and bring up a Nation that is not yet developed, to a stage where it can stand on its own feet. I will not now deal with the Convention of 1894 but I will refer to the Order in Council which enjoins Government that when they make laws in the country they will respect Swazi law and custom.

Thirdly, as I mentioned, I don't think that the Advisory Council can join together with us. The set up, the way of life of the European is such that it is individualistic and he has his own practices which are peculiarly his own. That is their tradition, but we have our own traditions too. No man can say that that one is not as good as the other one but I will say that mine is the better tradition.

By way of illustrating what I am saying I'd like to point out that in the European culture you find that if I married a wife, my wife is my own and she is not a woman of the household of my family. A wife does not belong to the family but she is my own. I'm her husband and nobody else has got anything to do or to say to her. According to Swazi custom she is your wife, she is your family's wife, belonging to the family as a whole. Among the Europeans if there is a misunderstanding in the house, the husband will run to the magistrate and report, 'Oh my wife does not want to share a bed with me.' If the wife has got some difficulty in the house she goes to report to the Court – and then the newspaper reporters are there and they are ready to report. And then the Court Order is given – you should make it up and if you are not able to make it up within so many days, come back to me. Among us Africans we feel that that is not good behaviour. With us, if the man had such a situation in the house he, if it is the woman that is becoming difficult, reports the matter to his parents. If his parents no longer lived, he reports to friends or relatives and they come and discuss the matter and get it over – it is not broadcast to the whole world so that everybody should know what's happening – that these are no longer sharing their bed, etc. A family matter of that nature is referred to the King, to the Court only as a last resort, and we feel that that is a better procedure than to report everything to the Court rather than have it settled amicably at home.

In so saying I am trying to point out that the Europeans and Africans are not yet at the stage where they would be able to meet and discuss things profitably in such gatherings as the Advisory Council. But I don't mean that they should not meet, I think that we should by all means find a way of making these two meet.

But we regard the Advisory Council as having a lower status than our Council. We cannot meet the Advisory Council in its present stage as an Advisory Council and in order that we should join it, let its status be raised to that of a Legislative Council. Only then can we come together. At that stage we'll come together on equal basis, discussing matters of the Territory of Swaziland as a whole. It would not lower our prestige, our dignity as a protected people who have their own institutions and rights, but it will raise us both to a stage where we could together confer on matters of state and legislate for the country. We would not be taking a retrogressive step there. Now there again, as I have mentioned, these people have been brought up on different ideas. How will they come together, join up only at the top levels? I think a solution to that would be that the Advisory Council, the European public, should elect their own men under their system of election, and we would get our men, chosen by us to meet and legislate for the country. They would all then join together. It would be better to call the method that of Federation, where we would not count how many represent so and so and how many represent that unit, but they will merely meet as a Federation together.

If we met on these lines and the Africans came with their own system I think it would solve the situation. I don't see how we can try to adopt European ways of doing things which we don't know. Yes it is quite true that we should copy those good practices that the Europeans have, but when we come to consider what is this democracy of which they speak you ultimately get lost in the idea – I don't even understand what is meant by democracy – because each man will display his wealth and say that he wants to do so and so and bring out certain monies with the idea to do so and so but one without capital will not be able to do any of these things or display. When people speak of democracy one wonders what democracy it is they want to maintain because we, the Africans as a matter of fact, have bigger numbers than the other people but one cannot understand what is meant by democracy when one thinks on those lines.

Let us regard this as a practice, as a European practice, because to speak of democracy, I don't think would be the correct word, because democracy is not there. A man promises his constituency that 'I will do so and so for you, I will certainly achieve so and so for you' and then he is not able to do it. I think it would be better democracy if people went into it in the same way as de Gaulle took up his position in France. He was called by the people to come to their rescue as they were in difficulty in this way. He came with that mandate. There's nothing that he has promised the people that he would achieve for them. Actually I appreciate it was the people that suggested that he should be appointed. I thought that was a good form.

If only we could be able to extricate Africa from this idea of one man, one vote, I'm sure we would have achieved our objective. Even this federation that I referred to, that we have heard of in Central Africa, if it aims at one man, one vote I'm sure it will not be a success. Whether it is a federation for the white or the black, it would not be successful. Because if the parties fear that the one party, the black or white, supersedes the other, then there will be fear that they will swallow all the others' rights, absorb them, nationalise all their institutions; and that's the fear. That is my own opinion, whether it is right or wrong, it is my opinion. I would like to hear from you, what you suggest could be done to save this country.

The Acting Resident Commissioner opened the discussion with cautious approval; it was 'a great pleasure' to know that the Ngwenyama thought along the same lines as 'he and many of his friends', and that he 'was sure that one day we will have the democracy which he finds so elusive'. Others spoke, Madevu expressing his support in religious terms: 'You have borne witness to the Word of God'; Sibiya, a former teacher and policeman, recounted personal but typical incidents of humiliation to stress the need to educate the young to be 'humane and kind', adding that in the schools white and black should study together. Dr Hynd stated that one man one vote was seen by whites as the best means of justice for the ordinary citizen, but Lewis disagreed, making the only *ad hominem* speech of the afternoon, beginning: 'Fortunately or unfortunately Dr Hynd is a churchman and churchmen do not always think the same way as we do.' He suggested scrapping the voters roll and starting afresh with perhaps an 'elected council, the Ngwenyama-in-Council, a High Commissioner and a few leading citizens', and re-emphasized that it was on the personal level that change must be implemented – 'let us shake hands with each other in the street – do not be afraid of it.'

When nothing new was being added Sobhuza closed the meeting; it was getting late, it was time to disperse to think of what had been said and come together again at a later date and clarify points that had not been understood. Lewis asked if they might talk to others and

Sobhuza agreed. The first seed was sown; it had to germinate and spread.

Marwick on his return was disturbed to find a matter of such importance had been publicized in his absence. In June the Secretary of State replied to the memoranda he had forwarded and instructed him to pursue the idea of establishing a legislative council on which European and Swazi interests would be represented, so that Swazi could more effectively play a part in government. It distressed Marwick that Sobhuza was moving in a different direction with Carl Todd, elected leader of the European Advisory Council, whom Marwick did not trust, as a strong supporter.

Further discussions took place between Sobhuza and a close circle of advisors as well as between members of the Council. On 25 July, Sobhuza called a second meeting at Masundvwini inviting a few more whites. He made the same points as on 23 April, repeating that 'the policy of "one man one vote" was fatal for Africa because the race with the largest numbers would swallow the other race, take away its rights and nationalize its institutions. The prospect of this brought about that fear which was the root of all the trouble in Africa' (*Times of Swaziland*, 27 July 1960). He tried to clarify what he meant by the word 'federation', a term used in the South African context by Sir de Villiers Graaff, leader of the United Party, who advocated race-federation as distinct from apartheid. The sense in which Sobhuza used the term was without the racist implication of the United Party leader's proposal since the United Party never contemplated full equality or African autonomy over their own nationals. At this meeting Todd spoke in favour of Sobhuza's policy.

Members of the Swazi National Council were holding their own discussions, and at an early meeting of the Council, Nquku created a stir by suggesting that it was time to introduce more fundamental changes to bring the Swazi system of government into line with western political developments. One of the few men who spoke supporting Nquku was the trusted Sifunti Matsebula. When Sobhuza was told what was taking place, he said, 'Let everyone speak'.

On 29 July the Swazi National Council publicly endorsed Sobhuza's proposal as the policy of the nation, but two days later the Swaziland Progressive Association, at its annual conference in the township of Kwaluseni, formed itself into the first 'modern' political party, the Swaziland Progressive Party (SPP), with Nquku as President. A delegation from the conference went to the nearby home of Dr Ambrose Zwane, inviting him to become its Secretary-General. Dr Zwane, who had recently resigned from his post as a Swaziland Government doctor because of the policy of racial discrimination at all levels, accepted Nquku's invitation, describing it as an opportunity to 'improve the condition of all African people'.

At that stage, Sobhuza did not regard the SPP as a serious threat to national unity, and far less as a challenge to Swazi Kingship. True, there was 'open and hot debating', but he still hoped to contain the opposition within a single national movement. He appreciated that Nquku had chosen to settle in Swaziland and had contributed to the social and educational development of the people. Nor did Sobhuza doubt the motives of Ambrose Phesheya Zwane. Sobhuza had helped pay his University fees and followed his progress with interest and pride. He was happy that Ambrose had accepted an appointment in Swaziland and he expressed indignation both personally and through the Swazi National Council, when he heard of the discrimination against him in salary, and of the humiliation inflicted on him by some of the white staff.

The fact that both Zwane and Nquku frequently expressed their personal respect and admiration for Sobhuza, at the same time that they criticized weaknesses in the system of hereditary chieftainship, did not make Sobhuza's position any easier, but gave him reason to believe that the new elites could be brought into the future political system without creating a major cleavage. He arranged to meet members of the Swazi Progressive Party at Masundvwini on 17 September and held a long and much publicized session with them. He spoke as usual without demagoguery or threat: there were difficulties throughout the world; Swaziland was caught in world problems, but had to seek its own solutions along its own path. He referred to the crisis in the Congo, warning that politics would lead in Swaziland as elsewhere to *umbango* – civil war. Instead of parties he advocated national congresses that would look after the interest of all the people. 'One man one vote' created leaders with selfish individual ambitions and led to sectional interests.

According to the *Times of Swaziland* (14/10/60), which expressed the views of the more liberal Europeans, Sobhuza called for 'the immediate abolition of parties'. But in fact he did not do so. He made it plain, as he had previously, that he was putting forward his suggestions as food for thought. Nquku made this point in a letter to the editor (28/10/60) in which he also wrote, 'The Swazi King is a democrat, and we as Progressives protest most strongly against anything that tends to point otherwise in the eyes of the world.'

Many members of the Progressive Party and of the European Advisory Council expressed support of Sobhuza, each hoping for his support in return. Sobhuza struggled to make his decision in terms of his own principles and political perception. Among the western educated whose initial position was not clear but for whom he had a special affection and in whose career he had taken a personal interest was Malabhane Allen Nxumalo, son of Benjamin, the trusted and wise advisor of his youth, who had died in 1941. Malabhane, like Phesheya Zwane, had spent many years in South Africa, and qualified, in 1957, as a medical doctor at Witwatersrand University. Burly, good-natured, well spoken, he soon made a wide circle of friends among the more liberal whites as well as western oriented

Swazi. He had struggled very hard to pass his examinations, and was not eager to be drawn into politics.

In October, Brian Marwick began formal discussions on the constitutional issue, meeting first with the European Advisory Council and members of the European public, and later with the Swazi National Council. He saw Sobhuza privately, and their discussions were courteous and friendly; but Sobhuza made his own position very clear: he did not accept the western model of elections, parties and caucuses, nor would he commit himself to go against the wishes of his people.

On 4 November the first official joint meeting of Swazi and Europeans was held in Mbabane with Brian Marwick presiding. Sobhuza did not attend and explained to me later that it was not appropriate. Instead he sent some of his councillors as delegates, keeping others with him to scrutinize their reports. In addition to representatives of the Swaziland National Council, he appointed three officials of the Swaziland Progressive Party to act in their personal capacity. The whites who were invited included elected members of the reconstituted European Advisory Council and a few individuals, considered influential or representative of special interests. Brian Marwick was accompanied by four government representatives.[11]

Marwick outlined the terms of reference and invited discussions.[12] As yet no government policy had been rigidly formulated. Differences in outlook soon became obvious. Particularly sharp were the exchanges between delegates of the Swazi National Council and Nquku who, supported by Zwane and Mabuza, spoke as officials of a political party.

At the end of the meeting Polycarp Dlamini, as Secretary of the Swazi National Council, announced that the *Ncwala* was about to begin and no further discussions could take place until the end of the ritual. The date of the next meeting was set for 17 February 1961.

At the capital of Lobamba the priests carried out the traditional

---

[11] The delegates were: (1) SNC: Makhosini (recently returned from a year of study in England); Lutfo (as senior prince); Polycarp Dlamini (Secretary of the Swazi Nation); Msindazwe Sukati (Senior Liaison Officer); J.S.M. Matsebula (Liaison Officer); A.K. Hlophe (Councillor); M.P. Nhlabatsi (Councillor); Douglas Lukhele (the first Swazi lawyer), and Dr Malabhane Allen Nxumalo. (2) SPP: J.J. Nquku (President); Dr Zwane (Secretary-General); Obed Mabuza (member of the Executive). (3) EAC: A. Millin (lawyer); J.H. Pearce (farmer); C.F. Todd (lawyer and farmer); R.P. Stephens (manager of Peak Timbers). (4) Dan Fitzpatrick (former civil servant and now shopkeeper); B.P. Stewart (shopkeeper); G. Bordihn (farm manager); Willy Meyer (farmer); Eric Wynn (farmer); E. Bowman; C.S. Hubbard (agriculture and forestry); and Dr David Hynd (missionary and educator). (5) Government: J.C. Martin, O.B.E. (Acting Government Secretary); W.E. Pitcher (Director of Education); H.J. Steward, O.B.E. (First Assistant Secretary); M.J. Fairlie (Acting Secretary for Finance and Development). The names listed in the *Times of Swaziland* (11/11/60) are not entirely identical with those recorded in the minutes of the SNC memorandum.
[12] The terms of reference were: (1) to examine the circumstances which militated against common purpose and co-existence; (2) to consider what form of constitution was desirable for Swaziland and to draft accordingly; (3) to consider the need for subordinate or local forms of government in Swaziland (*Times of Swaziland* 11/11/60).

rituals to unite and strengthen the nation through the Kingship. Sobhuza danced with his warriors. Zihlathi and the Queens reaffirmed the central position which he held, as head of the nation and head of the Malangeni.

But behind the scenes other political activities were being enacted. On 16 December 1960, anniversary of the defeat of Dingane, King of the Zulu, by the Boers, a day of victory for white nationalists and of protest and mourning for blacks, the Swaziland Progressive Party, under Nquku, called a meeting at Msunduza Hall in Mbabane. The most eloquent speaker was a young man, Prince Dumisa Clement Dlamini, son of the late Mkukwane, younger son of the Ndlovukazi Nukwase, almost as high in the royal genealogy as Sobhuza's own children. Dumisa had spent many of his early years at the capital with his grandmother, where his own mother, also a Nxumalo but closer to the Ebulandzeni branch, was a welcome visitor. Dumisa, bright, sparkling with vitality and enthusiasm and ambition, had taken his matric in Swaziland, going first to national schools and then, because of his interest in Latin, doing his last years at a Catholic mission school in Bremersdorp. He had gone for further education to Basutoland where the King was paying for his education at the University of Roma. There, as he said, a new world opened. He started reading history and was inspired by debates, and worked with the anti-colonial Basutoland Congress Party. At the meeting at Msunduza Hall he made an impassioned plea for the rights of all people, pointed to the racial inequalities in Swaziland, and advocated radical changes and new alliances.

When Sobhuza heard of the Msunduza meeting and Dumisa's speech, he made no public comment. He no doubt noted that Dumisa did not dance the *Ncwala* that year with his peers and that there were others too who did not attend. Before dismissing the warriors, he warned them against grasping at strange customs because they belonged to those in power, and pointed to the danger of national strife through individuals who were 'power greedy'.

The majority of the Swazi National Council was adamant that Nquku could not continue as an official representative, and Sobhuza could no longer hope that he would work within the constraints of the traditional system. He was therefore formally dismissed from his position on the National Council and found himself excluded from the next session of the Constitutional Committee. The two other members of the Progressive Party walked out in support. The Swazi members of the Constitutional Committee, which was to carry on the major task of formulating and discussing proposals, thereafter consisted only of members of the Swazi National Council.

At the meeting of the Constitutional Committee on 17 February, three major political viewpoints emerged – that of members of the Swazi National Council, that of settlers on the European Advisory Council, and that of the British through its senior civil servants. New leaders were struggling for power on the African continent, leaders linked ideologically with Pan-Africanism as well as nationalism. In Swaziland, ideologies ranging from racial conservatism to radical socialism were being expounded. Sobhuza's own position became extremely difficult.

CHAPTER XIV
A Constitution Imposed

The following years, 1961-1963, were heavy with danger of violence. Brian Marwick relied increasingly on the advice of senior officials in the service who had worked for 'progress on the British model' in other countries. Anxious to transform what they described to me as 'a feudal society' and also as 'a top-heavy monarchy' into a 'modern democracy' under a constitutional king, they underestimated the strength of the Swazi system.[1]

Sobhuza acknowledged that these men were not racists, but he realized that their sympathies were with the self-styled progressives on the assumption that 'west was best'. He could not convince them otherwise. 'Freedom' was seen by them as possible only in the 'democratic' system of competing political parties, each with its own leaders; and they contrasted this unfavourably with an 'aristocratic nepotism'. Sobhuza saw this type of individual freedom and competition as a threat to the rights of others; his basic premise was that the ideology of kinship, extending from the family to the nation, imposed essential moral constraints and reciprocal obligations. 'Freedom' allowed one to flout constraints and shirk obligations; it was not a contrast between a democracy and a tyranny, but between an egoistic and a communal approach.

There were among his supporters some who would have had him act with more aggression to the 'politicians'; but he resisted them. He avoided as much as possible direct confrontation with either the British or the 'politicians', using when necessary the indirect approach – the 'mouth' of such diplomatic intermediaries as the Secretary of the Swazi Nation or the Chief Liaison Officer – and relying largely on reports by his trusted 'eyes'. He had learnt that to show anger would not help his cause. 'When he was most angry, he would not want to speak; and when he spoke in his most polite way you knew you were in for the high jump.'

[1] Two senior expatriates who were particularly influential in shaping his policy were Michael J. Fairlie and Atholl Long. Fairlie, a man of strong convictions but rough mannerisms, committed to non-racialism, interested in encouraging interracial cultural activities, believing in trade unions as the best method of protecting and advancing workers' interests, came in 1957 with recent experience of Bechuanaland. He was largely responsible for developing the Department of Labour. Atholl Long came in 1961 as new Government Secretary with experience of Burma and Northern Nigeria. Cynical and intelligent, polished and cosmopolitan, he found it impossible to accept Swazi values or culture.

Again events in South Africa provided a counterpoint to developments in Swaziland. In April 1961 Verwoerd attended the Prime Ministers Conference in London and withdrew South Africa from the Commonwealth. Back in Pretoria, in May, he told the Nationalist Party Congress that the relationship of the new Republic with the High Commission Territories was as that to 'foreign states'.

The British government continued and intensified its efforts to develop the Territories economically as well as politically. The foundations of a modern economy were being firmly laid by improving transport and communication, and the Constitutional Committee was busily at work. There was one principle on which Sobhuza's representatives on the Constitutional Committee and the British officials were in general agreement: racial discrimination with its assumption of African inferiority was unacceptable. How to bring about a fundamental change in attitudes and actions was a different matter. The first step suggested by representatives of the Administration was to remove discriminatory legislation. In October, 1961, an Anti-Discrimination Proclamation was passed, prohibiting segregated facilities in bars, banks, cinemas, hotels and theatres. The unofficial white members gave support with different degrees of acceptance.

To Sobhuza some of these 'concessions' were symbolic rather than basic and would 'not necessarily help his people'. Racism was too deeply imbedded to be removed by proclamations; it would take time and strict enforcement, in addition to the revision of almost every statute in the country. Moreover, in itself the proclamation did not affect the more fundamental issues of redistribution of wealth and power. He warned his people that they might be 'swallowed' by the more powerful race, their economic rights and their culture be taken from them; he considered the best way to protect themselves was by cooperation, 'on a basis of equality'. Political parties would destroy Swazi national unity by making cooperation more, not less, difficult.

Each group worked with its own legal advisors. Sobhuza, following his customary caution, was in contact with more than one lawyer inside and outside Swaziland. One of the Swazi representatives on the Constitutional Committee was Douglas Lukhele, the first Swazi lawyer, who had worked in the legal offices of two leading members of the African National Congress in South Africa, Nelson Mandela and Oliver Tambo. Sobhuza also made contact with Jan van Wyk de Vries who, as Sobhuza's critics pointed out, had ready access to Verwoerd. But Sobhuza argued that if his advice was sound he would take it; if not, he was under no obligation to follow it nor did it prevent him hearing or considering other legal opinions.

The British sent out their own legal advisors to help guide discussions. In September 1961 Sir Charles Arden Clarke met the Committee. Marwick introduced him to Sobhuza at the Matsapha National School. Sobhuza turned the conversation from the specifics of the Constitution 'since the Committee which he [Sir Arden Clarke] had come to advise had been appointed for that purpose'.

The Swaziland Progressive Party engaged the services of Professor Denis V. Cowen, then Professor of Comparative Law at the University of Cape Town. The Cowen Report,[2] submitted to Arden Clarke, was most in accord with the outlook of senior government officials, and was a direct challenge to the traditional monarchy.

Two members of the European Advisory Council, including the chairman Carl Todd, were lawyers. Todd expressed support of the Swazi system 'as far as practicable', and urged the Committee to work on a plan that 'would not damage Swazi tradition', so as not to allow 'the new forces in Africa to control the situation'. He argued that there were not enough members of the Progressive Party to dictate changes but they were enough to catch the ear of the British government. He was largely responsible for the proposals passed by the Constitutional Committee on 6 November 1961.

Described later as the '50-50 Constitution,' it proposed *inter alia* the establishment of a Legislative Council consisting of 24 unofficial members of whom twelve would represent Europeans and twelve Swazi. Of the twelve Swazi, eight would be nominated by the Ngwenyama according to Swazi tradition; of the Europeans, eight would be elected by Europeans on the lines of the existing elections for the European Advisory Council. The remaining four Swazi and four Europeans would be elected on a common roll in four double member constituencies. These proposals were not acceptable to members of the Swaziland administration, whose representatives withdrew from the meeting when the vote was being taken.

Makhosini Dlamini, A. Khuseni Hlophe, Carl Todd and Dan Fitzpatrick were selected to go to London to present the proposals of the Committee; Marwick travelled separately taking with him confidential suggestions from the administration. Mr Reginald Maudling, Secretary of State, received the delegation on 13 December. This First London Conference was formal and preliminary; a reply would be received from the British government when the documents had been studied.

Sobhuza was shrewd enough not to interpret 'politics' at the superficial level of representation in government. Political representation was a symptom of power; the real crux, the issue of major importance, was who holds power over economic resources, more especially land and minerals. Numerical racial differentiation in representation was not an end in itself, but a means of controlling future developments. Polycarp Dlamini, as his spokesman before the Secretary of State, stated that the difference between the Swazi National Council and the 'politicians' was that the SNC was more interested in economic advance than political argument, but denied

<hr>

[2] D.V. Cowen, *Report on Constitutional Reforms*, Swaziland Progressive Party, Mbabane, 1961.

that the traditionalists were opposed to political advance – 'participation and growing political consciousness of the younger elements are inevitable and must be given recognition.' He pointed out that the issue of land and mineral ownership had been given little publicity compared with the publicity given to the system of representation, and he reiterated that 250,000 Swazi owned 51% of the land, 8,000 Europeans the rest, and that the mineral resources brought little advantage to the Swazi people (*Africa Diary*, vol. 1, no. 25, Dec. 16-22, 1961; *Times of Swaziland*, 22 November 1961). Sobhuza did not want the Swazi nation that he represented as Ngwenyama to lose control of its economic resources to others, white or black, British or South African, or to be subordinated to foreign leadership.

The 'confidential paper'[3] submitted by the Swaziland administration put forward the goal of 'a democratic non-racial stable form of government provided with checks and balances to safeguard all civil liberties'. To achieve this they considered it necessary to build one nation by western political procedures. They made no specific reference to the Swazi monarchy, but stated that the traditional local government system should be replaced gradually by elected town councils, trade unions, and other western institutions. The document gave little recognition to the viability and flexibility of the Swazi structure, and directed economic policy whether in industry or agriculture towards foreign models.

The whites of Swaziland were involved in their own power struggle. The proposals of the Constitutional Committee had not been published but the contents had been leaked to the public. The *Times of Swaziland* became a forum for antagonistic factions. Opening the controversy was a copy of a letter signed by Vincent Rozwadowski and 14 other citizens, who claimed that they were 'members of no political party'. The original of the letter sent to the Secretary of State indicated the influence of the Cowen Report and contained detailed criticism of the proposals 'which were originally suggested by the Paramount Chief and possibly favoured by the Constitutional Committee'. In their view 'the proposed racial division – strongly resembling apartheid – would entrench social and racial differences'. The first to reply was Carl Todd who began his letter, 'As a Traditionalist I support orderly development in political affairs and would prefer the safe course of carrying the bulk of the people with me than introducing innovations that may have support from a minority of theorists' (*Times of Swaziland*, 2 February 1962). Sobhuza was aware of this controversy, and watched while others joined in the dispute.

The public was informed in mid-February that the long awaited

[3] Mimeographed – Mbabane, 7 February 1962. It did not matter that the document was labelled 'confidential' since nothing was in fact confidential at that time; and even 'secret' discussions of the working committee were known almost as soon as the doors closed at the end of each session and the members went in their different directions.

response from the Secretary of State would be received at the end of the month, and from the SNC offices notices went out calling the nation to assemble at Lobamba, on 27 February, 1962. The Secretary's response took the form of releasing the contents of the Constitutional Committee's 'Proposals for a Swaziland Constitution'. These were then made known to the nation, at a meeting of some 3,000 people in the *sibaya*. Both the Ngwenyama and the Ndlovukazi were present. The SNC representatives were vigorously challenged for submitting proposals without a mandate from the entire nation and were accused of not expressing the King's ideas. Not only spokesmen of the political parties but members of the Council argued that it gave a 50% representation to the whites who numbered less than 5% of the total population.

Politicians mushroomed as political parties struggled to establish roots and propagate new ideas. Sobhuza knew of the confrontations at public meetings held in halls in the urban centres, at which allegations and counter allegations were made, each party publishing its own pamphlets, manifestos and letters. But he would not allow himself to be personally embroiled. He watched the new leaders who were emerging and wondered how long they would last. Nquku and Zwane had reached a point of mutual distrust. Dumisa had joined with Zwane and formed a youth wing. The day the Constitutional Committee Report was published, a Swaziland Democratic Party (SDP) came into the open, its prime mover Simon Sishayi Nxumalo, a son of Mgcobeya, with Rozwadowski as secretary-general. Sishayi had already shown his ability as a community teacher and in September of 1961 had started the Swaziland Sebenta Society to further education and community development. The SDP policy followed the lines of the non-racial South African Liberal Party. As the Swaziland Progressive Party split into factions, senior government officials felt more confidence in the Swazi Democratic Party and their ideal of a common society. Superficially closer to the views of Sobhuza was the more historically labelled party of Dr George Msibi and Clifford Nkosi,[4] who in July 1962 formed the Mbandzeni National Convention. By emphasizing the position of the monarchy and by calling themselves a convention instead of a party, they reflected Sobhuza's own interest in a national movement. But the leaders were not members of the Inner Council of the Nation, and they argued for 'one man one vote'.

Marwick had hoped that once the proposals had been made and discussed, the Constitutional Committee, having completed the task for which it was established, would dissolve, but Sobhuza pointed out that it was essential that their conclusions be reported to the entire

---

[4] Msibi had returned with a degree in medicine from India and a wider experience of political systems than most of his countrymen. An eloquent and impressive speaker, he had formed the 'National Convention' in April of 1962. Clifford Nkosi, a Swazi who had worked in a law firm in the Republics had started 'The Mbandzeni Party'.

libandla. The gulf between Sobhuza and Marwick had widened. Msindazwe Sukati, in his capacity as Liaison Officer, bore the brunt of criticism from both sides.

Shortly after the meeting at the *sibaya*, when the proposals had been announced, Sobhuza called the Swazi members of the Constitutional Committee together with some of his councillors to Masundvwini and informed them that the proposals were not acceptable to him and the nation, and that more work needed to be done to try to prevent civil strife created by leaders openly advocating organised opposition. He wanted more discussion with people in the outlying districts, so that he could better express national interests to the British government. Some of his younger supporters pointed out that the hostility shown at the meeting was against those men who had agreed to the proposals, and that if the proposals were to be changed new emissaries were needed. In Swaziland, as elsewhere, the Establishment was being challenged from within. Sobhuza replied that 'old oxen are needed to teach the young to pull the plough', but he recognized the practical value of the suggestion, and acted on it later.

In May 1962, the Ngwenyama held a further meeting of the nation in the *sibaya* of Lobamba at which he stated specifically that when in his initial suggestion he had mentioned 'equality' he had *not* meant actual numbers since 'equality is not a question of numbers'. Giving the small white community the same number of representatives as the Swazi did not constitute equality. He again urged national unity. At this meeting there were heated protests and interjections.

But despite the vocal opposition of party members Sobhuza was aware that Swazi support for him as Ngwenyama remained firm. He also received letters from a number of whites expressing their allegiance; he had previously put to the Swazi National Council the need to incorporate coloureds and whites into the Council to indicate that he was not working for a single section but for the entire nation. He made it clear that he wanted to cooperate with non-Swazi. He had chosen an extremely difficult path, but the confusion within the parties enhanced his own power. Sobhuza's denial that he had ever intended a literal numerical equality of representation allowed him greater freedom to manoeuvre and negotiate with the more flexible of the politicians. He called a special meeting of teachers to Masundvwini, and having made his position clear, he asked them to think about the situation, because 'teachers are those to whom one is entitled to look for guidance'.

Swazi National Council mistrust of the British increased as friendly contacts between individual senior officials and members of political parties became conspicuous. Since traditional Swazi society is bound largely by personal ties, a racially mixed social gathering at a hotel or in a private house, especially at that period, assumed added political significance. In an effort to improve official relationships, the Resident Commissioner, Brian Marwick, asked the Ngwenyama-in-Council to discuss the whole situation with him personally. They met at the Lobamba office. Different meeting places carried their own messages. The office, built after the passing of the three proclamations in 1950 and sited about a quarter mile from the capital, was suitable for western British-style communication; the *sibaya*, arena of the *Ncwala*, was the Swazi ritual centre, symbolizing Swazi tradition. The meeting between Marwick and Sobhuza was courteous enough but did not achieve the desired end. Marwick explained that the Legislative Council would give the Swazi a greater share in the government and would not destroy their system or culture. The Council remained unconvinced. Sobhuza replied politely that the intentions of Government were appreciated but the most important issues of land and minerals were still to be discussed.

Sobhuza held no further public meetings with the members of the European Advisory Council. When individual whites came to see him privately 'as a friend', he would not change the stand he had taken on basic points – the meaning of 'equality'; the importance of federation to safeguard the rights of both groups; and his duty as he saw it to protect land and mineral rights for his people. He ignored the letters of extremists,[5] expressing strong anti-British views.

The annual meeting of the Swazi National Council was called for 3 July. Sobhuza was not expected to attend each session but to be kept informed of the discussions, and to express the general consensus at the end of the meeting. He had agreed to a request put by Councillor Sifunti Matsebula that the views of the politicians be heard. Nquku accompanied by Albert Nxumalo, another son of Mgcobeya, representing the SPP, had pleaded before the United Nations against the proposed Constitution. The views they had expressed there were similar to those of local British officials who had described the Constitutional Committee's proposals as 'completely outdated by the United Nations and British Government policy: unimaginative, unelastic and dangerous, if not naked autocracy' (*Times of Swaziland*, 30 March 1962). Some of the councillors did not want Nquku to be allowed to speak but Sobhuza had replied that he did not want an underground movement. It would be better to know what was being said in criticism. However, he was doubtful of the value of foreign interference. Nquku began his address by saying 'I am *simaku senkosi*'. The *simaku* is a small dog that in the hunt is able to enter the hole of the prey and by barking loudly drives it out to the big dogs which can finish it off. He claimed, 'We [the SPP] are under the stick of the King.' When the audience pressed for information on the funding, the

---

[5] For example, there was the following letter: 'This is to assure you that you have in Swaziland at least one European friend who trusts you, and feels sorry for you because it is clear to me that the Englishmen who in the past you have regarded as being your friends and allies are now going to turn against you. I am dead set against all politicians and political parties. I am a 100% Sobhuza man. As far as I am concerned I am a resident in your country, and Marwick, Macmillan, Duncan Sandys and the rest of the gang can go to hell ... They are a barrel of fools and England is a fourth-rate nation.'

membership and the political alliances of the party he replied with spirit, even when 'he dodged the truth'. All this was reported back to Sobhuza.

While a few of those close to Sobhuza had defected to the parties, an increasing number of educated Swazi were returning to Swaziland from the Republic either at his request or on their own initiative. The views of Swazi who remained in South Africa were conveyed to him through his representatives, including Swazi chiefs in the Transvaal. But Sobhuza did not encourage mass migration; the question of the boundaries between Swaziland and the Republic was to be a matter for future discussion.

Marwick came on 21 July to the Swazi National Council office to introduce D.S. Stephens, appointed by the Colonial Office as another constitutional advisor, and three members of the Commonwealth Parliamentary Association. Sobhuza was not present. As Secretary of the Nation, Polycarp reported that he regretted that the Ngwenyama was 'indisposed' and would be represented by the Ndlovukazi. Marwick expressed his concern about the Ngwenyama's health, and introduced Mr Stephens who spoke of the need for progressing along lines already acceptable to the rest of Africa, adapted to the needs of each country.

It was about this time that Balthazar J. Vorster, then South African Minister of Justice, was visiting Swaziland unofficially and was given permission by Sobhuza to hunt at Ehlane. Sobhuza, who had acted as 'host', made no political commitment. His attitude to the South African government policy was expressed characteristically. 'If you have two bulldogs in a kraal, and you chain them up facing each other, when you release them they will fly at each other's throat. But if you let them roam around the kraal they will get to know each other and there will be no fight' (Marjorie Juta, *Boundless Privilege*, 1974:194).

Negotiation between members of the Swazi National Council and the European Advisory Council continued over the following months, and, on 3 September they passed several resolutions, one of the more important being that 'the Ngwenyama be recognized as King of Swaziland'. However, it went on to state that 'the Europeans would continue their allegience to other governments but would recognize and respect the position of the King therein'. What exactly this would mean would be decided in the future. There were obviously going to be many points of difference between the two bodies. They also resolved to request the Secretary of State to withdraw his restrictions over mineral rights so that the Swazi nation would be in control. Sobhuza, the most powerful figure, remained in the background and his signature appeared on no document. He accepted the support of the EAC without endorsing their viewpoint.

The next move was taken by the British government. The Secretary of State called a second Constitutional Conference in London, inviting a wider range of representatives than had been at the first London conference. Sobhuza was specially requested to attend. He refused. He could not commit his people without consultation with his full Council, nor did he feel he could absent himself from his country at a time of internal crisis and for an indefinite period. Moreover, many of the councillors were opposed to his flying. 'He is not a bird', and he agreed: speed is dangerous.

He confirmed their choice of SNC members – Makhosini Dlamini, Polycarp Dlamini, Msindazwe Sukati, Mfundza Sukati, Mabalizandla Nhlabatsi and A. Khuseni Hlophe. At the last moment Bhekimphi Alpheus Dlamini was appointed as leader in place of Makhosini, who was ill. Bhekimphi was a member of the wider Constitutional Committee, but he had not been on the working committee. However, once his name was included in the list the wisdom of the choice was acknowledged. A keen, intelligent man, son of Chief Mnisi of Nkhaba, with a background of traditional discipline and loyalty and a good school education, he had served in the Second World War for four years, and became a sergeant at the age of 20.

Apart from the six members of the Swazi National Council, the British invited four members of the European Advisory Council (Carl Todd, R.P. Stephens, Dan Fitzpatrick and C.S. Hubbard), one from each of the three political parties (Nquku for the Swaziland Progressive Party,[6] Sishayi Nxumalo for the Swaziland Democratic Party, and Dr George Msibi for the Mbandzeni National Convention); and two unaffiliated participants (A. Selstroom for the EurAfrican Welfare Association,[7] and Dr David Hynd as an independent member of the European community). Brian Marwick went over in his official capacity together with M.J. Fairlie who had been very active in formulating with him the broad outlines of government policy in Swaziland.

That year the *Ncwala* had been more than usually significant.[8] Increasing numbers of Swazi were demonstrating their national identity with Sobhuza in the subtle language of dress and participation in Swazi customs. Leading men, notably Prince Makhosini, Polycarp Dlamini and Msindazwe Sukati, who had never taken part in the *Ncwala* because it had been prohibited by the churches to which they each belonged, donned ritual costume and danced with their age regiments in the *sibaya*. Men who absented

---

[6] The split in the ranks of the Progressive Party put the government in the difficult position of choosing between Nquku and Zwane and Mpangele Obed Mabuza; the decision was made in favour of Nquku.

[7] The SNC selected David Hynd Stewart as an 'observer-delegate' for the Eur-Africans.

[8] The meaning of the *Ncwala* is even misunderstood by a man as knowledgeable as Dr David Hynd, who when in London, expressed his surprise that the delegates were presented at a moment's notice with a resolution passed 'at the cattle kraal' on far-reaching proposals for the nation. 'To draw an analogy,' he continued, 'it was like asking the kilted competitors at the Braemar Gathering to approve some important legislation for Scotland' (Minutes, Swaziland Constitutional Talks, 3rd meeting, 30 January 1963).

themselves did so more deliberately than before and the distinction between Swazi and non-Swazi Africans was more evident. The formalities of British representation were maintained and the Resident Commissioner accompanied by senior staff in official uniform made their brief appearance on the main day. Sobhuza walked Marwick along the lines of chanting warriors and the Ndlovukazi sent the guests the traditional bowl of beer as welcome. The day Sobhuza dismissed the regiments from Lozitha he addressed them on the principles that guided Swazi traditional government, and informed them of the proposals that the Swazi delegates were taking to England on their behalf.

The delegates arrived safely, and though it was English winter and bitterly cold, the Swazi King's men appeared at the meetings in Marlborough House barefoot and wearing Swazi dress of decorative cloth and loinskins, their chests bare. Subtle ornamentation indicated their individual status and taste. All other participants, Swazi as well as European, wore dark formal suits considered by the British more appropriate for serious discussion.

In addition to the delegates, each group had its legal advisors in London.[9] The legal representative of the Swazi National Council was John Foster, Q.C., a former Minister of Commonwealth Affairs, recommended by Carl Todd. The political parties had formed a loose alliance, initiated by Sishayi Nxumalo, who appealed to them to join together in face of 'a united front formed by black privilege and white privilege'. But differences in viewpoints of the political leaders were not resolved, and Nquku refused to join.

The first session, on 20 January, was presided over by Mr Duncan Sandys, Secretary of State, most subsequent meetings by Lord Lansdowne, Minister of State for Commonwealth Affairs. After announcing that the British had no preconceived plan, Sandys put forward a compromise formula on both the political and economic fronts. This was rejected by all delegates, whose various statements revealed a complex mixture of idealism and realism, of sincerity and double talk. The meetings continued without clear direction. No one seemed prepared to change his own mind and so no one could really influence the mind of another. The speeches were often long and discussions heated and personal. The deepest passions were involved – nationalism, self-interest, fear.

Sobhuza was kept informed of what was happening by telegram and phone, but he himself never spoke on the phone and communication was laborious. At one point the British again urged him to fly over and attend in person. He again refused. When the discussions seemed to be getting nowhere, the Secretary of State became increasingly impatient, and on Sunday 12 February, at about

[9] Rozwadowski, as well as Zwane, was in London, and there were many members of both the Labour Party and the Africa Bureau, as well as personally disinterested lawyers ready to advise the parties.

10:00 p.m., he came into the meeting and announced harshly that since agreement could not be reached, he would have to impose a constitution. There was a brief stunned silence. Then vehement reaction. Mr Sandys, apparently rather taken aback, suggested an adjournment for half an hour. When the meeting reassembled, Lord Lansdowne tried to smooth over the incident, but the damage had been done. The Second Constitutional Conference ended in a stalemate on 13 February. When the Swazi National Council delegation returned and made its report, Sobhuza commented to Polycarp, 'You took the box but forgot the key.' Then Todd went to see Sobhuza. He gave his version, adding that 'It is essential to demonstrate that the whole nation is behind you', and he suggested that Sobhuza send a letter to the Resident Commissioner, asking Government to conduct a referendum of the entire population. According to Todd, Sobhuza responded, 'Do me the letter now.' Todd did so, inserting with Sobhuza's consent, 'But you may find it inconvenient to conduct the referendum; in that case, I will do so myself.' Todd left the letter with Sobhuza; he would discuss it with the Council and it did not mean that they would accept it or that he would send it. A referendum was not a new idea; the point was: should it be used by the Swazi?

It was time to send out some of the younger trusted men of the Swazi National Council to sound out the attitudes of the people and to convey his own views. Again the decision was taken by Sobhuza-in-Council; and twelve picked men, of whom only three were the old guard who had served on the Constitutional Committee, left in two vehicles from Masundvwini, one group going to *tinkhundla* (regional committees) in the South and West, the other covering the East and North. Their strategy had been carefully planned, and their speeches shaped by many preliminary discussions. National unity under the Ngwenyama, the need for stability in a world endangered by strife, were the dominant themes. On their return they reported that he had overwhelming support at all *tinkhundla*; western political ideas were rejected by the masses. A committee of seven men was appointed by the Inner Council to draft a national resolution.

On 9 March the Constitutional delegates reported to a meeting held at Lobamba and attended by the Ndlovukazi and some 4,000 Swazi. A few days later (13 March) the Resident Commissioner came to explain the provisional conclusions of the Secretary of State. The next day the response of the Swazi National Council was announced by Prince Masitsela supported by Councillor Mndeni Shabalala who spoke on behalf of *tinkhundla* delegates. 'We, the members of the SNC herein assembled in the Council Chamber, Lobamba, this 14th day of March, 1963 resolve that:

1. We are very grateful for the report on constitutional talks in London, notably, the provisional conclusions of the Secretary of State for Colonies.

2. As they are a complete departure from our proposals of a Legislative Council (Legco) based on racial federation or communal representation, these provisional conclusions of the Secretary of State must be referred to the people for whom we speak who will give us a fresh mandate.
3. Another meeting will be called for 15th April, 1963 to crystallize these ideas.
4. Government will be furnished with the views of the Swazi Nation by the 23rd April, 1963.'

In the meantime Todd went ahead and polled the opinion of white voters on the Constitutional Committee's proposals. This exercise held in May 1963 was not difficult. The result was an overwhelming majority in favour of the proposals.

In the midst of the political manoeuverings Sobhuza found himself confronted with critical labour problems. African wages were generally low and working conditions poor. Two spontaneous strikes had occurred in December 1962, followed – from March until June in 1963 – by a series of strikes and demonstrations in urban and industrial centres throughout Swaziland.

Many of the British officials were in favour of trade unions, which they saw as part of the overall western democratic system to which they were committed. Legislation for the establishment of trade unions had been in the statute books since 1942 but employers were not in favour of them and it was not until September 1962 that the first active trade union was registered. The impetus behind union organization was given by M.J. Fairlie, who had come to Swaziland in 1957. Sobhuza, however, continued the pattern of appointing a representative to each major industry and company town to communicate grievances expressed by workers and to support their complaints. Specialized trade unions were outside the traditional system, and he associated them with the techniques of strikes and boycotts; his opposition to these reached back to his reaction to student strikes in schools in Swaziland in the 1950s where, he pointed out, the main losers were the students themselves, who wasted hard-earned educational opportunities. He also feared a repetition of the situation in South Africa, where Africans were excluded from trade unions and strikes were illegal; both had been attempted, usually with dire consequences – loss of pay, loss of jobs, hardship on the workers' wives and children, destruction of property, physical injuries, death of innocent people, and reprisals by the authorities. In a colonial system where only the ruling 'race' had access to arms and the subordinate people had been deliberately effectively demilitarized, Sobhuza feared that any organized movement by workers, like any other signs of opposition, tended to evoke a demonstration of superior force.

Conditions for effective trade union organization – workers wholly dependent on wages, uprooted from the soil – did not exist in rural areas where the majority of Swazi had their roots, and where conditions of work were associated with rights to land and regulated by numerous obligations within a total political community. The situation was different in urban and industrial centres where many of the workers were non-Swazi who had neither loyalty nor interest in the traditional Swazi system. It seemed clear to the non-Swazi workers that they would be excluded from full political participation in a system built along lines suggested by the Swazi National Council, and that it was only through the vehicle of the political parties that they would have the opportunity to participate and improve their own conditions.

Nquku's branch of the Swaziland Progressive Party became interested in union organization as a means of improving conditions of work, but it was Zwane's branch, which in April 1963 titled itself the Ngwane National Liberatory Congress, that recognized the potential advantages of using the legitimate grievances of workers for political ends by supporting and, if necessary, initiating strikes.

In April Lord Landsdowne came to see Sobhuza in Swaziland. It was a private meeting at which Sobhuza reiterated his position. No meetings had been arranged for Lord Landsdowne with the leaders of the political parties, but shortly before his arrival an incident occurred in the Mbabane market which was to have serious consequences. A government health inspector closed the stalls of market women who, without the requisite licences, had been selling sour milk and sour porridge for their livelihood. The women protested, and Prince Dumisa, who chanced to be near, espoused their cause and organized a spontaneous gathering. The police, called by the District Commissioner, ordered the crowd to disperse immediately. They were slow to do so, and began to sing political songs; Dumisa and several others were arrested. The following day, leaders of the political parties and their followers – about 400 strong – marched to the Residency to protest the arrests and the constitutional proposals. This time the Government Secretary, A.C.E. Long, ordered them to disperse and when they refused, the police, who had come prepared for trouble, used tear gas.

On 2 May Sobhuza publicly appointed his son Prince Masitsela as his chief labour representative.[10] Masitsela's position was delicate and difficult. He stood between Fairlie, who represented the trade unions and whose personality was in sharp contrast to his own, and Dumisa, who described himself as 'prince of the oppressed' and talked gaily of revolution. The potential dangers of the situation crystallized in a strike on 19 May involving 1,400 Africans at the Havelock Mine. Dumisa again appeared to support the workers. When the management attempted through a court order to ban him from the

[10] Prince Masitsela had grown up at Lobamba and was known for his respect for custom. He had been employed as a clerk-typist at the Lobamba Appeal Court and then as a clerk in the Mbabane post office, where the treatment he received gave him an experience of racial prejudice especially humiliating for a young prince trained in courtesy and conscious of his royal birth. He was however without knowledge or experience of modern labour organizations and the history of workers' movements in other countries.

premises, the workers chose him as their representative. He took part in the subsequent discussions but these produced no settlement and the strikes continued. Sobhuza sent the workers a telegram: 'No true Swazi would talk to me through the strike. If any misunderstanding existed arrangements for delegates to visit headquarters should have been made through Mntfwanenkhosi Masitsela' (John Houlton, Board of Inquiry into the Trade Dispute at Havelock Mine. Mbabane: Government Printer, 1963).

On 31 May, when relations between Sobhuza and government were seriously strained, and tension between management and workers was high, the Secretary of State presented to the British Parliament the proposed constitution. It began with the forbidding statement that 'the present Constitution of Swaziland is contained in the Swaziland Order-in-Council of 1903'. A copy was sent to Sobhuza, who with his close councillors studied the document clause by clause, discussing its implication. The Secretary of State contended that, since the lengthy discussions and consultations had failed to reconcile differing opinions, he had been obliged to decide on his own responsibility what form the new Constitution should take. He also claimed that he had endeavoured to take account of the traditional Swazi institutions, the contributions of the European community to the economy of the country, and the need to provide opportunity for political expression to those who, while respecting the position of the Ngwenyama and the Swazi National Council, did not feel themselves adequately represented in the tribal structure.

Clearly there was to be no change in the structure of power. On the contrary, even greater authority was to be accorded the Resident Commissioner, whose position was to be changed to that of Her Majesty's Commissioner for Swaziland, appointed 'like Colonial Governors, by the Sovereign,' and directly responsible to the Secretary of State. The Legislature was to consist of Her Majesty's Commissioner and a Legislative Council composed of a Speaker, twenty-four elected members, four official members nominated by the Queen's Commissioner, and up to three nominated members. Of the twenty-four, eight were to be Swazi certified by the Ngwenyama-in-Council as having been elected by 'traditional methods'; eight Europeans of whom four were to be elected by voters registered on a European Roll and four by voters registered on a National Roll; eight persons of 'any race' elected by voters registered on the National Roll; and finally, up to three members also nominated by the Queen's Commissioner. Qualifications of voters and conditions for voting were stipulated. Executive powers would be vested in the Queen's Commissioner, assisted by an Executive consisting of three ex-officio officers and five members of the Legislative Council appointed by him, but he was not required to consult with them in cases in which, in his judgment, Her Majesty's Service 'would sustain material prejudice' or in matters which, 'in his judgment, were of insufficient importance', and he was especially 'empowered to act contrary to the advice given him by the Executive', subject only to the condition that the matter be reported to the Secretary of State.

The power of the Queen's Commissioner was made potentially absolute; he would have power to prohibit the Legislative Council from proceeding with any Bill relating to taxation; all Bills passed by the Legislative Council would be submitted to him and in his discretion 'but subject to Royal Instructions' he could assent, refuse assent, or refer the Bill 'for the signification of Her Majesty's pleasure'. A general power of disallowance of laws was reserved to the Queen, and the power to prorogue or dissolve the Legislature was vested in Her Majesty's Commissioner.

'The powers and privileges of the Ngwenyama' were then elaborated. Compared with those of the Queen's Commissioner they were negligible. He would be 'entitled' to be provided with all papers and minutes of meetings of the Executive Council, and also with copies of every Bill passed by the Legislature, and he was empowered to require the Queen's Commissioner to have any matter considered at a Council Meeting, unless excluded by discretion of the Queen's Commissioner after consultation with the Executive. 'The foregoing privileges and powers' were made conditional upon fulfillment by the Ngwenyama of a solemn undertaking set out in an Agreement to be concluded between him and Her Majesty's Commissioner.

On a different key, creating a new trend in the system, were provisions by which the Ngwenyama was entitled to a number of non-traditional Swazi privileges modelled on those accorded the tradition-oriented British sovereign: the establishment of royal emoluments and a Civil List, exemption from taxation of personal income and property, immunity from compulsory acquisition of his personal property, and immunity from civil process in his personal capacity. The King was placed in an economic position distinct from any of his subjects, and at the same time he could acquire private property, distinct from national property or family property, which he could dispose of as he pleased.

On vital national economic issues, limited concessions had been made to Swazi requests. 'Swazi nation land was to be vested in the Ngwenyama on behalf of the nation', but with qualified rights of allocation and disposal. Mineral rights were covered in a similar formula but the Legislature was given overriding power of control, and rights to exploit minerals would be granted or refused by the Queen's Commissioner in the name of the Ngwenyama after consultation with him and the Executive Council.

The Legislature was declared not competent to legislate on the following matters – the office of the Ngwenyama, of the Ndlovukazi, the appointment and suspension of subordinate chiefs, the composition and procedure of the Swazi National Council, the annual *Ncwala* Ceremony and the *Libutfo* (regimental system). This anomalous situation was described to me as 'covering with the left hand what had been stolen by the right.' The document included entrenched provisions: the protection of human rights; the continuation of existing laws until changed by a competent legislative authority; arrangments for the inclusion of the Swaziland Public Service Commission established under Order-in-Council of 1962; and provision for a High Court in Swaziland, the appointment of a Chief Justice and Judges.

The proposals produced by the Secretary of State in his effort to give something to everybody satisfied nobody, and the leaders reacted typically and differently. At the one extreme, Dr Zwane, Dumisa Dlamini and Macdonald Maseko of the Ngwane National Liberatory Congress (NNLC) increased their technique of encouraging the masses to protest by direct action; at the other, Sobhuza-in-Council pursued the more peaceful technique of appeal and persuasion.

On 8 June, 1963 the SDP called a mass meeting in Mbabane of domestic servants, a generally poorly paid category of workers, essential to the colonial situation. The market women joined their 'sisters' and the NNLC took over the platform. On Sunday, 10 June, there was a call for a general strike. The following day some 3,000 men and women, led by Dumisa, demanded to see the Resident Commissioner, who agreed to talk to 15 representatives. No agreement was reached. That night prisoners in the Mbabane jail rioted and ten escaped. A number of white residents formed a special guard and Mbabane was described by one white as 'a town in a state of siege'.

The police force was small and relatively weak. There were 40 senior and 293 junior ranks spread over 6 district headquarters and 22 district stations and posts. A mobile unit, improvised from the trainees at the Police Training School, was not considered as effective as it should have been. When the Mbabane strike broke out the main force was concentrated at Havelock Mine and it was necessary to draw in detachments from outstations (Ballenden, et al., 1963, *Report of the Commission of Enquiry into Unrest in Swaziland*. Mbabane: Government Printers).

This was the situation Brian Marwick confronted on his return from Britain where he had been knighted in recognition of his meritorious service. His closest officials warned him that if he did not act immediately the South African government might intervene. Brian, now Sir Brian, was reluctant to call for help from outside the country and requested Sobhuza to assist the police in quelling the strikes. Sobhuza refused; to do so would have embroiled his people in civil war. The British had provoked the situation through their support of the parties; and had then rushed through legislation under which they arrested leaders they themselves had encouraged, thereby inciting the masses to violence.

The next thing that Sobhuza knew was that 37 police were being flown in from Bechuanaland, and on 13 June, some 600 British troops, a battalion of Gordon Highlanders, arrived from Kenya. When the huge planes flew over Mbabane, strikers and people from the surrounding villages flocked to Lobamba. Dumisa and Zwane, realizing the danger of a possible clash between the strikers and the troops, appealed for an audience with the King. They then asked him to call out his regiments against the troops since, in their viewpoint, the conflict was no longer between Swazi politicians and traditionalists, but between the Swazi and the colonial administration. The King refused. It was not only because his warriors had no modern weapons and open confrontation could have been a massacre, but it would have meant civil war and the end of any hope of national unity; and he still had sufficient faith in Sir Brian to believe that if the strikers did not resist by force, force would not be used against them. Sobhuza addressed the nation in the *sibaya*, sternly warning the strikers to return to work and telling everyone to keep the peace; and the *mlamuli* – the symbol of protection – was raised in supplication.

The troops were billeted in schools in and around Mbabane and Manzini. Sir Brian made no further contact at that stage with Sobhuza, who remained a calming personality among his own warriors. Within a fortnight after the arrival of the soldiers, most of the men, many of whom had been reluctant to strike in the first place, were back at work, and 'peace' was restored without bloodshed. The strongest resistance had been at Havelock where some hundred men were arrested. The rest returned to work; 244 Africans in all were in custody, but most were soon released. Fifteen leading members of the NNLC were charged with public violence; the SPP and SDP had disassociated themselves from the NNLC and the alliance against the SNC had virtually disintegrated. The troops remained explicitly to maintain peace for the elections to be held in terms of the White Paper, and implicitly as a statement to South Africa of British commitment to a policy distinct from apartheid.

Sobhuza pursued his struggle against the White Paper. The SNC met at Lobamba, and three members – Makhosini Dlamini, as leader, Polycarp Dlamini and A. Khuseni Hlope – were sent to England to urge the Secretary of State to reconsider the constitutional proposals, and more particularly the clauses relating to land and mineral rights. Marwick was angered by this action taken without his knowledge, and the Swazi on their arrival found that messages had been received by the Colonial Office saying they were 'the wrong people' and no one should listen to them. It was agreed that 'they may have been sent by Sobhuza' but they were asked, 'Who is this Sobhuza?' According to the government official report, he no longer enjoyed the support of his people.

At that point Todd, who had come over independently on behalf of the European Advisory Committee, came to their assistance and

helped the delegation arrange a press conference which aroused
sufficient interest for them to be asked to address a parliamentary
committee and to have questions raised by Sir William Teeling of the
Conservative Party.[11] In a written reply, Sir William was informed by
Mr Sandys that he was not prepared to reopen negotiations. After
waiting in London for two and a half weeks the Swazi delegates were
able to see Lord Lansdowne. Their session with him lasted some $2\frac{1}{2}$
hours, but the result was the same. Duncan Sandys finally agreed to
see them at the Colonial Office on 29 July. The hearing was brief and
before they left he told them bluntly that he 'was not changing a
paragraph, not even a sentence'. If they had the support they claimed,
they should readily go to the electorate. The deputation telephoned
home and received instructions to return immediately. The next day,
30 July, the Swazi National Council passed a resolution at Lobamba
to petition the Queen to request the British Government to stay the
enactment of the White Paper until the British Parliament itself had
been afforded the opportunity to go into the matter.

Relations between Britain and South Africa were hardening. In
September (1963) the South African government unilaterally limited
the freedom of aircraft flights between the High Commission
Territories and imposed stricter controls at the borders. Britain in
turn made certain adjustments in the definition of its own position,
abolishing the ambivalent office of High Commissioner to the three
territories and subsuming it into the single and less equivocal office of
British Ambassador to South Africa.

Verwoerd, who had given up talk of incorporation but still hoped to
bring Basutoland, Bechuanaland and Swaziland more closely into his
sphere of influence, stated:

I am now making an offer to Great Britain – I might almost call it a challenge – to
allow us to put the essentials of our policies before the inhabitants of these Territories.
Let us demonstrate to them what our policies really are, that our real feelings towards
them are friendly, how we would view their future, and how we could cooperate.

We should have the opportunity of presenting our case to them. It means a new
and a better deal than that which they are getting or can get – not through ill-will on
the part of the United Kingdom, but merely because the United Kingdom is not in a
geographical position to do for the High Commission Territories what the Republic
of South Africa can do for them (*The Road to Freedom for Basutoland, Bechuanaland,
Swaziland*, Fact paper 107, South Africa: State Information Office 1963:11-18).

He also offered to restore part of the Eastern Transvaal to the Swazi,

[11] In a letter to the *Times of Swaziland* (26/5/65) Todd stated that he had visited London to
negotiate some 'improvements' from the European point of view and not to question the main
features of the proposal, but 'he thought the Swazi delegation had a valid case and had offered a
fair and generous solution and the Secretary of State's summary rejection of their proposals was
unstatesmanlike, and we now find ourselves with a total rejection by the SNC of the White
Paper, with consequent uncertainty to our future in the Territory ... Whilst I have been a
moderating influence upon the Swazi delegation in these negotiations I must make it quite clear
that I am not their adviser and the decision at all times is in the hands of the SNC, who have
definite and intractable views of their own.'

to buy out white farmers, and to set up South African industries on the Swaziland border.

But Sobhuza went on working on the new petition to present to the British Parliament. He had told the Council that he would express the consensus of ideas which selected councillors should then reduce to writing in consultation with his legal advisor in Johannesburg. However, when he received the document he was disturbed to find that several passages did not truthfully reflect his ideas or record the facts accurately – as for instance the words 'The Swazi were silent' for 60 years appeared in place of 'the Swazi were silenced ...' It was clear that the document had to be redrafted and Sobhuza decided to do it himself, working with Douglas Lukhele, a man he could trust and who knew the law.[12]

Polycarp went ahead to brief Foster, who had agreed to present the petition which was to be brought over by Makhosini. The petition was read to the *libandla* at Masundvwini since everyone had to be satisfied. On 19 November 1963 'The Humble Petition of the Ngwenyama Sobhuza II, C.B.E., Paramount Chief of Swaziland' suitably inscribed to 'The Honourable the Commons of Great Britain and Northern Ireland in Parliament Assembled' was duly presented by Patrick Wall. It dealt specifically with three vital issues: the mode of election; the constitutional status of Swaziland including the position of 'your humble petitioner as Paramount Chief under the constitution'; and Swazi land and minerals. It sought relief 'in the name of justice', from the new Constitution which 'seeks to impose a system of electing members of the Legislative Council which is wholly unsuitable to and unacceptable by the people of Swaziland'; ignores its protectorate status, and his rightful position as King of Swaziland; takes away from the Swazi nation its rights to land and minerals, and from the Nation, the National Council and the Ngwenyama-in-Council powers in regard to its own institutions.

It contended that the election procedure was complicated and confusing, and would 'force the majority of people to participate in a form of political activity which it does not want and does not understand'. It suggested a simpler and more flexible formula for voting and also proposed a system of proportional representation.[13]

---

[12] Douglas Lukhele was the obvious choice, but Douglas had returned to his practice in Johannesburg, and the King felt he should not take him from his livelihood. So every Friday Zonke Khumalo was sent by car to bring him to Lozitha and Sunday night would drive him back to Johannesburg. Throughout the weekend the King and Lukhele worked on the Petition, with councillors at their call.

[13] Any qualified European had the right to register on either the European or National Roll, not on both; any qualified Swazi could participate in the traditional Swazi manner but would have the free right at any time to claim to be registered on the National Roll in which event he would cease to take part in the traditional manner; and any qualified Eur-African would have the choice of either taking part in the traditional manner or of being enrolled on the European Roll or the National Roll.

'Each European member elected from the European Roll represents a certain number of

Sobhuza argued that this new formula gave each person the right to 'decide for himself' (thereby meeting the criticism made against his earlier formulation – 'that the Swazi evoluée and minority groups were not provided for'), and that, 'in the spirit of a free, multi-racial, democratic society', it provided 'ample scope for the natural development of the political society in Swaziland'.

As to his own authority, he 'respectfully' pointed out that his position had been 'relegated to one of very minor importance' whereas the Constitution clothed the Queen's Commissioner 'with virtual dictatorial powers'. He therefore submitted that 'the Constitution should accord him his rightful place as King of Swaziland in the Executive and the Legislature'.

In regard to land and minerals he reiterated that promises and undertakings of the past had not been implemented, and that in effect the White Paper dispossessed the Swazi Nation of its rightful property including land purchased by the Nation which, for all practical purposes, becomes 'state property under a Legislative Council which will not be responsible to the Swazi nation but to the overriding power of the government'. In contradistinction the proprietary rights of the Europeans were expressly guaranteed (Section 23J).

This petition received little support; antagonism to 'traditionalists' and 'conservatives' was strong. In December, by Order-in-Council under authority of the Foreign Jurisdiction Act of 1903, the Constitution was promulgated and the date for the first western-style elections was set for June of 1964.

During this turbulent period Sobhuza observed his duties as Ngwenyama yemaSwati with scrupulous care and made it easy for the Ndlovukazi to fulfil the public roles expected of her: she herself had acquired more self-confidence with experience. When chiefs or old national priests died Sobhuza accepted successors chosen by their kin from the same ancient clans and he never directly overruled the decisions of the Councils. The responsible post of Governor of Lobamba had finally been bestowed on Deka of the Khumalo clan, who had been serving at Zulwini, the royal village started by Sobhuza I.

No woman had been sought for Sobhuza as main Queen, nor had been married with a ritual indicating that she would be the mother of the heir, but his children – 'the eggs of the nation' – were many and, in spite of high mortality, increasing in number. His sons chose their own wives, and sometimes the King helped them with the bridewealth; but even if no bridewealth had been given, the children belonged to the royal family. For the princesses, arranged marriages were considered more appropriate, and the responsibility for these

---

European voters and each Swazi member elected from the Swazi system represents a number of Swazi voters. As soon as the National Roll gains that number of European voters, it will gain that seat from the European Roll; and as soon as the National Roll gains that number of Swazi voters it will gain at the expense of the traditional representation' (Sections 14-16).

21. Sobhuza dancing with his regiment, the Balondolozi. On his right is Lomafasa Dlamini; on his left Chief Bafana Maseko, Chief Mpetsambalo Shongwe and Cuługwane Dlamini

22. Dressed for *butimba* (a ceremonial hunt) at Ehlane. Left to right: Prince Lonkhokhela, Chief Manyakatane Mdluli, Lomafasa Dlamini, the Ngwenyama, Chief Bafana Maseko, Mshelevu Dlamini with guards and police in the background

23. The First Anniversary of Independence, 6 September 1969. Princess Alexandra and her husband, Angus Ogilvy, were the guests of honour. On the right is the Ndlovukazi Zihlati

24. Opening of the Ncwala by the ancient Mandanda Mtsetfwa as *ndvunankulu* (traditional Prime Minister). With him are other governors and attendants of royal villages, including his son Velabo Timothy Mtsetfwa (later first Swazi Commissioner of Police)

marriages was delegated to a specially appointed man, Prince Mambiwe, son of Jokova.

With such an extensive family it was not surprising that there should have been a few defectors to the parties at this time. Much publicity was given to the fact that in addition to Dumisa, his own oldest daughter Betfusile had joined the NNLC and, for a short period, Myingili and Pholile did as well.

The sorrows of his intimate life – the deaths of a queen, children, siblings, friends, and close kin – could not interfere with his national duties. One of his deepest losses was when Fongofani Motsa died suddenly. Mazini, her son, was on his way home after two years of study in England. Sobhuza spent as much time as he could comforting the young man, who was very deeply affected; but he could not give way to his own grief or extend his own period of mourning. He believed that particularly in time of strain it was necessary to have faith (*titsemba*) and 'do the best one could'.

A most pleasant event during the otherwise unhappy period of 1963 was the celebration of the arranged marriage of Gcinaphi, the daughter who had gone with him to England. She had taken her B.Sc. at Roma in Basutoland, the first of his children to obtain a university degree, and he was immensely proud as well as fond of her. The husband chosen for her was Nkominophondo Khumalo. To the uninitiated the choice might appear strange. Nkominophondo was not an important chief, nor was he one of the new educated elite nor even of the main house of Khumalo. But he had served for several years as 'a boy of the king' (*umfana wenkhosi*), trusted with confidential matters, and had proved his fine character, quiet strength and honesty. Gcinaphi was the third wife of Nkominophondo, but, by reason of her high birth, was recognized as main wife. Her father had built for her a western home not far from Lobamba, beautifully situated near the river and the hot springs, and in walking distance of her own mother's home in the *sigodlo*. The King helped establish her husband in businesses, which he would manage with his 'brother' Zonke, who was later to become Swaziland's second Deputy Prime Minister.[14]

It was a superb wedding celebrated on an unprecedented scale, combining full Swazi ritual with selected western ceremonials. It took place soon after the annual Reed Dance which brought maidens from different villages to perform their services for the Ndlovukazi. The wedding culminated in three days of public festivity (18-20 July) alternating between *sibaya* and reception hall, leather skirt and satin gown, feathers and tiara, beer and champagne.

In addition to Swazi personages a number of whites (including Sir Brian Marwick and his wife Riva) and Eur-Africans were among the invited guests.

[14] Zonke Khumalo is a son of Mashambo, special attendant of Labotsibeni. When the village of Zombodze moved to a new site Mashambo was left to look after the grave of Labotsibeni. Sobhuza had 'observed' Zonke from childhood.

Sobhuza's approach to economics, to politics, to social life, to religion, was not designed to please any one section. He was too independent in his thinking and though he did not force his ideas on others he was not afraid to express them. The result was that he had enemies, not many but dangerous, and over the years he had grown increasingly aware of the possibility of assassination.

There had been an alarming episode when an unknown white man appeared inside the residence at Masundvwini and asked to see the King. Though he did not succeed, the Inner Council on investigating found that the intruder had been brought in a van driven by a son of a Prince high in the hierarchy. Several councillors wanted to expel him from his position in the Council and banish him. Sobhuza had previously said that the Prince was entitled to a district in which he could also exercise local authority as a chief; two men were now delegated to find a place which would satisfy him. The police had been called in to trace the identity of the white, who was not from Swaziland and had indeed already returned to South Africa. The Resident Commissioner, hearing of the episode, approached Sobhuza, who said he appreciated his concern and told him as much of the story as he thought necessary; he added that he too had heard 'rumours' and was expecting the Prince to come to him and explain. But he said, 'Nobody in Swaziland can expel him – even I cannot.' To those councillors who also wanted drastic action taken, he argued that whatever the Prince had done, the position of his (late) father had to be considered for had it not been for him 'the country would not have been here as it is today'. He could not banish the Prince: 'he is me.' After this a lock was put on the gates to Masundvwini and the guards, armed with spears, were told to be more vigilant and to let no one in without permission. But access to the premises from different angles was easy, and Sobhuza still frequently moved around the countryside without official security, attended by only a couple of little boys.

There had also been a more organized and serious attempt which again was given no official publicity and never reached the courts. One night driving from Lobamba to Lozitha he was warned that an *impi* was waiting near the Mtilane bridge to kill him. He got out of his car and into another. The car in which he was supposed to be was stopped. The traitors were there. They included men in whom he had great trust. The case was heard privately by the princes at Lobamba, and the men were banished from court but not from the country. All have since been reinstated.

These were challenges against the greatness of his position. At a different level and more humiliating was a public case in which two subjects – Mpangele Mabuza and Sifunti Matsebula – were accused of selling a large number of cattle, among which were some belonging to the King. The men sent him a cheque which he refused to take, saying he did not know about the deal and did not authorize anybody to go and sell his (national) cattle. Mabuza was called before the court, and the magistrate at Manzini heard the case. The King was asked to give evidence. The Council felt it was against Swazi custom to call their sacred King to such a court since 'it is a place where people who have killed others appeared.' So it was arranged that the magistrate go to the High Court at Lozitha. When the King confronted the two men Sifunti said, 'I have nothing to say. I know that I made a mistake'. It was not Swazi custom to look the King in the eyes and argue with him. But Mpangele stood up and claimed to be a lawyer and kept on asking questions, and saying to the King, 'Did you see me selling your cattle?' Finally the magistrate said that if he was going to ask such questions he would impose a heavy sentence because he knew it was not the responsibility of the King to see what he was doing. The case went back to Manzini after the hearing and the men were ordered to pay back the cattle. But the King said, 'Oh no, such poor people, where can they get cattle?' And he finally took the cheque.

The case is remembered to this day because of the different attitudes of the two men – Sifunti, who said he would rather admit guilt than have to question the King, and Obed Mpangele Mabuza who, to the anger and horror of the loyalists, cross-examined him arrogantly, looking him directly in the face. And it is also stressed that the King himself replied without anger and acted without vengeance. It was as a result of this case that the councillors insisted that in the new Constitution the Ngwenyama be given the privilege of immunity from civil process in his private capacity.

CHAPTER XV

Sobhuza Leads a Modern National Movement

When Sobhuza had sent off the petition with Makhosini and Polycarp he was optimistic, but on their return it was clear that few if any concessions would be made. They told him of the discourtesy with which they, as his envoys, had been received by the Colonial Office, of widespread rumours discrediting his approach, and of the allegation that he had no support from the masses. They also recounted how, when invited to speak to a student body at Oxford, they had accepted gladly. But when they had finished, a young African stood up and said, 'I also am a Swazi and these men have no right to speak for the majority of the people. They represent the uneducated reactionaries. They are nobodies.' The emissaries were surprised; the students confused. Then, unexpectedly, a man from the audience said, 'I have worked in the Secretariat in Swaziland and I know these men. They are important men and not uneducated, and whether you like it or not, the facts are as they have reported.' The speaker was J.R. Stebbing, a former Government Secretary in Swaziland. Later, they took the opportunity to see Sir John Maud, the former High Commissioner and friend of Sir Brian, who was now Master of a college at Oxford, and to discuss with him their objections to the White Paper. Sir John responded in the end that he had not fully understood that the proposal from Sobhuza referred to equality of opportunity and not equality of numbers. Once he understood, he was willing to support the Swazi cause.

Sobhuza had then approached Sir Brian in the following way: You say I am isolated from my people, and that the petition represents the wishes of a few chiefs and others whom you describe as reactionaries. But I do not think so. Let me hold a plebiscite and put this issue to the test. What I am saying is also the wish of my councillors and we would like the Government to help us to see that there is no cheating and no fighting. Marwick did not agree. Sobhuza tried to persuade him, pointing out that a referendum was a technique recognized and acclaimed by westerners. Later he mentioned specifically and deliberately a statement by the Under-Secretary of State, Nigel Fisher, in the British House of Commons on 10 December 1963, who, referring to the acceptance of a constitution by the people of Malta, described a referendum as 'a very democratic way of deciding what people wanted'. If the Government had a real interest in the wishes of the people, Sobhuza contended, it should welcome the suggestion rather than try to suppress it and discredit him in advance, especially since the Government was trying to introduce the system of voting through the Legislative Council.

For a moment Sir Brian hesitated, then replied firmly that the Constitution was already drafted and some concessions made. If Sobhuza was so sure of the support for his viewpoint he should not fear the result of an election. Sobhuza saw there was no sign of his relenting. Exercising the utmost restraint Sobhuza said he thought Sir Brian was doing wrong and that if the Government would not help carry out the plebiscite, the Swazi would do so on their own. Marwick replied with a hidden threat that if they did, there might be trouble and the Ngwenyama would be held responsible. Sobhuza answered that the Queen's Commissioner was responsible for keeping law and order, and that if Marwick felt so sure there would be trouble, he could issue a proclamation and prohibit the referendum: he had the police and British troops were still in the country. However, to refuse to allow an open plebiscite would run counter to all claims of supporting democratic procedures.

Sobhuza found Sir Brian's attitude 'harsh', but when he saw A.G. Marwick and the old man said with bitterness that he could not understand the change in 'his child', Sobhuza tried to comfort him, saying, 'This happens to children. They rejoice us when small, as they grow up they may listen to bad ideas and cause us much sorrow. But we cannot throw them away. They are ours, ourselves. We can only hope that in time they may return to us. Sometimes they do things that they themselves do not really like because they are forced by their position. I think that this is the case with your child. He is a brave man, loyal to the Government that appointed him.'

The form of the referendum agreed to by Sobhuza-in-Council was simple, direct and graphic. There would be only one question: Do you or do you not agree with the petition submitted by the Ngwenyama to the British Government? Since over 75% of the Swazi voters were illiterate the vote was to be expressed through symbols – the lion and the reindeer. The lion stood for the King, and the Council considered it appropriate to use it to symbolize any activity of the Swazi nation. The reindeer was a foreign animal. A picture of this unknown creature, 'with many curving horns and no straight direction', had hung in the office of the Swazi National Council. Sobhuza had previously used it to describe political parties.

The Swazi National Council issued a dignified public statement to the press expressing regret at the stand the Government had taken, and indicated their determination that the election be fair and orderly, without intimidation, coercion or violence. Sobhuza had insisted that 'the name Marwick' should not be identified with the reindeer, and in its statement to the press the Swazi National Council made it clear that 'the Council disassociates itself from any abuse of the name Marwick because the issues involved are not Sir Brian's personal affair, and it reassures the public as well as the Government that the name Marwick has not been associated with the reindeer. For purposes of the plebiscite the reindeer stands simply for those who are opposed to the petition' (*Times of Swaziland*, 10 January 1964).

This was the first time that the Swazi people would vote in a secret ballot. Sobhuza speculated – would it reveal that which men were afraid to show in the open? Was it not better to have free discussion with the opportunity to confront and persuade the opponent? Was not the secret vote closer to the hidden techniques of poison and witchcraft? There was something sinister in this secret way of putting people in or out of power. But he was curious rather than afraid of the outcome. He had made the decision to go ahead, and set the date for 19 January.

On 6 January eighteen NNLC members – including Dr Zwane and Dumisa – were charged with public violence in the Mbabane strike. Ten accused, including Dr Zwane, were acquitted; judgment on the remaining nine, including Dumisa, was reserved until 21 January. The evidence before the court had shown conclusively that Dr Zwane, on his return from Addis Ababa, had in the words of the Crown Counsel 'found the tiger held by the tail and was involved in attempting to extricate it'. Dr Zwane urged his followers to maintain peace but abstain from voting in the referendum.

Sobhuza instructed the representatives of the Swazi National Council to explain the referendum and its significance. Balloting was organized through *tinkhundla* (regional committees) and voting took place at strategic and accessible points. There were no voters rolls and no formal constituencies, but each applicant was asked his name and nationality, and tax receipts served to identify Swazi citizens. When the votes were counted, 122,000 out of a total adult male population of 125,000 had chosen the lion; 154 the reindeer.

Sobhuza received the results with outward calm and restrained relief. Having thanked his supporters, he said the victory was not his but that of the people, and described it as 'the rebirth of the nation'. He then added that it was not the end but the beginning of difficult times. The Constitution stood fundamentally unchanged. The agreement attached to the Constitution still awaited his signature. Though it referred to him as the Ngwenyama, King of Swaziland, most of the objectionable conditions remained. By using a recognized democratic procedure, the referendum, he had disarmed many of his critics, and even those who had objected to the way in which it had been organized had to admit that the Government had underestimated the strength of Swazi Kingship, and more particularly, the support of the people for their King, Sobhuza. But the referendum still did not decide his future role nor the policy to be adopted in the proposed elections. Faced with a Constitution that he and his Council opposed, he had three alternatives: to take no part in the elections; to support a general boycott; to enter the struggle as the Ngwenyama, King of the Swazi.

Sobhuza had been prepared to abide by the initial reaction of some of his advisors in the Council and ask his people to boycott the election. But to be effective such action would have had to be total, or an unwelcome political minority on the basis of a few votes could claim victory. Three days before the referendum Dr Zwane announced that the Ngwane National Liberatory Congress had decided to fight the election. For Sobhuza to abstain from participating at that stage would satisfy only those who argued that he, as King, should not actively associate himself with politics. The decision to lead his people into modern politics was consistent with the traditional role of Swazi kings.

The expressed aims of the Ngwane National Liberatory Congress – change in the Constitution within the first six months of the Legislative Council, followed immediately by responsible government and independence – were not at variance with those of Sobhuza himself; his objection was to the proposed methods of achieving the goals, and to the new political rhetoric in which the NNLC described itself as the 'champion of all oppressed masses of Swaziland' and the Swazi National Council as having a 'Bantustan approach to politics'.

Sobhuza still hoped to maintain national unity, realizing that there were many points on which all Swazi and many whites were agreed. One of these was the rights of women. For reasons which were difficult to fathom and which appeared to run completely counter to British assertions of democracy, the first Constitution excluded as voters all but the senior wife of a polygamist, as well as unmarried women and widows. When the Swazi first realized this they thought it might be bad draftsmanship, or an oversight, and brought this to the attention of the Government Secretary, but the exclusion was repeated in the formal registration proclamation. The women, including his Queens, reacted, and Sobhuza gave them his full backing. He had on various occasions tried to explain that the European interpretation of the position of women in Swazi society was distorted by their western perspective. Polygamy was an honourable custom, in which women were taken publicly and legally, not as prostitutes or mistresses, but as wives and mothers of legitimate children. The men who had the most wives were of highest standing, and the women shared the benefits of their husband's wealth and status. For Government to recognize only the first wife would humiliate and antagonize her 'sisters', and if the husband had to make the choice, he would bring upon himself as well as on the chosen, the favoured, the poisoned barb of jealousy. It was also paradoxical that the professional women, especially nurses and teachers and businesswomen, would be penalized since they married later than their more tradition-rooted sisters with fewer years of schooling. As to widows, their exclusion would seem to punish them for the death of their husband as if they were guilty of his death.

On Sunday, 1 February, a large group of women from different churches came to Lobamba to express their views on public matters. They gathered first in front of the shrine hut and were joined by the Queens and many of the other residents. In the presence of the Ndlovukazi, they all prayed for the twin rulers, their people and the country as a whole; and they prayed that changes would be made peacefully. The Ngwenyama sent word that he wanted to hear their suggestions, but not in the sacred centre, so towards noon they moved, chanting hymns, to the plantation of gum trees on the outskirts of Lobamba, a place for more secular modern political activity. There, Sobhuza and his councillors joined them, and the women requested A. Khuseni Hlophe as the King's Private Secretary and also as a man active in church matters to serve as master of ceremonies. The women addressed the meeting with great dignity and eloquence, drawing inspiration from texts in the Bible, and before returning, passed a resolution demanding the vote also for every woman twenty-one years or over. When they asked the Ngwenyama to convey this resolution to Her Majesty's Commissioner to forward to the Secretary of State, he willingly agreed, and in thanking them, urged them to 'continue their efforts to uplift the people,' adding, 'it is not true that in world affairs women do not play any part. In the family, whether they are monogamous or polygamous, a man may not enter into an agreement without consulting the other members. Invariably the wives give sound advice.'

On 16 April 1964, before a meeting attended by more than two thousand people, Sobhuza announced that he had agreed to the request put to him by a delegation of princes and councillors that the SNC organize its political strength and nominate its own candidates under the name of *Imbokodvo* – the Grinding Stone. He emphasized that this was not a new party, since he was against the principle of parties, but a *movement* of the nation. He explained that the Imbokodvo was a traditional symbol, an essential piece of equipment in every home, used to break down separate grains into a single paste, and that the full name should be *Imbokodvo lemabalabala* – the Grinding-Stone-that-brings-together-many-colours.

On another occasion he related the name Imbokodvo to a story of the folk hero Chakijane, the marvellous hare, who, pursued by hunters, came to a river which he could not cross. He tried this way and that; the hunters were close. He turned himself into an *imbokodvo*. The hunters rushed up; Chakijane was nowhere to be seen. One man picked up the *imbokodvo*, saying, 'If I saw that Chakijane I would kill him like this', and he threw the stone across the river. They were amazed to see it become Chakijane, who shouted, 'Thank you, you helped me cross the river!' It was, Sobhuza explained, the politicians,

behaving like the hunters who had forced him to form the Imbokodvo
to save the nation. It did not matter if members of the opposition
described the Imbokodvo as the stone grinding people down; he knew
the majority of the people understood his meaning. In the final symbol
representing the movement, the Imbokodvo was placed in the centre
of a great *sibaya*.

Sobhuza familiarized himself with the new constitutional
procedures by studying books and pamphlets issued by Government
and discussing the implications for different groups, black and white,
foreign and local, with his Council. Registration for both European
and National Voters Rolls had opened on the 1 February. Sobhuza
publicly instructed every Swazi to register, and he told the chiefs to
keep a register of all their subjects including the women excluded by
the British from voting. Of the total African population of 270,000,
7.25% were born outside Swaziland; of 8,040 Europeans, 81.09%
were born outside Swaziland; and of 2,260 EurAfricans, 30.53% were
born outside Swaziland. Most of the foreigners in all categories were
born in South Africa.

The Swazi referendum had brought Sir Brian's career in Swaziland
to an unhappy close. Sobhuza no longer consulted him or felt it
helpful to inform him of his decisions. When Marwick sent a message
through Msindazwe Sukati that a strong argument existed for
withholding the salaries of SNC officials paid from taxpayers' money
but using their services and offices for electioneering purposes, back
went the two-edged question: How is it then that you and your
officials, who receive salaries from public funds, continue to interfere
in politics?

Before Marwick's return to England for his next assignment,
Sobhuza invited him and his wife to Masundvwini for a formal
farewell. It was a small gathering – senior civil servants, a handful of
old friends, and a few representatives of the Swazi National Council.
Sobhuza did not know that Sir Brian had prepared a formal speech
criticizing the SNC for stifling progress, and rebuking the King for
entering politics. On arrival Sir Brian handed a copy to the
Ngwenyama who, when he absorbed the contents, asked Sir Brian not
to deliver it. But it was already in the hands of the Press. In it Sir
Brian stated that the developments in economic, health and other
fields

owed little or nothing to the Swazi National Council, which for the most part was
content to contemplate the imagined wrongs of the past and to be critical of the
Government's efforts to bring progress and stability to the people of Swaziland ... I
leave Swaziland dissatisfied with the results of my efforts to produce leaders amongst
the Swazi people capable of supporting their King with sound, objective and fearless
advice, or capable of removing from his shoulders the heavy burden which he has
carried for so long (*Times of Swaziland*, 24 April 1964).

Sobhuza made a short speech regretting that their long association should have an unhappy end, but wishing him and his family well in the future. Though Sir Brian did not read his carefully written speech he expressed its substance spontaneously and angrily to the distress of most who were present. This was not the occasion for public denunciation; it violated a fundamental code of Swazi manners which he more than any other white should have appreciated. The Swazi in particular felt wounded and insulted by the words of a man whom they had once trusted. The tea provided by the King was drunk perfunctorily and without pleasure. And the guests left silently and sadly. In some Swazi circles the name Marwick is still anathema. Others appreciated all the help that Sir Brian had given over the years, and they remembered particularly that as Resident Commissioner he had conceded at a meeting of the Minerals Committee in 1958 that Mbandzeni did not sell the land, but that it had been alienated from the Swazi by Orders-in-Council. He was thus instrumental in publicly clearing Mbandzeni's name of slander. Sir Brian and Lady Marwick came to the Independence Celebration as special guests at the invitation of Sobhuza.

Sir Brian's successor Francis Loyd (later Sir Francis) came with experience of Kenya, as had Beetham and Morgan, men with whom Sobhuza and the Swazi National Council had continued cordial relations. Sir Francis – dapper, formal, correct, diplomatic – was charged with the task of keeping the peace and healing the breach. He was officially sworn in as Her Majesty's Commissioner in Mbabane on 12 May. From his first meeting with Sobhuza he was 'charmed and impressed' and did not underestimate the strength of purpose behind the courteous manner and musical voice. Though Francis Loyd did not realize the depth of suspicion which was the legacy of the past he was eager to be placatory. First the elections would take place.

As political animosities continued, Sobhuza remained convinced that 'parties' were divisive. But the die was cast; and he found himself increasingly involved in negotiations through Carl Todd with members of the European Advisory Council, who formed themselves into the United Swaziland Association (USA). This party of white settlers expressed uncritical support of King Sobhuza on the ground that his government would maintain their economic and political security. Other whites founded the Swaziland Independent Front, ideologically closer to the Swaziland Democratic Party (SDP), which was committed to non-racialism in a common society and to open rejection of South Africa's racist policies.

Nominations for representatives on the Legislative Council were made public a month before the elections. Fifty-eight names representing six parties were finally accepted by the electoral officers for the 24 seats. It was a complicated procedure, as Sobhuza had pointed out in his petition. Ten whites were standing for four seats on the European Roll for which the whole of Swaziland was a single constituency. Forty-eight representatives of six different political groups stood for the twelve seats on the National Roll of which four were reserved for whites, with the whole country divided into four constituencies. Eight Swazi for the National Roll were elected by traditional Swazi methods from the *tinkhundla* divided into twenty-five constituencies, each of which sent two representatives to the Swazi National Council, which in turn chose from these ranks the Imbokodvo candidates.

Sobhuza did not pick these candidates, but he scrutinized the names, listened to reports on the qualifications and made suggestions before giving his approval. For the four seats reserved for whites on the National Roll, the Imbokodvo sponsored Carl Todd, standing as an Imbokodvo, Dan Fitzpatrick, as an Independent, and R.P. Stephens and C.A.B. Mandy, more moderate members of the USA.

More important from the Swazi viewpoint were the eight Imbokodvo representatives for the National Roll whose names were announced to the nation at a public meeting in the *sibaya*. These were: William Magongo, Meshack Hlatshwako, Mfanasibili Dlamini, Mateus Gamedze, A. Khuseni Hlophe, Zonke Khumalo, Prince Masistela Dlamini and Bhekimphi Dlamini. The crowd listened with intense interest, silent for the most part. But now and then there were loud and angry interjections, accusations that the candidates had not been elected by the people but had been nominated by a few conservatives on the Swazi National Council. Vocal and conspicuous was Dumisa, released the previous day (17 February) after sixteen months in jail in Mbabane.[1] Dumisa tried to address the meeting, and finally held a small gathering of his own outside the *sibaya*.

Electioneering went ahead, each party holding meetings, issuing pamphlets, and indulging in intrigues, strategies (including deliberate circulation of false rumours, and cancellation of meetings by unauthorized persons) and a new public rhetoric. But from all parts of the country reassuring reports came back to Sobhuza, who kept to his usual routine, reading in the morning and accessible in the afternoon.

As electioneering increased in intensity and acrimony, criticism was directed at the Imbokodvo and at times at Sobhuza himself, verbally and in print. A typical letter, published in the *Times of Swaziland* (5 June 1964), accused him of descending into the political arena and taking sides with one group of his people against another, and warned him of the danger of siding with South Africans and reactionaries and thereby endangering his position in the nation. For the time being he abstained from any public defence, leaving it to his supporters to make his case. Dr Msibi, then Secretary of the Imbokodvo, pointed out that Sobhuza as King of the Swazi had been in the political arena since his ascension, and his politics had always been national and not

---

[1] He had been found guilty of inciting to strike but sentence was postponed for 18 months on condition that he was not cited for the same offence during the interim period before the case came up for review by the High Court. A description of events of this period is given by Potholm, *Swaziland: The Dynamics of Political Modernization*, 1972.

party politics. Sobhuza himself stressed that 'political parties were an anomaly in a country without independence because before independence people have one goal – freedom – and not ideological differences' (*Times of Swaziland*, 12 June 1964).

In its manifesto issued in the first week of June, the Imbokodvo advocated goals originally stated by the other political parties: the end of colonial rule, independence as soon as possible, a programme of crash training including adult education, training of Swazi administrators, and raising the standard of Swazi living. It also included the more controversial issues – the forming of a constitution along traditional lines; the recognition of the Ngwenyama as Head of State; and the right of the King of the Swazi to control land and minerals. Leaders of the opposition were not won over nor did they think they would be defeated. They appealed for support to African and European sources outside the country, and tried to discredit the Imbokodvo at the Organization of African Unity.

Elections took place on 16 June for the four European Roll seats, and on 23-25 for the twelve National Roll seats. Strict Government surveillance was maintained, with the troops and the Swaziland police in charge of radio communications. There were heated arguments at some of the booths, but no fighting. Each party had its symbol, and each voter was identified by a photograph and an inanimate object drawn by lot. This time no animal symbols were allowed. Since over 75% of the electorate was illiterate, a procedure was introduced by which each voter poked a nail attached to a string into the image of his or her choice; voting henceforth has officially been translated as *kuhlaba*, literally 'to stab'.

Sobhuza waited for the results at Lozitha. 60% of whites and 85% of Swazi went to the polls. The United Swaziland Association swept all the European Roll seats, the Imbokodvo-sponsored candidates every seat on the National Roll. For the National Roll the Imbokodvo received 79,683 votes (85.45%), NNLC 11,364 (12.3%), SDP 1,271 (1.4%), Nquku's SPP 589 (0.46%), Mabuza's SPP 368 (0.25%). It was clear that the NNLC was the only sizeable opposition party. Thirty-one of the 37 opposition candidates lost their deposits. Zwane received only 2,438 votes, Macdonald Maseko 928, Dr Malabhane Allen Nxumalo 237, Simon Sishayi Nxumalo 147, Nquku 56, Mabuza 34.

On 26 June, the Swazi National Council announced the names of their eight representatives chosen by acclamation through the *tinkhundla* system: Makhosini Dlamini, Polycarp Dlamini, Duma Dlamini, George Mabuza, Chief Mbatshane Mamba, Dr George Msibi, John Rose and Mfundza Sukati. The choice of Imbokodvo 'leader' and Swazi National Council spokesman in the Legislative Council would be difficult to make. The position would carry considerable authority and it was essential that the chosen be true to tradition, and at the same time be able to deal with the subtleties of foreigners. Finally Sobhuza announced that Prince Makhosini was appointed as the *indvunankhulu*, Prime Minister.

Prince Makhosini did not oust old Mandanda Mtsetfwa – *indvunankulu* of the royal villages in the traditional system, nor did the members of the Legislature replace local chiefs.. Positions in the western administrative hierarchy complemented rather than replaced the traditional offices; and the persons chosen to fill the new positions represented a subtle blend of qualities essential to each sphere. Every member of the Imbokodvo was automatically a member of the Swazi National Council, and nearly every Swazi elected or appointed to the Legislative Council had a trusted position in the traditional hierarchy.

In the first executive appointments by Francis Loyd, A. Khuseni Hlophe was made Member for Local Administration and Social Development, and Polycarp Dlamini, Member For Education and Health; two former members of the European Advisory Council, Dan Fitzpatrick and Carl Todd, were appointed members for Public Works and Communications and for Natural Resources respectively. The remaining members were initially all white officials of the government.

The King accepted the election results as a justification of the Swazi national policy and as evidence that he had correctly interpreted the wishes of the majority of his people. But he also recognized that he had to consolidate the national victory. He read angry denunciations of his approach in liberal papers published in South Africa and Britain. The *Times of Swaziland* regretted that the 'dynamic parties' did not win any seats and stated bluntly that 'vigorous opposition is a good thing'. Opposition parties were still vocal, and some of the leaders had tried to form a new united front against the 'traditionalists and white settlers' who, they claimed, had managed to exclude from the Legislative Council 'the representative, progressive and democratic elements' (*Times of Swaziland*, 19 July 1964). Appeal was made to the Liberation Committee of the Organization of African Unity at Dar-es-Salaam (*Times of Swaziland*, 7 August 1964) and cables went to U Thant, to the British Colonial Secretary, and to the British Prime Minister, protesting the election results and alleging malpractices by candidates and intimidation by chiefs in rural areas. Ironically, in the light of previous protests, the British Government was requested to take strong and immediate action 'to restore our democratic freedom, to redress abuses of power and to create conditions under which truly free elections can take place' (*Times of Swaziland*, 10 July 1964).

But the attitude of the British had changed as support for the Ngwenyama had become increasingly apparent, and the Colonial Office had replied, through Francis Loyd, that redress for alleged malpractices lay in an appeal to the courts, that the parties should seek legal advice, and that the Ngwenyama-in-Council exercised rights in Swaziland and could prohibit any act which might disturb the peace (*Times of Swaziland*, 10 July 1964). Following legal advice, the parties attempted to reverse the results and unseat fourteen Imbokodvo members, but the suit was dismissed for lack of evidence.

As King of the Swazi and head of a potentially new African state, Sobhuza began to clarify his political stance in relation to South Africa, other African countries, Portugal and the rest of the world. He had gained sufficient confidence to formulate for himself an overall strategy and also to re-evaluate relations with white settlers.

One of his first actions was to make it officially known that the Imbokodvo represented the majority of all people in his country and to deplore the fact that no Imbokodvo official had been invited to the meeting of heads of African states held in Cairo in July 1964. At that meeting resolutions were passed for a boycott of Portugal, and to assist guerilla movements in Southern Africa.

Sobhuza was no longer isolated in his techniques of diplomacy. He had common ground with other African leaders whose countries were on the verge of independence; but his outspoken criticism of racism was tempered by an awareness that to refuse to cooperate with South Africa in the economic field would be economic suicide, and to allow his country to be used as a base for armed aggression would be political suicide. As long as England was in control Sobhuza was able to evade major political commitments in international relations. Now it was becoming increasingly difficult.

Rumours had been circulated that Sobhuza himself had yielded to the bribes and promises of Verwoerd and supporters of his policy in Swaziland. These rumours were reported to Sobhuza, who at first dismissed them with the reply that his people 'knew better than to believe lies.' The rumours persisted. When people he respected appeared almost ready to credit them, he could no longer remain silent.

He called a meeting of the nation, and in what he described as his 'authentic statement', published in the local *Times of Swaziland* (24 July 1964), described a visit from his 'old age-group mate', the Reverend Jonah Mndzebele. The minister had been so worried by things he heard that he left a church meeting still in progress 'because he could not say his prayers with any benefit with his spirit wandering and so depressed', and came direct to the King to find out the truth. He had heard that Sobhuza was planning to sell his people to Verwoerd, or negotiating to have his country annexed to the South African Republic.

How does one reply to such lies? By anger? Or emphatic denial? Or in the 'Swazi way'? Sobhuza began with an analogy that, he said, 'made us roll with laughter'. Do you remember? he asked, 'when you and I were young?'

There were in this country hyenas which pulled kids out of the huts. Sometimes the hyena would howl from a distance and the unwary would think it was too far to bother about only to find that all of a sudden it had broken into the hut and snatched its prey.

Today we have hyenas that walk on two legs. They are to be heard howling and yelling around homesteads, frightening our children out of their wits so that some of them desert their homes in an effort to escape only to find themselves landing right into the snarling teeth of the hyena that is ready to draw them to its masters. And the child will not be able to turn one way or the other as he is now in the clutches of this formidable animal.

If you set snares for game, closing all possible openings except one, you then set a bait attractive to the victim – so, for a bird the rich white ant, or similar tempting decoys. It is only guinea fowl which shows true caution; when it sees something enticing it stops to consider the motive behind this unknown friend's generous act, and leaves without eating of the gift.

Prosperity that suddenly springs from nowhere and shoots up overnight like mushrooms must be looked at with the same suspicion.

He then confronted directly the accusation that he had been bribed with £25,000 to 'hand my people and the country over to the Republic'. He asked, 'Is this country and its inhabitants worth only this amount?' He had requested the author of the story to come out openly 'if he had anything genuine to say. If no one comes forward this would be an indication that his story was a lie. No one took up my challenge'.

I do not remember the Swazi nation meeting in the royal kraal to give me the mandate for the annexation or incorporation of Swaziland into the Republic. I cannot endorse or act on issues for which I have received no mandate from the Swazi nation. I am like a rubber stamp. What is surprising is that while all the nations are clamouring for freedom, we, the Swazi nation, should wish to go from one domination to another.

And he warned his people against listening to the promises of 'foreigners who pretend friendship', advising them to think and judge for themselves as Swazi, for

Woe unto those who are lazy to think independently, to those who become easily convinced and to those who follow others for the sake of following, for they will learn by bitter experience ... But in the case of real Swazi, not those who are light-hearted or prostitute-minded, you can never really mislead, seduce or buy them by whatever means, and no one can sell them away. Thus you should not be worried or troubled by untruths and false statements where it is quite clear that they are intended for a certain mischievous purpose. You should be able to weigh all the facts independently and individually and realize what action would befit a person in the position of a King.

Having expressed his attitude on South Africa, he had still to reaffirm his position in relation to the British. Despite the fact that Francis Loyd was personally anxious to please, the nation still awaited the outcome of the petition, and the imposed Constitution was soon to be put into operation.

The official opening of the Legislative Council was set for 9 September 1964 at the High Court in Mbabane. The Ngwenyama was scheduled to deliver the opening speech. Before the meeting

Makhosini presented the Swazi members of the Legco as 'representatives of the Nation' to the Ndlovukazi at Lobamba to receive her blessings and good wishes.

Everything had been arranged for what the British hoped would be a very splendid occasion. The order of arrival and the allocation of seats had been carefully decided by Western protocol. A large crowd looked on expectantly as the notables arrived. Some thousand warriors in Swazi attire had marched to Mbabane and stood outside in a section cordoned off for the public. Facing them, separated by police and British troops, were some seven hundred members of the opposition with Prince Dumisa and Macdonald Maseko in the forefront, occasionally chanting Congress protest songs and calling on the King to stay out of politics. The Ndlovukazi with two attendants arrived in state. But the King did not appear.

When Francis Loyd opened the proceedings he announced that the King was 'regrettably indisposed'. Msindazwe Sukati, M.B.E., read the King's speech, carefully worded, critical rather than hostile, dwelling on future hopes rather than past failures:

It was after many years of government by proclamation which was far from being satisfactory that we initiated the constitutional talks on 23 April 1960 ... There followed many disappointments and tribulations ... the refusal to grant the petition, the imposition of the Constitution ... so that it would be hypocrisy to deny that our confidence in Her Majesty's Government has not been shaken. It is, however, our wish that the relationship will change for the better. Let us not dwell on the past, let us cast our eyes to the future and let us seek there that which is good for our nation.

The events of the past contain the one irresistible truism – if we desire our country's future to be placed on a firm footing, we must be the masters of our own destiny – realizing all the time, that Swaziland is strongly surging forward towards its independence. Our people will calmly but fearlessly strive to achieve this objective, undaunted by problems and difficulties. It is the will of our people to be independent within the Commonwealth of Nations; and the present Constitution shall be made a vehicle to reach this goal as soon as possible. This must be done without estranging our people from their Swazi heritage and national tradition.

As to the elected members, he urged them to carry out 'the duties which their position placed upon them in the light of the trust which was being shown in them and the ideals which they should uphold'. He concluded:

Yours is indeed a grave responsibility for the eyes of the people of Swaziland, the eyes of the people of Africa, and indeed the eyes of the people of the world are upon you. Do your duty with impartiality before God for the fate of our nation is very much in your hands. May we wish you and Swaziland good rains, good crops and good government. (Swaziland Legco 1st Session, 1st mtg. 9-14 September 1964).

The King's speech expressed the national ideals. Prince Makhosini as leader of the Imbokodvo then put forward its policies. The first thing required was a new Constitution which was not based on racialism, which did not want an alliance with apartheid, and one which accorded the King of Swaziland his 'due position'.

There is opinion expressed in some quarters, which we do not accept, that the King should not enter into politics. Imbokodvo would like to explain that it is the King's duty to discuss political affairs, especially when the country is in political turmoil. This is so because as King he is by tradition leader and mouthpiece of the Nation. Even during his minority, Swazi poets used to sing – 'grow up and speak for yourself'. In the last two years it became obvious that an unwanted Constitution was being imposed upon us, and how could the King remain silent? We shall continue to ask for the amendment of this law so that the King be accorded his rightful position (*ibid.*).

As he elaborated points which had been put forward in the Imbokodvo manifesto, it became increasingly clear that the Swazi National Council would no longer be subservient to white opinion, and that the Imbokodvo would be able to use its majority to free itself from its alliance with the United Swaziland Association and move closer to the national aspirations previously expressed by opposition parties.

Some saw in the King's conspicuous absence from the opening of the Legco a symbolic protest against the imposed Constitution. That he was ill was admitted. He had suffered greatly from the strain of the past few years. But had this been the *Ncwala* all his people knew he would have 'hidden' his illness, and 'danced the Kingship'.

The public direction given by Sobhuza and reaffirmed in the policy statement by Makhosini made its impact on Swazi nationals who had opposed the Imbokodvo. The first leading opposition politician to respond favourably was Sishayi Simon Nxumalo. Sishayi, idealist and realist, an astute politician with a fine sense of history, perceived that at least in his case it was not because of what he had said that he had suffered a crushing defeat in the elections. He, like others of the Swazi Democratic Party, had publicly stated that he recognized the authority of traditional chiefs, and he wanted the eight Swazi National seats on the Legislative Council to be filled by chiefs or their councillors. Moreover, he, Sishayi, had stood in a constituency in which he was not only well known but popular as a person and admired for his work as a teacher. He realized that he had lost because, as a member of a political party, he had put himself into an enemy camp and so was described as 'fighting the King'. He remembered how his father, Mgcobeya, had stood his ground from within the Council, and his criticisms and suggestions had been effectively followed.

Sishayi announced through the press that he had resigned from the SDP to work for wider national unity. He also handed to the King a first-class air ticket to Taiwan explaining that it now belonged to Makhosini. Before the election results Sishayi had been so sure of victory and so convincing to others, that the Vice President of Taiwan, whom he had met at Malawi's Independence celebration, had invited him to visit his country as future Prime Minister of Swaziland. Sobhuza appreciated Sishayi's gesture and showed his trust by sending him on tour as his personal emissary to explain his (Sishayi's) change of heart, correct misrepresentations of royal policy, and 'put Swaziland into its true position'.

In March 1965, when the First Legco was in recess, Makhosini, accompanied by Dr Msibi, went on his first 'state visit' on the VIP invitation given to Sishayi. In Taiwan, he asked his hosts to convert his first-class ticket to economy class so that he could also visit Nigeria, Ghana and Ethiopia. The Taiwan government was so impressed that they included these other countries in his itinerary. For Prince Makhosini it was a wonderful and broadening experience.

After Sishayi's resignation the SDP began to disintegrate. The overzealous Rozwadowski was expelled for sending a letter to the Secretary of State without consulting his Swazi colleagues; and in April 1965 after a long period of negotiation, Dr Malabhane Nxumalo, who had become President of the SDP, was accepted by the Imbokodvo. The SDP dissolved, and many of its members sought, and obtained, admission into the Imbokodvo.

It was an ideal of Swazi society that rivalry between political parties could not destroy or obliterate kinship bonds. Politicians remained friendly with kinsmen in other parties and fulfilled their obligations towards them. Years later, a high British official, speaking to the King at the State House, rather indiscreetly enquired about the past conflicts. The King did not reply directly but asked with apparent innocence if it were true that England was facing civil war in Ireland and could his visitor explain the reason. The answer was given as a struggle between Catholics and Protestants. Sobhuza sympathized with England's problems and said how fortunate his country was that among his people one member of the family could be a Protestant, another a Catholic, another a Traditionalist. Even if they belonged to different political parties they retained family responsibilities.

In all these events in which politics, kinship and economics were inextricably intertwined, Sobhuza sought traditional guidelines through the twisted paths of modernization, attempting to protect his people from exploitation, and at the same time trying not to jeopardise the economic stability of the country. Foreign investments were increasing. The first rich deposit of iron ore had been extracted and the controversial railway from the mine to Lourenço Marques in Mozambique completed at a cost of sixteen million rand. It was with obvious pleasure that Sobhuza blew the whistle to officially open the new railway and set the train on its course. That same year a R 500,000 hydroelectric scheme was inaugurated by the internationally known South African financier, Harry Oppenheimer; a new coal mine was started; and irrigation was introduced in the lowveld permitting the establishment of large-scale sugar plantations. A new type of urban centre emerged – the company town associated with the exploitation of particular resources and built to house and provide services for employees. 15% of Africans (41,000), 69% of Europeans (5,570) and 55% of Eur-Africans (1,240) lived in designated urban areas.

But the modern sector was being built up and controlled by white investors, and the sharp duality between haves and have-nots which had led to support for the strikes in the previous year continued. Sobhuza tried to work in two directions – to raise the level of wages of Swazi employees, and at the same time to extend Swazi participation in the economy. He encouraged the Commercial Amadoda, urged that Swazi be trained for managerial positions in the white private sector, and he told employers of labour that people should not be paid wages that come under the category of 'cheap labour'. He warned them that 'anyone who cares only for his own well being will destroy the good will and understanding in the territory'.

But 1964 brought one of the worst droughts in memory! He and the Queen Mother had performed all the necessary rituals without the desired results. Rains, expected in late August, did not fall until late October, by which time thousands of cattle had died and crops had not been planted. This was not all. In the middle of October foot and mouth, a highly contagious cattle disease, broke out in Mozambique. The Veterinary Department was unanimous in insisting that to prevent it from spreading into Swaziland, border areas be cordoned off and livestock crossing the borders or suspected of contamination be destroyed.

Sobhuza reluctantly accepted the necessity of drastic measures put forward by experts and supported by whites who had started large-scale ranching. He appealed to the nation to safeguard the entire cattle industry. The people most directly and immediately affected were Swazi under the Mahlalela and Sifundza chiefs, Ngudvumane and Majembeni, in the area near Nomahasha with a cattle population of over 40,000. The area cordoned off limited both the grazing and the water supply. The people wanted to move their cattle to an adjacent farm, owned by an absentee European. His manager, afraid that the cattle had already been exposed to the disease, refused permission. The situation was complicated by the fact that Ngudvumane Mahlalela supported the NNLC, and that Sobhuza's daughter Betfusile and Dumisa led a demonstration of resistance in the area against the preventive measures. The local District Commissioner described the situation as explosive. Sobhuza endorsed the decision of the Swazi National Council to fine Ngudvumane, and at the same time to resume negotiations with the farmer through their own nominees to obtain temporary relief for the people. The confrontation reflected the continuing hazards and festering resentment created by the initial land division between whites and Swazi, but Sobhuza considered that in this instance the NNLC were trying to make political capital out of a highly emotional issue.

Sobhuza sent for the chiefs to appear before the *liqoqo* at Lozitha. Ngudvumane defied his order; police were sent to fetch him; they brought him by force, which the King lamented as 'something we all hate to see and do', but circumstances had driven him into a position in which 'force was necessary to preserve the peace'. At the enquiry

Sobhuza asked the men why they had followed the leadership of 'these two children of mine. Did they say they were coming from me?' And he continued, 'Be that as it may, will you please take note that we in this Council do not use nor have ever approved of aggressive methods in matters of state. We always prefer evolution to revolution. I wonder who are these people who have come up with aggressive and violent methods. I ask you this question: Who is your friend? Is it he who incites you to fight a formidable enemy when you are unarmed, or is it he who advises you to use peaceful means of negotiation? I should say it is the latter who is the friend' (*Times of Swaziland*, 9 October 1964).

What would his rebellious 'children' do next? The answer was not long in coming. The troops who were still in the country had little to do, and some spent their free time and money in the bars to which they attracted local Swazi girls and women. Public mixed drinking was condemned by all respectable Swazi; Sobhuza described it as 'shameful'. The newspapers published letters by parents expressing bewilderment, sorrow and anger at what was happening to the morality of the women. On the evening of 3 November, Dumisa and a fellow worker in the NNLC went into a bar of a hotel in Mbabane notorious for its unseemly revelries, and dragged out four Swazi girls and beat them. Dumisa was arrested and released on R20 bail. Two weeks later he assaulted a woman in Msunduza Township whom he accused of misbehaving. The two cases were set for a hearing on 14 December.

The moon of the little *Ncwala* was approaching. Dumisa would never dare to attend; if he did, how could his safety be guaranteed? But what about the more foolhardy Betfusile? The majority of Queens were adamant that she should not come into their quarters or dance with their own daughters. Senior Princes of the Inner Council called her to Lobamba, and when she came asked her why she had 'branched away' from other royal children. They reported that she had answered 'aggressively without respect', and so they told her not to enter the *sigodlo* or the *ndlunkulu* any more. Sobhuza as King of the Nation had to agree to their verdict.

On the day of the little *Ncwala* Betfusile arrived together with Princess Myingile; the guards told them they would not be allowed to dance, that they were politicians, and mocked them 'go and dance Dumisa's *Ncwala* – he is your king'. Angrily they challenged this. 'The *Ncwala* is for every subject of the King no matter what their politics may be.' But it was to no avail. A senior councillor stated that the King had confirmed the exclusion. He could not do otherwise; but when it was suggested that he inflict further punishment on his children 'who were Communists', he replied, 'They are my children and if they are Communists they are my Communists.'

The *Ncwala* drew an immense crowd. On the main day the elected Swazi members of the Legislative Council participated in full Swazi regalia; white members of the Legco attended; the Queen's

Commissioner and his wife together with senior staff put in a formal appearance; and Sobhuza danced Kingship. Symbolically though not yet in fact he had amalgamated the two systems, paving the way for the next stage in the creation of a new independent African state. But outside the capital he knew that there were people who were jealous and people who were suspicious and people who were opposed to the movement he had started.

CHAPTER XVI
The Legco Period

The Legislative Council was only in existence from September 1964 until March 1967 but it influenced the directions, in law and policy, for many years to come. It was a period in which there was an effort by the British to make effective a political model which would be more compatible with western ideals.

For Sobhuza, as Ngwenyama, it was a strange period – not only was greater formal authority vested in Sir Francis Loyd, the Queen's Commissioner, but his own representative, Prince Makhosini, appeared more frequently before the general public to express national interests in the Legco, while the standing committee of the Swazi National Council remained less conspicuously at Lobamba. Yet everyone also knew that he, Sobhuza, was the power behind the scenes; that Swazi members dashed down the hill from Mbabane to Lobamba or Masundvwini at all hours of the night in response to his summons 'Ngemandla'; that because of him, the new Secretary of the Swazi National Council, Sibusiso Motsa, was in effect as influential as the Chief Secretary, Atholl Long; that the discussions in Legco as well as the decisions were considered by Sobhuza in his appraisal of individual members for future office. But he was not yet given official recognition as King, and the country was not yet politically independent.

At the opening meeting of the Legislative Council, 3 September 1964, Prince Makhosini had made it clear that the Imbokodvo National Movement would press for constitutional changes, but the strategies that would be employed, and the exact nature of these changes, were less obvious. Only one thing Sobhuza constantly reiterated – changes must be peaceful, bloodshed avoided.

In Britain, the Labour Party, which had been voted into power in October 1964 after thirteen years of Conservative rule, had set 1966 for the independence of Basutoland and Bechuanaland; it could not – nor did it necessarily wish to – refuse the request of Makhosini, as leader of the majority of elected members in the Legislative Council, to reconsider the 'imposed constitution'. It could only delay the date.

At first Sobhuza had been prepared to move towards independence slowly, but soon he appreciated that this was not necessary. He had the support of the majority of his own people and other African leaders. Makhosini, returning in the middle of March 1965 from his first world tour, during which he had attended a session of the OAU Council of Ministers in Nairobi, recounted to Sobhuza the reactions of other 'Third World countries' and made a public speech for 'Independence Now'. When British officials argued that the Swazi had neither the knowledge nor the trained personnel necessary for modern government, Makhosini replied with the impassioned indictment, 'You have left us naked', at the same time rejecting as antiquated the notion that Swazi were not ready to guide their own affairs.

Sobhuza expressed himself with more moderation: 'It is you not us who were guilty of neglect; now we must try to work together to remove that guilt'. Neglect of education should not justify the continuation of colonialism. The Swazi were ready for independence, and he had no doubt that they could run their affairs like any modern state. By Swazi he meant white Swazi as well as black Swazi. He often mentioned by name some of the white Swazi – mainly former high officials who had settled in Swaziland and were ready to help the country 'if they were needed'. He did not think 'the affairs of the nation should be jeopardized by differences between individuals of different colour. People who have those kinds of thoughts should excuse themselves and leave the country. Human feeling has no colour boundary and I might find a white Swazi selling the country down the drain just as I might find a black Swazi selling the country down the drain' (*Times of Swaziland*, 20 August 1965).

Sobhuza was sufficiently secure to move forward without the direction from whites represented by the United Swaziland Association (USA). They had supported the initial request that the Secretary of State be asked by the Queen's Commissioner to reconsider the Constitution on the assumption that their own interests could in this way be best served. Carl Todd had written Sobhuza a confidential letter trying to obtain from him promises that their existing position be safeguarded. However, Sobhuza had not replied, and by the time a copy of Todd's letter, stolen by an NNLC supporter from national files, was publicised in the press (in November 1966), it could be used to discredit the tactics of the opposition, since the new direction of the Imbokodvo had been made more explicit.

Makhosini, Sishayi Nxumalo and Dr Msibi, not Sobhuza, bore the brunt of criticism by the conservative whites, who openly condemned their visits to 'centres of radicals and communists'. In the Imbokodvo itself a few influential old guard were afraid that former party leaders – particularly 'the Nxumalos and Msibis' – were struggling to capture the country, using Makhosini for their own ends. For different reasons the NNLC directed its most bitter criticism against the Swaziland Democratic Party, and in particular against Sishayi Nxumalo.

Sobhuza realized the danger of dissension; as leader of the Swazi he saw his role as building a strong and unified Swazi nation. In his address to the nation at the annual meeting at Lobamba in July, he stressed that the Swazi people would never get independence unless they spoke with one voice. He went on to explain that it was not criticism itself which was destructive but the party system. Drawing his usual analogy he said, 'In every family there are arguments, but later when the time comes for meals, the meal is taken together and the family does not break up into separate houses' (*Times of Swaziland*, 23 July 1965).

Nationalism and patriotism, he argued, did not exclude friendship and cooperation with people of other countries and cultures but set the necessary guidelines for mutual respect. At the opening of the Swaziland Credit and Savings Bank (August 1965), having stressed that the Swazi were ready for independence and were capable· of running the country, he expounded on this theme:

There are people who might say they are black Swazis who ask if the white Swazis should be here, and white Swazis who ask if the black Swazis are chasing them out. This is out of date, and we don't want that sort of talk in Swaziland ... We are living in the modern age where geographical and parochial boundaries are falling away. All people belong to the human race, ... there is no time for people who take a short view of things and look at the colour of a man's skin ... We respect and welcome everybody who has the welfare of Swaziland and the people at heart and identify themselves with Swaziland (*Times of Swaziland*, 20 August 1965).

On 18 August 1965, Sir Francis announced that the request for a review of the present Constitution had been granted. The Secretary of State for the Colonies authorized him as the Queen's Commissioner to appoint a committee to submit proposals for the stage of internal self-government preparatory to independence. He appointed eight Imbokodvo, four USA, and two senior civil servants; he himself became chairman.[1]

The automatic exclusion of the opposition from membership, and hence from the full deliberations and final decisions, evoked inevitable and predictable reactions of protest and appeal,[2] but the British were now committed to negotiate with Legco representatives and their recognized leader, Sobhuza II.

As in the London conferences, Sobhuza deliberately did not participate directly in the discussions but everything of importance was reported to him by his men. From these reports he knew how each member of the Committee viewed controversial points in the system of representation, the qualifications for voting, and the appointment of officials. He carefully weighed the arguments with individual

[1] Sir Francis appointed the Chief Secretary (Atholl C.E. Long) and the Attorney General (J.J. Dickie) as official members; the unofficial members were Princes Makhosini, Masitsela and Mfanasibili; A.K. Hlophe; Polycarp Dlamini; Mfundza Sukati; Dr G. Msibi; Carl Todd; D.H. Fitzpatrick; R.P. Stephens; W. Meyer; and E.G. Winn. The Assistant Chief Secretary (H.M. Roemmele) and the Senior Liaison Officer (Rev. A.B. Gamedze) were Joint Secretaries.

[2] The SPP, under Nquku, the NNLC under Zwane, and a 'Joint Council of Swaziland Political Parties' under O.M. Mabuza, made separate submissions to the Committee and sent memos of protest to the OAU and to sympathizers in different countries.

councillors of the Swaziland National Council, and became increasingly guarded in his attitude to the white settlers as he noted their reservations on issues agreed to by his own people. It was hard, he once said, to separate the sheep from the wolves. When the Queen's Commissioner consulted with him, Sobhuza reminded him of British promises in the past, reiterated the national desire for independence 'as soon as possible,' and made no concessions that might commit his Council to unacceptable compromises.

He himself moved adroitly from one role to another, steadily building up the base of his future power. The second session of the Legislative Council opened on 12 October 1965. Since the British had officially recorded their decision to reconsider the Constitution, Sobhuza saw no objection to attending in person. Sir Francis, who began, 'Mr. Speaker, Ngwenyama', surveyed the present position, informed the listeners of policies Government wished to pursue, announced that he hoped the recommendations of the Committee would be ready early next year, and concluded on a personal and optimistic note, declaring his belief that 'there was enough wisdom in this territory ... for the right decisions to be taken'. He had made no reference to the role of Sobhuza. When the Council adjourned for business, Sobhuza and his retinue returned to Lobamba, determined that it would not be long before the Swazi sovereign would take precedence over any foreign official.

The previous Friday, on 8 October, he had driven with a large entourage, including several of the younger Queens and children to Shiselweni, to officially open a new royal residence. This was a gift from his people in the South. Modern, built entirely by Swazi labour, it was paid for mainly from the cattle of achievement (*tinkhomo takaqoza*) presented him by his people on his return from the Coronation of Queen Elizabeth, in 1953. To the house, well equipped but pleasingly unpretentious, the whites of the South contributed an impressive wrought iron gate inscribed with his name. The site was some five miles from the little town of Nhlangano and some twenty miles from the royal village of Old Zombodze, now under the senior chief, Phuhlaphi Nsibandze. The ceremony was attended by about 2,500 people, a cross-section of the entire population, with Swazi warriors in traditional finery. Sir Francis had sent a deputy, Pat Forsyth Thompson, Secretary for Local Administration, who apologized that His Excellency had been prevented from coming by pressure of work.[3] For the Swazi, however, as made explicit by Msindazwe Sukati who had been largely responsible for the plan and its execution and was acting as Master of Ceremonies, this was more than the opening of a new house; it marked a new page in Swazi history. It was a *sibimbi*, an occasion for the performance of ancient dance-songs reserved for major national occasions and rituals.

---

[3] For a fairly full report of the event, see *Times of Swaziland*, 15 October 1965.

Sobhuza in his address named the house the New Shiselweni, which he explained would represent 'the presence of a King'; people who came there even in his absence 'must sing the praises of Kingship'.

The King stayed at Shiselweni for a couple of days, holding court in the afternoons, and familiarizing himself with developments in the area. Before coming to the house, he had visited the site of a projected sawmill, the first factory in the South, which would employ some 150 people. Though the South had some of the most progressive chiefs, the roads, communication, marketing and social services were poor, and people felt neglected. Sobhuza's visit was extremely welcome, and the women brought beer and uncooked foods and there was much jubilation. He promised he would visit more frequently and include Shiselweni in his circuit of royal villages.

The following October he kept his promise. Much of the previous traditional ritual was repeated, for the residence was to be completed by the addition of a *sibaya*, built with special trees of the country. This time I was in Swaziland and was fortunate to see it and hear it all – the regiments in their costumes performing the ancient dance-songs, queens and princesses married to local chiefs dancing forward to greet them, the King watching with obvious enjoyment. Then he gave an address. It was windy and bitterly cold and the dust blew so that the recording over the loudspeaker was poor, but the message came across and the *emabutfo* – 'the strength of the nation' – whistled their piercing responses as he made his points, and thundered 'Bayethe' at the end.

In March 1966, Sobhuza II was in the birthday list of honours bestowed by the British Queen. In a dignified ceremony at the Oval in Mbabane, where he had met Edward Prince of Wales, Sir Francis invested him with the insignia of a Knight Commander of the Civil Division of the Most Excellent Order of the British Empire, KBE.

A few days before, on 3 March, the report of the Constitutional Committee was published, in English and siSwati, informing the public that 'the non-official members had repeatedly affirmed their "desire and intention for complete independence as soon as possible," and the Secretary of State, accepting this "in principle", had made it clear "that this should not be later than the end of 1969"' (Swaziland Government, Report of Swaziland Constitutional Committee, 1966:2). As a first stage, the status of Swaziland would be changed from that of a Colonial Protectorate to that of a Protected State under a Treaty of Friendship with the British Government; and the Committee made specific and detailed proposals which combined in their view the essentials of a modern democratic state with the traditional institutions of the Swazi Nation and Swazi Kingship.

It proposed returning certain rights of traditional sovereignty and at the same time building up foreign institutions, that imposed certain restrictions. The Ngwenyama was to be recognized as King of Swaziland and Head of State; until full independence Her Majesty's Commissioner should retain responsibility for external affairs, defence, finance and internal security (including the use of the police), and conditions of public service. The Swazi National Council was to continue to advise the King 'on all matters regulated by Swazi law and custom,' but legislative, judicial and executive authority would also be vested in separate bodies.

There was to be a Parliament of two houses. The House of Assembly would consist of a Speaker, 24 elected members and 6 members nominated by the King 'having regard to interests not already adequately represented'; the Attorney General would be present but would have no vote. The Senate would consist of a Speaker and 12 members, 6 elected by members of the House of Assembly and 6 appointed by the King, again having regard to interests not otherwise adequately represented. The principle of universal franchise on a common roll was accepted. The vote was extended to citizens of the United Kingdom and British Colonies (a category which did not include South African citizens) resident in Swaziland for not less than three years during the five years immediately preceding their application for registration. The Ngwenyama would appoint the Prime Minister and Cabinet, although British colonial separation of political office from civil service would be maintained and developed through the Public Service Commission and a Judicial Service Commission.

This complicated document – which was being widely discussed and criticised from different angles when in September 1966 after an absence of five years I returned to Swaziland – met with cautious approval from Sobhuza. I recall from my notes our meeting when we touched on this matter. I had spent a relaxed afternoon with the Queens of Masundvwini, drinking 'Fanta' (a non-alcoholic cold drink) and eating crackers. We sat on mats on the ground in a new large square room built in the yard behind the main house; the little children came in and out from play. Geese wandered around and peacocks paraded. Huge iron pots boiled on an outside cooking space. I mentioned that I would like to *'vusela'* (greet) Ngwenyama, and one of the Queens, laMgometulu (junior), acting as *'lincusa'* (intermediary), reported this to him.

He told me he had not been very well – 'the usual stomach trouble' – and had just come back from seeing a traditional Zulu doctor of very good reputation, who was from South Africa but had now settled in Swaziland. We sat on chairs in the front room; three of the Queens joined us, sitting decorously and naturally on the floor. Fat pigeons strutted in and out of the rooms. We exchanged news of our families; talked about the approaching *Ncwala* and the possibility of my daughter Jenny (to whom he had long ago given the name Lahlekile) filming it as a private record. When I asked if he was pleased with the new constitutional proposals, he replied, 'Of course,' then said more guardedly that they were still being 'considered'. 'But we are going forward as before; we have to watch these things carefully.' And he lightly changed the subject with an inquiry about American immigration laws.

The Report of the Constitutional Committee embodied in an official White Paper published simultaneously in Swaziland and London (Swaziland Constitutional Proposals 3119, October 1966) reflected the opinions of the Imbokodvo rather than the reservations of the USA members. The Committee had identified as its 'fundamental problem' 'the restoration of what the Swazi regard as the original treaty relationship which Swaziland had with Britain in the 19th century and the recognition of the Kingship of the Ngwenyama (Paramount Chief).' This original treaty relationship referred to the Pretoria Convention of 1881, signed by British, Boers and Swazi recognizing the independence of the Swazi under their own King. While the British set the proposals in the context of their view of the present constitutional status of Swaziland and described their role as 'granting   independence',   the   Swazi   spoke   of   'regaining independence', translated as *inkhululeko* – freedom.

Reconciliation of the views of the British and the King-in-Council had been reached on all but one major issue, an issue ostensibly centred in the control over rights to minerals and mineral oils, but fundamentally revealing the subtle distinction between the British interpretation of the role of a King and the Swazi concept of Kingship. The Secretary of State finally agreed that control over minerals be vested in the King, advised by a committee; but who was to constitute the committee? The Swazi were adamant that in accordance with traditional Swazi Kingship the committee be appointed by the King in consultation with the Swazi National Council. The British argued that since Government would be in the hands of a Cabinet drawn from a Parliament mainly elected by universal franchise, the committee should be appointed from the Cabinet. In the opinion of the Secretary of State, it was

essential that the central Government which was responsible for other aspects of the economic development of Swaziland should also control mineral development. To provide otherwise and to vest control in the traditional authority might well result in a clash with the central Government which would have far-reaching effects in Swaziland. Furthermore in view of its unique position, events in Swaziland would come in for close scrutiny and it was desirable to avoid creating procedures which would enable people to say that a traditional, rather than a democratic, system was being adopted. Clear ministerial responsibility would dispose of this criticism (Swaziland Constitutional Proposals [Cmd. 3119], Oct. 1966:6).

The Swazi interpreted the refusal of the British to accept their viewpoint as indicating a lack of faith in the Ngwenyama and depriving him and his people of the right to control revenue in accord with their real national interests. To critics who considered that Britain was being asked to recognize a traditional model of Kingship existing some 100 years back under totally different conditions,

Sobhuza pointed out that Britain was applying its own traditional concepts of constitutional monarchy.

The opposition did not object to control over minerals being vested in the committee of the Cabinet, but they objected to the limited number of constituencies (eight in all), each represented by three members; they urged sixty constituencies each represented by one member. Their own supporters, scattered in small pockets, among the urban and industrial centres, would constitute a minority in large predominantly rural constituencies. They also disagreed with the definitions of citizenship which they felt would exclude a number of their own supporters and give to the white immigrants privileges denied their black compatriots. The approach of Sobhuza and of the parties to the British was therefore very different.

Imbokodvo's suspicion of British motives was not allayed by the fact that Basutoland and Bechuanaland, neither of which at that time was believed to have the minerals or general economic potential of Swaziland, were approaching political independence. On 30 September 1966, Bechuanaland became the independent Republic of Botswana; on 4 October 1966, Basutoland became the independent Kingdom of Lesotho. Sobhuza had been invited to their celebrations but sent Makhosini as leader of the Swazi delegation.[4] John Stonehouse, then British Parliamentary Under-Secretary for the Colonies, having attended the Independence celebrations in both countries, came to Swaziland in the hope of reconciling different viewpoints on the Constitution. He met Sobhuza, local officials, political leaders and delegations from the political parties, but was not able to persuade the King-in-Council to accept the British proposals for the control of mineral rights. The British reaffirmed their policy on this particularly controversial issue. Sobhuza and his men were not daunted, only (temporarily) frustrated.

Addressing the nation at Lobamba on 11 November (1966), Sobhuza declared in an allegorical speech that 'the bride has not yet been taken from her father's home'. His audience understood that he referred to deficiencies in the proposed constitution. He again emphasized the need for national unity and hard work to make a success of independence. He never promised them Utopia. Makhosini, speaking after Sobhuza, proclaimed: 'Those who could never agree that there should be two kings, now see only one, our King, who will bring back the country to the people.'

The British troops, which had been in Swaziland since the disturbances of June 1963, were unexpectedly evacuated at the end of November 1966. The last replacement, some 400 officers and men of the Royal Irish Fusiliers, had been there only since April of that year. According to Sir Francis Loyd, the move had been planned for some

---

[4] Others included Sishayi Nxumalo, Bhekimphi Dlamini and Makula Shongwe of the Administration, distinctive in Swazi attire.

time as the British had never intended to keep a force in Swaziland after the granting of independence to Botswana and Lesotho. But Sobhuza was only informed a few days before the event.

His reactions were rather mixed. English soldiers represented a foreign military force. At the same time, the soldiers had become a familiar part of life. They in no way oppressed the people, their relationships were friendly and courteous, at times too friendly. He had been impressed by the discipline and courtesy of their commanding officers and delighted by the military band. However, he was essentially relieved when they were recalled.

No Swazi had been trained by British troops. It had been the great ambition of Prince Gabheni, son of Sobhuza by Lomadlozi Nkambule, to go to Sandhurst. But the local officials had refused him permission: they had firmly denied his request on the grounds that there was no modern Swazi army, nor for economic reasons would there be one in the foreseeable future. They suggested instead that he join the police, which was a paramilitary force, and, particularly in recent years, well trained and well equipped. When Makhosini as Sobhuza's messenger suggested that the barracks which had been built for the troops be left for a Swazi army of the future, the idea was dismissed as unrealistiç, ridiculous and childish. 'The country can't afford it. Besides, whom would you fight?'

The police force had been increased to 600 in 1966, and every effort had been made to attract young men of above average education, who received special training at the police college; some were even sent to the United Kingdom. But the police force was not yet integrated into the national structure and there was a feeling that the allegiance of some of the officers was to the British not to the Swazi monarchy. In 1964 there had been no African gazetted officer; in 1966 four out of thirty-three were Swazi. The senior positions were still held by white officers. (By 1968 the Swaziland police had been renamed the Royal Swaziland Police; and later, Timothy Velabo Mtsetfwa, son of the great governor Mandanda, became the first Swazi Commissioner under Sobhuza, the Commander-in-Chief.)

The Government anticipated – and rightly – that there would be no trouble in the coming elections. Whereas the Imbokodvo was united under Sobhuza, who dealt kindly even with people whom he did not altogether trust but whose special talents he appreciated, the opposition was weakened by bitter personal squabbles and accusations. The NNLC was about to lose its most charismatic and active member – Prince Dumisa – and Sobhuza had to decide his future.

Meanwhile Dumisa jumped bail while waiting trial on charges of assault and, 'trying' in his own words 'to increase his knowledge and gain experience of revolutionary methods'. He visited Moscow, Peking and Cuba. After some eleven months of wandering and searching he 'longed for home', and returned, via Mozambique, to give himself up on 13 February 1966 to the police at Siteki. He was put in jail, charged with assault, tried (in May) and convicted, and sentenced to nine months' imprisonment, of which two had already been served while awaiting trial. In the new modern prison, built on a large open site, and under an enlightened British director who considered that prison should be rehabilitative rather than punitive, prisoners worked in the gardens, learned crafts, and had literacy classes. Dumisa was permitted to read selected books and encouraged to write down his ideas. He also ran classes for other prisoners, received news from outside, and was allowed visitors. Among them were his relatives, Sishayi and Dr Malabhane Nxumalo, and his friend and political colleague, Arthur Khoza, who had been appointed in Dumisa's absence as Secretary General of the NNLC.

Khoza, intelligent, well educated, shrewd, had been disturbed for some time by the disruptive factionalism in the NNLC,[5] and was finding Zwane increasingly erratic and difficult. Dumisa admitted separately to both him and his kinsmen that he too was 'disillusioned'. Soon rumours circulated, and reached Sobhuza, that there would be major defections from the NNLC. These rumours were confirmed when, in September 1966, Khoza publicly resigned.

Soon after, Dumisa asked Sishayi to go to the Ngwenyama and beg his forgiveness. Sishayi enlisted the support of Makhosini, and together they approached Sobhuza on behalf of his errant 'child.'[6] But Sobhuza was also 'Father' of the nation. The Prince had challenged this position. Yet he, Sobhuza, had accepted others, including Sishayi, and Malabhane, and Dr Msibi, all of whom were now serving the cause of national unity. Sobhuza knew that the royal family would be divided about Dumisa; some – particularly a few of his own sons – were bitter against his 'brother' who they felt had brought the nation to the brink of civil war; a few others were more tolerant; some even sympathetic; and the Ndlovukazi and Princess Mnengwase were ready to accept him back. All, however, would be guided by Sobhuza. Dumisa's fate was in his hands.

Dumisa was still in jail, his defection from the NNLC not yet public. His followers denied the rumours as 'lies of traitors', and, informed that he would be released on the first of November (having received maximum remission for good behaviour), prepared a reception at Msunduza Hall to welcome him, and also to question him. But the Government officials, better acquainted with his new views and fearing for his physical safety, agreed to other arrangements. Very early that morning Sishayi Nxumalo came by car to the jail and drove Dumisa straight to his mother, of the Ndwandwe

[5] Arthur Khoza had received his first degree at the University of South Africa and studied politics for a period at the Ideological Institute of Winneba in Ghana. On his return to Swaziland, he had been appointed to the Civil Service. In October 1965 he had written to the *Times of Swaziland* appealing to the nation to unite against separatism and racialism.

[6] Brothers' children are covered by the same terms as one's own children.

clan, who was waiting to welcome him. For the next few days he was kept virtually hidden from all but a few of Sishayi's trusted friends. On 15 November he was driven to the office at Lobamba to appear before a special meeting of the National Council.[7]

Sobhuza, by custom, was not present; it was necessary that his advisors find out first what the young rebel had been doing, the extent to which he had involved the country with foreigners, his past transgressions and the sincerity of his present appeal for forgiveness. They would report; the Ngwenyama would decide. There was no need for any formal charge, or specific definition of treason; the issues were understood by all, but the facts needed to be verified.

Dumisa sat at the side of the front row, facing members of the Inner Council, conspicuous in his tailored suit that contrasted with the traditional clothing worn by the Princes Sozisa, Lutfo, Ncabaniso and many of the chiefs. Sozisa, solid, calm, heir of Logcogco, now himself senior prince of the Swazi nation, began by politely asking Dumisa to tell them where he had been since he had left Swaziland, and if it was true that he had visited Communist countries. Dumisa replied respectfully, and then with considerable eloquence made the point that after seeing all those countries he had 'wanted to be home'. The interrogation continued: the probing was thorough; details demanded; contradictions on statements quickly noted. The Council had possession of a letter in which he had written: 'If you can't defeat the enemy from outside, infiltrate from within, through the schools, the administration and all possible avenues.' Was this not the reason for his present plea? Would he bring his followers with him as an enemy army?

The atmosphere was tense, but even the most critical and hostile refrained from loud abusive insults. Most gave advice as well as warning. He answered each question fully, presented a graphic picture of political intrigue and of corruption in different countries, and expressed his disillusionment with 'policies in which party officials tell us where to live and what to do'. He said he now regretted his early 'blind belief and trust'.

To the direct question: Will you leave 'politics' (i.e., the parties) and join us? he answered, 'I will help strengthen the Council.' It was nearly sunset. Makhosini speaking very earnestly said, 'We are glad that you have returned with your new knowledge. We must cleanse our hearts, that the spirits of our ancestors remain at peace. Imbokodvo, not the parties, is the regiment that will win us Independence. We move slowly because we take the people with us.' Prince Sozisa closed the meeting and went with Makhosini and a few others to report to Sobhuza, who was with the Ndlovukazi at

---

[7] The main speakers at this meeting were Princes Sozisa, Makhosini, Lutfo, Masitsela, Charles; Chief Pica Magagula; Councillors Ngangenyoni Tfwala, Mabalizandla Nhlabatsi, Mndeni Shabalala and Sishayi Nxumalo. The meeting was not taped, but I was permitted to take notes.

25. Sobhuza, relaxed with his people in the *sibaya* of Lobamba. On his right are Mfundza Sukati, Polycarp Dlamini, Prince Makhosini; immediately behind Sukati is Dabede Dlamini. At far right is Prince Mazini. The girl in the foreground is his daughter, Msindvose. July 1970

26. Opening of parliament 1972. At the rear on the left is J.S.M. Mkulunyelwa Matsebula; in front, Ian Aers (Speaker of the House) and Sir John Houlton (Speaker of the Senate). To the left of His Majesty is Superintendent Mfanawenkosi Maseko and to the right is V. Smithyman (Commissioner of Police). On the steps with knobkerrie is Nganganyoni Tfwala

27 Three kings at Independence celebrations 1973. On Sobhuza's right, King
    Moshoeshoe of Lesotho; on his left, King Zwelithini of Kwa Zulu

28. In 1973 after the King had repealed the constitution he held national meetings with his
    councillors in the *sibaya* of Lobamba

Lobamba. Dumisa returned with Sishayi to his home; he was not free to enter the capital until he was ceremonially reconciled with the King and the royal family.

A Shakespearian meeting took place on 10 December 1966 in the privacy of the Queen Mother's quarters; I felt deeply privileged to be permitted to attend. Those who had been specially summoned were sitting on mats on the cement floor of the verandah of a rectangular house where the Ndlovukazi gave audience. The King came from the sanctuary with his personal ritual attendants, heralded by praises dramatically recited by his son, Prince Mahlaba. Clad in brick-red patterned *mahiya*, barefoot, carrying himself with immense quiet personal dignity, he took his place at the end of the long side of the wall beside Mazini, born of laMotsa, his deceased ritual Queen. Other senior sons, beginning with Prince Makhungu, followed in order of age – and between Makhungu and Mkhatjwa sat Dumisa, again conspicuous among the princes by his western clothing; contrary to the customary respect usually shown by Swazi when in any hut of the Queen Mother, he was even wearing shoes. Next to the 'sons' on the shorter side of the rectangle were Sobhuza's 'brothers' and 'fathers' and other members of the blood royal. Opposite them, on the King's right-hand side, sat the Queen Mother Zihlathi, his laMatsebula Queen, and two other classificatory 'mothers'; opposite Sobhuza, to the left of the steps, were his 'sisters', including Princess Mnengwase, and to the right of the steps a national priest and governors of the main royal villages; between the governors and the princes sat the two Nxumalos – Sishayi and Malabhane.

Sobhuza took his time, observing all who were present before he began, 'I have called you, Children of the Sun, you and not the whole Council to discuss our troubles.' Then, in a voice deeper than usual with emotion, he recounted the family history, and how when Nukwase, affiliated wife of his own mother, gave birth to the Princes Mshengu and Mkukwane, the question was raised, 'Would this not cause trouble?' But his mother had replied, 'No, they will support and protect you; they are part of you. If Mshengu fails, Mkukwane will be there.' He dealt briefly with the trouble between the brothers; it was known to his listeners, but he mentioned that Mkukwane (Dumisa's father) had picked up 'bad habits of drink and foreign ideas'. Then, directly rebuking Dumisa, he continued, 'If Kingship overwhelms me, it will overwhelm you. For I am you and you are me. We are one, and Kingship is the strength of the nation. If the burden of Kingship is too heavy, and I have to flee, you will have to go with me.

'Do not think you could stay behind and rule in my place. Sishayi and Malabhane are in the same position – they are of me, and I of them. Others, outsiders, may be the opposition. Whites try to govern with an organized opposition, foreign and unknown to us.'

Then he developed, in a lighter voice, with occasional humorous illustrations, his idea of the meaning of patriotism, and how it needed to be bolstered by the economy for his people to keep their self-respect. 'If you are poor, you can be told "get up," "sit down" – you cannot fight on an empty stomach. You must be armed before you can overcome someone who is armed. Long ago a High Commissioner showed me on a map how Swaziland was part of the Union of South Africa; the geography has not changed. If we drive the whites out of here, they will still rule us from outside the border. We cannot afford to be so foolish; we do not have the trained people. Those who are educated must join with us, not against us.' Ending on a deeply religious note after speaking for almost an hour, he said, 'The country is not mine, it is for the ancestors. The ancestors see us. To them evil is not acceptable, and those who are evil are not welcomed by them. Dumisa is a child of the home, he allowed himself to be led astray. Now he is begging forgiveness. Can we throw him away? I have finished.'

The audience responded, 'Bayethe', and Princess Mnengwase, in the role of 'female father' of Dumisa, shuffled on her knees to Zihlathi, the Queen Mother and Dumisa's grandmother, and whispered to her; she half-smiled, and nodded. Then Mnengwase went to Dumisa, who came, crouching respectfully, and knelt before Zihlathi. She took his right hand tenderly, and pressed her lips to his wrist, a traditional gesture of affection and greeting to one who has long been absent. LaMatsebula, his 'grandmothers' and the 'mothers' who were present did the same. Sobhuza watched them closely, deep in thought.

Back in his place among 'the sons', Dumisa spoke briefly, beginning, 'I, Dumisa, was young, but a child grows up'; and he confessed that it was not easy to find words to express his sorrow at the pain he had caused the family. The gentle Mazini responded first and asked his brother 'not to do it again.' When other princes began stating their views and pressing Dumisa to justify what he had done, Sobhuza intervened, 'We have accepted Dumisa back. Now it is over.'

Subsequently Sobhuza explained to me, 'When a child has done wrong and you have corrected him, and then you ask him to speak and he knows he has done wrong, he either remains silent or speaks nonsense. Dumisa could not say more.' And then he added, 'It was very sad and very moving especially when his mother kissed him.' But, commenting on how his own late mother, Lomawa, had assured him that Mshengu and Mkukwane would support and protect him, he wondered 'if I or my mother spoke the truth ... this will be judged not by us but by the ancestors'.

He suggested to Makhosini that Dumisa be given a position in Government where he could prove his worth. It soon became clear, however, that this would be unwise. Stones were thrown at him at a meeting; his life was threatened by former comrades who felt betrayed by his 'self-styled' conversion. It would be best for all concerned that he be sent out of the country, at least for the time being. The American Consul organised a six-week tour of the States, and the

British arranged that he be admitted to an English university to continue his studies. The Ngwenyama called him to say goodbye, and he left before the elections for the first Parliament took place, but in the meanwhile he had been allowed to dance at the *Ncwala* of Sobhuza, in the *sibaya* of Lobamba.

When John Stonehouse left, Sir Francis Loyd still hoped to persuade the Ngwenyama of the wisdom of the British approach to minerals, and to 'appreciate the concessions' made to Swazi demands. But the Ngwenyama was not prepared to discuss matters further. The *Ncwala* came at a most opportune time. Reverend Sibusiso Motsa as the Secretary of the Swazi National Council informed the Chief Secretary of the Government that 'according to Swazi custom the Ngwenyama would be in seclusion and all routine administrative matters would be suspended for the duration of *Ncwala*'.

The fact that for approximately eight weeks the Ngwenyama would not meet members of the British administration for private discussion created a situation which the Queen's Commissioner found 'most awkward and inconvenient' and which one senior expatriate civil servant criticized as 'putting the *Ncwala* show before the political interests of the country'. They did not get the unspoken message: seclusion served as exclusion. The fact that Ngwenyama was throughout that time close to his own advisors, issued his own directives, and gave audience to personal friends, demonstrated his position as upholder of Swazi customs and his identification, not with the colonial government, but with Swazi national aspirations.

At the same time the Ngwenyama made it clear – as he had on many previous occasions and as he has subsequently shown by his political appointments – it was not on a racial basis that he was taking his stand. Immediately after seeing him at his residence, Masundvwini, on 8 December, i.e., during the period of *Ncwala*, I recorded his words thus:

The cry of many leaders in troubled countries in Africa was 'Get rid of the Europeans; drive them to their own homes; let only Africans remain in Africa.' I see no sense in such talk. There are whites who have been here for generations, and cases where whites formed firm friendships with Africans. What good is there in chasing away our friends? If the Africans tried to chase all the Europeans from Africa, it would have to be expected that the Europeans would chase out the Africans who lived in their country, and then access to the outside world would be denied to the Africans together with the opportunities such access offered for education and broadening views.

I had last witnessed the *Ncwala* in 1942; in 1966 it was like taking part in a new production of a drama based on a holy and ancient script. Mandanda Mtsetfwa, now bent with age and almost blind, again had the honour as *indvuna* of Zombodze of starting the first sacred song; his voice was still incredibly sweet and clear. Though many of the earlier actors had died, their understudies were selected from the same clans to play their stereotyped roles in relation to the King, the hero and symbol of national unity. A few minor innovations did not contradict the uniquely unalterable core of the ritual. Sobhuza once said, 'Each year it is like hearing something new at the same time it is something we all know.' *Ncwala* cannot grow stale, nor can it be interrupted.

The *Ncwala* is a time for happiness; grief must be hidden and conquered, particularly by the King. That year on 16 December, the tragic news came of the death of Qondzaphi, his daughter by laFakudze, senior Queen of Lozitha, who had been given in marriage to Chief Ncephu, heir to Tikhuba Magongo, one-time governor of King Mbandzeni's village of Mbekelweni. Three months before, Ncephu himself had died. Qondzaphi's mother had lost her younger daughter when ripe for marriage, and for over a year she herself had been under medical treatment in the village of a traditional specialist. How would she take this blow? Sobhuza could not speak to her or see her to comfort her. No one could condole with him, nor could he let himself mourn in public. As he explained, 'During the *Ncwala* tears must not be shed; you have to perform and not show sadness. You hide your heart and sing. You must not pollute Kingship.' As Father of the Nation he had to conquer his feelings as father of the child.

On Christmas day he came to welcome to Swaziland my daughter, Jenny, who had arrived from America and was staying with me in the guest house of Princess Gcinaphi and her husband, Nkominophondo Khumalo. I had received from the King permission for her to film the *Ncwala*. His visit was altogether a wonderful surprise and honour. Our household was having a most jovial party. The Khumalos had provided two huge goats, large pots of beer, porridge, potatoes, as well as bottled liquor and cold drinks, and guests in uninvited numbers arrived in a happy mood from the morning onwards. I had bought the traditional western turkey (a bird not normally domesticated by Swazi and unknown to the mouths of most), which Phumuzile Mhlanga, the talented assistant selected for me by Prince Masitsela, had roasted deliciously. Princess Gcinaphi's mother, laMngometulu senior, and several other Queens from Lobamba, were being royally entertained in a separate room of the house.

In the middle of the festivities, a messenger came to me, '*Ngemandla laBhima*'.[8] Ngwenyama was outside in his car with the youngest of his Queens, the charming laTfwala, and two lovely little daughters. In a separate car were three of his sons. Sobhuza's presence caused immense excitement. The King, laTfwala, Jenny and I, the Khumalos and a few others, not too many, went into the guest house. Sobhuza was genial and being himself relaxed put everyone at ease. He introduced a range of topics – the best colour of necklace for Jenny to

---

[8] My maiden name was Beemer, and following Swazi custom I am known as laBhima, or as Nabo Lahlekile. Lahlekile (The Lost One) refers to sadness on my leaving Swaziland.

wear when dancing at the *Ncwala* (and decided that *lijuba*, a soft blue, would be right), to the meaning of Christmas. He told of the experience of a herdboy, now an old man, who had seen The One Legged, Mlentengamunye, descend in a flash of light; the imprint of his single foot is still visible in the Peak. He described vividly some of the old customs for pleasing Mlentengamunye, whose one limb symbolized 'unity in one body', he asked to see my camera (a handwound Bolex) and laughed at it as much too clumsy (how right he was!). He again asked about the American immigration quota, saying that too many undesirables were coming into Swaziland. He moved skilfully from one subject to another, immensely sensitive to his listeners' reactions, and quick to respond to their comments. Before he left we drank toasts, and everyone felt pleased and happy.

On the opening day of the main ceremonies a phone call came from Lesotho with very distressing news. An old dispute between the young King Moshoeshoe and Chief Leabua Jonathan, the Prime Minister, had erupted in open violence. 'Blood had been spilt.' Moshoeshoe was under house arrest. He sought Sobhuza's help. Sobhuza did not want to support one side against the other, but found it difficult to refuse his friend's appeal. He would talk the matter over with those of his people who were acquainted with the situation and who appreciated the problems. In the meantime he sent an urgent message to both parties to 'quiet their strength; fighting and bloodshed would not help anyone but outside enemies.'

On the climactic day, before dawn, the Ngwenyama, vulnerable and majestic, walked from the sacred enclosure to the hut of his first ritual wife. And as he passed the people over whom he ruled, the women wept, and the solemn theme song rang out with penetrating melancholy.

That afternoon the capital was crowded for the main events and everywhere there was excitement and people dressing in the glory of the full *Ncwala* costume. Among the performers were many civil servants, former members of political parties and ministers of churches. When Sir Francis, in full regalia, was taken by Sobhuza to inspect the singing and dancing warriors, he remarked that it was not easy to recognize some of the members of the Executive in their present costumes, and Sobhuza joked back, 'It depends on how well you know them.'

When Sir Francis joined his wife and other guests, the King took his place in the regiments. The visitors watched awhile, and drank from the bowl of beer brewed in the Queen Mother's quarters, which as far back as Sobhuza could remember had been offered 'to welcome and refresh' the highest British officials attending the main day of the *Ncwala*.

Then Sobhuza, flanked by royal kin and backed by the regiments, moved rhythmically towards the sanctuary. The warriors alternatively drove him forward and lured him back, all the while singing a sacred song, the wildest and saddest imaginable, until at last he disappeared through the low arched doorway. The visitors were asked to leave; the rest of the drama was for the Swazi Nation alone.

Some minutes later Sobhuza emerged in the costume of Silo, fearsome, awe-inspiring as the monster hero of ancient legend. Eventually he threw the evergreen gourd onto the black shield held by a pure youth; the earth shook with the stamping of feet and the thumping of shields, and the air was rent with a frantic hissing. The King had survived the trials of the past year.

Throughout most of the *Ncwala* period, apart from roughly two weeks of holiday covering Christmas to the New Year, secular politics continued publicly outside. The Legislative Council was in session and the office of the Swazi National Council remained open. During the day vital issues, immigration, localization, urban developments, employment, labour, industry, were debated in the courthouse of Mbabane; in the evening and on weekends members of the Legislative Council would drive down the hill to Lobamba or Masundvwini in response to Sobhuza's call or to ask his advice. Generally he would have with him other members of the Swazi National Council.

Sobhuza's contacts with British civil servants in Swaziland were increasingly limited to official meetings over technical issues and to ceremonial occasions, the *Ncwala*, the Queen of England's birthday, the opening of a new institution or industry. The relationship was cordial but always rather distant, and those officials who were most interested complained rather sadly that they knew little of what was happening 'down the hill'. The early pattern of deference expected from a Paramount Chief of a small colony to the highest representative of a great British empire was changing to one in which a Swazi King extended diplomatic courtesies to senior officials of a foreign country.

Sobhuza's opinions were increasingly being heard, and listened to, in neighbouring states. Though he no longer travelled outside Swaziland, he sent emissaries with instructions to establish the friendliest possible relations with other African leaders. In September 1965, the Imbokodvo had received its first official invitation, including travel tickets, to attend the meeting of the OAU at Accra, 14-21 October. His representatives, Prince Makhosini and Dr Msibi, were the guests of Dr Nkrumah; the leaders of the three political parties (Nquku of the SPP, Dr Zwane of the NNLC, and Obed M. Mabuza of the Joint Council of Swaziland political parties) were guests of the OAU Liberation Committee.

The meeting was especially concerned with the crisis in Rhodesia where the white minority led by Ian Smith obdurately refused to recognize the rights of the African majority, and put their leaders into prison. The OAU Council of Ministers, 'considering the situation constituted a serious danger to world peace', expressed strong disapproval of the British, 'whose deliberate failure to take drastic political and military action against the white minority government bent on usurping power in Southern Rhodesia now exposes the African people of Southern Rhodesia to servitude under a settler government' (OAU, 1965:1). During the debate, various tactics ranging from diplomatic sanctions to military intervention had been advocated. Sobhuza's rejection of Ian Smith's racist policy did not blind him to the futility of threats by African countries that could not be put into effect. He was not prepared to compromise the standards he upheld in his own country by supporting a more popular radical rhetoric outside. This was his stand on South Africa as well; while he openly expressed his 'total rejection' of apartheid, he made it perfectly clear that it was unrealistic to expect Swaziland to boycott South Africa.

He also wanted to clarify his attitude to guerrilla warfare and to refugees. While he expressed sympathy with 'victims of oppression in any country', and was glad to offer refugees political asylum in Swaziland, he would not agree to their using Swaziland as a base for guerrilla attacks, thereby provoking retaliation. Nor did he want them to take part in local politics: asylum was not citizenship. When I asked if he distinguished between those for and those against the policy of Imbokodvo, he answered, 'They are not Swazi and we do not know them. When a hungry man asks you for food, you should not refuse, and if you serve him food he does not like he can refuse to eat it, but he has not the right to say "bring me other food".' His direction was clear: Swaziland was vulnerable and he did not want his people to be destroyed by war or hunger.

Sobhuza genuinely believed that changes should be and could be brought about by 'reason and peaceful negotiation around the table.' Lesotho was a case in point. He was one of the few African leaders who did not condemn Chief Leabua Jonathan for going to South Africa to try through person-to-person discussions (first with Dr Verwoerd and then with Vorster) to obtain conditions most advantageous for the people of his impoverished, landlocked and politically divided country. In 1967 the OAU accepted Nyerere's formulation that the Council 'should distinguish between those states which embrace their captors and those which seek merely to survive' (Africa Report, June 1967).

To Sobhuza, the lesson of Lesotho was clear. Political independence alone was a mockery; political authority needed the backing of economic power. He did not want to be in the same vulnerable position as either King Moshoeshoe or Chief Leabua Jonathan. So far, he was fortunate. There was, at least for the time being, no dynastic rivalry in Swaziland. Dumisa had come back to the fold. The once powerful independent clans were incorporated into the nation and none were threatening to secede. The Magagula, Maziya, Maseko, Mnisi, Gama – all were kin as well as subjects and neither he nor they could forget this. In addition, Swaziland was potentially rich.

It remained for the Swazi to realize that potential for themselves together with their political independence. When the NNLC predicted that the name Swaziland would be changed to Ngwane on independence, Sobhuza asked, 'Why? We are known as Swazi and this is our land. Both Mswati and Ngwane were Swazi Kings, and there is no sense in getting rid of the name of one King and replacing it by that of another. Swaziland is already widely known and accepted.'

It was during this period that localization became a crucially controversial issue, a struggle between locals and expatriates and also between Swazi and other Africans.[9] The British sympathised verbally with Swazi ambitions to take over the reins of government but argued that until the supply of 'suitably qualified local officers' could be increased, it would be necessary to look for expatriates both within the civil service and from outside Swaziland. Sobhuza and his people were not sure what was meant by suitable qualifications, more especially in the administrative positions. They knew that Swaziland was pleasant and peaceful and one of the last places in Africa to which British civil servants from former British colonies could be transferred and accorded favourable conditions. Some of these officials were immensely able, dedicated and idealistic, others were more limited. Sobhuza indicated his personal attitude in a message sent through Sir Francis to the annual meeting of the Swaziland Civil Service Association:

I greatly appreciate the valuable contribution to the development of Swaziland made by expatriate civil servants over a long period, and I hope that many of you will continue to serve the country for many years to come (*Times of Swaziland*, 20 August 1965).

In theory the appointment of officials by the British was guided by education, and promotion went by experience and seniority. To take family background and connections into consideration was labelled nepotism, condemned as unethical and dismissed as irrelevant, whereas for the Swazi these criteria were relevant. The conflict in views became more obvious and critical during the period of the Legislative Council and was accentuated by the fact that the government interpreted localization as Africanization and did not distinguish between Swazi and non-Swazi Africans. Some non-Swazi, mainly from South Africa, were among those granted scholarships and promoted to coveted positions.

Sobhuza was concerned with the tensions set up through the greater rewards – financial and social – accorded civil servants

[9] The term 'expatriate' replaced the term 'British civil servant' in a new anti-colonial language. The importance of building up a local civil service was recognized by the Colonial Office in the early '60s, and by 1965 sixty-five posts formerly held by whites were filled by Africans. In November 1965, the Swaziland government appointed a Localization Commission headed by T.C. Luke, a senior civil servant from Sierra Leone. His main recommendations, detailed and moderate, were not implemented.

employed by the British compared with the permanent officials of the Swazi National Council. The contrast was physically visible in the two local centres – Mbabane, which had grown into a modern town with large comfortable homes for civil servants and all amenities; and Lobamba, where the men of the Nation[10] had smaller, inferior quarters.

Sobhuza's older sons were more in evidence in the Swazi National Council, most of the younger were still at school. It became important to him to see that they obtained the educational qualifications necessary to ensure that they would not be inadequate for the new regime. Pedigree was not sufficient to secure entry into the new elite even if combined with good character.

His concern was also with those of his people who would not benefit by the higher educational facilities. Over 75% of the population were illiterate. Sobhuza had encouraged the Sebenta Society, an organization to promote adult literacy, in which Sishayi Nxumalo played a leading role together with liberal whites. In February 1965, Sobhuza became patron, with Sishayi as director, of a broader National Voluntary Service, 'to gather into one organization the energies of all the men and women of Swaziland irrespective of race, creed or political allegiance, to fight against disease, poverty and ignorance through modern community development and education' (*Times of Swaziland*, 19 February 1965). The Sebenta Society, like other separate welfare associations, was seen as part of the great centralized scheme visualized as a national service organization.

Sobhuza had always emphasized the need for 'practical education'; and had 'dreamed a long time ago' of an agricultural college for Swaziland.[11] On 28 October 1966 the Agricultural College was officially opened by Sir Francis Loyd.[12] The gathering was impressive – senior Government officials, heads of relevant departments, leaders of industry and agriculture, representatives of overseas organizations that had helped finance the building, consuls of two countries, the United States and Portugal, with offices in Swaziland, the Vice Chancellor of the University of UBLS, the staff of the college,

---

[10] Among these influential men, well known to Swazi but not to whites, were Princes Sifuba, Sozisa, Lutfo, Ncabaniso, Mckiseni, Charles and Mkhatjwa; Chiefs Pica Magagula, Nganganyoni Tfwala; and Governors Deka Khumalo and Maboya Fakudze.

[11] He had developed a rather sceptical approach to proposed agricultural innovations, advocating the need to experiment first before introducing hybrid strains or new crops or more effective pesticides. He was willing to try things out for himself, as well as encourage his people to accept innovations that were indeed successful. Thus he carried out his own experiments on a particular strain of maize that the Agricultural Department claimed ripened more quickly than those that were being cultivated. He found the claim not true and the new strain was dropped. He accepted from observation that certain pesticides appeared effective, but he wondered if they were not also poison and in the long run more harmful than some of the less effective old-fashioned techniques.

[12] The money for the buildings had come from Oxfam and the people of Cardiff, in Wales, supporting the Freedom from Hunger campaign; fourteen scholarships had been provided by private industries in Swaziland. The Government would be responsible for teachers' salaries and much of the upkeep.

members of the Legislative Council and of the Standing Committee of the Swazi National Council, and a selected number of students. Many of the Europeans were accompanied by their wives. Sobhuza arrived looking like an elegant Gandhi in an orange-bordered patterned cloth, two red feathers of the royal lourie in his greying hair, his only adornment a simple traditional beaded necklace, and he carried in his hand a tiny pitch-black stick like a long pencil; of course he was barefoot. He brought with him laTwala, who was accompanied by some of his daughters of the same age, all dressed in Swazi style.

The principal, David Brewin, set the new tone of the country when he began his speech: 'Your Majesty, Your Excellency, and distinguished guests from overseas.' There were many speeches. Sobhuza's face lit up and he nodded his head vigorously when Wyndham Lewis of Cardiff cited the Chinese proverb: 'If you give a man a fish, you feed him for one day; if you teach him how to fish, you feed him for many days.' He would quote this on subsequent occasions. He was the only one who spoke impromptu, holding a sheet of paper in his hand. He told very simply how he viewed the college and the difficulties that it had overcome. He paid special tribute to the people who had moved from their land in response to his appeal for a fertile site on which to establish the college. He had promised them that their resettlement would be to their advantage and indeed this was the case. They were developing into successful dairy farmers in the new area. To move was not easy; they had acted 'like true Swazi'. Then he took the opportunity to emphasize to the students that they must appreciate this opportunity to build firm foundations for the nation. 'People,' he said, 'can fly in planes to the moon, but they can't do this without food.' The courses at Luyengo were to be agriculture, forestry, and home economics. The following year Luyengo would serve as a centre for an advanced agricultural diploma to students from Botswana and Lesotho, as well as Swaziland. He saw it as the beginning of a university in his country; a centre for seminars dealing with practical matters, drawing together chiefs and people eager to apply knowledge to the problems of the day.

After the speeches ended, he and his small group were taken on a tour of inspection. He was interested in everything – the equipment, the library, the kitchen, and the staff. It pleased him to learn later that the matron was the daughter of Lancelot Msomi, once his tutor, whose father had named her Sibhimbi after returning from celebrating Sobhuza's *sibhimbi sekutfomba* (Puberty Jubilee).

He came again to Luyengo on 3 March 1967 to inaugurate the first seminar, 'Planning for Independence', organized by Government. The participants included persons of different political viewpoints, and organizations selected for their knowledge of government, economics and education. To them Sobhuza said:

One striking fact about planning is that there is no end to it – you plan since you are small and you plan until you die because human progress is always there. Once a good foundation has been laid those that build on it and build well will build until they come to their lifetime. The next generation will continue where they left off and so will the next until the whole house is completed.

We wish that we will build so well that we will not be blamed by the next generation, because if you build badly and the house crumbles, then the next generation will be questioning and say, how did they build? The best thing is to dismantle the whole thing and start afresh. We would not like to see that in our planning today.

As to his own plans for the future – they filled his thoughts and came into his dreams, and he often prayed 'with his heart' for the right road to independence. But what was independence? It was not a thing to see, to touch, to hold; it was a thought, a hope, a promise, a responsibility. For people to grasp its meaning, it had to be given names, images, music, words, buildings written in the soil of each nation, fashioned in its mould. The British, familiar with the process of decolonization, appreciated the need for symbols. They organized competitions for a national anthem and a flag. These would be found not through competition for new designs, new songs, new sites, but in adaptation of symbols already cherished.

During the final session of the Legislative Council, which lasted from 16 February to 7 March 1967, members dealt with twenty-one bills and raised questions on many vital issues – immigration, irrigation, citizenship, education. The meetings were often stormy and occasionally antagonistic currents swept so strongly through the house that the Speaker would ask for a short recess for members to cool off. The Ngwenyama was never present in person; but he knew which of his men could rouse passion and who could assuage and placate, and his approach was constantly in evidence.

For the Swazi, the Legislative Council was a battlefield not a debating ground; while they accepted the formalities of British parliamentary procedure, they manoeuvred towards their own vision of the future. Few issues raised such deep emotions as the choice of a site for the buildings of Swaziland's first House of Parliament. British officials took it for granted that Parliament would be, and should be, at Mbabane – the administrative capital and a centre of commerce, a modern town. They refused to treat seriously the objection conveyed by Prince Makhosini, as member of a civic Committee, that the nation wanted the buildings to be at Lobamba on land allocated by the Ngwenyama. The Committee went ahead, a site was chosen, the plans drawn, and heavy expenses incurred before the matter came to the Legislative Council in full assembly. The Swazi protested sharply, and at times eloquently, resting their main argument on sentiment and historic associations. Atholl Long, Chief Government Secretary and Chairman of the Committee, replied with contempt and even denied that he had received any objections in writing or verbally until Makhosini. gave, with impassioned restraint, a totally convincing

account of the negotiations, and reiterated that the Swazi National
Council had made it clear it would like Parliament buildings to be
established at Lobamba 'and nowhere else'.

The period of Legco was drawing to a close; the period of 'self-
government' was approaching. So it came about that Parliament was
built in the ambience of Lobamba, on the site from which the
Ngwenyama had sent out his soldiers in the Second World War to
remind the British of promises made in the reign of Mbandzeni.

CHAPTER XVII

From Self-Government to Independence

While the position of the Ngwenyama was secured by the Constitution promulgated in March 1967, everyone realized that his effectiveness would depend to a large extent on his relationship with members of the new Parliament. Elections had been set for 19 and 20 April 1967.

In addition to the Imbokodvo, which Sobhuza still refused to call a party, the NNLC, the SPP and the SUF (Swaziland United Front) contested the election but only the Imbokodvo could, and did, follow traditional channels of selecting candidates. As in the previous election, it derived much of its strength from cooperation with, and access to, the institutionalized resources of Chieftainship. Though Sobhuza publicly introduced Makhosini as the political *ndvuna*, his position was obviously different from that of Dr Zwane or John Nquku or Obed Mabuza, who were leaders of their separate parties. Makhosini was one of many councillors, as well as one of many chiefs and one of many princes.

Only the Imbokodvo and the NNLC registered the full number of twenty-four candidates (three for each of the eight constituencies), the SPP mustered seven, and the SUF five. This time no white was included in the Imbokodvo list and the initial reaction of most settlers was one of dismay and anxiety. But Sobhuza had considered the matter very carefully. Race was an explosive issue, and the white minority in Swaziland was at least as diversified as and more divided than the black majority. The United Swaziland Association, rejected by the Imbokodvo as a political ally, had split into factions. A few diehards directed their hostility against a politically more liberal group, 'a committee of 12', not a party, which explicitly disassociated itself from the policy of the USA. Prominent in the Committee were Leo Lovell, Peter Braun and Ronnie Black, all of whom preferred the political climate of Swaziland to that of South Africa, which they had left more or less permanently in the early '60s. At a request made through Makhosini, these three convened a meeting at Mbabane which was attended by about 150 people, and addressed by Mhlangano Matsebula, Prince Masitsela and Sishayi Nxumalo. They explained that the Imbokodvo had to contend with pressures which were at times 'illogical', and since many 'people regarded the white man as a symbol of a white colonial government', no white had been nominated by the Imbokodvo.

This was followed shortly after (11 April 1967) by a special meeting at Lobamba National offices to which Sobhuza invited representatives of all organizations, businesses and industrial concerns. Some five hundred people responded, hoping for reassurance. In a speech frequently referred to on subsequent occasions, he put forward his own attitude on the future of foreigners in the country. The speech was not that of a glib politician, but of a statesman confronting the reality of racism in the process of nation building. He explained that he had invited them because he had heard of the fears of some about their future security in Swaziland. 'I think,' he said, 'the fears were caused by enemies of the country's unity who sowed seeds of distrust and sometimes hatred. I would like everyone to ask himself, am I an asset or am I a liability to Swaziland? If your answer is an asset, there lies your security. Everyone who is good for the country is welcome. Those who are not good and those who are dangerous are not welcome. Who would say that I would like the sugar industry to pack up and go? Who would say get rid of the forest industry, Usutu Pulp and Peak Timbers? Only an enemy of Swaziland would make such a suggestion. When I refer to big industry, I am not belittling the contribution made by the small man, Swazi, White or Eur-African. In his small business he is an asset to the country. If there are people who sit back and feed on the blood of the country while others are working hard to make it prosper, the sooner Swaziland gets rid of them, the better.'

Race tensions existed and could not be ignored. 'Since they were played upon by irresponsible politicians, it had not been possible to put whites into the election at this stage'. He went on to ask, 'Will it be the policy that Europeans will never be represented in this country? I say No. I repeat, No. I repeat once more, No.' He concluded by requesting those present to send names through the Secretary of the Swazi nation, recommending people for appointment to represent their interests. Leo Lovell (invited on the advice of Makhosini) thanked him for his address.

Eighty percent of registered voters came to the polls, though the number who registered was lower than anticipated. The King did not register and when he heard that the Queen Mother was on her way to the polling station at Lobamba, he sent a message asking, 'Which party will you vote for? You are recognised as Head of State; therefore, all parties belong to you' (*Rand Daily Mail*, 21 April 1967). But, this same injunction did not apply to the Queens of whom some twenty went 'to stab' for their candidates. Voting procedures were already familiar from the last election, apart from minor modifications. No animal imagery was permitted but, in addition to personal symbols and photographs, party symbols were introduced at the request of both the Imbokodvo and the NNLC. The Imbokodvo selected the grinding stone imposed on the map of Swaziland; the NNLC a knobkerrie, a traditional fighting weapon; the SUF a bundle of faggots; the SPP decided against a party symbol. The elections were quiet and orderly. The Deputy Chief Electioneering Officer, Huw Jones (an expatriate who had also run the census), described the elections as 'arousing interest but no fever'; he suggested that the calmness was because there was no hard struggle to gain independence, and because the desire for independence overrode all other considerations.[1]

The Imbokodvo won every seat in the election, polling 79.4% of the vote, as against 20.2% for the NNLC. Sobhuza's hope that there would be no formally institutionalized opposition within Parliament was fulfilled.[2] In only one constituency was voting close: 10,242 votes for the NNLC and 11,266 for the Imbokodvo. This constituency, Mphumalanga, had the highest percentage of foreign-born Africans and also the lowest number of Swazi actually born in the district; these Swazi were mainly employed on two sugar-growing complexes with no immediate ties to adjacent rural areas. Even so the support for the NNLC 'surprised' the Imbokodvo, which had put forward strong and well-known candidates: Prince Mfanasibili, Mfundza Sukati, and Aaron Duba. The three NNLC men – Kingsay Thulasizwe Samketi, Nimrod Malaza, and Mageja Masilela – were acknowledged forceful speakers and politically experienced. The results as a whole indicated the overwhelming support for Sobhuza as Ngwenyama of the Swazi; both Sishayi Nxumalo and Dr Malabhane Nxumalo, who as leaders of the SDP in the 1964 election received 384 votes between them, were returned as candidates of the Imbokodvo with large majorities in different constituencies. Dr Zwane was badly defeated in Mbabane and both Nquku and Obed Mabuza lost their deposits.

Though it had long been decided that Swaziland would become a Protected State after the election, irrespective of the results, the Imbokodvo victory undoubtedly gave added relish to the occasion. The Protected State Agreement was signed on Monday, 24 April 1967, by Sobhuza as King of Swaziland and Sir Francis Loyd on behalf of the Queen of England; privileged to sign together with the King was Phuhlaphi Nsibandze, Governor of Old Zombodze in Shiselweni, whose ancestors had throned Dlamini Kings of the past and, when need be, died for them.

The main celebration took place the next day, 25 April 1967, henceforth the annual public holiday of Somhlolo or Flag Day. It was a great occasion. Before a crowd of some 20,000 on the plain of

[1] For a full report on the elections, see *Report on the House of Assembly Elections, 1966-1967*, published by the Chief Electoral Officer, Mbabane, Swaziland, April 1967. On the basis of the 1966 census, it was estimated that a total of 147,000 persons were eligible to register. Of these, only 106,121 actually registered. *Op. cit.*, pp. 12-13.

[2] For details of all the Parliamentarians, see *Profiles of Parliamentarians* by Sishayi Simon Ndwandwe (n.d.)

Lobamba from which twenty-five years before he had sent Swazi troops to fight together with the British to remind them of past promises, Sobhuza was sworn in as King of Swaziland, and the old kingdom of Swaziland was symbolically reborn. He wore the unassuming everyday dress of his regiment, the Balondolozi; only a few bright red feathers of the lourie in his hair showed his royal birth, and two long strong feathers of the thunderbird showed his unique position among princes. He took his place on the platform with dignitaries of both governments – the Ndlovukazi; Deka Khumalo (Governor of Lobamba); Prince Makhosini; Prince Sozisa Dlamini (senior Prince of the Swazi Nation); Chief Phuhlaphi Nsibandze; Reverend A.B. Gamedze (Liaison Officer); Sir Francis Loyd; Atholl Long (former Government Secretary and then Deputy to the Queen's Commissioner); Chief Justice Elyan and three Appeal Court judges (Justices Roper, Schreiner and Maisels); W.A. Ramsden (the Attorney General); G.K.W. Oscroft (Master of the High Court); and W.G. Syer (Commissioner of Police). Judge Elyan, in the dark robes and white wig of his office, administered the oath to the King. Soon after, he announced the appointment of Makhosini as Prime Minister, who was sworn in by the Attorney General.

In siSwati, translated by Polycarp Dlamini, Sobhuza began his speech smiling gaily, 'This is a day of rejoicing', and then in a firm voice that rang clearly through the bright crisp air, he declared, 'It is the tradition of all African kingdoms that their Kings are leaders as well as Kings. It is also true for Swaziland. Now rightly or wrongly some people have mistaken this dual capacity as a dictatorship. I would like to assure you here and now that the King both leads and is led by his people. I am my people's mouthpiece ... There can be no peaceful progress without cooperation and unity of the people; if the people are divided into camps and go to the extent of undermining one another, such a state is doomed to catastrophe no matter how good and wise the leader may be. Demagogues of the world too often under the cloak of liberty and democracy have successfully undermined the spirit of unity and cooperation in the nation and have set one group against another only in the interest of gaining a brief day of power for themselves. When they succeed they trample upon the very fundamental rights which it is our duty to protect.'

The ceremony moved on through speeches and symbolic actions. The flag of the new Kingdom of Swaziland, which would replace the Union Jack, was flown for the first time – red at the base, blood of life; yellow in the centre, prosperity; and at the top blue, peace and fruitfulness, adorned with shield and weapons of the Emasotja regiment. To some the flag was new, but others recognized it as essentially a copy. The original was the standard sewn in silk by four princesses – and given by the King to the Swazi soldiers of World War II.[3]

[3] When a flag for the Kingdom was required, well-intentioned British officials, who had not

In the final scene Sobhuza stood alone on a small dais for 'the salute'. Thousands of chanting warriors loped past, their shields raised in deference, and some hundred western-trained police marched by, looking directly at him in western fashion, as they raised their right hands. When the ceremony was over, the protocol of departure which had operated on all previous occasions was reversed, and instead of the representative of the British government taking precedence, the Ngwenyama's car went first, followed by the car with the Ndlovukazi, and then the British Queen's Commissioner.

Sobhuza had still to appoint members to the Assembly and the Senate for interests not adequately represented. Since the Imbokodvo now held every elected seat this was not of such concern for the Swazi majority as for the whites. The whites regarded this as a test of the King's good faith and an indication of their own future. He indeed kept his promise. On the day the House of Assembly met for the first time, the names of his nominees were publicly announced: four whites – Leo Lovell, Robert Stephens and Reverend Robert Forrester of the former Legislative Council, and J. Springh Murphy, an old Swazilander and Chairman of the Swaziland Tobacco Cooperative; David Hynd Stewart, a Eur-African who had served as Imbokodvo observer at the First Constitutional Conference in London; and Duma Dlamini, a successful Swazi businessman. The House elected Dr Msindazwe Sukati as Speaker, and six Senators – Polycarp Dlamini; Jethro Mkhulumnchoti Mamba; Mabalizandla Nhlabatsi; Bhizeni Dlamini; Peter Braun; and Magangeni W. Magongo.

To these the King added his own nominees, again indicating in his choice his awarenesss of his responsibility to different sections of the nation. He appointed a Swazi woman, Mrs Mary Mdziniso, known throughout the country for her work in welfare organizations and an eloquent speaker at the women's prayer and protest meeting against exclusion from the franchise; George Mabuza, a committed rural development officer and formerly a member of the Legislative Council; Douglas Lukhele, the lawyer who had helped draft the 1963 petition; Reverend A.B. Gamedze, minister of religion and educator; and two whites with whom he had worked over many years, Carl Todd and Dan Fitzpatrick. Sobhuza had thought about all these appointments for some time, but he had kept his ideas so much to himself that the final decision came as a pleasant surprise to those he selected and a great disappointment to others who had anticipated their own selection. The list did not tally with that published in the South African press which had included some of the extreme members of the United Swaziland Association.

---

been told of the previous flags, organized a competition and received many entries. But when Prince Makhosini and Msindazwe Sukati, members of a Protocol Committee established by the government, met with the Swazi National Council, several of the elders recalled the earlier composition and all agreed that it be the model. For the history, see 'Old Flags over Swaziland,' a letter by James Matsebula and George Murdoch, *Times of Swaziland*, 26 May 1967.

From these Parliamentarians he selected his Cabinet: Prince Makhosini as Prime Minister; Mfundza Sukati as Deputy Prime Minister; Leo Lovell as Minister of Finance, Commerce and Industry; Prince Mfanasibili as Minister of Local Administration; A. Khuseni Hlophe as Minister of Agriculture; Rev. A.B. Gamedze as Minister of Education; Dr Malabhane Nxumalo as Minister of Health; and Polycarp Dlamini as Minister of Works, Power and Communication. He also appointed four Assistant Ministers: Zonke Khumalo in the Prime Minister's Office; Sishayi Simon Nxumalo in the Ministry of Finance, Commerce and Industry; Prince Masitsela (in charge of labour) in the Deputy Prime Minister's Office; and Bhekimphi Dlamini in the Ministry of Local Administration.

Sobhuza had toyed with the idea of including Dr Zwane as one of his appointees in a government which he hoped would draw together all sections of the people, but Dr Zwane indicated that, unlike Sishayi Nxumalo and Dr Malabhane Nxumalo, he would not accept an appointment as an individual without a party. He continued to appeal to international organizations and political figures overseas[4] against the election, the Constitution and Imbokodvo policy. When Dr Zwane called on all workers to strike for an indefinite period, Sobhuza endorsed the warnings of the Prime Minister and the Commissioner of Police against the possibility of violence. The opposition to Dr Zwane's tactics was so strong and came from so many quarters that he went no further than insisting on an interview with Sir Francis Loyd to whom he and his executive presented a memorandum of grievances. Later he made tentative efforts to link up with the Imbokodvo, but these càme to naught. Dr Zwane still attended public meetings of the Swazi National Council and continued to protest; he also came to the *Ncwala* albeit in western clothes.

With the establishment of a Legislative Council, later a single parliament, British constitutional lawyers assumed that the Swazi National Council would be redundant and disappear. To them it was a symbol of a dual system in which the traditional structure served as an obstructive shadow government. However, at every constitutional discussion Sobhuza's men insisted that the SNC be continued and receive recognition. Its function continued to be defined as dealing with all matters regulated by Swazi law and custom. With the approach of Independence it continued to serve as the 'cultural watchdog' of a Parliament confronting new issues and passing new legislation.

It was one of Sobhuza's difficult tasks to keep the two bodies distinct, but complementary, and not let their lines of authority

---

[4] Dr Zwane cabled Diallo Telli, Secretary of the OAU in Addis Ababa, U Thant in New York, and Harold Wilson in England, protesting the 'fraudulent Constitution' and calling for 'fair elections'. Nquku also protested to the United Nations and his friends in the Labour Party in England. The OAU had decided not to support parties which were not representative of the majority.

conflict. When it was reported to him that certain members of the Swazi National Council exceeded their authority, using his name to back their actions, he called a meeting of those involved and affirmed the higher legislative authority of Parliament. The Secretary of the Swazi National Council could not act as Secretary of the entire nation. The Swazi National Council was the foundation, not the total structure.

Throughout this period Sobhuza and Sir Francis behaved towards each other with considerate circumspection. Sobhuza never used any crude anticolonial slogans to rally national support. On the contrary, he explained he was 'not fighting the British, he was trying to get them to work with him for the best conditions at independence.' There were many difficulties inherent in the conditions imposed during self-government. Control over internal security and the Civil Service, as well as finance and external affairs, was still reserved to the British.

It had come as a great shock to learn, at the last meeting of the Legislative Council, that at self-government every permanent secretary would be a British expatriate, with five Swazi in 'supernumerary posts'. The British did not seem prepared to hurry the process of localization, and the Swazi were not prepared to wait. Sobhuza commented: 'The British will change, but will take their time and will not move as quickly as we desire. We understand how unpleasant it must be to sacrifice one's own livelihood for the sake of the next man and give up something nice which you already possess. The British attitude is a natural one, but it is the human material on which the wealth of the country must be based. Foreign training is necessary but good teachers as well as good pupils are needed. And we must find people with the right attitude as well as skills to keep up the standards of efficiency.'

The British had promised independence not later than 1969; but the Swazi leaders asked, 'Why delay so long?' Prince Makhosini, speaking on behalf of the new Kingdom at his first press conference after he had been sworn in as Prime Minister, stated that the conditions of 'so-called self-government' were difficult to accept, changes in the Constitution were essential, and his government would demand full independence at an early date.

July 7th, 1967 marked the official opening by Sobhuza, as King, of Swaziland's first Parliament. The Courthouse in Mbabane could accommodate only a select section of the huge crowd. However, the proceedings were broadcast live from Swaziland's own station (opened in 1965), so those outside would be able to hear his speech.

He was dressed for the occasion with western formality – in full, morning dress, black waistcoat and white tie, shoes shining, and holding in a white-gloved hand a thin and potent stick. *Emabutfo* who had marched, singing, up the long hill from Lobamba very early that morning were there to greet him with the royal whistle. Accompanied

by Sir Francis and the Commissioner of Police, W.G. Syer, Sobhuza
then inspected a Police Guard of Honour, and the band played.
Ministers and a few councillors of the Swazi National Council and
other guests, among them representatives from Lesotho and
Botswana, were shown their seats.[5] Leaders of the opposition parties
had been invited, and both Nquku and Obed Mabuza were inside.
Only Dr Zwane remained on the roadside with his followers, who
cheerfully waved the Congress flag and placards with slogans of
protest against the Constitution. Sir John Houlton, President of the
Senate, escorted Sobhuza to the door of the House and left him there
with Msindazwe Sukati, Speaker of the House of Assembly. The King
waited for the next step in a ceremonial developed in seventeenth-
century Britain and performed at every subsequent opening of British
Parliaments to signify the supremacy of the elected representatives of
the people over the arbitrary actions of an individual King.[6]

The usher announced, 'Mr Speaker, King Sobhuza II of Swaziland
seeks admission, Sir.' Came the reply, 'Let His Majesty, King
Sobhuza II, King of Swaziland, be admitted.' He had been groomed
for his part and given the origin and meaning of the ancient British
custom. Everyone stood as he entered and was shown his chair,
behind the long table with its microphone, facing the onlookers. He
read his 'Speech from the Throne' in English. Sukati translated it into
siSwati. Having expressed the gratitude of the people for the present
'unique constitutional arrangement', he announced that 'my
government is already looking forward to further constitutional
advancement and is therefore proposing that Swaziland be granted
Independence in September 1968.' Moreover, 'fully aware that
constitutional advancement alone will not satisfy the legitimate
aspirations of the people [it] is planning for solid progress in the
economic and social spheres.' The plans he outlined did not introduce
any radical changes in policy, but the focus of concern had subtly
shifted from material to human resources.

[5] Lesotho was represented by the Assistant Minister of Health, J. Rampeta, and the Assistant
Minister of Education, J. Monaleli, and Botswana by the Assistant Minister of Finance, M.
Segokgo, and the Deputy Speaker of the Senate, G.G. Sebeso.

[6] In England during the reign of Queen Elizabeth I, the conflict between the Commons and
the Monarchy began with the Commons claiming that they had the right to deal freely with all
matters of grievance or policy, a claim challenged by James I, who with his own hand tore out
the pages from the journal on which this had been recorded. When, in January 1642, his son
Charles I came to St Stephen's to arrest and impeach five members, the House defied him and
the Speaker, on being asked where the missing members were, replied, 'I have neither eyes to see
nor tongue to speak in this place, but as this House is pleased to direct me.' The civil war
between King and Parliament which followed Charles' attempt to arrest the members resulted
in the triumph of the Parliamentary army and, ultimately, in 1649, in the trial and execution of
the King. Neither the war nor the execution, however, produced a stable or representative form
of Parliamentary government. It was not until James II had fled from the country that the
conflict between King and Parliament was finally resolved. In 1689, William and Mary of the
House of Orange accepted the 'Declaration of Rights' made by the two Houses which stated the
supremacy of Parliamentary law. Parliament then proclaimed them King and Queen and under
the Bill of Rights passed later in the year, Parliament became the supreme and only lawmaker,
and by the Act of Settlement of 1701, regulated succession to the throne.

He returned to Lobamba, leaving Parliament to deal in the first instance with the problems confronting a country in the simultaneous process of decolonisation and modernisation. Bills were sent to him for his assent. He took his responsibility very seriously and, in addition to reading the debates in both Houses, he would seek the opinion of his councillors. He also had his own legal advisors, who did not include the Attorney General appointed by the Public Service Commission. The Attorney General, however, had a considerable influence on discussions in both Houses and on the formulation of legislation.[7] Expatriates complained of the long delay in receiving Sobhuza's responses, but he was more sensitive to the criticism of his own people, who were sometimes divided amongst themselves.

Proposals for the final Independence Constitution, passed by the Cabinet and published as a White Paper, were presented by the Prime Minister at special meetings first to the House of Assembly, on 22 January 1968, and then to the Senate. At the same time that the Prime Minister put the motion that the proposals be accepted he indicated that there were still some unresolved grievances relating particularly to minerals and land. He dwelt on the difficulty experienced by the Cabinet in reaching a compromise between the 'two irreconcilable views' – those of the Swazi and the British. Since the Swazi considered minerals to be the rightful property of the Swazi nation held in trust by the Ngwenyama, he argued that the benefits deriving therefrom should accrue to the Swazi nation and be used for its benefit. The British maintained their old stance that control of these valuable assets should be vested in the Cabinet, and indicated that they were obliged to consider interests other than those of the Swazi. The argument again revealed the contradiction in the role of Sobhuza as Ngwenyama of the Swazi and Sobhuza as a King constrained by the British model of a constitutional monarchy. The mineral issue was a symptom, not a cause of the conflict. The compromise put forward by the Cabinet was that the Minerals Committee consist of the Commissioner of Mines (a government official) and four or six members, half of whom would be appointed by Sobhuza as Ngwenyama in consultation with the Swazi National Council, and half by him as King acting on Cabinet advice.

The first to speak from the floor was Elias Dladla, who condemned bluntly the authors of the White Paper for 'the nerve, the temerity and audacity to grant power to Cabinet to exercise control over Swazi private property which is under the trusteeship of the Ngwenyama.' He proposed an amendment returning to the 'Ngwenyama-in-Libandla (SNC)' the right to appoint all members of the Minerals

---

[7] At that time, the post was held by William Ramsden, who had replaced the late J.J. Dickie in 1967. Ramsden, British-born but South African trained and new to Swaziland, had little understanding of the depth of Swazi grievances. Until Independence, the Chairman of the Public Service Commission was appointed by the Queen's Commissioner.

Committee, and hinted that the Cabinet 'should rather resign than meddle with what is thought to be so dear to us'. His seconder, S. Mndeni Shabalala, made a more restrained but no less firm statement of Swazi wishes. The discussion that followed was acrimonious. The Minister of Finance, Leo Lovell, who had seconded the motion of the Prime Minister and had been largely responsible for formulating the compromise and for persuading Cabinet to accept it, reacted strongly and predicted that 'if one thought of a way of creating friction with the British, if one worked a method of raising their suspicions, one couldn't have done it better than has been done with this amendment'. Those who supported him argued that the Committee was *only advisory* so that irrespective of its composition full authority remained vested in the King. But the amendment was carried by 21 votes to 9. The next day the Prime Minister presented the same address to the Senate; the reaction was almost identical. The amendment, put by Senator Magongo and seconded by Senator Mabuza, passed by 8 votes to 4, the strongest opposition being voiced this time by Senator Braun.

When Sobhuza was told of the division, he did not refer to the fact that none of the whites had voted for the amendment, but replied to the argument that the Committee was only advisory and that he was not obliged to accept its advice by saying 'that was not in line with Swazi democracy.' From previous experience he was 'afraid that white friends might mislead my people with the best of intentions'.

Makhosini's support of an amendment to the Cabinet's proposal on minerals provoked from Leo Lovell the comment that a British Prime Minister would have resigned in similar circumstances. Makhosini retorted privately that Swaziland was not Britain, and perhaps the objecting minister might want to resign instead. On this question, Sobhuza subsequently expressed himself as follows: 'Some Europeans advised us to vote on the basis of factions, but we asked them, "How can we rule on disputes and factions?" There have been disputes on the question of minerals even among the Cabinet ministers. But some warned against the dangers of division. When Prince Makhosini appreciated this, a certain sector complained and blamed him for having accepted advice and suggested that he be expelled because he had opposed their own authority. But African procedure is that a person in authority must be advised by the Council and the people who put him in a position of authority. He is not a dictator. European rule is that of dictatorship. In African procedure, if someone opposes you he is your brother, he is helping you, pointing out the dangers to you. This is our custom. Advisors should not be expelled because their opinions are different from those in a position of authority and those in authority should not resign if they change their opinions on the advice of the councillors' (Speech at Lobamba, 2 March 1968).

A conference to discuss the final Constitution was convened by the Secretary of State for Commonwealth Affairs on 19 February 1968 at

Marlborough House.[8] In addition to the proposals and the amendments, Prince Makhosini had been instructed by Sobhuza and against the wishes of some of the members of the delegation to raise at that conference the delicate land issue. The national economy was growing fast, but the gap between 'the two sections, the haves and the have-nots', remained – and, unfortunately, this division was mainly between whites and blacks. Forty-three percent of the country was still in the hands of whites, many of whom were absentee landowners with vast acreages for grazing their sheep in winter. Others, as individuals or corporations, were engaged in cultivating or ranching on a large commercial scale. But Sobhuza's own people needed land for food; Swazi areas were congested, farm tenants were insecure and the grievance of concessions was kept alive by their discontent.

One of the great fears of whites was that after Independence their land would be expropriated 'for a song'. Sobhuza recognized their fears but pointed out that since the time of his grandmother the Swazi had been buying back their own land often at inflated prices. Now his approach was different; he placed the onus on Britain and citing as precedent the British purchase of the White Highlands in Kenya for the Africans suggested that whites and Swazi together ask the British Government to compensate local farmers whose land the Swazi needed. 'We can't blame the farmer who was following the law of this country and really believed he had bought the land and had paid for it with his own money.' This was the approach his government would pursue and that Prince Makhosini presented at the conference in London.

Prince Makhosini warned that the land shortage would increasingly cause economic pressure and racial problems which the Swaziland government would have to face after Independence: if not solved, it might disrupt local peace and stability. The Swazi delegates claimed compensation for the alienation of land under the Partition Proclamation and a further 500,000 acres which had been sold by the British to finance its administration of the country. The British rejected this claim. Before Makhosini left London, he expressed himself rather frankly at a press conference, saying: 'It was as if the British Government had planted a time bomb in Swaziland and were giving Independence before the bomb exploded.' However, he 'hoped that in one way or another the British would help defuse that bomb and, in any case, the Swaziland Government certainly does not intend to sit idly by and watch it explode.'

---

[8] Cabinet delegates were Prince Makhosini, A. Khuseni Hlophe, Polycarp Dlamini, Leo Lovell and Dr Malabhane Nxumalo; the British representatives were Sir Francis Loyd, the Attorney General (William Ramsden), and the Secretary of the Cabinet (H. Roemmele). The Swaziland political parties protested their exclusion in vain. Dr Zwane and his deputy, Samketi, dramatised their exclusion by lying on the steps of Marlborough House from which they were good-naturedly raised by British police. A photograph of the two men smiling happily, their thumbs raised in the 'African salute' as they were being carried out, appeared in several papers.

Prince Makhosini and the Swazi members of the delegation were met at the border by a crowd of supporters, and, after stopping briefly at the Secretariat, drove on to Lobamba, where the Ngwenyama, the Ndlovukazi, and members of the Council were waiting to receive them. Makhosini reported that the delegation had been cordially received; agreement had been reached on most matters, and the British had finally recognized the 'strength of Swazi claims' to control of minerals. Only the land issue had not yet been satisfactorily resolved. Though recognizing that the Swazi had a legitimate grievance, Britain rejected outright the Swazi claim for restitution of the land and instead suggested a series of land projects. Negotiations were not yet at an end, further discussions were envisaged, and the granting of Independence would not be delayed.

Sobhuza praised the delegates as an *impi* returning successfully from battle. He reminded them too of the warning of Somhlolo, who said, 'Oh Swazi, my children, there are foreign nations coming to your country. Do not spill their blood. If you do, that will be the end of your country.' When some wished to take up arms, wiser counsel prevailed: 'The dog's sweat is wasted on its hair [The outcome is not worth the effort]. Patience and persistence are always necessary.' The first objective was to regain Independence.

Neither Sobhuza nor his Council wanted Swaziland to enter Independence with 'a feeling of grievance'. The tone of Prince Makhosini's opening statement on the next round of land discussions, held in London in July, was diplomatic:[9] the King of Swaziland and his people recognized the 'financial stringencies in the United Kingdom and hoped that times will improve to enable the British Government to help us generously ... it is not a matter calling for immediate payment, but could be extended over 5, 10, or even 15 years' (*Times of Swaziland*, 9 August 1968). What was needed was a final assurance that 'this grave problem was already being tackled'; as yet, the proposals of the British had 'not committed it to anything'. In fact, they tended to prejudice Swaziland's expectations of aid to solve its social problems. When Britain agreed to consider the more detailed proposals on land shortage and land use put forward by the Swazi, and to send a team of experts to examine the situation, the news was received by Sobhuza as a step in the right direction.

Preparations for Independence were going ahead. As early as August 1967 the government had established an Independence Celebration Committee of five members of the Cabinet under the chairmanship of Mfundza Sukati (Deputy Prime Minister) and appointed as Planning Officer Mark Patey (a District Commissioner

---

[9] His team this time (July, 1968) included Dr Malabhane Nxumalo and Arthur Khoza, then Makhosini's Private Secretary, and the government expert was Tony Venn, Director of Agriculture.

then acting as Permanent Secretary in Sukati's office).[10] Mfundza Sukati and Mark Patey, both ex-soldiers, approached this assignment with the enthusiasm of commanders engaged in battle. Mr Patey explained to me, 'Every section must be strategically deployed, everything must go with military precision. We must coordinate strength and strategy and not waste our personnel.'

The day chosen by the Swazi for the main celebration and agreed to by the British was 6 September 1968. The month was auspicious, the date had historic associations, and the moon would be full. Never had there been such excitement and activity as in those last months. New roads were laid, old roads repaired, hotels were rushing up additional rooms booked long in advance.

Key buildings, given historic names, were rising on ancient sites. As far back as 1957, Sobhuza had allocated forty acres of land on the plains of Lobamba for national development. The Legislative Assembly at its last meeting had decided to erect a stadium as well as the Parliament buildings on the site. Since no money had been allocated for this by the Government, it was to be a self-help project supported by voluntary contributions – big money from big firms, smaller donations from men of lesser means. The response was tremendous. A superb stadium for 40,000 people was built in record time. Sobhuza named it Somhlolo Stadium.

When Sobhuza opened it officially, on 25 August 1968, he replied to critics who had asked why so much money (200,000 Rand) should be spent on a sports ground and not on schools: 'To be healthy, one needs the whole body, not just the head or arms or legs. A project such as this was necessary. It does not mean that education is ignored or despised.' The opening also served as a rehearsal for the Independence celebrations, with performances by school children, police, traditional warriors, veterans of the Second World War, and maidens from the Annual Reed Ceremony (*Umhlanga*), which had been postponed to coincide with the great celebration. 'The princess' of these girls was Sabisile, daughter of laMaziya, who was now finishing high school. The King hoped that she and her sisters would continue their education in both cultures, and would perform traditional dances at Independence.

Parliament voted money for a State House, where the King would receive visiting notables and dignitaries. He would not move into the elegant residence in Mbabane which the Queen's Commissioner was to vacate on Independence. That would be for the Prime Minister, for whom a less elaborate home had been planned, but which, from the Swazi view, would be more suitable for the Deputy Prime Minister.

Sobhuza had little desire for an extravagant mansion and had first suggested that perhaps Masundvwini could be remodelled. It was a

[10] Other members of the Committee were Dr Malabhane Nxumalo, A. Khuseni Hlophe, Prince Mfanasibili and Reverend A.B. Gamedze.

home in which he was comfortable. The palms and old trees were
beautiful. A committee of Queen laMasuku, his daughter Gcinaphi,
and his Secretary Mkhulunyelwa Matsebula were instructed by him
to look over the place. They recommended a new building. The King
agreed and worked through the plans, making suggestions. It was not
a palace. On the upper floor, three bedrooms; downstairs a dining
and living-room. The final cost was roughly 46,000 rand, which was
no more than the imposing residence the British were erecting high in
the hills of Mbabane for the High Commissioner who would replace
the Queen's Commissioner. There was virtually no one who did not
feel that a State House for the King of Swaziland was not only
essential for the occasion but a tribute to a man who had worked so
hard for his people and his country. Following a traditional
consecration, a 'pegging' of the site, building began on 15 May, and
was barely completed in time for the celebrations. Sobhuza named it
Embo, commemorating the mythical centre of Dlamini origin.

In the end he seemed pleased by the result, though not altogether
satisfied with the fixtures and fittings. He liked particularly the effect
of the inner courtyard with a fine sculpting, *The Giver of Life*, a long-
horned steer with two herd boys at a small fountain, with lines of dark
blue tile spreading outward from the sculpture like the rays of the sun.
But for many years he did not really enjoy Embo; it was somehow
confining and isolated from his people, and it had the associations of a
political necessity at a time of economic stringency.

The ritual capital of Lobamba retained its basic form and structure,
and there, in the *sibaya*, the nation gathered on Saturday, 2 August
1968, for the last annual meeting of the Swazi National Council prior
to Independence. In his speech, the Ngwenyama emphasised the two
aspects of Independence: one was joy in the rebirth of the nation, and
the other, the struggles that lay ahead to make Independence
meaningful. He instructed the regiments to wear the *umqhele, sigeja*
and *ingwe*, explaining that this regalia, worn on the main day of the
Ncwala, also symbolized 'a time of war.' For this reason there should
be no public display of personal bereavement, and all mourning
clothes should be put away at the beginning of the last half of the
present moon. This did not mean the denial of inward grief and pain.
It signified that they needed all of their strength in time of national
warfare or struggle.

He reminded his people of the responsibilities of 'freedom' and the
effort needed to make Independence work. In the Official Programme,
his message reads, 'While my people celebrate this great moment in
the history of our nation, I know they are thinking of the future, a
future in which we must work hard if Swaziland is to become a
prosperous country dependent on no one.' His photograph on the
opposite page shows the grey in his hair, the deep lines of
concentration on his forehead, and as he looks away from the camera
into the distance, there is an expression of worry and thoughtfulness

in his eyes and his smile is tight and stern. A somewhat different image appears in the large, more popular portrait widely exhibited in shops and offices: a full face, benign and majestic beneath the *Ncwala* headgear.

The lists of guests had been prepared, and approved by the King. The British delegation would include the Duke and Duchess of Kent and Mr George Thomson, the Secretary for Commonwealth Affairs. The Duke of Kent, representing the British sovereign, was expected to hand over the final instruments of Independence. Since he was a cousin of both Queen Elizabeth and the Duke of Edinburgh, the choice was considered a signal tribute. Unfortunately, his mother, Princess Marina of Greece, died late in August while the Ngwenyama's instructions on mourning were still ringing in people's ears. There was no alternative but for the King-in-Council to indicate that it would be 'out of Swazi custom to receive a royal guest so soon after bereavement'. Someone else, hopefully equally royal but less close to the dead, would have to act as the British Queen's representative.

In official circles there was consternation as well as sympathy. Programmes and brochures elaborately detailed, too expensive to change, were already in print. The photo of the Duke was prominent and all the activities in which 'their Royal Highnesses' would take the stage were listed. Who could be sent in their place? Speculations were rife until the phone rang in the office of Sir Francis Loyd to say that he had been appointed as Her Majesty's Special Representative at all official functions. He had already said his farewells. Sobhuza had sent him a long letter, dated 28 August, expressing appreciation for his 'keen interest in the development of the country' and wishing him well in the future. Though Sir Francis had become fairly widely liked, and his tact, particularly in handling some of the difficult situations of the past year, was admired, the general reaction was disappointment. Sobhuza, however, accepted the decision philosophically: there would be celebrations of Independence in the future, 6 September would always be a public holiday, and British royalty would be very welcome.

The list of guests who had accepted was impressive. Invitations had been sent to the heads of fifty-two countries; of these, forty-two had agreed to send representatives – the largest number would be from Great Britain, followed by South Africa, Portugal and the United States.[11] Sobhuza was sorry that Tanzania and Algeria though invited

---

[11] Twenty-three were members of the Commonwealth. In Africa they were Ghana, Nigeria, Lesotho, Botswana, Kenya, Uganda, Zambia, Tanzania, Malawi, Sierra Leone and The Gambia; outside Africa were Britain and Northern Ireland, India, Pakistan, Australia, Canada, New Zealand, Ceylon, Guyana, Malaysia, Mauritius, Malta and Singapore. Countries not in the Commonwealth, but in Africa, were Algeria, Cameroon, Ethiopia, Congo Brazzaville, Congo Kinshasa, Ivory Coast, Liberia, Somalia, South Africa. Foreign countries outside Africa were the Republic of China, Denmark, Belgium, France, West Germany, Israel, Italy, Japan,

would not be sending delegates, but was satisfied that contact would be maintained with them through the Organization of African Unity to which Swaziland would seek admission immediately after Independence. All Communist countries were excluded: every visitor would have to cross the border of either South Africa or Mozambique. The South African government had agreed that official guests be allowed in without visas, and that the border gates be open for longer hours during the week of celebrations.[12]

Invited guests included industrialists (among those well known to the outside world were Harry Oppenheimer, Chairman of the Anglo-American Corporation; Dr Van Eck, Chairman of the Industrial Development 'Corporation of South Africa; Dr Anton Rupert, Chairman of the Rembrandt group of companies; and David Lewis, Chairman of the Edward Hotels Limited); churchmen (among them, the Archbishop of Cape Town, the Most Reverend R. Selby Taylor); judges (including the judges of the Appeals Court for Lesotho, Swaziland and Botswana); scholars; farmers; lawyers and former government officials (including Sir Brian and Lady Marwick). Sobhuza's personal guests on the public list were few: Lancelot P. Msomi, his old teacher at Zombodze, now in South Africa; A.G.W. Champion, a successful African businessman and a one-time political leader in South Africa; Major Patrick Wall, who had helped to get the land and mineral petition heard in the British Parliament; and Leo Kuper and myself. Sobhuza's special private guest was King Moshoeshoe of Lesotho. Then there was another circle, less official, less conspicuous, to Sobhuza equally important – priests, chiefs, kin and non-kin, many of whom lived in South Africa, some of whom came at his request and at his expense, others to show their respect.

Official guests were accommodated at the luxurious Royal Swazi Hotel in the Ezulwini Valley, taken over and enlarged for the occasion; King Moshoeshoe and his entourage stayed with Princess Gcinaphi and her husband. Swazi veterans of the Second World War camped in tents between Lobamba and the State House, and other visitors squeezed happily into huts at the royal villages. Masses of people – including a swarm of press and cameramen – flooded Mbabane and Manzini, whose town boards had rivalled each other in effective publicity. The Prime Minister opened an impressive 'Independence Exhibition' at Manzini, and recounted, with understandable pride, the country's recent developments and spoke of its future potential. For every day there was a full programme of entertainment: horse racing, football, tennis, theatre, film, traditional dancing and, for official guests, additional formal functions.

Sobhuza spent much of his time holding unofficial court and giving

Norway, the Irish Republic, Portugal, Sweden, Switzerland, United Arab Republic and the U.S.A.

[12] On the morning of Independence the Prime Minister signed a Criminal Extradition Treaty with South Africa. This did not affect political refugees, who were still granted asylum.

personal interviews. The day before Independence, he drove, in a new tractor, around the Exhibition, stopping at the different stands, examining with keen interest the new machinery, the handicrafts, the prize cattle, and spending a few moments watching the entertainers. From there he went with the King of Lesotho to the stadium to watch the Cup Finals of a football match between Swaziland and Lesotho. They stayed on, each wrapped in a colourful blanket for warmth, to watch a dazzling display of fireworks presented by the governments of West Germany and Japan.

On Independence Day, exercising his prerogative of mercy under the Constitution, he granted an amnesty to all short-term prisoners and reduced by six months the sentences of all long-term prisoners. Long before the official guests arrived, the stadium was crowded, the arena alive with choirs singing, acrobats and gymnasts performing, maidens in traditional dress dancing and chanting, and police bands playing. It was a gorgeous spectacle of brightness and colour, the air crystal clear, the sun burning in a light-filled sky, flags of all the countries waving in the background. Rows of plumed warriors faced the grandstand. A special section was occupied by the royal women, the Queens and Princesses, married and unmarried, each group in traditionally distinctive dress. When they walked to their seats in single file, heralded by bards, they were indeed a beautiful sight to see.

The notables made their entry, each in a car of symbolic status: Chief Justice and Mrs Elyan in a Rover, the British Secretary of State for Commonwealth Affairs and Mrs Thomson in a Rolls Royce, the Prime Minister and his wife, laMkhonta, in a Dodge Monaco, the Ndlovukazi and her attendant, widow of the late Prince Mshede, in a large Buick, the Queen's Commissioner and Lady Loyd in a Rolls bigger than that of the Secretary of State and flying the Union Jack. Sobhuza's car was an enormous '68 Cadillac limousine and, like all the other vehicles, it was deep black, but he stepped from it into a dazzling white open Landrover while the people roared their welcome and the warriors gave ear-piercing whistles. He was in full *Ncwala* costume, with its high plumed headgear and he looked exceptionally majestic as he was very slowly driven round the stadium track. He acknowledged the welcome with a graceful, unaggressive gesture, not a salute or a thumbs-up. After circling the arena, he moved to the dais where he took the Royal Salute, and then inspected the Guard of Honour, mounted by the Swaziland Police. The Malawian Police Band played Swaziland's new national anthem, and at the arrival of the Queen's Commissioner, *God Save the Queen*.

At high noon, with the sun blazing hot, there was an air of controlled excitement and expectation. Over the loudspeaker came the next announcement. George Thomson stood up; as representative of the British government he delivered an address of goodwill, beginning with a message from the Queen welcoming Swaziland to the

Commonwealth of Nations. Then, almost unobtrusively, he handed
over the general 'articles of independence.' The King received the
document in both hands, Swazi style, and read his acknowledgement
in English: 'This formal act is a climax of our celebrations and returns
to the Swazi people the sovereign independence they enjoyed 65 years
ago. The act also terminates a long and friendly association with the
British people in one form but I hope the association continues in
another form between our people in the future.' All speeches were
translated from one language to the other and the crowd applauded
formal assurances of mutual goodwill.

The transfer of sovereignty was solemn but rather mundane until
from the throats of the thousands of warriors came the haunting
sound of the epic anthem *inqabakanqofula*. Then the King rose with the
Prime Minister at his side and left the grandstand to join the
regiments in their dance. Piercing whistles greeted their arrival.
Visitors gasped with surprise and delight. The royal women
responded. First the young Princesses left their seats and danced
towards him; then came the Queens and married daughters. It was
superb, euphoric, an African Ballet Royal, in a grand natural setting.
In the final movement the warriors, the King in their midst, crouched
low, and hidden by their shields, leapt forward in unison. The ground
shook to the rhythmic thud of their feet. Then they raised their shields
high above their heads. To applaud would have been indecent. A
western-designed political ceremony had been temporarily
transformed into a sacred ritual rich in allusion and associations.
Later, Sobhuza said simply, 'A true Swazi cannot just sit and watch
inqabakanqofula. It is a wonderful song and I like to dance to it.' So he
had danced. Then back he went to his formal role.

Standing alone on the dais, facing the warriors, he took the salute
from each of the many and varied groups assembled in the arena. The
dignitaries then left in a cavalcade. Sobhuza, in the huge Cadillac
with two of his adolescent daughters, drove direct to the State House
to receive foreign diplomats. The British High Commissioner
designate, Peter Gautry, formally presented his credentials.
Mkhulunyelwa Matsebula brought the guests, in order of arrival, to the
reception hall where Sobhuza welcomed each personally, with
charming informality. After the interview they were taken into the
main living room to meet members of the National Council and enjoy
refreshments. Later the King joined them. He was a delightful host
and everybody stayed on until someone politely mentioned that they
should leave: he had still to attend the State Banquet.

The night was velvet dark and the fires blazed on the mountaintops
as he arrived at the Royal Swazi Hotel. Many visitors considered the
banquet the highlight of all the social activities; he accepted it as
necessary and in keeping with such occasions. It was an elegant,
sumptuous, and formal affair. Each place carefully assigned. Dress
regulated. A menu in French. The best of wines. The King came in

full dress suit except for the special 'Independence necktie' – a few tiny Swazi shields on a dark blue background. He ate sparingly and kept his drink for the toasts – his to Her Majesty the Queen of England, Sir Francis' to His Majesty, King Sobhuza II, the Prime Minister's to the distinguished guests, the British Secretary of Commonwealth Affairs to Swaziland. Two hours later the guests left. For some the night was still young, the bars and casino open. Sobhuza went straight back to Lobamba. The Ndlovukazi and the Queens had remained there with kin and friends.

In England and in America, Swaziland's Independence was also being officially celebrated. In London, Douglas Nkomeni Ntiwane, Swaziland's First High Commissioner to Britain, and in Washington, D.C., Dr Msindazwe Sukati, Ambassador-designate to the United Nations and Swaziland's first permanent Ambassador in America, hosted parties for friends and well-wishers and drank to the health of their King and the prosperity of the country.

From the official viewpoint the main celebrations ended with the banquet, and any events that followed were inessential. But for Sobhuza and many of his people, a traditional finale was absolutely necessary. Early in the morning, the inhabitants of Lobamba started their preparations for a *sibhimbi* ritual. Old women – the King's 'mothers' and 'grandmothers' – who knew the words, tunes and movements of ancient dance-songs performed at his puberty ceremony (*sibhimbi sekutfomba*) had been brought specifically for this new *sibhimbi* of Independence. It began at Somhlolo Stadium and then moved – led by the elderly Princess Lozinja, daughter of King Mbandzeni, followed by the Queens and then other sections of the populace – to the *sibaya* of Lobamba. There Sobhuza joined them, and as he danced with his people, many of the royal women wept tears of joy. Later that day there was feasting from cattle provided from royal herds. Each section of the nation received a portion, no individual was excluded, and the ancestors were remembered. Tradition would later again be reaffirmed in a great ceremonial hunt, a *butimba*, with its appropriate costume and songs.

Other religions could not be forgotten and on the following Sunday converts of all denominations, many from independent African churches, gathered at Lobamba to pray and sing hymns.[13] In a short speech the King thanked *Nkulunkulu* for what he had done, asked His blessings for the future and counselled the ministers not to be divided amongst themselves since 'there is but one God and He is the God for everyone'.

Monday 9 September brought business as usual, but with a

---

[13] Among the key speakers were Reverend Nicholas Bhengu of the Assemblies of God, whose headquarters were in the Cape and whose local preachers included John Nxumalo, another son of Mgcobeya, and Reverend Jeremiah Mncina of the Zionist section started by the late Reverend Stephen Mavimbela, who had worked so closely with the late Queen Mother Nukwase. Dr Hynd of the Nazarenes was the main speaker for the more conventional churches.

difference. The Civil Service had changed dramatically, but peacefully. Sir Francis and most of the senior expatriate officials had left or were leaving – some with resentment, most with sadness. Sobhuza spent the day at Lobamba with members of the Swazi National Council and Cabinet, finding time in between to say goodbye to the last of his guests. He had sent Prince Masitsela to call the 'Kuper family' to see him. When we arrived, rather later than expected, he was coming through the gateway of the Queens' quarters with the Prime Minister, the Deputy Prime Minister, the Governor of Lobamba, and some of the Princes. He said that he could not talk to us then as he had to address the soldiers but we could go along and he would see us afterwards. As we went, stumbling over the stubble, the wind began to blow and the clouds to gather. The veterans of World War II were all lined up ready for inspection, gazing straight ahead and very erect. Isaac Dlamini struggled with the loudspeaker; Sobhuza's speech was impromptu; the message was important. 'You are the soldiers,' he said, 'who have helped win Independence and the Nation is grateful to you. Whites call people who are no longer in the army – 'ex-soldiers' – that is not our custom. A Swazi is never out of a regiment; he is always a soldier ready to defend his country. You who have been trained in the guns of the Europeans will be able to teach our own young people.' The new regiment of young people was to be called the *Gcina*, literally 'The End' (of an era); and it would have, as in all Swazi regiments, a junior section that would be the *Inkhanyeti* (Morning Star). The soldiers gave the royal Swazi whistle. I wonder how many of us listening to the King's speech that night realized the role the veterans would be called upon to play in a few years' time.

On our return to Lobamba, Prince Masitsela took us into a house in the Queen Mother's quarters where the Ngwenyama joined us.[14] His Majesty looked very tired and I asked how he was feeling after all his activity. He answered, 'It is not so much doing things that tires me, but reminding others of what should be done. The school-educated are not very reliable – perhaps they were not properly taught. Education is no good if it does not teach self-discipline and respect, respect to others, to yourself, to your country. Those are qualities that used to be acquired through the *emabutfo*.' He asked very earnestly if we as teachers tried to develop these qualities in our students. 'Older people,' he said, 'can teach some things to the young, but to be a man is also to be advised by others, even by your own children.' We touched on many topics and as we left the village I found myself praying that his sons would learn from their father wisdom and humility.

Immediately after Independence the new Kingdom of Swaziland became the twenty-eighth member of the British Commonwealth, the

---

[14] With him were Prince Sozisa, Reverend Motsa, Prince Nqaba, and Velabo Timothy Mtsetfwa (his A.D.C.) in police uniform.

29. Sobhuza at the graduation ceremony of university students at Swaziland's first university campus as part of the University of Botswana, Lesotho and Swaziland (U.B.L.S.). Left to right: Professor C. Rodger (Vice-Chancellor); King Moshoeshoe II (Chancellor); King Sobhuza; King Zwelithini. 1973

30. President Samora Machel, President of Mozambique, visits King Sobhuza at Ehlane in March 1976

31. King Sobhuza with his youngest children at Lobamba. 1974

fortieth member of the Organization of African Unity, and the 120th member of the United Nations. But Sobhuza knew well that 'happy ever after' was a fairytale ending. The new Kingdom of Swaziland remained, like its colonial prototype, surrounded on three sides by the Republic of South Africa, and to the east, by Mozambique, which was still a Portuguese colony. The Prime Minister, enunciating the foreign policy of the new Kingdom, had made it very explicit that his government was 'constrained by geographic and economic circumstances to follow a policy of enlightened self-interest, relying upon a maximum of acumen and a minimum of heroics ... It would maintain a policy of nonintervention in the internal affairs of other states since it was in no position to enter the lists of international power politics in the spirit of a medieval crusade.'

It is a truism that the future of a country depends on its leadership, and in the Swazi monarchy the conduct of the King was obviously crucial. Sobhuza had kept the peace and retained his own honour, dignity, humour and humanity in the long struggle for national sovereignty. He had led his people to 'Independence'. What would happen to him in the years that lay ahead?

CHAPTER XVIII
Are We Truly Independent?

'Independence' at last. What fulfilment would it bring to him as a King and as a man? Would the Constitution make it possible for him to relax after the years of leadership and leave to others the struggle to achieve and maintain his ideals of a prosperous non-racial nation in which neither wealth nor colour would be the measure of a man's worth, a state in which order and discipline would be maintained without force, a culture in which the best of Swazi tradition would thrive in a modern world? Or would the complex Constitution which he had finally accepted prove a handicap and further obstacle? Would it provide the substance for a traditional sovereignty or merely a Western reflection in a Swazi frame?

Superficially, the Constitution made it easy enough for him to withdraw and simply give his sanction to decisions made in Parliament, but he knew well that to do so would jeopardize the unity and the ideals for which he had worked. 'Parliament was not the nation', and in a speech, made to chiefs at Lobamba in 1969, he likened it 'to a train which is directed by the railway line. A train only goes where the railroad leads it. It is not turned to different directions by needs; where the railroad bends, it also bends. This is the nature of the Constitution we have been given by the British. There are binding and unchangeable rules, which we have to abide by under all circumstances. The Swazi may not agree with what we do but we realise that we are bound by the Constitution. *Sitawufela umnyama wentsambama* – we will die in the evening darkness – which means that we will suffer for things that occur late in life and for which we are not responsible and in which we have no choice ... unless the non-Swazi clauses are changed, we specifying what we want according to our custom and not just take the white man's ways, we shall have hardship. It is the Swazi themselves who will say, "We want Swazi custom and procedure." With independence we want to change the Constitution to comply with what we want. The government in Mbabane does not have such powers to change the Constitution on their own. It is only the nation which has such powers ...' 'The nation' consisted of citizens of different clans, colours, creeds and class; and the changes that were envisaged were interpreted by him in the traditional idiom of nationhood.

Sobhuza described the first year of independence as 'an exciting one, our independence has been recognized'. For the first anniversary the British accepted the invitation to send as guest of honour the Princess Alexandra, whose husband, the Honourable Angus Ogilvy, included in his business interests Lonhro, which already had investments in the asbestos mines in Swaziland. From the point of view of the outsider the presence of British royalty gave a greater glamour than the celebrations of the previous year; but though Sobhuza was also enchanted by his royal guests, he made it clear that 'Independence was regained only once. Our anniversaries remind us of how hard we fought for it and how far we are pushing ahead with it.'

It would be necessary to begin by taking stock of available personnel, professional, technical and administrative, to carry out the development required for national independence. A report completed in September 1969 by Chief J.O. Udoji, C.M.G. of Nigeria, who had been brought in to advise on localisation of government posts, revealed the extent to which key positions were still held by expatriates, and made far-reaching recommendations for training and reorganizing the entire civil service.[1] The King-in-Council accepted these as realistic and specific – the search for talent among Swaziland nationals, intensive on-the-job-training, a time limit for certain jobs to be vacated by expatriates and filled by the new men, the coordination of post-school education and occupational opportunities, the urgency of certified directives regarding positions necessary for effective change, and the setting up of a new Department of Establishment and Training.

Of the limited number of trained Swazi personnel, many had been members of the political parties in the '60s and critical of the Imbokodvo. Sobhuza stressed they be given responsible positions in the civil service and welcomed them for the contributions they could make. He also sent messengers to ask Swazi who were still in South Africa or further afield to return. Among those were Dr Pym Dlamini, Swaziland's first dentist trained on a government scholarship in Britain, who became Minister of Education in 1973, and Ethan Mayisela, an economist who worked in Tanzania as Director of Budget Management, before joining the Swaziland government in 1971.

To Sobhuza, contrary to the wishes of some of his men, localization did not mean Africanization or Swazi exclusiveness. Any person 'irrespective of his colour or creed who has genuinely become a citizen of this country and identifies with us is a Swazi. You may think it means the colour of a man's skin. It you think that way, you are mistaken.'

There were Swazi efforts, and achievements, in all fields – economic, social and cultural. The three newly independent

---

[1] Chief J.O. Udoji, *Training and Localisation of Swaziland Civil Service*, September 8, 1969.

territories, Botswana, Lesotho and Swaziland, were able by joint effort to exert pressure on South Africa to enter into a new Customs Agreement, signed on 11 December 1969. Swaziland was the main beneficiary, and for the first time since the colonial era was able to balance her budget. Swazi took the initiative in extending trade links to other independent African nations and to other continents. Foreigners who showed an interest in the small and stable country, rich in natural resources, were encouraged to invest on condition that they realized that, as the King said, 'It is in the interest of all who work and earn in Swaziland to give full participation to the indigenous people so that they may not see industry or any other business as a foreign exploitation but as part of their own work.'

Visitors were increasingly attracted by the beauty of the country, and tourism was being promoted by different interest groups in and outside government. Sobhuza supported the general idea of using tourism as an economic resource but was also aware of the disadvantages, particularly the potential danger to the morality of the people and the likelihood of economic exploitation. In 1970 the first of a chain of Holiday Inns in Southern Africa was built in the beautiful Ezulwini Valley next to the Royal Swaziland Hotel (and Casino). Leading people of the country as well as many visitors from South Africa were invited for the opening. The King consented to be present and in an impromptu address, having first thanked the director of the hotel for the beautiful tape recorder with which he had been presented, indicated very politely the obligation of people who ran hotels in the country to the people who lived there. Referring to a speech made a few days before in which a Swazi member of government had criticized the persistence of racism in the country and advocated rapid localization (a speech which angered a section of the white population), he gently reiterated the substance and reaffirmed the truth of the minister's remarks, summing up his own approach in the idiom 'Two hands wash each other'.

Education, technical and academic, had been accelerated by large grants from general revenue and assistance from abroad. The regimental age group system which had been the traditional institution of major educational value was being revitalised. At a camp started by Israelis on a site allocated by the King, youngsters who were not in school or employed were being trained for rural community development. The King hoped that each batch of recruits would 'pass on the agricultural skills and techniques they had acquired, and like salt in the cooking pot go home to their areas and help improve the farming there'. (Speech by Sobhuza, April 1971.) Because of the discipline, the youths were being regarded as the equivalent of *emabutfo* who formerly stayed in barracks at royal villages and rendered national service. In 1970 the Ngwenyama gave the camp the same name he had bestowed on the new regiment he formed at Independence – *Gcina* (The End of an Era) and he also gave to the camp the hawk (a royal bird) as its emblem. The project was in accordance with his attempt in 1934 to develop a national educational system based on the regiments and binding together all sections of the people.

The education of the girls was equally important, and in 1969 the King gave his support to the celebration of an *umcwasho* on an unprecedented scale. This time objections of churchmen were dealt with more openly and effectively. The term *likholwa* (believer) was no longer restricted to orthodox Christians, and now most churchmen praised Sobhuza as 'a true Christian', a *likholwa* par excellence, while he continued to tolerate and respect different denominations, and at the same time to perform the ancient rites of his people.

Despite progress and promise, the added revenue from the customs union did not make for real economic independence – solvency was but a first step. Much more was needed to meet the demand for modern development whether it be in education or health services or housing, and to bridge the conspicuous gap between the white minority and the majority of Swazi blacks, the historical legacy of colonialism. A serious obstacle to harmonious national sovereignty and development was still the land issue. More than 40% of the total area of the country was still owned by non-Swazi; the majority of the Swazi were still part-time peasants, crowded in communal areas (now under title deeds held by the King on behalf of the nation), or squatters (now termed 'farm dwellers') subject to harsh restrictions and limited security, on 'farms' owned mainly by foreigners. Though there had been considerable agricultural development, recognized as benefiting the whole country, large areas had remained undeveloped since the initial acquisition by concessions, and some had been bought by speculators interested in subdividing and selling small plots at high prices. Both in the countryside and in the developing urban areas the cost of land was high and beyond the means, but not the legitimate aspirations, of black Swazi citizens.

The 'time bomb' about which Makhosini had warned the British had to be defused. Some Swazi suggested outright confiscation of white-owned farms, others advised farm dwellers not to move when evicted by the landlords. The King, backed by his more moderate councillors, openly opposed these modes of action and sought for 'a peaceful as well as just solution. ... God the Creator gave you this land and it will be rightly restored to you. You can't take a shortcut to it. A shortcut in taking jumps leads to death.' He recalled the time when 'a Resident Commissioner came to divide the land, and some said "If we kill this man we would end the dispute over land," not realizing that this would perpetuate the dispute and Europeans would instead plant their roots more deeply into the country. Always bear in mind that other people's property should be respected. The question of land is no single individual's concern that should let him adamantly build his home or refuse to move off. Such a person is like a careless dancer who dances on a snare which catches him. Squatters who refuse to leave when ejected are knocking their heads against stones.'

He knew that some of his people rejected this view: 'As I'm talking to you now there will be someone who says, "the King is just talking, there's nothing he knows." But you know when I started this task, most of you are younger than I am.' And he compared himself to General Smuts, who first fought against the English in the Boer War, and then with the English in the Second World War, and in both cases 'fought to the end for the same goal.' He spoke with unusual bitterness and sarcasm of people 'who claim that I am a sell-out. They are wiser than I am and see things which I don't see. Where were they then? Where were they then? There are those who advise you to encroach on European farms and remain there obstinately. *They* are selling the land; they are selling *you.*' And then he said firmly, 'I am the one to decide on that issue. It is I who will face the *Libandla*, if I am failing we will discuss the matter further and you will advise me. Now we have put our case to England ... Mbandzeni was promised the return of the land as payment for the part the Swazi played in helping the British at the battle of Mshadza. I ordered the delegation to ask about that promise. We shall never stop asking that question from Britain, saying, "Britain, since you admit that Mbandzeni gave away no land and sold no land, no land was ever taken away from him." All we were told was "You have lost your land." We must handle this issue kindly and patiently and ask Britain, "Is this human or not?" To act otherwise is to challenge a champion who will kill you. Then you will be blamed because you have been aggressive. I will not agree to this. You must follow the rule as it has always operated. We shall patiently continue to ask [Britain] for our land. We hope that we shall finally succeed. It is not evident how we lost the land.'

The negotiations with Britain were progressing slowly. The British government had offered a specific area for major resettlement, but the purchase was conditional on retaining certain controls over its use and developments. The King-in-Council asked, 'Are we still subjects?' The controls were humiliating to an independent nation, as well as reminiscent of the experiences of the earlier post-Second World War schemes in which some land was bought at inflated prices and too much was spent on administrative costs and buildings for non-Swazi personnel.

By 1971 the price of land had rocketed; several large land deals were being negotiated by non-Swazi, while more land was urgently needed for the Swazi. After much thought and long private discussions with certain members of the Cabinet and of the Swazi National Council, Sobhuza agreed that a law be introduced through Parliament to control all land transactions involving non-Swazi.

The early harmonious cooperation within the government was being disturbed by differences of opinion in the Cabinet and in the Inner Council of the Swazi National Council on a variety of issues relating to development – appointments, qualification and salary of staff, investments, licences, citizenship, as well as land policy. In July 1971 there was a major reshuffle of ministers and senior civil servants. Mfundza Sukati had been removed from his position as Deputy Prime Minister (with authority over immigration as well as other crucial areas), to the less controversial Ministry of Power, Works and Communication. His place was given to Zonke Khumalo, former Minister of State for Foreign Affairs.

In many countries removal of colonial masters released individual ambition submerged during the common struggle for independence and opened, particularly for government officials, temptation and opportunities for personal aggrandizement. The King, caught between rival personalities in and outside of Parliament, expressed his disillusionment. 'You appoint *bafana* thinking they will help each other remove the thorns from each other's feet. Instead you find each trying to get more for himself.' And on another occasion he said, 'A stone stays where it is put, but the heart of a person changes, it moves.'

An increasing number of matters were dealt with by Parliament and the administration without Sobhuza's knowledge. Decisions not always acceptable to him or to councillors active on the Swazi National Council were taken before he could intervene. The Prime Minister explained that this was often necessary because of the complexity and pressures of time in the modern world. 'Cabinet makes the decision on public matters and then takes them to the King for approval. It doesn't ask-him first; sometimes he doesn't approve.' 'And then?' I asked. He replied, 'Then we discuss it further,' and he quoted the axiom, 'A King is not argued against, he is advised. But,' he added, 'a King is King by the Council.'

The publication of the Land Speculation Control Bill produced panic among many whites, who feared for their personal property and also argued that the proposed mode of control would frighten off investment. Their anxieties were intensified by the fact that the Minister of Finance, Leo Lovell, together with two other ministers (Mfundza Sukati and Sishayi Nxumalo) who were known to be particularly sympathetic to the private sector were out of the country when the Bill was to be discussed by Parliament.

Sobhuza had realized that many of the whites who claimed they were against land speculation had a different approach (or was it different interests?) from his own people. 'How are investments tied with speculation in land? Genuine investors are not speculators. It seems that those who are objecting are those who are benefiting from the speculation. There are foreigners who do not wish the country to develop nor have any interest in helping it develop, only in selling land at a high price. It is from those we must protect ourselves; others will not feel their land threatened.' Had they forgotten how, over the years, in the face of opposition from some of his own councillors and at the temporary sacrifice of Swazi individuals and families, he had encouraged such innovations as timber plantations, irrigation schemes and the introduction of new crops? He had supported these as investments, trusting they would be of ultimate benefit for the people, 'the major asset of the country.'

The bill was presented on 7 December 1971 by A. Khuseni Hlophe, Minister of Agriculture, under a certificate of urgency, first to the House of Assembly and then to the Senate. It was in the process of being debated when the three ministers returned. At the second reading before the Senate, the Minister of Finance, Leo Lovell, though not a member of the Senate, asked in a passionate speech to move an amendment which he well knew was not acceptable to Cabinet. He sought to justify his request on the grounds that he had been away for twelve days on official government business, and on his return had found the bill had been through Cabinet and was having its second reading in the House of Assembly.

The following day the Prime Minister came in person to the Senate 'to correct certain statements' alleged to have been made by the Honourable Minister of Finance. With biting anger he dealt with the allegations, and pointed out that the Minister had acted against the basic Cabinet principle of collective responsibility. 'To me, Mr President, all His Majesty's ministers are useful but none of them is indispensable. Cabinet must at all cost follow government policy; if not, they must bear the consequences of their action.' And he concluded, 'that no responsible government will continue to allow its entire land, the only God-given asset, to be swallowed by foreigners and its national wealth exploited by speculators.'

The Land Speculation Control Bill passed the final reading without amendment on 16 December 1971, and the Minister of Justice announced that members were going on to Lobamba for the opening of the *Ncwala*. Parliament was accordingly adjourned.

The King postponed his assent to the Bill until February when the *Ncwala* ritual was over. The Bill itself would only become law in December 1972. Opinions on the drafting and contents had been obtained unofficially from legal experts. The King received the assurance that the weaknesses were not irremediable; clauses could be amended, additional clauses introduced, the warning to speculators had been given, guarantees to genuine investors written in. Let criticism be voiced. Let tempers cool. The banks, over which government as yet had no control, would recover from their initial nervous reaction and again be prepared to grant loans and receive mortgages on landed property. Confidence would be further restored through the quality of members appointed by the Prime Minister to the two Boards, a Lower and an Appeal, acting independently of the courts of law.

In the last brief session after the *Ncwala* several other important bills were passed but tempers were controlled. Leo Lovell had not resigned and the King calmed down those councillors who would have liked him to indicate publicly that he was displeased with the Minister's conduct. To do so at this point would have exacerbated hostility. A general election, required under the 1967 Constitution, was close. Besides, the King pointed out, Lovell had acted in accord with his principles and had done good service.

Sobhuza dissolved Parliament with effect from 15 March and announced that elections would be held on 16 and 17 May 1972. He had already told the warriors after their final service at the *Ncwala* that they were all to vote again. 'If not the nation would suffer for there are two ways of electing a person. In Western procedure you go to vote to elect a person. If you abstain from voting, thinking that by staying away you are not electing, you are in fact electing another by increasing his total against the one you really wanted in power.'

The population had become increasingly diversified. It was part of the King's policy to meet separately and often informally with different groups of teachers, businessmen, preachers, converts, farmers, workers, ex-soldiers, police, school children, princes, chiefs, and sons-in-law. To each he carried his message of the need for unity, his long-time theme, adapting his idioms, parables and metaphors to the audience, showing awareness of their particular interests but pointing at the same time to the need to subordinate these for national development and peaceful survival. In 1969, when he had addressed the Royal Swaziland police force, he had compared it to the American astronauts 'who returned from the Moon only yesterday. Who,' he asked, 'is the greatest of the three? I wonder whether it is Neil Armstrong. That is the man who first set his foot on the surface of the Moon. Whether it was his left foot or his right foot which set there first? From the time the scheme was initiated I wondered who should be regarded as the greatest of all. And I said to myself, no one is greater than the other. This is team work and cooperation and what we must do is praise the whole of America, the wise and the foolish, because no one deserved to be praised more than anyone else. All American citizens were taxed for the project for educating the astronauts and the other members of the team.'

During the Colonial period it was easier for him to stand out and express the wishes of his people; he was the recognized mouthpiece, speaking for an oppressed section of the population. The institution of Parliament changed his position. His information and contacts were more indirect, his obligations to different sections more difficult to disentangle, the process by which these obligations could be met more complicated because of the diversity of groups simultaneously putting forward contradictory claims.

The months between the dissolution of the first Parliament and the new elections was a time for him to take stock before giving – and receiving – new guidelines. The names he had bestowed on two of his children indicated his view of changes in the situation: Makhosetive – literally 'rulers of foreign countries' – born in 1968 when foreign diplomats were gathered to celebrate Swazi independence; and Ncengencenge, born in 1971. He explained the second name in a bitter indictment of new attitudes among some of his people – 'by the way this country begs. It is a pity because I can't beg ... I named one of my children Ncengencenge because I realized that there are those who condone bad actions and behaviour.'[2]

At a farewell party to the outgoing Parliamentarians at his home at Embo on 15 March, to which he also invited senior civil servants and members of the Public Service Commission, so that 'all the organs that formed part of the government be present,' he took the opportunity to make a major policy speech which he began with the parable of an aged king who felt he was about to pass away and wondered which of his three sons could be entrusted with the task of looking after the kingdom.

He called his first-born son and said, 'My son, tell me how much do you love me?' The son replied, 'O,'my King, my love is immeasurable. There is no scale on earth that I can use to measure my love for you.' The king called the second son and asked him: 'My child, how much do you love me?' The son replied, 'O, my King, my love for you is as wide and as deep as the sea that you see. There is no other deep and wide thing to which I can liken my love.' The king called the last, third son and asked him, 'My child, how much do you love me?' The son answered, 'O, my King! I love you. That is all. I have nothing to compare with.'

The king then went away on a pilgrimage. Before he left, he charged his sons to care for the well-being of state. During the absence of the king the eldest son busied himself with horse races and hunting. He did not bother about state affairs. The second son spent all his time dancing and playing the guitar. He too did not pay the slightest attention to the affairs of state. The only son that took his duties seriously and conscientiously was the youngest. It was rumoured that the king was dead. The horse races, hunting, guitars and dances continued. The youngest son persevered with the worries of the affairs of state. Then a poor old man was seen daily for a few days at the gates of the palace walking about. He saw all the activities of each.

One day people heard sounds of trumpets and drums at the palace. The king had returned from his pilgrimage. The king then called his sons to recount how they had looked after affairs of the country during his absence. The eldest and the second had nothing to report. The king found that the only son who sincerely looked after the business of the country was the youngest. The poor old man who had been seen at the palace gates had been the king himself. This parable clearly shows that what you say with your mouth cannot reveal what is truly yourself.

Then he congratulated the Parliamentarians – 'highly educated and less educated, white and black' – for working together as if they were 'all members of one family', demonstrating that the absence of an official opposition did not stifle differences of opinion since 'everyone of you knows that there has been a type of opposition which emanates from within hearts of members. Such opposition was spontaneous, genuine and constructive, born out of facts rather than out of fear and jealousy. You did not oppose for the sake of opposing

[2] The verb *ncenga* implies begging with a sense of humiliation or subordination, not asking for help with self-respect. My committee says the English equivalent is 'spare the rod and spoil the child'. (King's Speech at Lobamba on 25 March 1972).

but because you had alternative ideas you strongly believed could better solve the problems put before you.'

He paid special tribute to Sir John Houlton as President of the Senate for his ability 'to direct debates because those who debate have different tempers.' He then addressed himself to the Public Service Commission, which initially had favoured expatriates, and now was under his own nominees:

The employer and the employee are the same when it comes to the well-being of the job done. There are bad employees and there are bad employers. I want to try and show you what are the criteria for bad employers. The criteria for a good servant are when you find that one servant has worked for the same employer for a long time. This is a trustworthy servant. Again, if you find that an employer has had the same servants for a long time you should know that he is a good employer. A person who moves about from pillar to post changing his job, is a bad employee. Likewise a master who always changes his staff must be a poor master. Therefore, you who employ should examine yourself in the same way as he who seeks employment should look at himself. Sometimes an employer keeps the same employee not because the employee is a good one but for certain reasons other than for good reasons. This may be a bad servant. The law of a country is meant to be applied for the good of the people. The law too is flexible and takes into consideration degrees of offences. Therefore, I want to warn the Public Service Commission, so that it should know that it should deal with employees considerately when they behave themselves well. But if the public servant misbehaves himself, the [Public Service] Commission should use all the power at its disposal to discipline such a servant because to punish a person is not to kill him but to make him repent, and to deter others who may be tempted to commit a similar mistake. If you condone such behaviour because you want it to be said you are a good employer the state is corrupt and it will be in disrepute. In some countries governments are toppled because they condone corruption in the public service. Through your actions the country can go from strength to strength, but through your failure to act the country can go to the dogs ...

He pointed to the defects in their interpretation of localization.

I have often wondered whether our national policy was being observed ... because when I ask how many white Swazis are in the Civil Service, I hear that there is only a handful of them. I don't know whether it is the white Swazis themselves who don't come forward or you make it difficult for them ... The most important thing which you should always keep in mind when employing a person, is his character. Next comes his experience. Then his initiative and devotion to duty. This is what I know to be the criteria for advancement to promotion. Not the colour of one's skin ... All people are equal. Sometimes I hear that a job has been given to a foreigner, thus by-passing a local who has all the prerequisite certificates and knows the job. That is why I am advising the Public Service Commission that they be wary and not spoil things for us. And I hope it will always have this piece of advice in mind whenever it considers new applications and applications for promotions.

Everyone listening knew exactly to what and to whom he referred in his various remarks, and while some left with a feeling of some discomfort, others felt reassured.

On 26 March he held a meeting of all his people in the *sibaya* of Lobamba, to hear the report of the Parliamentarians, and to give his advice. The meeting was scheduled for 10:00 a.m. but everyone knew it would not open until after noon. People drifted in throughout the morning and the praises of Swazi kings rang intermittently like a theme song through all the casual conversations. The people waited patiently in the hot sun, occasionally drifting off to try to buy food from some of the little stores nearby. When the King arrived (about 3:00 p.m.) he went to the Great Hut to see the Queen Mother, who was too ill to attend, and to tell her what was taking place. With him were senior councillors of the Swazi National Council and Parliamentarians. He instructed the Parliamentarians to enter the *sibaya* through the main gateway. He remained with the Governors of royal villages and other councillors, who took him ('their person') into the arena where a huge crowd of some 3,000, among them a sprinkling of women and whites, was waiting. He sat on the ground facing them, his back against the fence of the *sibaya* near the sanctuary. The Swazi Parliamentarians then came in, five abreast, in a traditional march formation, with the Prime Minister Makhosini in the centre. He and the Minister of Justice carried sticks, symbolic weapon of Swazi warriors, though the stick of the Minister of Justice was a silver sitting stick which he had bought in England five years ago. As they moved forward they chanted the anthem, 'We are the Fortress.' It was an impressive entry, and Prince Mahlaba, in the blue overalls which he always wore when driving the King's cars, dashed forward lifting an ornamental spear and shouting praise songs. He was followed by Prince Mazini, the official first-born. Then some of the Princesses 'could not restrain themselves but had to rejoice the warriors who had returned', and danced towards them.

When everyone was again seated, the Ngwenyama welcomed the Parliamentarians as an *'impi'* that had returned from battle, and whose report people at home were waiting to receive. The Prime Minister, standing in front of a microphone, informed the audience of the difficulties that they had confronted in Parliament. The Ngwenyama then commented that he could detect that the Prime Minister was 'heated up', and said he sympathised with the Parliamentarians 'tied by a Constitution which in fact limited the power of Parliament ... a Constitution which had tried to marry two systems but there was a lot of discord in the union because it was difficult to know what was the best to select from both cultures. When the sun is bright and warm it is easy to decide to get into a pool, but on arriving there one becomes frightened in case there may be a crocodile in it or a python or *imfingo* (legendary serpent), then you change your mind on your initial approach. It is necessary for us now to rectify what we considered wrong ... There are things done here which were and are not done even in Britain itself, and some things which were not done even during British rule. When they handed over independence to us they then decided that we should do those things in our country. They tell us to do certain things which they did not do and bound us by working these things into our Constitution.'

He expressed his view of Kingship and of his responsibility to speak up when he saw things going wrong. It was on this occasion that he told how he 'had once abdicated.' His attitude had not changed. He would never be terrorized into doing what he did not think best for the nation. 'I am not begging for Kingship or anything else. I only beg for the truth which I see, so that even if I'm misled it is God who is misleading me ... I am not bothered about begging to be a King nor do I fear being deposed.'

He likened political parties to nations, 'each fighting a battle to be in power; each wanting to rule the other. This is what a political party is – wanting to rule. As to elections, you will find all the inhabitants of the country intoxicated, drunk for power, each one spending his last money so they may get into power. Whereas finally only one person will get into power, the other five will constitute the Cabinet – that is all. To hell with the rest. [laughter] You have only elected a few into power. Once they are there they don't care for you.'

A few days later, on 28 March, a small crowd which included the Queens and other women gathered outside the arena to hear the report of Swazi emissaries to the All African Trade Fair held at Nairobi. The girls who had danced in the *umcwasho* had already performed successfully in South Africa; in 1972 they travelled further afield and attracted wider acclaim. Prince Mfanasibili, Minister of Local Administration, who had gone as their escort, gave a glowing account of their reception, and Sishayi Nxumalo, Minister of Commerce, spoke of the appreciation of the Swazi exhibits and of the orders that had been placed for Swazi products. Sobhuza, sitting on a canvas chair, smiled happily as he listened, and thanked the emissaries for the way they represented the Swazi nation, which he likened to 'a child who admires its mother's beauty and does not envy another as being more beautiful than its own mother and deserts her to follow the more beautiful'. He recounted with much vivacity the origin of the Swazi saying, 'he abandoned his rabbit and chased the eland'. Of course the hunter lost both.

His next public address was on Good Friday, before a large crowd of *emakholwa* to whom he put the problem of personal responsibility in a confused and violent world. 'When I listened to the news last night there was fighting between Ireland and England over religion. Even where religion came from the issue of religion is still hot. Therefore it is each one's duty to search for the truth – the basis of truth is in your own heart.' He was confronting the fundamental dilemma of individual conscience and national goals. And when he asked each person to look into his own heart for guidance and for truth, he placed on them the moral obligation to disobey those things which they considered wrong in principle. As King he had to accept that the nation take priority over the individual. The encounter between the sovereign individual and the sovereign state is always terrifyingly unequal, and yet he hoped that those who objected on principle could be accommodated within the totality and 'differences of opinion would not destroy an entire friendship'.

In spite of his objections to the parliamentary party system and Western style of voting, he accepted the general election as an essentially peaceful move to final sovereignty. The procedure was now familiar; no changes in the boundaries or numbers of the constituencies had been made and the qualifications for voters had been stated simply to be any person who had attained the age of 21 and 'was a Swazi citizen'.

But who was a Swazi citizen? Citizenship was a privilege not a right, a commitment not a label. As early as 1930 Sobhuza had warned the Colonial government that the presence of people born outside the country, who were not brought into the Swazi nation through the traditional channels, would create problems. But Colonial rule produced subjects not citizens; no national citizenry was integrally involved in government and no unified policy had been laid down.

After independence the approach had changed and different techniques of distinguishing between citizens and non-citizens were more rigorously, and at times arbitrarily, applied. The great mass of citizens, people recognized as 'belonging to Swaziland,' were Swazi by birth and residence, but the traditional mode of incorporating by *kukhonta* (giving allegiance), sanctioned finally by the King, became more cumbersome. Swazi born outside of Swaziland as well as non-Swazi Africans had to apply through their chiefs to the Swazi National Council and have their acceptance validated by papers. Non-Africans could apply for naturalization through the Immigration Office, which fell under the aegis of the Deputy Prime Minister, and in most cases the personal procedure of the past took on the impersonality of modern bureaucratic complexities and accompanying individual frustrations, except in the few cases in which the King himself directly interceded. The position was generally confused, and in 1970 the King appointed a committee from the Swazi National Council to investigate the different categories of people and of citizens. They reported back that some 6,000 people in Swaziland were without any of the necessary evidence of traditional citizenship or documents entitling them to residence. The majority were non-Swazi Africans who had been brought into Swaziland as employees of the Colonial government, white settlers or contractors for the railway. But there were also several hundred Swazi born outside of Swaziland. When registration of voters which had begun in July closed on 31 January 1972, the final number was lower than calculated in terms of the population.

The Imbokodvo candidates were again chosen by the regional committees (*tinkundla*), accepted by the King, and presented at a huge meeting at Lobamba. It was stated explicitly that each candidate was appointed to represent the interests of the country as a whole, not simply his own constituency or his own local district, and therefore would not necessarily stand in the area from which he came or in which he was well known.

This time the 24 elected seats were contested by five political parties. The Imbokodvo, headed by Prince Makhosini; the NNLC (which had split on personal rather than ideological grounds into separate parties, one led by Dr Ambrose Phesheya Zwane, the other by his former Deputy K. Thulasizwe Samketi); the Swaziland United Front led by Obed Mabuza;and the Swaziland Progressive Party. John J. Nquku, the veteran leader of the Progressives, did not stand. He could not document his status as a Swazi citizen. He did not appeal against his exclusion to the King but accepted it as contrary to the King's own outlook.[3]

The Imbokodvo nominated the full quota of 24 candidates; the NNLC (Zwane), 19; the NNLC (Samketi), 14; the Swaziland United Front, 6; the Swaziland Progressive Party, 5. Of the Imbokodvo candidates, 17 had been in the previous Parliament, 7 were new nominees.

The King was assured by the Imbokodvo that it would gain an overwhelming victory and he himself felt confident that this would be the case. It had achieved much and was the only group with carefully thought out and realistic plans for the future, plans which he considered were in keeping with the ideals of the Swazi nation. Zwane's NNLC, recognized as the strongest opposition, simply reproduced the document of 1964 on the grounds that it did not need to be changed 'since the NNLC's goals were still the same'.

The organization of the election was effective; the Chief Electoral Officer, Patrick Forsyth Thompson, was well experienced. The King waited in the Great Hut at Lobamba for the results. It had rained heavily the first day, creating some disorganization in communication, but it did not stop some 40% of Swazi registered voters coming to the polls.

The early results were all in favour of the Imbokodvo. But in one constituency, Mphumalanga, which in the previous election had been the most closely contested, the NNLC (Zwane) candidates – Mageja

---

[3] After independence the SPP voiced no public criticism of the Imbokodvo and when asked in 1970 why the SPP was not active, Nquku replied, 'We have achieved our goal of regaining independence. We were the spearhead. Now let us give the ruling party a chance to see what progress they will make. But we are marking down all their sins. We've seen African states in action and the tragedy of coups through imperialist colonization. We've seen political parties engineered by the same colonialists and seen them broken down and we're not going to assist the imperialists and colonialists break down the Swazi government. All the imperialist powers are present here – the British, Americans, Germans, Portuguese, Italians, South Africans – so we're silent; we are not dead. We'll come out again in the next election. Ours is a non-racial policy and the Imbokodvo is not racist in any way, only the tribal instinct is there. The opposition which is engineered in African states is a destructive opposition. It is killing the leaders, killing the country itself. This we don't like. We want a constructive opposition as in London. Here in Africa they say kill the leader, but our leader is Sobhuza. He is the King of the Swazi and he is a wonderful man' (Interview 4 June 1970).

Masilela, Thomas Bhekindlela Ngwenya and Dr Ambrose Phesheya Zwane – defeated the Imbokodvo candidates – Prince Mfanasibili, Mlungeli Naphthal Mahlalela and Ndawonde Sikhondze. This came as a great shock to the King-in-Council. It was the first time that an organized opposition party had won a single constituency and it did not make any difference that the vote in that constituency was close. Several explanations were offered,[4] but did not mitigate the effects of a visible opposition in government. Though the final result was an overwhelming majority for the Imbokodvo, which obtained 78.3% of all votes with Zwane's NNLC winning 18.2% of the remaining 21.7%, an official opposition was equivalent to having in one's midst a subversive and persistent enemy, committed not by conviction but by organization.

The King and the Prime Minister indicated that they hoped the position would still change. The victory message of the Prime Minister expressed this viewpoint:

To my adversaries I have nothing to say but point to the indisputable verdict of the people. This is the third time. They should now search themselves very carefully. Their road leads but to the wilderness. But the doors of the movement are ajar and wide open, they are welcome like the prodigal son. A word of caution may be necessary. Their activities purport to divide the nation and this is an ill wind which benefits no one. To the Imbokodvo it should be stressed that this victory does not call for complacency (*Times of Swaziland*, 26 May 1972).

The election of Thomas Bhekindlela Ngwenya had initiated a bitter and dramatic battle in which two issues, the one related to the rights of a particular individual, and the other to the broad interpretation of national sovereignty, became inextricably confused.

At the time of nominations, Prince Mfanasibili, who had been on the 1970 committee examining claims to citizenship, had complained to the local Electoral Officer that Ngwenya, though a Swazi, was born on the South African side of the border and hence not a citizen of Swaziland. The matter had been mentioned to the Chief Electoral Officer, but since Ngwenya had voted in previous elections and was a progressive farmer at Vuvulane – a scheme sponsored by the Colonial Development Corporation – he did not treat the matter seriously, and no formal objection had been lodged. Once elected, however, the position changed. Prince Mfanasibili took his complaint to the Deputy Prime Minister, Zonke Khumalo, who, without informing the King, declared Ngwenya a Prohibited Immigrant, described him in the *Gazette Extraordinary* as a South African, and had him deported

---

[4] The Prince had made a speech strongly attacking missionaries and the area itself was one in which their work was appreciated; he had also expressed himself against trade unions and this was an area in which the workers were politically oriented. Some party members thought the Imbokodvo organization in the constituency was weak, and that the Imbokodvo should have won, more particularly since the opposition had split into two factions, with both leaders competing for the same seat.

across the border on 25 May, the day before the opening of the new Parliament.

When the King questioned the deportation, the Deputy Prime Minister, who found restrictions on his independent actions irksome, referred to the need to deal effectively with illegal immigrants and people who had no claim to citizenship under the existing Constitution. The King felt no hostility to Ngwenya. He had committed no crime and had in fact demonstrated the qualities of work and enterprise which the King himself admired. Ngwenya was in some ways irrelevant, a victim of a wider political situation. The King accepted the winning NNLC candidates; this was the result of the party system he condemned but which was embodied in the Constitution. The defeat of the Imbokodvo candidates was not in his opinion a justification, nor the opportune moment, to introduce the changes he considered necessary. When a number of people came to him requesting that Prince Mfanasibili again be given a position in the government befitting his rank and his qualifications (which they rated high) he initially refused, but eventually he agreed. The argument that finally persuaded him was that in Botswana and Tanzania there had been similar situations in which candidates who had lost in elections had been given high office by their presidents, internationally respected Sir Seretse Khama and Julius Nyerere.

When Parliament opened on 26 May the members were duly sworn in and the King's nominees to both Houses and to the Cabinet were announced.[5] In the new Cabinet were many familiar figures, though

[5] The elected members of Parliament for the eight constituencies were:

Mlumati:	Bekhimphi Alpheus Dlamini
	Prince Mnikwa Dlamini
	Mfana Lawrence Mncina
Mbabane:	William Magangeni Magongo
	Mhlangano Stephen Matsebula
	Sishayi Simon Nxumalo
Usutu:	Prince Gabheni Dlamini
	Amos Zonke Khumalo
	Saul Mndeni Shabalala
Mbuluzi:	Bhizeni Wilson Dlamini
	Prince Makhosini Dlamini
	Abednigo Khuseni Hlophe
Mkhondvo:	Prince Masitsela Dlamini
	Mphithi Luke Dlamini
	Chief Mantungwini Ndlangamandla
Ngwavuma:	Velaphi Richard Dlamini
	Meshack Nkoseluhlaza Hlatshwako
	Esau Mateus Gamedze
Lihlanze:	Khanyakwezwe Henry Dlamini
	Samson Msunduzeni Dlamini
	Elias Sipho Dladla
Mphumalanga:	Mageja Masilela (NNLC)
	Thomas Bhekindlela Ngwenya (NNLC)
	Dr Ambrose Phesheya Zwane (NNLC)

some were in new positions: Prince Makhosini, Prime Minister; Zonke Khumalo, Deputy Prime Minister; Polycarp Dlamini, Minister for Works, Power and Communication; R.P. Stephens, Minister for Finance; Sishayi S. Nxumalo, Minister for Industry, Mines and Tourism; A. Khuseni Hlophe, Minister for Agriculture; Prince Masitsela, Minister for Local Administration; Dr Malabhane Nxumalo, Minister for Educaton. Prince Mfanasabili had been appointed to a new ministry, Commerce and Cooperatives. There were also three Ministers of State: – Foreign Affairs, Mhlangano S. Matsebula; Establishments and Training, Khanyakwezwe H. Dlamini; Education, Sipho E. Dhladhla; and two Assistant Ministers – Bhekimphi Dlamini, in the Deputy Prime Minister's Office, and Mndeni Shabalala, Ministry of Local Administration.

The King again appointed Prince Makhosini as Prime Minister. He 'had proved very able'. As in the first Parliament Sobhuza deliberately tried to mix the highly educated and the less educated, 'to yoke experienced oxen with the unbroken young', to include white Swazi with black Swazi, and to get a cross section of opinion by having a variety of people work together over particular issues. By sharing responsibility he hoped to stop factions from developing and to achieve the unity necessary for peaceful progress. People of different attitudes and personalities would be able to watch each other and check each other and the responsibilities of their positions would hopefully make them put the national good beyond their personal antagonisms.

When the names had been announced two were conspicuously absent from the new Cabinet – Leo Lovell and Mfundza Sukati. Lovell realized in advance that he would not be included and wrote a letter to the King thanking him for his previous appointment and saying that he was ready to rest but would do all he could if called upon. The Ngwenyama sent for him and received him most graciously and told him that though he had not called him previously for an audience, he had followed his speeches and appreciated what he had done.

Mfundza Sukati accepted the change in his fortune stoically. Though he objected to the fact that he had been arbitrarily and cruelly virtually evicted from his house by order of his successor, he made no complaint, and it is unlikely that the King knew of his humiliation. To me he said, 'This is not the work of the Ngwenyama but of my enemies for reasons I do not know and have not been told.' He

---

To the House of Assembly the King nominated Dr Malabhane Nxumalo, Reverend Robert Forrester, R.P. Stephens, Prince Mfanasibili, J. Springh Murphy and Princess Msalela. To the Senators elected by the Assembly (Polycarp Dlamini, Dr G.L. Msibi, Douglas Luhkele, M. Nhlabatsi, J.S. Mavimbela) he added Dr V.S. Leibbrandt, C.F. Todd, N. Tomlinson, Prince Mekiseni Dlamini, J. Mamba and Mrs Mary Mdziniso. Sir John Houlton had been prevailed upon to continue temporarily as President of the Senate for the first period with Senator J. Mamba as Deputy to the President.

had his suspicions: he was very friendly with certain whites, and perhaps too ready to grant licences and work permits to South Africans. But his loyalty and devotion to the King were unshaken and appreciated. Even after he had lost his position with the government, the King entrusted him with many tasks at different times and always recognized him as a brave fighter, with the courage to say what he thought irrespective of consequences.

The King came to Parliament on 2 June 1972 to give his speech from the throne. In it he hinted at new economic directions – increasing production through big producer-cooperatives on national farms and giving government a stake in the banks of the country. Economic sovereignty was essential for national sovereignty; and the achievement of the goals he had in mind required 'overcoming human weaknesses – lethargy, lack of the acquisitive spirit, lack of a spirit of experimentation and fear of the unknown'.

Superficially Parliament was set to continue as before but the presence of two NNLC members was a constant reminder of organized opposition and the atmosphere was frequently tense. In his maiden speech Dr Zwane attacked the government policy of trying to obtain loans from Great Britain 'to buy land which rightly belongs to the Swazi anyway', and also objected to the creation of the new ministry for which he said he could see no reason except to provide a job for the Minister he had defeated at Mphumalanga. The Prime Minister reacted to the criticism of the land policy with a sharply reasoned rebuttal, and he justified the new ministry. The rapid growth of industry had placed a heavy burden on the Minister who had formerly carried both industry and commerce, and commerce itself was logically linked with cooperatives which the King-in-Council had over many years advocated as a suitable form of organization compatible with Swazi traditional structure.

Hanging over parliamentary discussions was the issue of Ngwenya, whose seat remained empty. The NNLC had decided to fight his case. Ngwenya had come back to Swaziland and been arrested by the Swaziland police on instructions by the Deputy Prime Minister, charged with being in the country illegally, found guilty and sentenced to twelve days' imprisonment. Ngwenya applied to the High Court in Mbabane to set aside the order pronouncing him a prohibited Immigrant. His lawyer was Musa Shongwe, whose parents, B.B. Shongwe and Emily Nxumalo, were Sobhuza's close and trusted friends and kin. Shongwe briefed advocate David Soggott of Johannesburg, who had acted for Dr Zwane and the NNLC at the time of the strikes. Advocate Soggott approached the situation as a political trial in which his client was being victimized because he had defeated a member of the Imbokodvo. The fact that Dr Zwane and Mageja Masilela, the other two members of the NNLC winning trio, were both admitted to and sitting in Parliament, did not affect his charge. South African papers in which the case was given publicity repeatedly referred to Ngwenya as 'the member who had defeated the candidate of the majority royalist party.'

On 12 July Dr Zwane tabled a motion of no confidence in the government and stated that he would 'give a long litany' on its 'sins of commission'. But the only members present in the House were the Prime Minister, the Deputy Prime Minister, the Minister for Finance, the Minister for Local Administration, and four ordinary members, two of whom were the NNLC representatives. The Minister for Local Administration interrupted Dr Zwane to point out that 'we seem to have no quorum'. The Speaker had to agree and 'had no alternative but to adjourn the House until tomorrow'. But that tomorrow did not come; the House was adjourned 'until further notice.'

Factionalism had intensified within the Imbokodvo, some criticising the actions of the Deputy Prime Minister, others supporting him for taking such a strong stand. The King regretted the 'unhealthy political activity', and the danger of violence evident in the rest of the world seemed closer than before to Swaziland. A book with a bogus bomb found its way by a series of extraordinary and rather ludicrous incidents from the office of Mkhulunyelwa Matsebula, the King's Private Secretary, to the desk of the new Minister of Education, Dr Pym Dlamini. Matsebula said that when he saw 'two things like torch batteries inside a fat book that had arrived by post I thought it was a new way of writing', and he left it on his table to read later. Dr Pym Dlamini, a firm but unaggressive man whose general attitude was in sharp contrast to that of some of his colleagues, had recently won the approval of the King, who had given him a Swazi name of honour – *Godolwezimamba* (Victor over a Mamba) since he had settled a conflict his predecessor had not been able to resolve. When the King heard the story of the book he was shocked. He also said, 'Why wasn't the book shown to me? I would have liked to see it', but it was still with the police who were investigating.

There were also politicians from other countries and agents of foreign powers active in Swaziland. The South African Special Branch presented evidence, more or less convincing, of threats to the peace of Swaziland and in one case of an alleged plot to kill the King.[6]

Sobhuza did indeed, and with good reason, fear assassination. The position of King was charged with danger. His personal popularity might be of little protection. 'It is the word King that many people hate. They think of a King living in luxury with huge palaces. They would never think of a King walking barefoot, dressed in *mahiya*.' As

---

[6] This involved Lionel Nikane, member of a political party banned in the Republic who later trained as a guerrilla, returned to South Africa, was discovered by the Special Branch and fled to Swaziland for asylum. The Special Branch got their message to the Swaziland Ambassador in Nairobi. Nikane was put in prison in Swaziland. The Prime Minister resisted pressure from the Deputy Prime Minister and others to hand him over to the South African police. The King urged that Nikane speak the truth, and Nikane in a long statement describing his movements ended by asking 'Why should I want to kill the King?' Arrangements were finally made to have him flown to Sweden, where he had been promised asylum.

Matsebula commented, 'King to those who don't know, means tyrant. But we here know that the King alone keeps the whole together.'[7]

To outsiders, however, Sobhuza gave the impression that everything was fundamentally safe and stable. He did not go around with a heavily armed guard and he kept to his usual schedule of ritual and administrative activities. His load had become increasingly heavy, receiving ambassadors, diplomats, missionaries, technical experts, industrialists, educators, speaking to different interest groups and also dealing with that other essential side of Swazi Kingship, the affairs of the royal family, whose troubles were brought to him and with whom he spent many hours giving advice and at times, comfort. But his private life could still be private. He was not dogged by photographers or the press and Mkhulunyelwa Matsebula as his Private Secretary was both discreet and considerate. At many audiences which received no publicity, matters of confidence were discussed. So it was that Carl Todd brought along Sir de Villiers Graaff, leader of the United Party in South Africa, accompanied by his lawyer, and party secretary. Several councillors were present when the visitors were brought in, and for a while the talk was general; then the *libandla* was asked to leave. The King and his Prime Minister remained alone with Sir de Villiers Graaff and Carl Todd. Negotiations were going on with the Vorster government on the question of a homeland for the Swazi. The United Party was not in favour. 'We as a party have fought against this policy; we fear it is dangerous to have independent autonomous states whose historical backgrounds would tend to be inimical not only to South Africa but to the relationship between the homelands themselves. And when you get in addition the hostility of the Russians and the Chinese creeping in as they are in East Africa and West Africa, one fears what the effect may be.' In the conference with Sir de Villiers Graaff and Carl Todd, the King made it clear that he was in touch with Swazi chiefs and opinion in the Republic, and no commitment could be made without their support.

The King's next interview was with Reverend Bhengu, head of the Assemblies of God, and two of his local ministers. Reverend Bhengu had returned from an International Conference of Independent Churches held in Canada. This interview was devoted to an interpretation of the scriptures as well as the role of the church in politics; it ended with a prayer for peace. No sooner had Reverend Bhengu departed than the new Minister of Works, Power and Communication, Dr Malabhane Nxumalo, arrived carrying a copy of a Johannesburg newspaper, the *Rand Daily Mail*, with headlines on

---

[7] At a meeting of African leaders President Kaunda of Zambia had referred to Sobhuza as 'his father', whereupon Quett Masire, the Vice President of Botswana, rebuked him for calling a King 'father' and went on to say 'we don't want kings'. Quett Masire was the candidate who had lost his seat against an opponent who was a chief; President Sir Seretse Khama, valuing Masire's ability, had appointed him Vice President.

Swaziland's Ambassador's 'Banking Adventure', a risky venture, from which the Swaziland government was subsequently obliged to disassociate itself publicly.

It had become the practice for the nation to celebrate the King's birthday at different centres. The festivities in 1970 had been at Nhlangano, and in 1971, the 50th year of his reign publicised as 'The Jubilee Year', at Siteki. This was the first time that the Swazi Guard of Honour, drawn from the Royal Swaziland Police Force, fired their rifles in a dramatic volley. In 1972 he celebrated his birthday with the usual colourful ceremony at Ntfonjeni. The house, modern, modest, secluded and comfortable, was made ready for him. Some of the younger Queens and children stayed in the house, others in the more traditional quarters of the historic royal village. They would be there for some two weeks and he ordered that cattle be slaughtered in the *sibaya*. On some days long lines of women arrived singing, carrying on their heads bowls of home-brewed beer or pumpkins or other foods as voluntary tribute for general consumption. Everyone was supposed to be happy and appropriately fed.

Visits like this to royal villages were his holidays but they were always working holidays and that year not a day passed but he was engaged with councillors, members of Parliament, princes, chiefs, advisors. Some slept in the barracks or in neighbouring villages and others drove from Mbabane and back the same evening. Everyone wanted to see him. One ambassador from overseas waited three days and two nights, sleeping in his car, and when I asked if he was losing patience received the reply, 'Of course not; when I see him I will be so glad.' Events at home and abroad required his attention and he kept himself informed through radio and newspapers brought up to him from Mbabane.[8]

He spent hours with the new Minister of Justice, Polycarp Dlamini, sitting on the ground in the sunshine in the private section of the *sigodlo*, studying papers, considering the advice received from lawyers with whom he was again in consultation on how to deal with the crisis created over the interpretation of citizenship. The Constitution, he repeated to me, was 'a confusion'. It was indeed a riddle with contradictions. 'It begins by saying that Swaziland is a sovereign kingdom, but when it comes to making changes there are entrenched provisions and 140 specially entrenched provisions for almost every one of its clauses; the lawyers can't agree amongst themselves.'

While he worked late into the night others were behaving 'with little

[8] On 24 July 1972, I sent a message through laZwane (the Queen who was acting as his messenger) that I too hoped to see him. He sent back the reply that as soon as Matsebula came we should go to the main house. Matsebula arrived bringing with him a big batch of the Sunday papers and together with Moses Mnisi, the liaison officer, formerly also a teacher, we went to the house. The meeting was pleasant and informal. He discussed various gossip items in the African papers and asked Matsebula to read him the report on a speech by Chief Gatsha Buthelezi criticising the apartheid policy in South Africa. At the end he commented, 'It is not wise to make a noise if it has no effect.'

sense of responsibility', and even people in whom he had great faith were 'thinking selfishly'. There were complaints that many people had received no food and on inquiring into this he found that not only more cattle had been killed than he had specified but much of the meat that should have gone to the people had been salted off by a few officials in charge. This was the final straw to a goodly number of irritations. 'Then,' as a friend put it, 'the lion roared.' A celebration feast and dance which had already been announced over the radio were cancelled. No explanation was given but everyone knew that he must be extremely angry. He did not lightly break a promise nor shirk a commitment.

From Ntfonjeni he went to Nkambeni to open a school built entirely by local effort. The area was under the young chief Madzanga, direct descendant of Chief Zidze of the Ndwandwe whose daughter had been main Queen of King Sobhuza I, and mother of King Mswati. Madzanga's own mother was the late Princess Sisila, Sobhuza's daughter by Lomacala Mgunundvu, and Madzanga had grown up at Lozitha and was educated at the National School at Matsapha. The first school at Nkambeni had been built some forty years back by Mgcobeya Nxumalo, father of the Minister of Industry, Sishayi Nxumalo. The King, invited by the community at the request of the Minister of Education, had consented partly because of kinship but mainly because 'it showed the development and the ability of the Swazi to build for themselves without outside help'. He did not want his people to accept charity; he always emphasized that if help were offered it should not be at the price of self-respect and dignity. Among the large number of notables, Swazi and non-Swazi, present were foreign experts – two Germans, a Swede, two Egyptians, a Czech, and two Englishmen – who were in the country as economic advisers.[9]

A few days later when he opened a secondary school at Zombodze – the area in which he had spent his childhood – the visitors included local representatives of the United Nations Development Programme, the British High Commissioner, the American and Portuguese Consuls, former British colonial servants who had settled in the country, as well as senior princes and old school friends. In his speech he said how pleased he was that the performance by the school children included traditional songs and dances and he also spoke of the traditional discipline which had been part of his own education.

The anniversary of independence was close and the elaborate

---

[9] One German was a U.N. adviser on economic affairs, and the other was also a representative of the West German government. The Swede was head at that time of the National Industrial Corporation; the two Egyptians were both U.N. officials, one working on tourism, the other on the process of extracting alcohol from molasses; the Czech was working on development of ceramics; one Englishman was a newly appointed Project Manager of Small Enterprise Development Corporation (SEDCO); the other was working on commercial uses of sugarcane by-products. After the school celebration the Minister of Industry invited the advisors and a couple of others to his house at Nkambeni. He made it clear that the message of the King was the guideline for the whole country.

arrangements were being handled by Prince Masitsela, as Minister of Local Affairs. Sobhuza never referred in public to the case of Ngwenya, which was occupying the time and thought of many of his people.

On the 29 August, a week before the actual anniversary, the Chief Justice of the Swaziland High Court, Judge Pike, sitting together with Judge Johnstone, declared in a 14-page judgment that Ngwenya was a Swazi citizen. There was deep consternation in many quarters and though the case could still be brought before the Swaziland Appeal Court, the King-in-Council realized that the judges would start off with the same assumptions and the same legal criteria.

The independence ceremonies were spectacular and no outsider would have suspected that there were any internal anxieties, or external tragedies. Independence Day itself was clear and sunny and the police kept order with competence and courtesy. The Ndlovukazi Zihlathi was too ill to attend, but standing in for her was laMatsebula, the King's ritual Queen, and with her in the assigned car was laZwane, mother of Betfusile who had stood again as an NNLC candidate and been defeated. In a separate car came Fikelephi Masuku with Lomzoyi Ndwandwe; the other Queens rode in the royal bus. When the King arrived, heralded by whistles and praises, he was not in the glory of the costume worn on the main day of the big *Ncwala* but in ordinary finery.

His speech that year was rich in subtle allusions: 'Our goal is to build on the foundations of the past a nation independent in spirit, secure in economy, and rich in culture, and a country in which every individual will strive to be worthy of citizenship. Our task is not easy ... Part of our strength lies in our persistence and faith and our approach is to work so softly and quietly that even our critics have been puzzled ... Let those who criticize our actions do so not from self-interest nor with evil intent but with genuine love for the country and respect for its people and an honest desire to help reconstruct the institutions of the future.'

In the afternoon he again received credentials and gifts from ambassadors who came to him at Embo, and in the evening he hosted the dinner at the Royal Swazi Hotel. No references were made to the news that had come through that morning of the murder of Israeli athletes at Munich, though it brought the violence as well as tragedy in the outside world close to home since Swazi runners were participating in the Games, and the Gcina youth, who had given a dazzling and colourful performance in the Somhlolo Stadium, were trained by an Israeli. He and the two Israeli advisors of the youth camp had carried out their duties until the end, masking their deep distress. The Ngwenyama commented to me later, 'They are indeed men. They cannot give up. There is too much to do. We must all continue to strive for peace.' And he elaborated on the ingredients that went into the making of peace.

It was these sentiments which he charged his emissaries to express abroad as well as at home. At the United Nations, Mhlangano Matsebula, Minister of State for Foreign Affairs and leader of the Swaziland delegation, told the General Assembly with the eloquence of sincerity unmarred by rhetoric, 'Swaziland would like to see all the oppressed people freed in the shortest possible time. This country feels that all people have a God-given right to self-determination. Denial of this right is not only wrong but inhuman. But the peaceful settlement of disputes is paramount and Swaziland cannot associate itself with any form of violence anywhere as a means of settling disputes. Interference by outside force is wrong. Violence whether in Northern Ireland or Africa, where some groups have used it as a major tool in a short-cut to power, must be condemned. And particularly violence in its global manifestations, as air piracy or hijacking, terrorism and kidnapping. These things are evil and uncivilized and divert natural resources from being channeled into means of improving the quality of life' (*Times of Swaziland*, October 1972).

Work on peaceful constitutional changes became increasingly urgent. At the annual conference of the NNLC, held on October 7-8, a motion of confidence in the leadership was passed and Ngwenya was elected one of the officers. A meeting of the House of Assembly had been called by the Speaker for 11 October on previous instructions from the Prime Minister. In terms of Judge Pike's decision, Ngwenya could take his place in Parliament. A senior expatriate police officer anticipating a possible assault on opposition members brought down a contingent of some 80 men. This could have provoked the very situation it was essential to avert – a fight between the *emabutfo* and the police. Sobhuza instructed his people not to respond with violence. The parliamentarians were in the House. When the Speaker wished to open the meeting, only Dr Zwane and Masilela – the two NNLC members – were present. All the Imbokodvo members stayed in their rooms. The Clerk rang the bell. They made no move. After a long wait, the Speaker 'regretted that there was no quorum,' and adjourned the meeting 'to a date and time to be fixed by the chair'.

Local newspapers reported the Imbokodvo action as a 'boycott'. The King, as well as the Cabinet, objected to the term. Who, he asked, were they boycotting? Themselves? The orders of the King? No. It was simply a technique to avoid violence and signify disapproval.

Two weeks later the King came to Parliament to celebrate United Nations Day, recognized as a new public holiday. Before a crowd of some 2,000 he spoke of the many historic events enacted on that site and expressed his hopes for the fulfilment of the high ideals of the United Nations.

When Parliament finally met on 13 November, a legal solution to the citizenship dispute was presented. An Immigration (Amendment) Bill, tabled by the Deputy Prime Minister under a Certificate of

Urgency, provided for the establishment of a special tribunal of five to decide cases of doubtful citizenship. The members of the tribunal would be appointed by the Prime Minister and an appeal could be lodged with him. The verdict would then be final and would also supersede and render ineffective any previous judgments of the courts.

The justification the Deputy Prime Minister gave for the tribunal having such extensive powers was that cases of citizenship 'often involved matters relating to traditional customs with which our courts are not familiar ... Moreover, we are anxious to protect our courts against the criticisms of the public in respect of decisions which although probably sound in law and in accordance with the evidence placed before the courts at the time do not in fact accord with our own people's views and our own knowledge of the facts. Such criticisms can only lead to a disrespect for our courts and their decisions. And I need hardly emphasise how important it is that such a situation should be avoided.' (House of Assembly, Reports of Debate 13/11/72, p. 270). In seconding the Bill, the Minister of State for Foreign Affairs, now back in Swaziland, pointed out that government was trying to meet the difficulties of the very delicate question of citizenship 'in a legal manner'.

Strong criticism of the Bill was voiced by Dr Ambrose Zwane, who raised two major objections. First, that the power of deciding who came into the country and who went out 'is reserved for the Prime Minister'. He did not elaborate on this. Dr Zwane as well as others wondered at the wisdom of this since the traditional right of accepting or rejecting subjects was vested in the King. Was the Prime Minister usurping the authority of the King? Dr Zwane also challenged the House's power over the rights of the individual entrenched in the Constitution, to make laws not subject to the jurisdiction of the courts. How much had been agreed to by the King? Did he know what he was being asked to sign? The Attorney General, David Cohen, responding to the challenge of Dr Zwane, specifically avoided comment on the political merits and demerits of the Bill, and limited himself to its legality. Very cautiously he gave as his considered opinion that the Bill did not intend to change the Constitution, and he compared the Tribunal to any other quasi-judicial body, 'such as the Liquor Licensing Board', the decision of which was not likely to be appealed in the High Court, 'though if it were to act in an arbitrary or unconstitutional and illegal manner, it would be subject to review'. So he had advised the government that the Bill was not inconsistent with the Constitution, it did not attempt to change the Constitution, and the question of the entrenched clauses did not arise.

The Bill passed all three readings in both Houses within thirty hours and was taken by the Prime Minister to the King. He already knew the contents, and having previously received the official reassurance of the Attorney General, gave his consent. The Bill immediately became law, the members of the Tribunal had already been selected, and their names were made public the following day, 13 November, in the *Government Gazette Extraordinary*.[10]

The first meeting was held at the Lobamba office that afternoon, but it would take some time finding witnesses and sorting out the evidence. All meetings were open to the public.

The Deputy Prime Minister's appeal against the decision of the High Court (lodged on 31 August) was still pending when, on 16 November, he further claimed an order setting aside the decision on the ground that it was obtained by perjured evidence. In response Ngwenya's lawyers applied to the High Court for an order against the Deputy Prime Minister and Chief Immigration Officer, on the grounds *inter alia* that the Immigration Amendment Act was *ultra vires* and the special tribunal unconstitutional.

On 1 December the controversial Land Speculation Bill became law and the members of the Board were gazetted.[11] The fears of many whites were allayed, and it was possible for the Prime Minister to describe the first reaction as 'a storm in a teacup'. At the same time another controversial Bill aimed at amending the Constitution by increasing the nominated members of the House of Assembly from six to ten, and of Senators by the same number, was before the House.

Tensions within the country were mounting. There had been mysterious accidents, and strange rumours heightened by a disturbing increase in murders practised by people, some in responsible positions, who believed that by using human flesh they could get more respect and influence for themselves. Among the accused was a chief and member of Parliament who was married to one of the King's daughters, and among the victims was one of his close nephews. No one seemed safe and no one immune from suspicion. Strains were obvious on all fronts. There was a pathological increase in theft, in disputes over property, in family conflicts, and threats of industrial unrest.

Cases had piled up in the courts and there was a shortage of judges and trained magistrates. All judges were in theory appointed by the King but continued to act in accordance with the advice of the Judicial Service Commission. Names of well-trained and highly-

---

[10] The President was J.F.G. Troughton, C.M.G., who had qualified as a barrister in England and practised law in Uganda before he came, in 1961, as a Magistrate to Swaziland. He had served as Acting Chief Justice (1965 and 1967), and though retired was at the age of 70 still very active on quasi-judicial bodies. He had the reputation of being a man of integrity, well versed in law, but harsh in his sentences. The other four were Swazi, all well known and holding responsible positions – Prince Sifuba, shrewd and widely-respected; Moses M. Mnisi, former teacher, then liaison officer; Chief Mlimi Maziya, an energetic progressive farmer; and Prince Sipho Dlamini.

[11] Members of the Land Control Board; Chief Sifuba Dlamini (Chairman) of Lobamba, Charles Dlamini (Kwaluseni), Maphevu Dlamini (Mbabane), Dr V.S. Leibbrandt (Nhlangano), Ben R. Forbes (Malkerns), and Paulos Ginindza (Mahlanya). The Land Control Appeals Board consisted of Michael Fletcher (Chairman of Big Bend), Prince Gabheni Dlamini (Mbabane), Ndawonye Sikhondze (Maloma), Martin Mdziniso (Manzini), B.M. Nsibandze (Mbabane), and H.K. Dlamini (Chief Immigration Officer).

respected African barristers suggested by the Swazi had been turned
down by the Commission. Early in December the Prime Minister
suffered a minor stroke. This was not made public and he appeared at
the *Ncwala*, but when he had a more serious attack his absence from
office was noted. The King had sent him for treatment to
Johannesburg (where Swazi officials received special expert care) and
on his return he recuperated at the home of Princess Gcinaphi, not in
his house in Mbabane.

On 9 January 1973, soon after the main public rites of the *Ncwala*
were ended, a new Chief Justice of the High Court (C.J. Hill) declared
that the establishment of the Tribunal was *intra vires* and dismissed
Ngwenya's case with costs. The government members were deeply
relieved. The opinion of the Attorney General appeared correct. The
hearings before the Tribunal continued. Several new witnesses had
been found, and on 29 January Mr Troughton, the Chairman,
delivered the Tribunal's unanimous decision, 'Ngwenya is not a
citizen of Swaziland. Although his ancestors may have been resident
in Swaziland, he himself was born in South Africa and therefore is not
a person who belongs to Swaziland in terms of the present law.' But
the matter was not at an end. Ngwenya appealed against the verdict of
Judge Hill to the highest court in the country, the Swaziland Court of
Appeal which had replaced the old British Privy Council.

Three leading South African judges, P. Schreiner, J.A. Milne and
J.A. Smit, heard the case in the Court of Appeal. Their decision,
expected on 17 March, was awaited with some anxiety. A routine
meeting of the nation had been called at Lobamba for the 19th. The
ex-servicemen were told to arrive a few days in advance and several
thousand people, anticipating a major constitutional announcement,
came to the capital. But the judges had not made their decision, and
the King, referring to 'the matter which they were expecting to hear
about,' told them that his 'advisers had not yet fully decided their line
of guidance'. He then posed to the nation a number of questions. 'Ask
yourselves (a) Are we really independent like the British, the French
or the Germans? Or are we nominally independent? (b) Do we have a
Parliament that is supreme like that of the British, the French and
other independent nations? Or do we have a token independence?'

On 27 March the answer came. Judge Schreiner, facing a crowded
and tense courtroom, declared the Immigration Amendment Act
'beyond the power of Parliament to enact, save in accordance with
Section 134 of the Constitution. Hence the Act was void.' What
should be done?

Parliament was due to meet early in April. The situation was
volatile. The King working with his Council reached a momentous
decision. On 12 April, at 2.15 p.m., Parliament unanimously passed a
resolution moved by the Prime Minister in the House of Assembly and
by the Minister of Justice in the Senate.[12] It declared that the

[12] In the House of Assembly the motion was supported by the Minister of Finance, the Minister

Constitution was 'unworkable', and called upon the King to consider ways and means of resolving the crisis. Individual members placed themselves 'entirely at the disposal of the King-in-Council'. The members of both Houses then went from Parliament to Lobamba. The King was expecting them. He had been waiting in the company of councillors including the Chief Immigration Officer and a minister of religion from South Africa who had come to visit and whom he asked to pray with him.

The Prime Minister and Cabinet fetched him to the *sibaya*, where a crowd of between 7,000 and 8,000 had assembled. For the first time Swazi soldiers equipped with modern weapons appeared before the public. It was a modern army albeit small in number, an army of defence, an army for protection, an army to show 'the dignity of the nation'. It was different in quality from the regiments of youths who now lived in royal barracks and acted as his messengers, described in traditional phraseology as 'the pillow of a King'. The King, barefoot and in *mahiya*, sat on the ground with his councillors – Prince Makhosini read the resolution of parliamentarians. Chief Sifuba Dlamini, prominent on the Swazi National Council, addressed the King in the name of 'the nation', which 'would like to be completely sovereign and independent and not have the Father Christmas type of independence'. The King remained seated; the microphone was adjusted. Slowly and quietly, he read this historic proclamation:

To all my subjects, citizens of Swaziland. Whereas the House of Assembly and the Senate have passed the resolutions which have just been read to us, and whereas I have given great consideration to the extremely serious situation which has now arisen in our country, I have come to the following conclusions:

(A) That the Constitution has indeed failed to provide the machinery for good government and for the maintenance of peace and order;

(B) That the Constitution is indeed a cause of growing unrest, insecurity, and dissatisfaction with the state of affairs in our country and an impediment to free and progressive development in all spheres of life;

(C) That the Constitution has permitted the importation into our country of highly undesirable political practices alien to and incompatible with the way of life in our society, and designed to disrupt and destroy our own peaceful and constructive and essentially democratic methods of political activity; increasingly this element engenders hostility, bitterness and unrest in our peaceful society;

(D) That there is no constitutional way of effecting the necessary amendments to the Constitution; the method prescribed by the Constitution itself is wholly impracticable, and will bring about that disorder which any constitution is meant to inhibit;

(E) That I and all my people heartily desire at long last, after a long constitutional struggle, to achieve full freedom and independence under a constitution created by ourselves for ourselves in complete liberty, without outside pressures. As a nation we

---

of Agriculture and the Deputy Speaker; in the Senate by Douglas Lukhele, Dr V. Leibbrandt and Dr Msibi.

desire to march forward progressively under our own constitution guaranteeing peace, order and good government, and the happiness and welfare of all our people.

Now therefore, I, Sobhuza II, King of Swaziland, hereby declare that in collaboration with my Cabinet Ministers, and supported by the whole nation, I have assumed supreme power in the Kingdom of Swaziland.

All legislative, executive, and judicial power is vested in myself, and shall for the meantime be exercised in collaboration with a Council constituted by my Cabinet Ministers.

I further declare that to ensure the continued maintenance of peace, order and good Government my armed forces, in conjunction with the Royal Swaziland Police Force, have been posted to all strategic places, and have taken charge of all government places and all public services.

I further declare that I, in collaboration with my Cabinet Ministers, hereby decree that: the Constitution of the Kingdom of Swaziland which commenced on September 6, 1968, is hereby repealed.

All laws, with the exception of the constitution hereby repealed, shall continue to operate with full force and effect, and shall be construed with such modifications, adaptations, qualifications and exceptions as may be necessary to bring them into conformity with this and ensuing decrees.

He then called upon the Attorney General 'to read out the decrees designed to provide for the continuation of administration, essential services, and normal life in our country' (*The Times of Swaziland* (Special Edition), 13/4/73).

The King's announcement was greeted by many with warm and obvious approval, and loud shouts of *Bayethe* and royal whistles. But there were some who were silent, and everyone listened intently to the Attorney General. There were to be no radical changes. All judges and other judicial officers, government officials, public servants, members of the police force, the prison service, and the armed forces were to continue in office; the Prime Minister, Deputy Prime Minister, Cabinet Ministers, Secretary to the Cabinet and Attorney General would remain in office at the discretion of the King; and all members of the Senate and the House of Assembly were entitled to receive the emoluments which they would have received but for the repeal. However, there were restrictions on individual freedom. Political parties were prohibited and political meetings, processions and demonstrations disallowed without prior written consent of the Commissioner of Police. The King-in-Council was given the power to detain a person without trial for a period of sixty days, which period could be repeated as often as deemed necessary in the public interest. This situation would be reviewed in six months' time.

The meeting ended quietly. The press outside of Swaziland reported – 'Swazi King Scraps the Constitution'; 'King Seizes Supreme Power'; 'Another African Dictatorship.' But inside Swaziland there was a general feeling of wait and see, and those who knew Sobhuza well trusted that returning to him and his Council full constitutional authority would indeed solve the difficulties that had become increasingly acute. It was not a military coup but an effort to turn nominal political independence into full sovereignty under a leader who had proved his wisdom and moral courage over the years, a man ready to listen to all sides before making a decision, a King who was not a tyrant, a King inspired by ideals of the best in a traditional African monarchy in which there was the interplay of councils and the King was the 'mouthpiece of the people'.

I came to Swaziland a few days later. It had been such a peaceful transition that had I not read the newspapers I would have been unaware that a change had taken place. As usual I went first to Lobamba to greet the Queen Mother Zihlathi. The village was quiet and tranquil. A guard in a pill box sauntered to meet me and inquired what I wanted. We did not know each other but somebody else came up and recognised me and we went along to the Great House. Zihlathi was very, very ill. We talked of family affairs; the state of the country was something that had passed her by. I then went to my friends, the Queens. There too nothing seemed to have changed. But one of them stated as a matter of fact 'Kingship has returned.' When I went to see the Prime Minister he was in his office as usual and he explained that government would be through the King by the King, with the ministers forming part of his Council; and the Attorney General would continue to draft the Bills. The following day I visited the Queens at Masundvwini. The King was sitting in the garden with B.B. Shongwe, father of the attorney who had appeared for Ngwenya. The relationship between the two friends seemed as good as ever. We talked about children, their choice of career, but did not try to foretell the future.

Epilogue

Three years have passed since the Westminster-styled constitution was repealed and the full burden of sovereignty was placed on Sobhuza at the request of the Swazi National Council and the two Houses of Parliament. He did not desire, or attempt, to convert his new position into a dictatorship. He would not rule by arbitrary fiat or autocratic decree, but, as far as possible, by decisions reached after consultation and deliberation. Much of the machinery of government has been retained. The Cabinet, officially renamed the Council of Ministers, continues to meet regularly; the Inner Council of the Swazi National Council[1] is involved in constant discussion, and new legislation generally initiated by the appropriate minister and drafted by the attorney general is submitted to Sobhuza at various stages. He has authority to accept, amend, or reject proposals but, knowing that there is no public discussion, he is more careful than ever not to sign any document blindly or impetuously, and insists on trying to understand the technicalities and the possible effects. The pressure on him has become increasingly heavy; unfinished work is mounting, important decisions are postponed, the demands of ritual performances become more exhausting.

The new Constitution which he had promised to provide is proving more difficult than he had anticipated. It was easy enough to state general guidelines and principles. It was much more difficult to make these specific. He decided to attempt to produce the ideal Constitution by stages. First he appointed a Royal Constitutional Commission, under the chairmanship of Polycarp Dlamini, as Minister of Justice,[2] to inquire into fundamental principles of Swazi history and culture, as well as the modern principle of constitutional and international law with which they needed to be harmonised. He insisted that the inquiry be thorough, some thought too thorough. In addition to inviting and receiving suggestions, the commission held regional meetings throughout the country, and, having sampled local

[1] The members of the Inner Council (*Liqoqo*) included: Ngangenyoni Tfwala, Chair; Chief Pica Magagula; Councillors Maboya Fakudze and Gaulela Zwane; and of the Royal family: Princes Sifuba, Ncabaniso and Mkhatjwa (a son of Sobhuza). Membership in the Liqoqo has always been somewhat flexible and the number not as rigidly circumscribed as for the Cabinet.

[2] The other members were R.P. Stephens, Dr George Msibi, Makobha Gamedze, Ndleleni Gwebu and J.F.G. Troughton; the Attorney General, David Cohen, as professional advisor; and Arthur Khoza as Secretary. Swaziland Government Gazette No. 6-7, 1973.

opinions, sent selected members to other countries in Africa – Malawi, Zambia, Kenya and Tanzania – as well as to Israel, England, Switzerland, and Denmark, to see other systems at work and learn from them. The report, which was finally presented to the King in July 1975, was not made public, but, on 26 November, he appointed, as a second stage, a Constitutional Advisory Committee under the chairmanship of A. Khuseni Hlophe, Minister of Agriculture, to make more definite suggestions for the actual Constitution based, it would be assumed, on the findings of the Commission.[3] Months went by, and it was not until July 1976 that the confidential recommendations (also not published) were handed to the King. The third stage – the appointment of a drafting committee – still remains.

Sobhuza has asked the people to be patient. He likens his position to that of a man who is carrying a clay pot of such value that he himself has to be carried lest he stumble and fall and the treasure break. There are some who tell him not to hurry, that there is no need to rush, that, in effect, the present system is working well enough, that a Constitution is indeed in operation, that laws are passed more expeditiously, without long-winded debates in Parliament; they say quite simply, 'As long as Sobhuza is with us, there is no need for a written Constitution.' Others, mainly those with less access to the King but not necessarily less loyal, point out that the public is presented with legislation on the most contentious issues without any opportunity for criticism; that every member of the repealed parliament is still (after three years) receiving full pay; that there are currents of uncertainty and dissatisfaction in key sections of the service; and that the formalisation of a Constitution is essential before patience is exhausted. But the 77-year-old King will not let himself be hurried or coerced; and postponement is a timely strategy when a rash decision on a fundamental controversy may divide the nation caught in the smouldering passions of a wider political contest.

At meetings of the OAU and UN Sobhuza's ambassadors and envoys express a viewpoint consistent with the principles of his policy at home: try to resolve problems by peaceful negotiations and compromise, condemn outside aggression, apply force only as an ultimate resort. Obviously this does not endear him to the more aggressive radicals either in his own country or abroad. But in Swaziland there have been no massacres, no cases of torture, and though the Sixty Day Detention Act has on occasion been invoked, the courts continue to administer the law and the jails are generally empty of political prisoners. The vote of the Swazi at the United Nations is based on principled directives, not slavish acceptance of popular resolutions by a majority.

[3] The other members were William Magongo, Prince Gabheni, Fred N. Dlamini, Sishayi Nxumalo, Prince Mahhomu, Jethro Mamba, with Martin B. Mdziniso as Secretary. This Committee was not gazetted.

The success of the long drawn-out struggles in Angola and
Mozambique against colonial domination by Portugal opened
possibilities for comparable dramatic changes in the structure of
power in the white settler regimes of South Africa and Rhodesia. The
OAU recognized Frelimo as the legitimate party in Mozambique. Its
leader, Samora Machel, established his political base at Maputo
(formerly Lourenço Marques) and proclaimed a policy of radical
socialism. With Swaziland geographically wedged between South
Africa and Mozambique it became both more difficult and more
necessary for Sobhuza not to jeopardize his people's independence by
committing them to action on either side. However, he had never
supported apartheid as an ideology and had always stood for human
dignity and self-determination.

Swaziland was officially invited to the independence celebrations in
Maputo, 20 June 1975. Sishayi Nxumalo and Dr Malabhane Nxumalo
were welcomed as official representatives and Swaziland's gifts – ten
head of fine cattle and money to build a clinic – were appreciated. A
request to establish firm and friendly diplomatic relationships through
an embassy in Maputo was granted. For this difficult and delicate
position Sobhuza selected Dr Msindazwe Sukati, deeply experienced
in diplomacy through his position as Liaison Officer in the critical
colonial years, and, subsequently, as Swaziland's first Ambassador to
the United States. On 29 November 1975, he presented his credentials
to President Machel on behalf of Sobhuza and the Kingdom of
Swaziland.

Mozambique could become a centre of international concern and
potential confrontation. Representatives from an increasing range of
countries, with East Germany, Russia, Cuba at one extreme and West
Germany, America, England at the other had established or planned
to establish offices in Maputo. Swaziland is physically close and
directly involved through its use of the railway and the harbour for its
main exports, and the shared interest in rivers that flow across
common borders. With the exodus of the Portuguese, food in their
former towns fell into short supply; Swaziland stores were relatively
well stocked and the economy was stable. The Swazi, struggling to
establish themselves in commerce, were threatened by an influx of
Portuguese as competitors and potential settlers hostile to Frelimo.
Immigration was a sensitive issue. Many people wanted to come into
Swaziland; few were eager to leave.

It had been a hard year. The Ndlovukazi Zihlathi died on 22 January
1975, and Seneleleni – co-wife and sister by the same father,
Vanyane of Elwandle – had been installed in her place. She had
submitted unwillingly; the high office carried heavy risks, she would
be the fourth Queen Mother to reign with Sobhuza. There had been
too many deaths, and inexplicable accidents. The governor of
Lobamba had been dismissed. The *Ncwala* was approaching; never
before had its function been more explicit – to protect the King,

symbol of the nation, against rivals from within, and enemies from without. At Lobamba, soldiers in uniform swelled the regiments of traditional warriors, and there were ominous and totally untoward happenings. On the Day of the Bull a son of Sobhuza shot himself in gruesome style, and on the following day there was a terrifying storm. The heavens roared and raged. But the ritual had to continue.

The whole world was in turmoil. The African continent was torn by war. Could the voice of reason still be heard? Soon after the grim *Ncwala* a Swazi delegation attended an emergency meeting called by the Organization of African Unity at Addis Ababa on the post-independence crisis in Angola. Three groups struggling for leadership, each with its foreign superpower backers. Sobhuza's views on the situation were expressed by Sishayi Nxumalo, spokesman for the delegation: Swaziland's main objective was to seek peace for the people of Angola; the Angolans should decide their future for themselves. To call for the withdrawal of one group of foreign soldiers only would not solve the problem, since wherever one of the superpowers and its allies were involved the other superpowers would also be involved. And each had its own self-interests. Moreover, by recognizing one of the warring groups, that group would be given licence to kill the others, and, in Sishayi's words, 'military aid to kill one's own people cannot be justified in any circumstances'.

Sobhuza hoped Mozambique would never become a second Angola; and that Swaziland could retain its neutrality. For the first time since 1908, following the division of land under the Concession Proclamation, sufficient maize had been produced in Swaziland for it not to have to be imported from South Africa, One thousand bags were sent as a gift to the people of Mozambique, and Sobhuza, through Dr Sukati, invited Machel to come to see him on a personal visit. The President accepted the invitation.

The meeting took place on 28 April 1976 at Sobhuza's secluded residence, Ehlane, eighteen miles from the border post of Lomahasha. Machel was met at the border and escorted to the house, where Swaziland police provided a guard of honour. Sobhuza met him with his usual warm smile. Machel responded. Sobhuza was in simple everyday national dress, Machel in western civilian attire. They clasped hands, and Machel, who had spent his boyhood and young manhood in the south, greeted the Ngwenyama in siSwati. As the two leaders stood side by side, a band of the Royal Swaziland Police played the National Anthems of both countries. In his welcoming remarks the King hailed the President and the people of Mozambique as 'heroes of Africa' in regaining their lost independence. After inspecting the Guard of Honour, the two men, each with a few trusted councillors, went inside the house. They were relaxed, the whole atmosphere was jubilant; bards who were reciting ancient epics would also record this historic meeting for posterity. At the end of the discussions, which lasted some two hours, Sobhuza presented his guest with a fine ox, a Swazi shield, a spear and knob stick, explaining that 'according to Swazi custom if a friend pays a visit, a beast is slaughtered for him'. As to the shield: 'This is what our fathers (including President Machel's) carried in olden days.' He walked with Machel to his car and when they said goodbye expressed the hope that they would meet again in friendship.

Though there is greater understanding and more goodwill than before, there remains the realistic apprehension that the fighting between Rhodesia and Mozambique, and the unrest in South Africa, may be a prelude to a more extended battlefield from which the Swazi could not escape. Sobhuza's dilemma would then be acute. Much as he desires peace, he has had to anticipate war. The small modern army, which made its first public appearance in 1973, has been increased in number and efficiency, but, compared with the forces available to neighbouring countries, it is insignificant and poorly equipped. It remains the Umbutfo Swaziland Royal Defense Force and, as its name implies, is designed for internal security, to protect not to attack. It cannot fight two strong opposing sides; and Sobhuza sees the price of alliance with either as intervention in non-military affairs. He is aware of the extent of existing economic neo-colonialism; he does not want ideological domination or, in his words, 'colonialism of the mind!' When he dismissed the regiments at the *Ncwala* he referred to the reputation of the Swazi as brave fighters in the past and indicated that they should be prepared to defend their hard won independence.

In November 1975, at about the same time that his ambassador, Dr Sukati, presented his credentials to President Machel, Sobhuza appointed the first Swazi Commander of the Army. His choice was Maphevu Dlamini. In March 1976 he also made Colonel Maphevu Prime Minister. He had prepared the nation for a change. At a public meeting months before he had thanked Prince Makhosini for his excellent service and indicated that he would soon be replaced. But the choice of Maphevu came as a complete surprise to many. There had been much speculation and many aspirants. Maphevu's name was not among them. Many asked, 'Who is this Maphevu? What are his qualifications for such important posts?' He was not a soldier of the Second World War, he was not well-known in political circles, and though he was of the royal Dlamini lineage he was not in the direct line of succession. But the choice was that of the king and could not be gainsaid.

The more people learned of Maphevu, the better they understood the reasons behind the selection. On his father's side he was a descendent of Mswati's brother, Ndwandwa; and on his mother's side he was from Gocweni, near Zombodze, home of the progressive Vilakati, and the base of Grandon, the stimulating and controversial teacher of Sobhuza's boyhood. Maphevu, who had been born in 1922 (the year that Sobhuza took the Swazi land case on appeal to Britain), heard oral history at the source, received a fair education at local schools, and was also trained in the values and discipline of regiments stationed at royal villages. At Lozitha, where his maternal uncle, Makweleni Raymond Vilakati, was Sobhuza's private secretary, Maphevu used the King's office as a classroom for teaching children to read and write. He had later been employed in the Republic, and on returning home in 1951 entered the Colonial Service not as a white collar worker but as a veterinary assistant. After independence he became Chief Stock Inspector, a responsible but back room position in a country where cattle were the prized wealth of the majority. He had also served on two important public committees: in 1968 the King appointed him Chairman of the Tibiyo (Mineral) Fund and in 1971 member of the Land Speculation Control Board. He had won the respect of those who worked with him for his integrity, seriousness and absence of interest in intrigue. He did not speak much, but was a good listener and strong enough to express his own opinions clearly and honestly.

To Sobhuza, warfare was but one of the functions of an army, and drill was but part of a soldier's peacetime duties. Maphevu, who was not a career soldier, had joined the Reserves of the Defence Force, spending his weekends at the barracks. He had started as a private, his promotion had been rapid. Sobhuza had on several occasions condemned military coups and was suspicious of military government; he was sure of Maphevu's loyalty. Hopefully the monarchy could be secure and the country peaceful, but prepared. Sobhuza realized that idle armed soldiers might be a national danger and their upkeep an economic liability. In the past every citizen was a soldier; now it was necessary that peacetime soldiers again serve as useful citizens. They should be encouraged in their patriotism by developing the national land. Farms bought with money from the Mineral Fund could be developed as model settlements. This was the topic Sobhuza discussed with Maphevu the evening before he announced his appointment at a special meeting in the *sibaya*. It was like Sobhuza not to make his main announcement immediately, but to speak of this and that for a long time while everyone waited expectantly. According to Maphevu he had no idea that he had been chosen and was totally unprepared. When he heard his name he could not believe it. People were staring at him. He felt confused, and when police came and escorted him out of the meeting he 'felt like a prisoner'.

Sobhuza, who had chosen him over all the Ministers and public servants, knew everything that he wanted to know about Maphevu – his family background, his education, his service, his sense of responsibility and his personal life. The fact that he had no experience as a politician and had not been involved in controversies was to his advantage. He was an outsider, not part of any clique. When introducing him, Sobhuza said that naturally he did not expect

Maphevu to be perfect in his duties, and he charged every Swazi to assist him by offering constructive criticism wherever and whenever necessary and not keep quiet if they realized that he was not doing things the right way but approach him directly and state their grievances. He also advised the new Prime Minister to approach the outgoing Prime Minister for help and advice, and Sobhuza saw to it that both men were present when he and selected councillors met with President Machel. Soon after, Maphevu was sent on a tour of friendship to other African heads of selected states, and represented the Kingdom of Swaziland at the Summit Meeting of Unaligned Countries, held at Colombo, in Sri Lanka, in September 1976.

Sobhuza's imprint is clear: Swaziland has distinguished itself from its neighbours politically and culturally. Economically it is still striving for its own identity and security through such techniques as continued emphasis on localization at all levels, the introduction of its own currency stamped with his portrait and known as *Emalangeni*, its own postal system, its efforts at establishing foreign financed factories and industries (in spite of South African opposition and competition), its development of independent trade with outside countries, its membership in its own right on international boards, its active participation on Conventions, from some of which South Africa is deliberately excluded.

The 'Sobhuza approach' has a special appeal to chiefs of the so-called 'homelands' in the Republic, who see their position as somewhat similar to that of the Swazi towards the end of British control. To the criticism that Sobhuza has developed a cultural nationalism which could result in balkanization of peoples who were being drawn together by the process of industrialization Sobhuza's reply is simple – 'You must know yourself and respect yourself before you can join with another and claim your share in the benefits of development'. His advice to the chiefs who are being offered 'independence' by the South African government on its own conditions is that they should not be divided in their negotiations, but should work together for genuine independence in an atmosphere of sincere dedication to the benefit of the people.

Sobhuza's extensive family – the weft in the web of traditional kingship – is integrated into modern politics. His singularly beautiful daughters and granddaughters are being sought after by men of status not only in Swaziland but elsewhere. Their marriages are state occasions, their bride-wealth substantial. Their position as main wives in the homes of their husbands is assured, and Swazi influence extended. A week of celebration culminating in a grandiose reception at a five-star hotel in Johannesburg marked the marriage of Princess Dlalisile to Vusa Shabalala, son of one of the few very wealthy African businessmen in Johannesburg. More traditional but no less elaborate was the betrothal of Princess Mantfombi to Goodwill Zwelethini, King of the Zulu; of Princess Siphila to Cornelius, Crown Prince of the

Mabhoko; of Princess Gcebekile to Nyalunga, a Swazi Chief in the eastern Transvaal; of Lombekiso, Sobhuza's granddaughter, trained as a librarian in an American University, to Mpondombini, Crown Prince of the Transkei; and of Princess Msindvose to Pilane, Chief of the Bakgatla of Rustenberg in the Transvaal. Sobhuza's sons claim their own privileges, and produce their own problems. Most of those who are adult have more than one wife, and all their children increase the royal clan. Sobhuza knows that, particularly in the modern world, there is less security for a hereditary aristocracy, and much internal jealousy and friction.

As a natural father he would like his own children to be well provided for, and is deeply concerned that they receive an education which would entitle them to positions to which they aspire, but at the same time, as Father of the Nation, he does not wish them to have privileges and opportunities denied the more needy and deserving of his subjects.[4] In 1976 he again extended the number of scholarships to schools, universities, and technical colleges.

Over the past three years in which his responsibilities have increased, he has become less accessible and more isolated, but it is extraordinary how many people, young and old, still come directly to him for help and advice in their personal troubles.

Sobhuza has become a legend in his lifetime. Innumerable stories are told of his kindness, his generosity, his humour, his homespun wisdom, his love of children, his interest in the conservation of nature. The Swazi motto 'Siyinqaba', translated as 'We are the fortress', could now more aptly be interpreted as 'We are the sanctuary'. To him all life is precious; it should be preserved, not wantonly destroyed. He does not like anyone to kill even wasps or bees or snakes, and when one of his men killed an adder in the grounds of Masundvwini he asked in real anger, 'What right have you to destroy a creature that is going its own way? How do you know it was not coming to seek protection?[5] Ask yourself what harm was it doing. Snakes help kill mice and rats. Nature balances itself.' Masundvwini has been recently renovated, but pigeons, geese, ducks, peacocks and snakes remain undisturbed. He stays more frequently than before at the State House, Embo, near Lobamba, and it has become more like home, with extra rooms for his queens and children; villages closer by; the same Royal Palms that he admired at Masundvwini established in the garden; exotic birds in large cages in the front; and people of all

---

[4] In 1973 Swaziland opened its own University campus, linked with Botswana and, until 1976, with Lesotho. As Chancellor, Sobhuza continues his interest in advancing higher education.

[5] Various kinds of snakes are said to be manifestations of the ancestors, others are simply snakes as animals. The distinction is partly in the species, and partly in the symbolic behaviour of particular snakes. Mambas are associated most frequently with kings, elders, diviners and women.

ranks waiting to see him. His favourite retreat is Ehlane, where wild life is now protected.

Sobhuza has accepted the idea that the country needs 'a palace' befitting a modern kingdom. It would be one of the many enduring structures he would leave to future generations; it is not for his own personal pleasure and entertainment. The plans, drawn up by an imaginative architect from the Philippines employed in the Public Works Department, have been approved, and the foundations laid with due formality and ritual. It will be more than a royal residence; it will include offices for councillors of the nation, reception chambers, meeting rooms, a place for the guards. Physically it adjoins Lozitha, Sobhuza's first independent village and administrative headquarters, situated on the ridge of Lancabane with a superb view of the surrounding country. When the new palace was described to me as 'The new Lozithahlezi' I recalled the original meaning of the name – 'Sitting surrounded by enemies.' He knows he must still be on guard, perhaps more cautious than ever before. 'I feel,' he recently said, 'like a man sitting in my home facing a poisoned snake. I am trying to be very calm and avoid sudden movement. Meanwhile my friends outside the door are throwing stones at the snake. I am the one endangered, not they.' He has always had enemies, but has not been intimidated. He has had the courage to face them, the ability to persuade them, the strength to survive without abandoning his principles. Recently he has given his sanction to the building of an international airport in the hope that in the years to come the little landlocked country will be in more direct contact with the whole world.

Unremitting toil, constant anxieties, together with his age, have affected his health, and he is quite often ill, but he shows remarkable stamina in fulfilling state obligations. The Queens say he is an obstinate patient, refusing to rest, objecting to medicines and ignoring doctor's orders. On my last visit to Swaziland, in August 1976, he was very ill and I could not see him to say goodbye. Since he could not *khulula* (free me) by wishing me good luck and a safe journey in person, he sent gifts, chosen with characteristic care, for each member of the Kuper family: a beautifully carved walking stick for Leo, exquisite bead necklaces for Lahlekile and Ntombincane (the names he gave our two daughters), and a photograph of himself, with his signature, for me. It is the frontispiece of this book. Less than two weeks later he appeared for his usual strenuous and exhausting role at the 8th anniversary of Swaziland independence. The crowd, some 50,000, cheered wildly as he was driven round the arena. In the photograph taken that day he looks terribly tired; and he did not dance. Soldiers in battledress were more prominent than the warriors or the police and he himself was in formal 'parliamentary attire' – top hat, tails, pin-striped trousers – in his hand a thin, elegant wand. In his speech he appealed to all nations in the world to find a new and vigorous approach to peace and war; Swaziland was greatly perturbed by events in South Africa; dialogue was necessary, and he warned, 'Talk for the sake of talking cannot help developing nations.'

The problem of his successor is never openly discussed, though it lurks in the shadows of the minds of all interested in the future of his country and his people. No queen has been taken in such a way as to indicate publicly that she will be the Queen Mother, and no son has the right to claim that he is the Crown Prince. But who can replace Sobhuza? He holds a unique position in modern African history – a hereditary King who developed traditional institutions in winning independence from colonial rule by peaceful means, and who subsequently gained recognition for the Swazi by selectively retaining their own ideals and concepts of humanity.

Though the continuity of the nation does not depend on the living presence of a particular king, kingship has been the core of Swazi national identity. Times are changing and monarchies are generally considered less secure than in the past, but is a monarchy necessarily less democratic than a Republic, a president preferable to a King? To this hoary question philosophers and political scientists gave no single answer. But this particular study runs counter to a self-satisfied and unfounded belief current in many circles, particularly in the west, that a traditional African King is a tyrant, that African monarchy is tantamount to African despotism, that an anointed monarch is less representative of the wish of the majority than an elected President. We find in Swaziland a King who built a modern nation within a political system in which leadership was not sought after, in which self-promotion was not admired, in which individual competition and rivalry were considered destructive, in which consultation at different levels was essential, in which national interests were considered more important than the freedom of the King himself. Power and privilege are inherent in the Kingship; but for Sobhuza, his inherited position spelt responsibility, self-restraint, respect for others, and also the courage to express unpopular opinions for unselfish reasons. He has filled his position with humility and dignity, and stands out in modern history as a good King, a wise statesman, a gracious man.

BAYETHE!

January 1976

Postscript

Since the completion of this manuscript, King Sobhuza has moved a step further in producing a model of government more in keeping with the Swazi idiom than the British-designed constituion repealed in 1973. On 22 March 1977, he informed the nation of the imminent termination of the five-year period of office of members of the Parliament elected in 1972, and announced that as 'an experiment' a new team would be chosen through the *tinkundla* (regional committees) expanded in number to incorporate educated and uneducated, rural and urban dwellers. Implicit was the understanding that the new men would not be voted in by secret ballot but by the familiar method of nomination, public discussion and majority acclaim, and that the final list would be scrutinised and approved by the King himself. While some might condemn the system as a regression to a backward and authoritarian past, the majority of Swazi consider it a good way not only of maintaining cultural identity, but of promoting peaceful development. According to the latest bulletins, Sobhuza's health has improved and his spirit remains undaunted.

September 1977

APPENDIX I

Joint Rulers for the Past Eight Generations

Kings	Queen Mothers
Ngwane III (d. circa 1780)	laYaka Ndwandwe
Ndvungunye or Zikodze (d. circa 1790)	laKubheka Mndzebele
Sobhuza I or Somhlolo (d. 1839)	Somnjalose or Lojiba Simelane
Mswati or Mavuso (d. 1868)	(1) Tsandzile Ndwandwe (laZidze)
	(2) File Ndwandwe (laZidze)
Ludvonga (d. 1872)	Sisile Khumalo (laMgangeni)
Dlamini IV or Mbandzeni (d. 1889)	(1) Sisile Khumalo
	(2) Tibati or Madvolomafisha Nkambule (laMbandzeni)
Ngwane IV or Bhunu (d. 1899)	Labotsibeni or Gwamile Mdluli (laMvelase)
Sobhuza II	(1) Lomawa Ndwandwe (laNgolotjeni)
	(2) Nukwase Ndwandwe (laNgolotjeni)
	(3) Zihlathi Ndwandwe (laVanyane)
	(4) Seneleleni Ndwandwe (laVanyane)

The names in parentheses refer to the fathers of the women.

APPENDIX II

Sobhuza's Petition Addressed to the People of England, 1941

Your Petitioner submits that there is no moral justification for the interference with two main aspects of the life of the people:

(a)   the methods by which the Paramount Chief and the other Chiefs succeed to their respective offices;

(b)   the powers exercised by the Paramount Chief and other Chiefs.

Your Petitioner submits that these two aspects are fundamentally rooted in the native customs of the people and should in no way be interfered with unless clearly injurious to the welfare of the people. For any other reason to tamper with the ancient heritage of the Swazi nation would be to break faith with all that has gone before, with the guarantees given by the British Government and the reiterated promises of good faith.

If the proposed legislation were to be passed in the form suggested it would mean not only that complete despotic power of deposition of Chiefs, Sub-Chiefs and Headmen would be placed in the hands of the High Commissioner, but also that he would be able to refuse to recognise as Paramount Chief that person who by all the rights of native law and custom is the rightful Paramount Chief.

It would mean that the voice of one man without any responsibility in law to the nation could make and unmake at his will and pleasure, a system so tyrannical and of such far-reaching consequences that Your Petitioner submits, the British Government fighting as it is for the liberty of all freedom loving nations, would not allow such to be forced upon an unwilling people.

Furthermore the powers of the Paramount Chief, should the proposed legislation come to pass, will be but the reflection of what the High Commissioner desires. The Paramount Chief will but become the mouthpiece of the High Commissioner and his ancient rights will no longer exist. He will no longer be the sole trustee and representative of his people.

Your Petitioner says that the Swazi Nation is indeed aggrieved that this proposed state of affairs should even be suggested. The Nation looks upon the Paramount Chief as being placed in his high office by the people themselves, and as being the trustee of their ancient rights.

Your Petitioner and the National Council would accordingly be failing in their duty to their people if they did not protest against this further inroad on the rights and customs of the Swazi Nation.

Your Petitioner desires for himself and the Swazi Nation to assure the members of the British Parliament of the Nation's sincere desire to continue the good relations which have existed in the past with the British Government.

Your Petitioner accordingly humbly prays that Parliament will give effect to the aforegoing Petition by either passing legislation to remove the grievances of the Swazi Nation or by appointing a commission with judicial powers to consider the aforegoing Petition and in particular with regard to the following:

(a)   To give effect to the promises and pledges which from time to time have been given by representatives of Great Britain as to the internal independence of the Swazi Nation and the due recognition of the Paramount Chief and other Chiefs and their succession and powers, according to native law and customs.

(b) To reject the proposed new proclamations taking away such internal independence and depriving the Paramount Chief and the other Chiefs of their rights according to the said native law and custom.

(c) To restore to the Paramount Chief his heirs and successors in law, the title and interests in the Harrington concession and to enter into an agreement binding in law with the Paramount Chief regarding the revenues payable thereunder as well as to secure the liquidation of the Trust Fund created by Proclamation no. 9 of 1906.

(d) To secure that steps be taken to remedy the urgent needs of the Swazi Nation with reference to land so as to save the people from retrogression and the much overstocked land from denudation and soil erosion.

(e) To secure that so far as possible the terms of all concessions be made to conform to the terms of the original grants with a view to protecting the rights of the natives in accordance with the intention of the grantor.

(f) To restore to the Paramount Chief and the Swazi Nation, title and interest in reversion over all concessions and that the radical title in all land be revested in the Swazi Nation.

(g) To restore to the Paramount Chief and the Swazi Nation its rights to land and minerals which have been taken away and vested in the High Commissioner as Crown Lands and Minerals.

(h) To authorise the definition of the Status of Swaziland under the provisions of the Convention of 1894 and the Protocol of 1898, such to be a declaration of the position of Swaziland under the Constitutional Law of the British Empire.'

(The Petition of Sobhuza II, Paramount Chief of Swaziland and the Council of the Swazi Nation, November 1941, sections 52-60, pp. 46-50.)

Bibliography

Bibliography on Swaziland, by John Webster and Paulus Mohome, published in 1968 by Syracuse University; Maxwell School of Citizenship and Public Affairs, provides a fairly comprehensive list of references until 1967. More recent publications also consulted are included in the comprehensive bibliography in *Swaziland; The Dynamics of Political Modernization*, Christian P. Potholm, University of California Press, 1972, pp. 157-176; and in *Historical Dictionary of Swaziland*, John J. Grotpeter, Scarecrow Press, New Jersey, 1975, pp. 198-243.

The following list is a brief selection of writings relevant to this biography. Reference to specific Reports by various government departments, official commissions and debates in the House of Assembly and Senate appear only in Footnotes.

Books

Barber, James. *South Africa's Foreign Policy* 1945-1970. London: Oxford University Press, 1972.

Best, Alan C. *The Swaziland Railway*. East Lansing: Michigan State University, 1966.

Bryant, A.T. *Olden Times in Zululand and Natal*. London: Longmans Green, 1929.

De Kiewiet, C.W. *Anatomy of South African Misery*. London: Oxford University Press, 1956.

Doxey, G.V. *The High Commission Territories and the Republic of South Africa*. London: Oxford University Press, 1963.

Dundas, Sir Charles, and Ashton, Dr Hugh. *Problem Territories of Southern Africa*. Johannesburg: South African Institute of International Affairs, 1952.

Fair, T.J.D.; Murdoch, G.; and Jones, H.M. *Development in Swaziland*. Johannesburg: University of Witwatersrand Press, 1969.

Forbes, David. *My Life in South Africa*. London: Witherby, 1938.

Garson, Noel. *The Swaziland Question and the Road to Sea, 1887-1895*. Johannesburg: University of Witwatersrand Press, 1957.

Hailey, Lord. *The Republic of South Africa and the High Commission Territories*. London: Oxford University Press, 1963.

Halpern, Jack. *South Africa's Hostages: Basutoland, Bechuanaland, and Swaziland*. Baltimore: Penguin, 1965.

Holleman, J.F. (ed.). *Experiment in Swaziland:* Report of the Swaziland Sample Survey. Oxford University Press, Cape Town & New York, 1964.

Hyam, Ronald. *The Failure of South African Expansion 1908-1948*. London: Macmillan, 1972.

Hughes, A.J.B. *Swazi Land Tenure*. Natal: Institute for Social Research, University of Natal, 1964.

Kantorowicz, E.H. *The King's Two Bodies: A Study in Mediaeval Political Theology*. Princeton University Press, 1951.

Kuper, Hilda. *An African Aristocracy: Rank Among the Swazis*. London: Oxford University Press, 1947.

——. *The Uniform of Colour*. Johannesburg: University of Witwatersrand Press, 1947.

——. *The Swazi: A South African Kingdom*. New York: Holt, Rinehart, and Winston, 1963.

Leistner, G.M.E., and Smit, P. *Swaziland: Resources and Development*. Pretoria: African Institute of South Africa, 1969.

Matsebula, J.S.M. *A History of Swaziland*. Johannesburg: Longmans, Southern Africa, 1972.

Marwick, Brian. *The Swazi*. Cambridge: Cambridge University Press, 1940.

Nquku, J.J. *Amaqhawe Kangwane*. Marianhill, 1939.

Perham, Margery, and Curtis, Lionel. *The Protectorates of South Africa*. London: Oxford University Press, 1935.

Plaatje, Solomon T. *Native Life in South Africa*. London: P.S. King and Son (n.d. c. 1915).

Potholm, Christian, P. *Swaziland: The Dynamics of Political Modernization*. Berkeley: University of California Press, 1972.

Scutt, Joan. *Story of Swaziland*. Swaziland Printing & Publishing Co., 1966.

Stevens, R.P. *Lesotho, Botswana, and Swaziland: The Former High Commission Territories in Southern Africa*. New York: Praeger, 1967.

Walshe, Peter. *The Rise of African Nationalism in South Africa*. London: Hurst & Co., 1970.

Watts, C.C. *Dawn in Swaziland*. London: Society for the Propagation of the Gospel in Foreign Parts, 1922.

Manuscripts and mimeographed collections

Daniel, J., G.N. Simelane and V.M. Simelane (eds.) *Politics and Society in Swaziland*. UBLS Readings. Vol. Three. (Prototype only. Kwaluseni campus.) 1975.

Honey, de S.G.M. *A History of Swaziland* (n.d. c. 1928).

Marwick, A.G. *The Attitude of the Swazi Towards Government and Its Causes* (September 1955, Mbabane).

Ndwandwe, Sishayi Simon (ed.) *Politics in Swaziland, 1960-1968*. African Studies Programme, Occasional Papers No. 5. Johannesburg: Witwatersrand University, 1968.

The Swazi Pioneers (Compiled by O.R.Q.M.S. Rigg of Group 54, Pioneer Corps (Not official). n.d. (c. 1947).

Articles

Coryndon, R.T. 'Swaziland.' *Journal of Royal African Society*, Vol. 14, 1915.

Baring, E. 'Problems of the High Commission Territories.' *International Affairs* 28, no. 2 (April) 1952: 184-189.

Bowman, Larry W. The Subordinate State System of Souther Africa. *International Studies Quarterly* 12, no. 3 (September) 1968: 231-261.

Cockram, Ben. 'The Protectorates: An International Problem.' *Optima* 13, no. 4 (December) 1963: 21, 177-183.

Houlton, John. 'The High Commission Territories in South Africa.' *Geographical Magazine* 26, no. 2 (June) 1953: 95-106.

Kuper, Hilda. 'A Royal Ritual in a Changing Political Context.' *Cahiers d'Etudes Africaines* 12, 1972: 593-615.

Landell-Mills, P.M. The 1969 Southern African Customs Union Agreement. *The Journal of Modern African Studies* 9 no. 2 (1971): 262-281.

Marvin, John. King Sobhuza II of Swaziland. *Optima* (Johannesburg), 23, no. 2 (June) 1973: 95-99.

Munger, Edwin S. Swaziland: The Tribe and the Country. *American Universities Field Service Reports* 10, no. 2 (August) 1962.

Potholm, C.P. 'Swaziland.' *Southern Africa in Perspective*, eds. Christian Potholm and Richard Dale. New York: The Free Press, 1972.

——. 'The Ngwenyama of Swaziland: The Dynamics of Political Adaptation,' *Kingship in Africa* (ed. Renée Lemarchard) London: Frank Cass, 1973.

——. 'Swaziland Under Sobhuza II.' *The Round Table*, no. 254 (April) 1974: 219-227.

Wentzel, V. 'Swaziland Tries Independence.' *National Geographic* 136, no. 2 (August) 1969: 266-295.

INDEX

Note on orthography The Swazi language (siSwati) is difficult to transcribe into Roman lettering or English spelling. Inconsistencies in the spelling of certain personal or place names (e.g. Ezulwini, Zulwini, etc.), reflect historical records. Sometimes I have retained forms which are more commonly used though grammatically incorrect (e.g., at Ehlane, not at Hlane).